DESIGN STRUGGLES
Intersecting Histories, Pedagogies, and Perspectives

PLURAL
Valiz, Amsterdam

In cooperation with the SWISSDESIGNNETWORK

DESIGN STRUGGLES
Intersecting Histories, Pedagogies, and Perspectives

Claudia Mareis and Nina Paim (eds.)

Danah Abdulla
Tanveer Ahmed
Zoy Anastassakis
Ahmed Ansari
Brave New Alps
Johannes Bruder
Cheryl Buckley
Sria Chatterjee
Alison J. Clarke
Sasha Costanza-Chock
Paola De Martin
Decolonising Design
depatriarchise design
Bianca Elzenbaumer
Arturo Escobar
Kjetil Fallan
Griselda Flesler
Corin Gisel
Matthew Kiem
Claudia Mareis
Ramia Mazé
Tania Messell
Anja Neidhardt
Nan O'Sullivan
Maya Ober
Nina Paim
Luiza Prado de O. Martins
Mia Charlene White

CONTENTS

PRELUDE

1 HISTORIES

II PEDAGOGIES

III PERSPECTIVES

INTRODUCTION
and PRELUDE

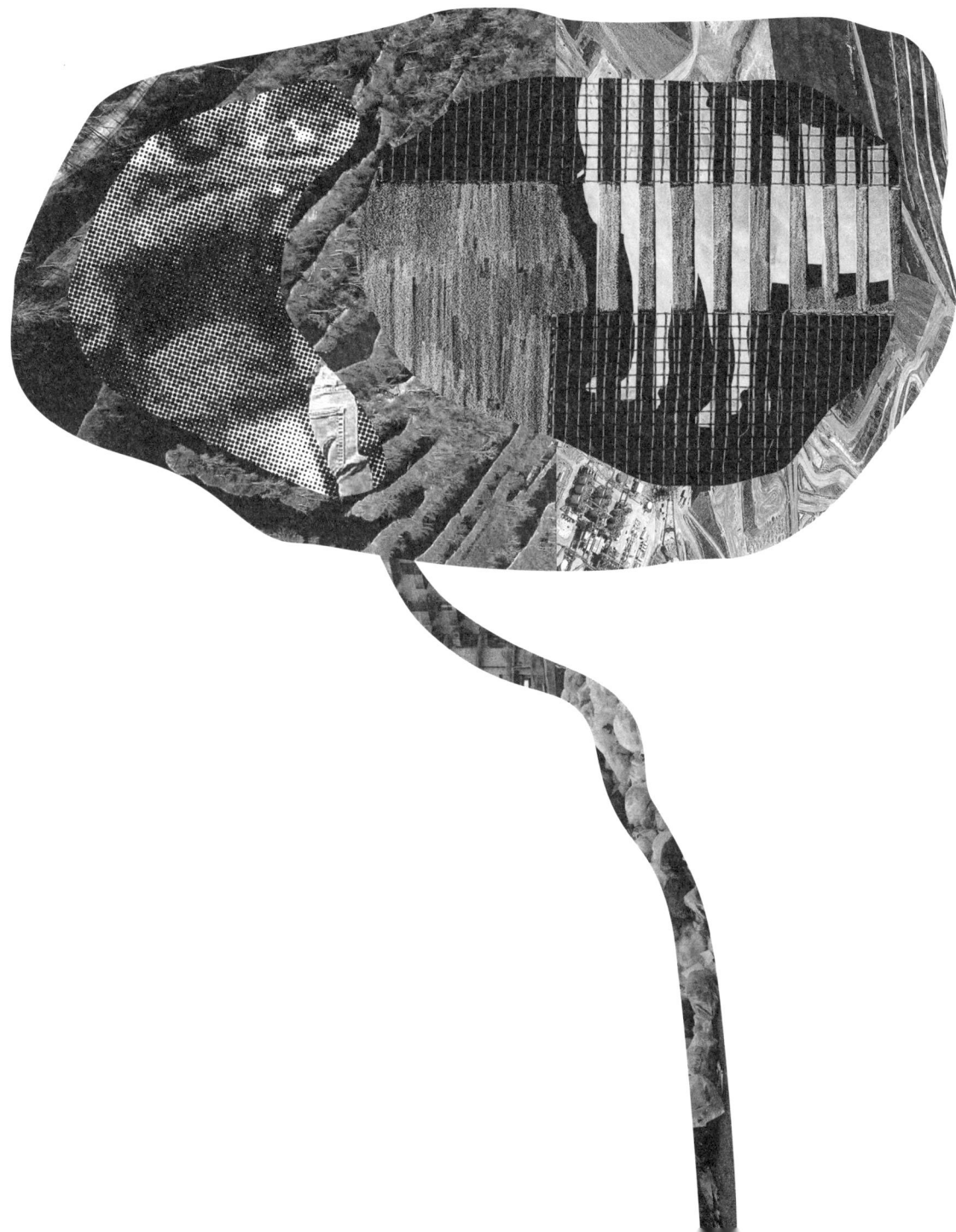

DESIGN STRUGGLES
An Attempt to Imagine Design *Otherwise*

Claudia Mareis and Nina Paim

1. The concept of *otherwise* has been making its way into design and design education most notably through designer, researcher, and educator Danah Abdulla and her Ph.D. dissertation "Design Otherwise: Towards a Locally-Centric Design Education Curricula in Jordan." The author and editors of this book are indebted to her framing. The concept of *otherwise* comes from Arturo Escobar's article "Worlds and Knowledges Otherwise" (2007), where, Abdulla says, he "discusses how decoloniality crosses borders of thought to craft another space for the production of knowledge. Thinking *otherwise* is another way of thinking that runs counter to the great modernist narratives. It locates its own inquiry in the very borders of systems of thought and reaches towards the possibility of non-Eurocentric models of thinking." Danah Abdulla, "Design Otherwise: Towards a Locally-Centric Design Education Curricula in Jordan" (Ph.D. diss., Goldsmiths, University of London, 2018), 16–17, research.gold.ac.uk/23246/1/DES_thesis_AbdullaD_2018.pdf. Most recently, this term has appeared in "Imagining Otherwise," a year-long "collaborative attempt to create an intersectional, fluid design laboratory," curated by Mayar El-Bakry, Claudia Mareis, Maya Ober, Laura Pregger, and Jörg Wiesel at the FHNW Academy of Art and Design in Basel, which fosters student-centered pedagogy through diverse learning and teaching formats.

This book was born out of the desire to think, teach, and practice design *otherwise*[1]. We believe that design, in its historical discourses, its pedagogies, and its practices, must come to terms with its troubling past and reimagine itself for the twenty-first century. Our volume foregrounds design's problematic and violent legacies and makes palpable current struggles to rework its material and conceptual logics. This difficult labor stems from a recognition that design and its thinking is deeply complicit in many structural systems of oppression, serving to concretize, perpetuate, and disseminate power and privilege. This book does not intend to propose solutions; instead it brings together an urgent and expansive array of voices and views from those engaged in struggles *with, against*, or *around* design, whether as professionals, educators, activists, researchers, or otherwise.

Historically, Western design as a professional and academic field has been a narrow and exclusive domain that often imagines itself as universal. Striving to define ideals and norms, the modernist lineage of design has proved largely ignorant of its all-pervasive anthropocentrism and exclusionary assumptions, projecting a vision of the world largely defined by a small number of mostly white, male, cisgender designers in the Global North. Instead, the diversity of life-defining aspects – gender, sexual orientation, race, ethnicity, religion, class, social background, physical or intellectual ability, and more – is routinely flattened or ignored in design's histories, pedagogies, practices, and objects. We believe that design is always a socio-material practice, one intimately linked to privilege and structures of inequality, white supremacy and heteronormativity, colonial power and epistemic violence, capitalist exploitation and environmental destruction. In order to rethink the discipline today, we must expand design's definition while avoiding its past universalisms, always situating and particularizing its historical claims. Moreover, the agency of design needs urgent reappraisal, a process of elevating, recovering, and creating perspectives and imaginaries beyond the dominant Western solutionist and anthropocentric model of thought.

Design is, in our view, intrinsically linked to the (re-)invention and (re-)production of material culture and the creation of the corresponding concepts, methods, media, and tools. Of course, material culture does not only include physical things, but is to be seen as an interplay of perception and materialization, of individualization and socialization, of culturalization and naturalization. The concept of ontological design[2], which we follow up to a certain point here, is based on the idea that we as humans do not only intentionally (and often unintentionally) design our habitats, but that this in turn affects our ways of becoming and being[3]. Design can thus be seen as a "powerful ontological tool capable of transforming the social and cultural reality, and modeling human experience, subjectivity and life style, and environment and social events."[4] A tool, however, with both positive and negative effects and enmeshed in universalist concepts of the "human" in need of explanation. As the Columbian-American anthropologist Arturo Escobar says, design is a process of world-making, and we must embrace a pluriverse of world-makings within our world: "all design creates a 'world-within-the-world' in which we are designed by what we design as subjects. We are all designers, and we are all designed."[5]

This book is the result of a collaboration between the Swiss professor and design researcher Dr. Claudia Mareis and the queer Brazilian curator and activist Nina Paim. It is an attempt to bring the generative potential of historical-critical, pedagogical, and activist approaches to design into dialogue and to make them productive in their similarities and differences. In what follows, we offer

2. Terry Winograd and Fernando Flores, *Understanding Computers and Cognition: A New Foundation for Design* (Norwood, NJ: Ablex Publishing Corporation, 1986); Tony Fry, *A New Design Philosophy: An Introduction to Defuturing* (Sydney: UNSW Press, 1999); Anne-Marie Willis, "Ontological Designing," *Design Philosophy Papers* 4, no. 2 (2006), 69–92.

3. In contrast to other authors in the field of ontological design who take a distinctly phenomenological position, we pursue the project of a Foucauldian "archaeology of knowledge," which questions the conditions of our becoming from a discourse-historical, genealogical perspective. In this sense, we would like to see a stronger problematization and historicization of some of the main sources of ontological design theories, e.g., with regard to Heidegger's anti-Semitism or the proximity of ontology and computer technologies in the work of Winograd and Flores.

4. Madina Tlostanova, "On Decolonizing Design," *Design Philosophy Papers* 15, no. 1 (2007), 51.

5. Arturo Escobar, *Designs for the Pluriverse: Radical Interdependence, Autonomy, and the Making of Worlds* (Durham, NC: Duke University Press, 2018), 133.

6. Cheryl Buckley, "Made in Patriarchy: Toward a Feminist Analysis of Women and Design," *Design Issues* 3, no. 2 (1986), 3–14.

7. Kimberlé Crenshaw, "Demarginalizing the Intersection of Race and Sex: A Black Feminist Critique of Antidiscrimination Doctrine, Feminist Theory and Antiracist Politics," *The University of Chicago Legal Forum* 1 (1989), 139–67; Kimberlé Crenshaw, "Mapping the Margins: Intersectionality, Identity Politics, and Violence against Women of Color," *Stanford Law Review* 43, no. 6 (1991), 1241–99. See also bell hooks, *Feminist Theory: From Margin to Center* (Boston, MA: South End Press, 1984).

8. Patricia Hill Collins and Sirma Bilge, *Intersectionality* (Cambridge, UK: Polity Press, 2019 [2016]), 2, 31ff.

9. On objectivity, see Lorraine Daston and Peter Galison, *Objectivity* (New York: Zone Books, 2010).

a partial but hopefully generative survey of issues and concerns that fueled our understanding and definitions of design struggles.

Despite a growing critical discourse, design today still struggles to acknowledge the complex interplay of mutually reinforcing social determinants and conditions, the dynamics of power and privilege that shape its role in everyday life. In the mid-1980s, British design historian Cheryl Buckley argued influentially that design history and practice is dominated by male worldviews and ideas, while women only play the role of consumers or advertising models[6]. This critique likewise benefits from Black feminism's subsequent articulation of intersectionality, recognizing the multiplicity of human experiences and ways of living. The term "intersectionality" was first coined by Black feminist scholar Kimberlé Williams Crenshaw in 1989 to describe how social identities, such as race, class, gender, and others, "intersect" and overlap[7]. It describes "the complexity of the world, in people and in human experiences" and can be seen both as an "analytical tool" and a "critical inquiry and practice."[8] Intersectionality is a prism for understanding how various forms of inequality often operate together and exacerbate each other. This interlocking of analysis and intervention provides access for more inclusive, situated design histories, pedagogies, and practices that confront their own struggles.

Despite the broader social visibility of womxn and LGBTQIA+ people, the field of design is still predominantly white and suffers from deeply entrenched heteropatriarchal institutional structures of education and practice, failing even modest targets for diversity among staff and students. Particularly in continental Europe, most professorships and teaching positions are still held by white cisgender men, leaving an absence of role models and a strong sense of a "glass ceiling" for historically marginalized genders in the field. In these contexts, it is still all too common to speak of the supposedly *objective* qualities of student portfolios, despite the long-standing recognition that "objectivity" is neither natural or neutral.[9]

Design's professed objectivity serves to make its subjective knowledge-power relationships appear self-evident and universal. In addition, its supposed forward-looking perspective and innovative thinking have proven enduring cultural myths surrounding its practices, even while design education clings to outmoded modernist paradigms. For too long, design educators have refused to understand modernist design as *situated* and thus restricted, rather than timeless and universal. An awareness of modernism's historical dissemination – starting from institutions like the Bauhaus (1919–33), the Ulm School of Design (1953–68), or the International Council of Societies of Industrial Design (founded in 1957), and moving into the Global South and postcolonial contexts – makes evident how its methods and pedagogies often failed to adapt to local conditions, thus undergoing modification or rejection. Nonetheless, the problematic narrative survives that design is an essential, developmental building block for a desirable (post-)industrial modernity. Since the postwar period, in many countries of the Global North, such as Germany, Great Britain, and the USA, a view of design as a generalist planning or problem-solving activity – capable of scaling to problems of any size and context – has developed and established itself.

In the late 1960s, the US-American sociologist Herbert Simon redefined design with the belief that its logics could be applied across various disciplines and professions. His oft-quoted formulation states that "everyone designs who devises courses of action aimed at changing existing situations into preferred ones."[10] Likewise for his colleague, the German design scientist Horst W. J. Rittel, design should not be seen as "the monopoly of those who call themselves 'designers.'"[11] Instead, he framed design as a plan-making activity. "Planners, engineers, architects, corporate managers, legislators, educators are (sometimes) designers," he believed. "They are guided by the ambition to imagine a desirable state of the world, playing through alternative ways in which it might be accomplished, carefully tracing the consequences of contemplated actions."[12] While expanded from its narrow, modernist definition, this postwar notion of design still excluded the vast majority of the world's peoples and lent increased authority to the policymakers and bureaucrats of the Global North.

Simon and Rittel certainly intended to broaden and democratize design with their definitions, and their work

10. Herbert A. Simon, *The Sciences of the Artificial* (Cambridge, MA: MIT Press, 1969), 55.

11. Horst W. J. Rittel, "The Reasoning of Designers," Arbeitspapier zum International Congress on Planning and Design Theory in Boston, August 1987 (Stuttgart: Schriftenreihe des Instituts für Grundlagen der Planung, Universität Stuttgart 1988), 1.

12. Rittel, 1.

Design Struggles

13. See Claudia Mareis, *Design als Wissenskultur* (Bielefeld: transcript Verlag, 2011).

14. See West C. Churchman, "Wicked Problems. Guest Editorial," *Management Science* 4, no. 14 (1967), B-141–42; Horst W. J. Rittel, "On the Planning Crisis: Systems Analysis of the First and Second Generations," *Bedriftsøkonomen* 8 (1972), 390–96; Horst W. J. Rittel and Melvin Webber, "Dilemmas in a General Theory of Planning," *Policy Sciences* 4 (1973), 155–69; Richard Buchanan, "Wicked Problems in Design Thinking," *Design Issues* 8, no. 2 (1992), 5–21.

15. Bruce Nussbaum, "Is Humanitarian Design the New Imperialism? Does Our Desire to Help Do More Harm than Good?," www.fastcompany.com/1661859/is-humanitarian-design-the-new-imperialism/ (accessed June 29, 2020).

16. Escobar, *Designs for the Pluriverse*, 213.

17. Richard Buchanan, "Education and Professional Practice in Design," *Design Issues* 14, no. 2 (1998), 63–66. See also Guy Julier, *Economies of Design* (London: Sage Publications, 2017).

18. Jason W. Moore, *Capitalism in the Web of Life: Ecology and the Accumulation of Capital* (New York, NY: Verso Books, 2015).

did foster cross-disciplinary collaboration and open up new perspectives on the very things that can be designed, including systems, services, and processes. Yet, as the field's sphere of action expanded from industrial goods to general problem solving, design took on an all-powerful agency and ever-more expanded universality, one that dovetailed with Cold War politics, military-industrial research, early computerization, and the heyday of cybernetics.[13] This constellation proved extremely pervasive and influential, and it is precisely this power that must be challenged and critiqued today. In particular, the idea of design as a method for dealing with intricate, "wicked problems" (problems for which there are no standard solutions due to their uniqueness) gained momentum far beyond the previous bounds of the field.[14] Today, supposedly universal "design thinking" methods are not only applied in management and business consulting, but also in the field of humanitarian aid, prompting the US-based author and professor Bruce Nussbaum to provocatively ask: "Is Humanitarian Design the New Imperialism?"[15] Somewhat more cautiously and optimistically, but pointing in the same direction, this concern was formulated as follows by Arturo Escobar: "is design not always about human projects and goal-oriented change, about an analytics and ethics of improvement and an inescapable ideology of the *novum*, that is, of development, progress, and the new?"[16] There are different answers to these questions – optimistic and pessimistic, hopeful and cynical – but certainly no unambiguous ones.

In short, design today struggles to confront this modernist and postwar heritage, which rests on colonialist and imperialist foundations. As a practice deeply linked to the rise of capitalism, industrial mass-culture,[17] and the exploitation of both natural resources and human labor (what Jason W. Moore calls "capitalism in the web of life"),[18] design contributes to the logic of Western modernity as both enlightening and oppressive, both productive and extractive. Right up to the present, the economic prosperity of the Global North is enabled through an exploitative capitalism that relies heavily on cheap labor and natural resources in the Global South. Nigerian curator Okwui Enwezor, for example, has pointed out that the image of an asymmetric production cycle still prevails, in which Africa is the recipient of the used, obsolete, and unmodern, while its valuable raw materials are taken abroad.[19] Moreover, as Clapperton Chakanetsa Mavhunga has shown, Western-centric notions of science, technology, and innovation hardly take into account the fact that Africa follows genuinely different, especially pre-colonial logics and approaches: "Today, our definitions of science, technology, and innovation (STI) originate from countries and cultures that have acquired their dominance of others through global empires — military, capital, and media — and are able to purvey to or even impose upon those without such power their definitions." Instead, he calls for different ways of thinking: "Imagine a positive Africa — creative, techno-logical, and scientific in its own way."[20]

Design feeds this asymmetrical globalization in its production and thought. Modernity's apparent progress, from the Enlightenment to the Industrial Revolution, was only possible via far-reaching colonization – not only of natural resources, but also of subjectivity and knowledge, bodies, gender, and sexuality, cultural practices and aesthetics. The assertion of a "colonial matrix of power" was, as Walter Mignolo, Aníbal Quijano, and others have argued, fundamental to the success of the "Western code" of modernity.[21] Colonialism, followed by imperialism, spread and installed Eurocentric epistemologies, ontologies, and aesthetics over centuries by claiming them to be "universal," and this power has by no means disappeared.

Decolonization, in part, means wrestling with the full breadth of such violence. Black Portuguese writer, psychologist, theorist, and interdisciplinary artist Grada Kilomba defines the term as the "undoing of colonialism," most often understood in political terms as "the achieve-ment of autonomy by those who have been colonized and … the realization of both independence and self-deter-mination."[22] But as the Puerto Rican sociologist Ramón Grosfoguel emphasizes, a decolonial epistemology should not simply replace Western universalism with another abstract universal, but instead aim for a "critical dialogue between diverse critical epistemic/ethical/political projects"; in so doing, decolonial thinking embraces "a pluriversal as opposed to a universal world" and "take[s] seriously the epistemic perspective/cosmologies/insights of critical

19. Okwui Enwezor, "Eine neue Sprache erfinden: Die Dimensionen afrikanischen Designs und ihre Dekodierung," in *Making Africa: A Continent of Contemporary Design*, ed. Mateo Kries and Amelie Klein (Weil am Rhein: Vitra Design Museum, 2015), 25.

20. Clapperton Chakanetsa Mavhunga, "Introduction: What Do Science, Technology, and Innovation Mean from Africa?," in *What Do Science, Technology, and Innovation Mean from Africa?*, ed. Clapperton Chakanetsa Mavhunga (Cambridge, MA: MIT Press, 2017), 1–27, here 1f.

21. Walter D. Mignolo, "Introduction," *Cultural Studies* 21, no. 2–3 (2007), 155–67; Aníbal Quijano, "Coloniality and Modernity/Rationality," *Cultural Studies* 21, no. 2–3 (2007), 168–78. See also Aníbal Quijano, "Coloniality of Power, Eurocentrism, and Latin America," trans. Michael Ennis, in *Nepantla: Views from South* 1, no. 3 (2000), 533–80, muse.jhu.edu/article/23906; Walter Mignolo, *The Darker Side of Western Modernity: Global Futures, Decolonial Options* (Durham, NC: Duke University Press, 2011), 8.

22. Grada Kilomba, *Plantation Memories: Episodes of Everyday Racism* (Münster: Unrast Verlag, 2008), 138.

23. Ramón Grosfoguel, "Decolonizing Post-Colonial Studies and Paradigms of Political-Economy: Transmodernity, Decolonial Thinking, and Global Coloniality," in TRANSMODERNITY: Journal of Peripheral Cultural Production of the Luso-Hispanic World 1, no. 1 (2011).

24. Richard Buchanan, "Design Research and the New Learning," Design Issues 17, no. 4 (2001), 4.

25. Tony Fry, Becoming Human by Design (Oxford: Berg Publishers, 2012), 91ff.

26. Anne-Marie Willis, "Ontological Designing," Design Philosophy Papers 4, no. 2 (2006), 70.

27. Anthropologist Tobias Rees has described the problem behind the idea of "the human" as follows: "'The human' – just as well as the category of 'humanity' – is not a universal, a timeless ontological category that has always existed. Instead it is a recently invented concept that emerged in Europe about 250 years ago and that became subsequently universalized." Tobias Rees, After Ethnos (Durham, NC: Duke University Press, 2018), 40.

28. Laura Forlano, "Posthumanism and Design," She Ji: The Journal of Design, Economics, and Innovation 3, no. 1 (2017), 16–29; Paul Coulton and Joseph Galen Lindley, "More-Than Human Centred Design: Considering Other Things," The Design Journal 22, no. 4 (2019), 463–81.

thinkers from the Global South thinking from and with subalternized racial/ethnic/sexual spaces and bodies."[23]

In the same way, a decolonial approach to design seeks to delink its practices from the modernist tradition, not to do away with this lineage entirely but to situate it as *just one practice* among a multitude, capable of providing insights while necessitating extensive critique. Design is still broadly regarded as something that belongs "naturally" to the Global North. As is argued at several points in this book, it is time to address the absences that colonial and imperialist entanglements still produce in the field of design.

Lastly, in tandem with these efforts, the field of design is likewise undergoing a thorough reassessment of its traditional ontology, stemming in part from the urgent discourse of the Anthropocene. The design historian Richard Buchanan has drawn attention to the idea that design research has been part of a tradition since the modern era in which "nature would be molded by art and human ministry in the creation of 'artificial things.'"[24] From an ontological perspective on design, however, it becomes clear how much both the touched and untouched habitats impact their designers. Representatives of ontological design, such as Anne-Marie Willis or Tony Fry, have argued that design is not just a unidirectional form of world-making, but a reciprocal mode "of coming into being," a process of co-constitution that troubles notions of causation and nonhuman agency.[25] As Willis puts it,

> designing is fundamental to being human – we design, that is to say, we deliberate, plan and scheme in ways which prefigure our actions and makings – in turn we are designed by our designing and by that which we have designed.[26]

But also from such an ontological perspective it is necessary to problematize on the one hand the universalistic idea of "the human"[27] and on the other hand to shift away from a human-centered perspective on design towards a post-human or more-than-human perspective.[28]

By understanding human intelligence and creativity, as well as the very notion of the "human," not as natural givens but as products of socio-material engagement and contingent assemblages of nonhuman and human actors, further questions about design's responsibility emerge. As in the humanities and natural sciences, we must develop in the field of design "sympoietic practices for living on a damaged planet."[29] Such a rethinking is increasingly urgent for grasping design's complicity with the global climate crisis and its role as a motor of extractive capitalism, mass-industrialization, and waste production. So-called design thinking routinely treats animals, plants, and the organic and inorganic environment as endlessly replenishable resources, devoid of agency and value beyond utilitarian ends. In so doing, it fails to understand the earth itself as a vulnerable, incredible, precious meshwork of nonhuman and human beings. It is imperative to find ways to learn from indigenous ways of knowing, without again exploiting them as a mere resource for design's continued conquest. Brazilian indigenous leader, environmentalist, and writer Ailton Krenak proposes manifold ways of relating oneself to the world, suggesting a process of "listening, feeling, smelling, inhaling, exhaling those layers of what was left out of us as 'nature,' but which for some reason is still confused with it."[30]

The critical picture of design that we have drawn is a pointed yet incomplete one. Design has a lot more to answer for, and many more ways to be understood and read. With the collection of essays in this book we want to provide a critical response to the tendency of seeing global crisis first and foremost as a worldwide design competition – without criticality, and without questioning underlying modernist biases and anthropocentric ignorance. In the face of today's political crises – the rise of fascist and nationalist regimes, social inequality, and environmental problems on a planetary scale – designers (and not only designers) are now more than ever confronted with the question of how they can contribute to the creation of a just and sustainable world. Against this background, we feel compelled to ask: How can design truly contribute to a more just society and more sustainable forms of living without compromising bottom-up initiatives and marginalizing the voices of those who are most directly affected? How can we reimagine

29. Donna J. Haraway, "Symbiogenesis, Sympoiesis, and Art Science Activisms for Staying with the Trouble," in *Arts of Living on a Damaged Planet: Ghosts and Monsters of the Anthropocene*, ed. Anna Tsing et al. (Minneapolis: University of Minnesota Press, 2017), M31. See also Donna J. Haraway, *Staying with the Trouble: Making Kin in the Chthulucene* (Durham, NC: Duke University Press, 2016), Chapter 3.

30. Ailton Krenak, "A humanidade que pensamos ser" in *Ideias para adiar o fim do mundo* (Companhia das Letras, 2019), 69–70 (our translation). Original text: "Esse contato com outra possibilidade implica escutar, sentir, cheirar, inspirar, expirar aquelas camadas do que ficou fora da gente como 'natureza,' mas que por alguma razão ainda se confunde com ela. Tem alguma coisa dessas camadas que é quase-humana: uma camada identificada por nós que está sumindo, que está sendo exterminada da interface de humanos muito-humanos. Os quase-humanos são milhares de pessoas que insistem em ficar fora dessa dança civilizada, da técnica, do controle do planeta. E por dançar uma coreografia estranha são tirados de cena, por epidemias, pobreza, fome e violência dirigida."

design as an unbounded, queer, and unfinished practice that approaches the world from within instead of claiming an elevated position? How, for once, can we see design as a situated practice instead of turning it into the Global North's escapist, problem-solving strategy? Our conviction: Design cannot change anything before it changes itself.

The essays in *Design Struggles* deal with many struggles, some in dialogue with the aforementioned critical framings, or entangled in their histories. Others take different framings completely. The essays deal with the struggles design must fight against, but also those that it produces and engenders. And struggle is not just our thematic focus, but also behind this project's very making and production. Gathering these essays – and supporting those involved, or who couldn't be involved due to precarious situations – has not been an easy or perfect undertaking, but one strewn with emotional and financial struggles relating to the structures of power in which we ourselves are embedded. That struggle is an invisible part of the story of this book, the underlying structure forming it as much as its glue and card or pixels, giving palpable rise to its shape and absences.

This book is organized in three sections: "Histories," "Pedagogies," and "Perspectives." These sections do not claim to be categorical or exhaustive, but represent an attempt to bring the contributions into a meaningful and lively dialogue. They also reflect the priorities and pressing issues *Design Struggles* stands for: How can we write design histories *otherwise*? How can we teach design differently? And how can we think and practice design in new ways?

The first section, "Histories," explores well-known design histories – i.e., the design canon – from a variety of critical perspectives. For instance, Cheryl Buckley revisits her influential "Made in Patriarchy" essay from 1986 from an intersectional perspective. Elsewhere, Alison J. Clarke reflects critically on the history of social design advocate Victor Papanek. These essays do not retell the same stories with the same restricted pair of glasses, but develop new, interdisciplinary, intersectional, and decolonial perspectives. They're written from the ground up, and seek to change how and by whom design histories are seen and told.

The second section, "Pedagogies," brings together contributions from design educators who, in different ways, open up slant perspectives on how design can contribute to a more just, inclusive, and sustainable society. The contributions in this section are often individual reports, narratives, or stories around experiences which do not claim to be generalizable, as there is no "one solution fits all" formula for learning and teaching. Many of these essays point to what design educators Danah Abdulla and Pedro Oliveira define as "minor gestures,"[31] those small, localized, and potentially subversive acts of kindness made in an enclosed system – such as a higher-education institution – which chip away to form a pathway towards structural change. Particularly inspiring are the stories from educators in Brazil and Argentina, from which we have much to learn through transcultural solidarity.

The third section, "Perspectives," is dedicated to both theories and practices dealing with design struggles. This section brings together a variety of topics and approaches related to reflecting and practicing in the midst of design struggles, and brings these differing activities into dialogue. These essays include critical examinations of contemporary issues, open-ended theoretical reflections, and practice-oriented models or pointers that gesture toward new futures. These perspectives, as we call them, have a special significance regarding the topic of this book: dealing with struggles is in theory and practice not only particularly complex and wicked, but also rich in experiential knowledge. Practice cannot merely be understood as the "execution of previously conceived or existing drafts, plans, ideas, routines, rules, structures, in short: as the representations of actions";[32] rather, practice is created by both "sayings" and "doings," by the direct interaction of spaces, bodies, and artifacts. In this sense practice is in no way opposed to theory or analysis. It is only in their interplay that situated, critical perspectives on design unfold, providing orientation but also calling for new directions to be taken.

The essays in this book were spurred by the lectures, workshops, and conversations that took place at "Beyond Change: Questioning the Role of Design in Times of

31. Pedro Oliveira and Danah Abdulla in an email conversation with the editors, December 2019.

32. Gregor Bongaerts, "Soziale Praxis und Verhalten: Überlegungen zum Practice Turn," *Zeitschrift für Soziologie* 36, no. 4 (2007), 249 (our translation).

33. The conference was held in March 2018 at the FHNW Academy of Art and Design in Basel, organized by Claudia Mareis and Nina Paim on behalf of the Swiss Design Network. For the conference program, see www.beyondchange.ch/. Of special importance here was the Building Platforms program, cocurated by Nina Paim and curator and journalist Julia Sommerfeld, which brought together three independent design platforms – the Decolonising Design group, depatriarchise design, and Precarity Pilot – to occupy the FHNW Academy's entrance hall. However, this book is not a conference report. Rather, it seeks to continue, expand, deepen, reroute, extend, and further the conversations started there. It includes selected conference contributions that were revised, as well as new contributions by voices not present at the "Beyond Change" conference. Also included are previously published articles that we think make a fundamental contribution to the concept of "design struggles." The inclusion of two interviews complements the unidirectional communication of singly authored texts. In this way, we hope to expand the network and broaden the knowledge first shared at the conference.

34. As Black Brazilian feminist, journalist, and philosopher Djamila Ribeiro says: "Waking up to the privileges that certain social groups have and practicing small perception exercises can transform situations of violence that before the awareness process would not be questioned" (our translation). Djamila Ribeiro in *Pequeno Manual Antirracista* (Companhia das Letras, 2019). Original text: "Acordar para af privilégios que certos grupos sociais tem e praticar pequenos exercícios de percepção pode transformar situações de violência que antes do processo de conscientização não seriam questionadas."

35. Ailton Krenak, *Ideias para adiar o fim do mundo* (Companhia das Letras, 2019), 33 (our translation). Original text: "Definitivamente não somos iguais, e é maravilhoso saber que cada um de nós que está aqui é diferente do outro, como constelações. O fato de podermos compartilhar esse espaço, de estamos juntos viajando não significa que somos iguais; significa exatamente que somos capazes de atrair uns aos outros pelas nossas diferenças, que deveriam guiar os nossos roteiros de vida."

36. From Gustavo Esteva's speech at "Planet Earth: Anti-systemic Movements," the Third International Seminar of Reflection and Analysis, San Cristóbal de las Casas, 2013, upsidedownworld.org/news-briefs/news-briefs-news-briefs/gustavo-esteva-recovering-hope-the-zapatista-example/.

Global Transformation."[33] By introducing people and bringing them together through various programs, we hoped to learn from each other and build networks of solidarity.[34] In short, we sought to stray *together* from the path most trodden, to carve out new routes completely by "cutting the bush with the machete," as the Brazilian saying goes; to build a movement, to form an ocean, while simultaneously reflecting on our different and varying positions and becoming all the stronger for it. As Ailton Krenak writes, "we are definitely not the same, and it is wonderful to know that each one of us here is different from the other, like constellations. The fact that we can share this space, that we are traveling together does not mean that we are the same; it means exactly that we are able to attract each other through our differences, which should guide our life paths."[35]

We hope that *Design Struggles* will prompt even more discussions and alliances. Editing this volume became an attempt to bring the perspectives and experiences of individuals geographically disconnected together in one space – this time not the space of a conference room, but the space of digital and printed pages. Thinking about and discussing the possibilities and limits of design should not be confined to the enclosed boundaries of the discipline and its institutions. For this reason this book is available to download for free, and its printed version has been resourcefully produced to limit the price tag. Moreover, while it is peer-reviewed and has been produced from the knowledge of a greater research community, it has simultaneously been compiled and edited in a way that hopefully allows for a larger, nonacademic readership to participate in its discussions. In particular, design has much to learn from activism, including what it means to struggle and the recognition that political work requires long-term goals rather than short-term, solutionist thinking. It also has a lot to learn about hope. As the Mexican activist Gustavo Esteva explains: "Hope is not a conviction that something will happen in a certain way. We have to nurture it and protect it, but it is not about sitting and waiting for something to happen, it is about a hope that converts into action."[36]

This book is dedicated to those who fight against the difficulties and struggles of design, knowing that

Claudia Mareis and Nina Paim

there will be no easy solutions or unambiguous answers. But it's also dedicated to those who are held back due to the struggles design creates. The struggles of design are daunting. They are especially daunting for isolated individuals working against powerful institutions. But limitations can also spur us to think *otherwise* together, and imagine futures beyond the present. As we prepare this book for publication, new struggles are emerging as a consequence of the COVID-19 pandemic, which is disproportionally affecting the poorest and most vulnerable populations. In that, historian of science Edna Bonhomme reminds us that pandemics are not isolated phenomena, but "part and parcel of capitalism and colonisation".[37] At the same time, the recent brutal killings of George Floyd, Breonna Taylor, and Tony McDade, amongst other unarmed African-Americans by the police, has ignited a global wave of antiracist protests and calls for institutional reforms. To think, teach, and practice design *otherwise* takes on a new urgency. It has become clear that we are one shared planet, our bodies networks just as much as our digital selves. We've also seen the power of coming together across borders, through the vital sharing of voices, resources, and research. Canadian author and activist Naomi Klein has written of the importance of the ideas *lying around*, which become those we most depend on when a crisis occurs.[38]

The ideas lying around in this book are radical, open, generous, caring; they're antiracist, antisexist, dedicated to abolition and liberation and imagining a pluriverse of worlds: we must lay them wide open, because these are ideas that can be used – and need to be used – right now.

37. council.science/current/ blog/covid-19-and-inequality-the-racialization-of-pandemics/.

38. Naomi Klein, "Coronavirus Capitalism – and How to Beat It," *The Intercept*, March 16, 2020, last accessed June 29, 2020, theintercept. com/2020/03/16/ coronavirus-capitalism/. See also Tony Fry and Madina Tlostanova, *Democracy and Crisis: Recasting the Political Now* (Launceston: Design Philosophy Provocation Press, 2020).

AUTONOMOUS DESIGN AND THE EMERGENT TRANSNATIONAL CRITICAL DESIGN STUDIES FIELD

Arturo Escobar

Introduction

This paper examines the seeming repositioning of design as a central domain of thought and action concerned with the meaning and production of socionatural life. It suggests that critical design studies are being actively reconstituted – perhaps more clearly than many social and human sciences and professional fields – as a key space for thinking about life and its defense from increasingly devastating anthropogenic forces. There is a hopeful recognition of the multidimensional character of design as material, cultural, epistemic, political, and ontological, all at once. Design, in short, is being acknowledged as a decisive world-making practice, even if often found wanting in this regard. The mood seems to be settling in, at least among a small but possibly growing number of design theorists and practitioners, for playing a more self-aware, and constructive, role in the making and unmaking of worlds.

   This means that the political character of design is being more readily acknowledged. New design lexicons and visions are being proposed as a result. The first part of this paper summarizes some of these trends, including the uneven but increasingly intersecting geographies from which they arise. Together, they are seen as constituting a transnational discursive formation of critical design studies. The second part shows the tensions, but also potential synergies and bridges, between approaches stemming from the Global South and those from the Global North, broadly speaking. The third part, finally, tackles the question of the relation between design and autonomy, examining autonomous design as a particular proposal within the transnational critical design studies field. While the analysis is offered as a hypothesis more than as a thoroughly substantiated argumentation, the paper hopes to contribute performatively to constructive articulations of the emergent trends.

On Critical Design Studies as an Interepistemic and Pluriversal Conversation

I believe we are witnessing a significant reorientation of design theory and practice at present. I am not suggesting that previous moments in design history have been immune to change; however, the current phase exhibits features that make this moment particularly transformative, theoretically, practically, and politically. I would highlight three of them:

The growing willingness on the part of a number of designers worldwide, although largely anchored in the Global North, to engage more deeply than ever with the interrelated crises of climate, energy, poverty, inequality, and meaning and the momentous questions they pose. These questions go well beyond the concern with the disappearance of species and the increasingly destructive effects of climate change, to involve the disruption of basic human sociality, the breakdown of social relations, the proliferation of wars and violence, massive displacement of people and nonhumans, abhorrent inequality, intensifying forms of intolerance, and the difficulty young people face today in crafting lives of meaning. I believe many designers are alert to this suffering and devastation and genuinely attuned to the Earth and to the fate of their fellow humans. They are more inclined than ever to consider design as central to the crisis and hence that it may be a crucial factor in confronting it imaginatively and effectively. Notions such as design for social innovation,[1] transition design,[2]

1. Ezio Manzini, *Design, When Everybody Designs: An Introduction to Design for Social Innovation* (Design Thinking, Design Theory) (Cambridge, MA: The MIT Press, 2015).

2. Terry Irwin, Gideon Kossoff, and Cameron Tonkinwise, "Transition Design Provocation," *Design Philosophy Papers* 13, no. 1 (January 2, 2015), 3–11, doi.org/10.1080/14487136.2015.1085688.

3. Tony Fry, *Becoming Human by Design* (London: Berg, 2012), doi.org/10.5040/9781474294041; Tony Fry, "Design for/by 'The Global South,'" *Design Philosophy Papers* 15, no. 1 (January 2, 2017), 3–37, doi.org/10.1080/14487136.2017.1303242; Tony Fry, Clive Dilnot, and Susan C. Stewart, *Design and the Question of History* (London: Bloomsbury Academic, 2015), doi.org/10.5040/9781474245890.

4. For a fuller treatment and references on these trends, see Arturo Escobar, Designs for the Pluriverse: Radical Interdependence, Autonomy, and the Making of Worlds (Durham, NC: Duke University Press, 2018). On design and democracy, see the ardent plea to the design community from Ezio Manzini and Victor Margolin, "Democracy and Design: What Do You Think?," DESIS network (website), www.desisnetwork.org/2017/04/11/democracy-and-design-what-do-you-think; and Virginia Tassinari's talks on "Regenerating Democracy" (DESIS Philosophy Talks), www.desis-philosophytalks.org/.

5. Susan Yelavich and Barbara Adams, eds., *Design as Future-Making* (London: Bloomsbury Academic, 2014), doi.org/10.5040/9781474293907.

6. Klaus Krippendorff, "Redesigning Design; An Invitation to a Responsible Future," in *Design: Pleasure or Responsibility*, ed. Pävi Tahkokallio and Susann Vihma (Helsinki: University of Art and Design, 1995), 138–62; Betti Marenko and Jamie Brassett, eds., *Deleuze and Design* (Deleuze Connections) (Edinburgh: Edinburgh University Press, 2015).

7. Tristan Schultz, "Design's Role in Transitioning to Futures of Cultures of Repair," in *Research into Design for Communities, Volume 2: Proceedings of ICoRD 2017*, ed. Amaresh Chakrabarti and Debkumar Chakrabarti (Singapore: Springer Singapore, 2017), 225–34, doi.org/10.1007/978-981-10-3521-0_19; Tristan Schultz et al., "What Is at Stake with Decolonizing Design? A Roundtable," *Design and Culture* 10, no. 1 (January 2, 2018), 81–101, doi.org/10.1080/17547075.2018.1434368.

8. Alfredo Gutiérrez Borrero, "El Sur del del diseño y el diseño del Sur," *International Colloquium Epistemologies of the South: South-South, South-North and North-South Global Learning Coimbra* (July 10, 2014); Alfredo Gutiérrez Borrero, "Resurgimientos: Sures como diseños y diseños otros," *Nómadas*, no. 43 (2015), 113–29, doi.org/10.30578/nomadas.n43a7; Ahmed Ansari, "Towards a Design of, from, and with the Global South," Carnegie Mellon University School of Design (unpublished paper, Pittsburgh, USA, May 2016); Tony Fry, "Design for/by 'The Global South,'" *Design Philosophy Papers* 15, no. 1 (January 2, 2017), 3–37, doi.org/10.1080/14487136.2017.1303242; Arturo Escobar, "Response: Design for/by [and from] the 'Global South,'" *Design Philosophy Papers* 15, no. 1 (January 2, 2017), 39–49, doi.org/10.1080/14487136.2017.1301016.

9. Elizabeth (Dori) Tunstall, "Decolonizing Design Innovation: Design Anthropology, Critical Anthropology, and Indigenous Knowledge," in *Design Anthropology: Theory and Practice*, ed. Wendy Gunn, Ton Otto, and Rachel Charlotte Smith (London: Bloomsbury Academic, 2013), 232–50; Ansari, "Towards a Design of, from, and with the Global South"; Madina Tlostanova, "On Decolonizing Design," *Design Philosophy Papers* 15, no. 1 (January 2, 2017), 51–61, doi.org/10.1080/14487136.2017.1301017; Rolando Vazquez, "Precedence, Earth and the Anthropocene: Decolonizing Design," *Design Philosophy Papers* 15, no. 1 (January 2, 2017), 77–91, doi.org/10.1080/14487136.2017.1303130.

10. See, for instance, the work of the Lakota-Dakota graphic designer, Sadie Red Wing, available at: www.sadieredwing.com/.

11. Hernán López-Garay and Daniel Lopera Molano, "Alter Design: A Clearing Where Design Is Revealed as Coming Full Circle to Its Forgotten Origins and Dissolved into Nondesign," *Design Philosophy Papers* 15, no. 1 (January 2, 2017), 63–67, doi.org/10.1080/14487136.2017.1303974.

12. Eleni Kalantidou and Tony Fry, eds., *Design in the Borderlands* (New York, NY: Routledge, 2014).

13. Escobar, *Designs for the Pluriverse*.

14. For instance, there is a clear overlap between those trends using a decolonial framework and the decolonization of design. On decolonial design, see "Decolonizing Design," ed. Decolonising Design Group (Tristan Schultz et al.), special issue, *Design*

design towards sustainment,[3] and redesigning the human are perhaps the most compelling expressions of this critical awareness and disposition.

Related claims call for a more explicit engagement between design and a host of important issues, including democracy, the speculative imagination, activism, expanding design spaces to include heterogeneous communities and temporalities, and collaborative and participatory design, among other appeals.[4] As Manzini unabashedly – and rightly, in my opinion – puts it, at stake in these new design orientations is nothing less than an emerging civilization. Design, succinctly, is about future-making.[5] It is, at least potentially, about laying down conditions for postcapitalist, postpatriarchal, and posthuman societies, or social systems that nurture a responsible anthropocentrism beyond the modern human. It is, finally, about philosophical and political discourses on design through which design itself is redesigned.[6]

The emergence of a transnational space, anchored chiefly but not exclusively in the Global South, that problematizes anew design's embeddedness in global historical relations of power and domination, variously explored in terms of design's relation to histories of colonialism and imperialism, its functioning within the modern/colonial matrix of power, the geopolitics of knowledge (Eurocentrism), racism, and patriarchal capitalist colonial modernity. This second feature is attested by novel framings of design praxes, such as those going on under the rubrics of decolonial design;[7] designs of, for, by, and from the South;[8] design by other names; the decolonization of design;[9] indigenous and multicultural design and visual sovereignty;[10] alter-design;[11] design in the borderlands;[12] and autonomous design.[13] It should be stressed that these trends often overlap; they are diverse and heterogeneous, in some cases even within each trend.[14] Taken as a whole, however, they can be seen as decentering design from Eurocentric accounts of the field, resituating it within larger histories of modernity and coloniality; making visible previously hidden or suppressed design histories and practices; redirecting design ontologically towards decolonial and pluriversal visions; and, very tellingly, addressing the implications of these repositionings of design for design education.

Attention is also paid in some of these tendencies to questions of care and repair; opening up multiple futures attuned to diverse temporalities and worldviews; imagining concrete decolonial design projects; and conceptualizing design epistemologies arising from multiple ontologies beyond the dualisms inhabiting the dominant forms of modernity.

As a consequence of the previous two processes, one can posit the existence of a transnational critical design studies field; it is not far-fetched to state that this nascent field is interepistemic and intercultural (one could even argue: interontological); in other words – and this is one its most promising developments – critical design studies has ceased to be an intra-European conversation, in the ontoepistemic sense of the term (that is, one that remains confined within the configurations of knowledge and world-views stemming from the European historical experience); it is becoming pluriversal.

In sum, what we are witnessing is the emergence of a domain of thought and action in which design might function as a political technology for a better, *and different*, world, or worlds. These trends reveal an open-ended attitude towards critique, reflected in a willingness to entertain radical ideas for the transformation of design; they infuse design with a more explicit sense of politics, even a radical politics in some cases; and they question anew readily accepted design solutions to contemporary problems, such as those on offer by mainstream discourses of development, sustainability, the green economy, social entrepreneurship, human-centered design, smart cities, technological singularities, and so forth.

As a discursive formation, this transnational field may be characterized provisionally in terms of three inter-related processes: interdisciplinary and transdisciplinary forms of knowledge, including newcomers in design studies, such as anthropology, geography, political philosophy, feminist and critical race theory, and political ecology, plus unprecedented engagements between long-standing design fields, such as architecture, and these other newly design-related disciplines; new forms of subjectivity that widen significantly the positions available to design subjects; and relations of power that regulate, albeit in shifting manners, the practices within the field.

and Culture 10, nos. 1–3 (2018), and the Decolonising Design group's website (www.decolonisingdesign. com/). There are related but independent efforts at decolonizing design that appeal to other subaltern experiences and concepts, particularly indigenous and Afro-diasporic, such as the work of Elizabeth (Dori) Tunstall and Sadie Red Wing; see, for instance, Elizabeth (Dori) Tunstall, "Respectful Design: Decolonizing Art and Design Education" (lecture in the Decolonising Design Lecture Series, University of Minnesota College of Design, November 15, 2017, www.youtube.com/ watch?v=iEUyGrgqaAM); and Elizabeth (Dori) Tunstall et al., "AIGA Respectful Design Video," October 17, 2016, www.youtube.com/ watch?v=sESVWI5aAHA&list= PLh-_JsB24Hqz3Y3U3Z992-UDmg5zhU7-K. There is also overlap between decolonial design and design for/by the Global South. On the latter, see "Design and the Global South," ed. Tony Fry, special issue, *Design Philosophy Papers* 15, no. 1 (2017).

15. Ansari, "Towards a Design of, from, and with the Global South," 3–4.

Bridging Design Discourses in the Global South/ East with Those from the Global North/West

Adopting the nomenclature suggested by Pakistani design theorist and activist Ahmed Ansari[15] I suggest that there is a rapprochement between design discourses in the Global South/East with those from the Global North/West. While there are convergences and potential synergies, the tensions between the two discursive fields should not be under-estimated. As Ansari puts it, "[f]ew texts within the lexicon of design studies or history have dealt with the question of what design *in* and *of* the Global South/East is and could be." His call is for "a hybrid design that navigates, negotiates and bridges North/West and South/East without asserting any kind of either/or hierarchy between the two" – in other words, design conversations that do not privilege either design history a priori, albeit acknowledging the Northern/Western coloniality of design knowledge. In what follows, I discuss three thorny questions that often muddle this conversation, while making it perhaps more stimulating even as it stalls: the question of modernity; the location of the designer; and the understanding of the communal.

The understanding of modernity. The Latin American decolonial perspective is one of the most radical critiques of Western modernity to emerge in a long time. It posits the existence of radical difference in relation to dominant forms of Euro-modernity. Less known in critical design circles are the arguments in the nascent field of political ontology. A key idea here is that dominant and subaltern worlds can be partially connected, even coproduce each other, while remaining distinct; said otherwise, worlds can be part of each other and radically different at the same time. The decolonial notions of "exteriority" and "border episte-mologies" and the political ontology notions of partial connections and of the "ontological excess" that subaltern worlds continue to exhibit in relation to dominant worlds are important in this regard. However, they are easily misunderstood as being against modernity, or as applying only to indigenous peoples. Neither of these claims is correct. At stake here, of crucial relevance for design, are the existence of worlds that do not abide completely by the separation between humans and nonhumans, even if the divide is also present in many of their practices.[16]

  While it is true that critics of modernity sometimes homogenize the modern experience, failing to see the plurality that inhabits it, it is also the case that moderns, whether in the Global North or the Global South and including those on the Left, have a hard time facing the ontological challenge posed by the idea of the end of modernity as a civilizational project; it induces a type of fright that is deeply unsettling. Interepistemic design conversations need to articulate this civilizational anxiety in effective ways. After all, many other worlds have had to exist with the fright, if not the reality, of their vanquishing. An important strategy by nondominant or alternative modern worlds would be to *effectively activate* their specific critique of the dominant modernity, which would place them in the position of fellow travelers, not enemies, of those who uphold more explicitly the possibility of a pluri-verse of social formations beyond modernity. Something similar could be said about the notion of change of civilizational model. This concept needs to deconstruct the dominance of Western civilization, pluralize critically other existing or potential civilizational models in open-ended ways, and be open to considering anew the critical retrieval of the history-making potential of multiple traditions, including the nondominant traditions that have existed within the West itself.

The identification of the epistemic location of the designer. Critical perspectives from the Global South/East share with feminist theory their decided emphasis on the situated character of all knowledge, against the claims of neutrality based on universal science.[17] For decolonial theorist María Lugones,[18] subaltern peoples always inhabit a "fractured locus" of enunciation. This politics of location is often found excessively politicized by scholars anchored in Northern/Western ontoepistemic locations, for whom the analysis of their own location would entail a deep understanding of eurocentrism and a decentering of all forms of modernity. At the same time, scholars and activists occupying Southern/Eastern positions (myself included) at times fall into the trap of limiting the complexity of their

16. Marisol de la Cadena, *Earth Beings: Ecologies of Practice across Andean Worlds* (Durham, NC: Duke University Press, 2015), doi.org/10.1215/9780822375265; Mario Blaser, "Ontological Conflicts and the Stories of Peoples in Spite of Europe: Toward a Conversation on Political Ontology," *Current Anthropology* 54, no. 5 (October 1, 2013), 547–68, doi.org/10.1086/672270; Mario Blaser, "Is Another Cosmopolitics Possible?," *Cultural Anthropology* 31, no. 4 (November 6, 2016), 545–70, doi.org/10.14506/ca31.4.05; Escobar, *Designs for the Pluriverse.*

17. Sandra Harding, "One Planet, Many Sciences," in *Constructing the Pluriverse*, ed. Bernd Reiter (Durham, NC: Duke University Press, 2018), doi.org/10.1215/9781478002017-003.

18. María Lugones, "Toward a Decolonial Feminism," *Hypatia* 25, no. 4 (October 2010), 742–59, doi.org/10.1111/j.1527-2001.2010.01137.x; and "The Coloniality of Gender," in *Globalization and the Decolonial Option*, ed. Walter D. Mignolo and Arturo Escobar (London: Routledge, 2010), 369–90.

19. See, for instance, Manzini's helpful concept of "SLOC" (small, local, open, connected) scenarios in Ezio Manzini, *Design, When Everybody Designs: An Introduction to Design for Social Innovation* (Cambridge, MA: MIT Press, 2015), 178–82; but also the Transition Town Movement.

20. Escobar, *Designs for the Pluriverse*, 176–85.

21. Manzini, *Design, When Everybody Designs*, 241.

own historical positionalities or the hybrid historicity of those groups with whom they work. Effective interepistemic dialogues across the entire range of positionalities requires more clarity and debate on these issues, including an ethics of generous listening and mutual care.

Understandings of community and the communal. Many transition narratives today acknowledge the deleterious effects of intensified liberal individualism and the spread of this model to most corners of the world via capitalist-induced consumption. Next to the relocalization of activities such as food, energy, transportation, and housing to the extent possible,[19] transition visions emphasize the need to recommunalize social life, taking nonhumans explicitly into account. In Latin America, new languages of the communal, such as *comunalidad*, aim to reinvigorate debates on the communal dimension of all social life[20] Yet each society, perhaps even each locality or region, has to invent a practice of the communal that might work best for them. Appeals to the communal are often resisted because they might resuscitate old ghosts thought long-ago discarded in some societies, such as the impingement on the rights of the individual, negative aspects of so-called traditional communities (including the predominance of elders and men), and so forth. But this need not be the case. In fact, recent debates in Latin America envision postpatriarchal, nonliberal, postcapitalist, and place-based but not place-bound forms of community.

Worldwide, groups need to grapple with the re/constitution of the communal in a pluriversal manner; they need to do so in ways appropriate to the specific conjuncture in which they are enmeshed within a domineering globalization. Manzini's call in this issue for a new view of communities, understood as open-ended spaces where individuals participate from their position of autonomy in conversations about possibilities, with an eye towards designing coalitions, is an instance of constructive rethinking of communities appropriate to a particular social and ontoepistemic formation. In his view, these communities imply forms of cosmopolitan localism coupled with distributed meshworked agencies.[21]

These are just three of the areas of tension but also

potential synergies that inhabit the transnational critical design studies field. There are other important areas that are beyond the scope of this paper, such as contrasting views of power and politics; the interplay between reformist and radical alternatives; the role of nonhumans in design frameworks; the tension between secularism, religion, and novel forms of earth spirituality, still scantly discussed in all-too-secular design and academic circles; the role of nonexperts; and so forth. In the last part of the paper, I explore a few of these open questions by discussing a current that brings the relation between design and politics to the fore, namely, the proposals for autonomous design that are at the heart of this special issue.

22. This section draws from Escobar, *Designs for the Pluriverse*, especially Chapter 6. See this book for an extended list of references.

On Bringing Together Design and Autonomy [22]

The idea of bringing together design and autonomy is not readily apparent. Is autonomous design not an oxymoron? To posit the idea credibly requires seeing a new design's dependence on modernist unsustainable and defuturing practices and redirecting it towards collective world-making projects, in all of their heterogeneity and contradictions. Design for autonomy thus springs out of an ontological design framework; it is centered on the struggles of communities and social movements in defense of their territories and worlds from the ravages of neoliberal globalization. Thinking ontologically about the current conjuncture implies examining the contemporary crisis as the result of deeply entrenched ways of being, knowing, and doing and their instantiation by patriarchal capitalist modernity; conversely, it implies nourishing design's potentiality to support subaltern struggles for autonomy, by opening up design to rationalities and practices attuned to the relational dimension of life, particularly those present among groups engaged in territorial struggles against extractive globalization. From this perspective, what we are witnessing is a veritable political activation of relationality. Relationality is also present, in the last instance, in the Earth itself, in the endless and ceaselessly changing weave of life on which all life depends.

The basic insight of autonomous design is

DESIGNING COMMUNAL AUTONOMY

23. Humberto R. Maturana and Francisco J. Varela, *Autopoiesis and Cognition* Boston, MA: Reidel Publishing Company, 1980); Humberto R. Maturana and Francisco J. Varela, *The Tree of Knowledge: The Biological Roots of Human Understanding* (Berkeley, CA: Shambhala Publications, 1987).

24. Francisco J. Varela, *Ethical Know-How: Action, Wisdom, and Cognition* (Stanford, CA: Stanford University Press, 1999).

25. Gustavo Esteva, Celebration of Zapatismo," *Humboldt Journal of Social Relations* 29, no. 1 (2005), 127–67; Gustavo Esteva, "The Hour of Autonomy," *Latin American and Caribbean Ethnic Studies* 10, no. 1 (January 2, 2015), 134–45, doi.org/10. 1080/17442222.2015.103 4436.

seemingly straightforward: that every community practices the design of itself. This was certainly the case with traditional communities (they produced the norms by which they lived their lives largely endogenously), as it is today with many communities, in both the Global South and the Global North, that are thrown into the need of designing themselves in the face of ever-deepening manifestations of the crises and the inescapable techno-economic mediation of their worlds. If we accept the thesis – voiced by social movement activists, transition visionaries, and some designers – that the current crises point at a deeper civilizational crisis, autonomously designing new forms of life appears to many communities as an eminently feasible, perhaps unavoidable, theoretico-political project; for some, it is even a question of their survival as distinct worlds.

Theoretically, the question of autonomy in relation to design can be grounded in the view, articulated by Maturana and Varela,[23] that autonomy is the most fundamental feature of the living; in these authors' jargon, autonomy is the key to the *autopoiesis* or self-creation of living systems. This proposition serves as a partial anchor for autonomous design. As Varela says, "[i]n fact, the key to autonomy is that a living system finds its way into the next moment by acting appropriately out of its own resources."[24] This resonates with Gustavo Esteva's definition of autonomy, based on the Zapatista experience, as the ability to create the conditions that enable communities to change their norms from within, or the ability to change traditions traditionally.[25] It involves the defense of some practices, the abandonment or transformation of others, and the invention of new ones.

The autonomous design framework may be considered a Latin American contribution to the transnational conversation on design sketched above. There is a range of forms of autonomous thought in Latin America at present. Together with the recrafting of communal forms of knowing~being~doing, these notions – *autonomía* and *comunalidad* – may be seen as laying down the ground for an autonomous design thought. The emergent concept of *Buen Vivir* (good living or collective wellbeing) as an alternative *to* development is an expression of such thought, and so are the *planes de vida* (life projects) being crafted by some indigenous, Afrodescendant, and peasant groups, and in some urban spaces. Experiences embodying the search for autonomy can be witnessed in many corners of the subcontinent where brutal forms of extractive globalization are taking place: in struggles for the defense of seeds, commons, mountains, forests, wetlands, lakes, and rivers; in actions against white/mestizo and patriarchal rule; in urban experiments with art, digital technologies, neoshamanic movements, urban gardens. Taken as a whole, these expressions of multiple collective wills manifest the unwavering conviction that another world is possible.

A fundamental aspect of autonomous design is the rethinking of the communal, in vogue in critical circles in Latin America and in transition movements in Europe. The realization of the communal can be said to be the most fundamental goal of autonomous design. Communal thought is perhaps most developed in Mexico, based on the experiences of social movements in Oaxaca and Chiapas. For Esteva, *la comunalidad* (the condition of being communal)

> constitutes the core of the horizon of intelligibility of Meso-American cultures… It is the condition that inspires communalitarian existence, that which makes transparent the act of living; it is a central category in personal and communitarian life, its most fundamental *vivencia*, or experience.[26]

It is important to mention that that in the context of many grassroots communities any type of design would take place under conditions of ontological occupation. But it is precisely in those cases where the idea of autonomy is flourishing and where the hypothesis of design for autonomy takes on meaning. Autonomía often has a decided territorial and place-based dimension; this applies to rural, urban, forest, and all kinds of territories in different ways. The place-based dimension of autonomía often entails the primacy of decision-making by women, who are historically more likely than men to resist heteronomous pressures on the territories and resources and to defend collective ways of being. There is often, in autonomía-oriented movements, the drive to re/generate people's spaces, their cultures, and

26. Gustavo Esteva, "La noción de comunalidad" (unpublished manuscript, Oaxaca, n.d.).

communities and to reclaim the commons. It could be said that autonomía is another name for people's dignity and for conviviality; at its best, *autonomía is a theory and practice of interexistence and interbeing, a design for the pluriverse.*

From this brief theoretico-political discussion we can propose the following elements for thinking about autonomous design. Autonomy-oriented design:

> has at its main goal the realization of the communal, understood as the creation of the conditions for the community's ongoing self-creation and successful coupling with their "increasingly globalized" environments;

> embraces ancestrality, as it emanates from the history of the relational worlds in question, and futurality, as a statement about futures for communal realizations;

> privileges design interventions that foster non-liberal, non-state-centered, and noncapitalist forms of organization;

> creates auspicious spaces for the life projects of communities and the creation of convivial societies;

> always considers the community's engagement with heteronomous social actors and technologies (including markets, digital technologies, extractive operations, and so forth) from the perspective of the preservation and enhancement of the community's autopoiesis;

> takes seriously the demerging design imperatives of place-building, relocalization, renewed attention to materiality and nonhumans, and the creation of interepistemic collaborative organizations;

> gives particular attention to the role of commoning in the realization of the communal;

> it devises effective means to foster diverse economies (social and solidarity economies, alternative capitalist and non-capitalist economies);

articulates with the South American trends towards Buen Vivir and the Rights of Nature and with related trends elsewhere (e.g., degrowth, commons, postdevelopment);

fosters pluriversal openings; it is, to this extent, a form of design for the pluriverse, for the flourishing of life on the planet;

creates spaces for strengthening the connection between the realization of the communal and the Earth (its relational weave at every place and everywhere), in ways that enable humans to relearn to dwell in the planet in mutually enhancing manners with nonhumans;

takes seriously the inquiry into, and design of, borderlands as the spaces par excellence where novel understandings and practices of design from ontological and autonomous perspectives might most effectively and radically take place.

Conceived in this fashion, autonomous design can be considered a response to the urge for innovation and for the creation of new forms of life arising from the struggles, forms of counterpower, and life projects of politically activated relational ontologies.

Conclusion

As a theoretico-political proposal, autonomous design may be considered as a particular trend within the emergent transnational critical design studies field. It suggests that design can be creatively reappropriated by subaltern communities in support of their struggles to strengthen their autonomy and perform their life projects, and that designers can play constructive roles in the ontological and political reorientation of design as an element in struggles for autonomy.

To restate the question in a way that might apply to communities and social groups in many parts of the world: how do we make effective weavings and foster mutually

27. Francia Márquez, "Situación que carcome mis entrañas: A propósito de la orden de bombardear el Cauca" (open letter, April 18, 2015). Francia was awarded the 2018 Goldman Environmental Prize for her actions on behalf of her community.

enhancing entanglements of worlds in the face of the catastrophe visited upon the planet by the current global capitalist world order? Earth's territories, including cities, is where we, humans and not, go on weaving life together. Design can thus become an open invitation for us all to become mindful and effective weavers of the mesh of life. To do so, design needs to contribute to creating conditions that dampen our compulsion to think and act like modern individuals in favor of an ethics of autonomous inter-existence, albeit without negating our capacity to operate in modern worlds at the same time – this, too, might be a question of survival. This entails designs that foster convivial reconstruction beyond the cultures of expertise and that promote a pluriverse of partially connected worlds in which all worlds strive for justice and craft autonomous relational ways of being, while respecting the ability of other worlds to do the same. This is a vision for sustaining the pluriverse.

Coda

In mid-April 2014, Francia Márquez, one of those struggling to defend the Afro-Colombian community of La Toma in Colombia's southwest against aggressive illegal gold mining, penned two brave and lucid open letters to the government and the public at large. "Everything we have lived," she said in her first letter,

> has been for the love for our territories, the love we feel when we see germinate the plantain, when we have a sunny fishing day, of knowing your family is close by … our land is the place where we dream of our future with dignity. Perhaps that's why they [armed actors, including the army, paramilitaries, and guerrillas] persecute us, because we want a life of autonomy and not of dependency.[27]

Acknowledgments

Arturo Escobar's text is a reworked version of an article first published in *Strategic Design Research Journal* 11 (2018): 139–46, originally published under Creative Commons 4.0.

Arturo Escobar

Bibliography

Ansari, Ahmed. "Towards a Design Of, From, and With the Global South." Carnegie Mellon University School of Design, unpublished paper. Pittsburgh, USA.

Blaser, Mario. "Ontological Conflicts and the Stories of Peoples in Spite of Europe: Toward a Conversation on Political Ontology." *Current Anthropology* 54, no. 5 (October 1, 2013), 547–68. doi.org/10.1086/672270.
—. "Is Another Cosmopolitics Possible?" *Cultural Anthropology* 31, no. 4 (November 6, 2016), 545–70. doi.org/10.14506/ca31.4.05.

De la Cadena, Marisol. *Earth Beings: Ecologies of Practice across Andean*. Edited by J. Foster and Daniel R. Reichman. Durham, NC: Duke University Press, 2015. doi.org/10.1215/9780822375265.

"The Coloniality of Gender." In *Globalization and the Decolonial Option*. Edited by Walter D. Mignolo and Arturo Escobar, 369. London: Routledge, 2010.

Escobar, Arturo. "Response: Design for/by [and from] the 'Global South.'" *Design Philosophy Papers* 15, no. 1 (January 2, 2017), 39–49. doi.org/10.1080/14487136.2017.1301016.
—. *Designs for the Pluriverse: Radical Interdependence, Autonomy, and the Making of Worlds*. (New Ecologies for the Twenty-First Century). Durham, NC: Duke University Press, 2018.

Esteva, Gustavo. "Celebration of Zapatismo." *Humboldt Journal of Social Relations* 29, no. 1 (2005), 127–67.
—. "The Hour of Autonomy." *Latin American and Caribbean Ethnic Studies* 10, no. 1 (January 2, 2015), 134–45. doi.org/10.1080/17442222.2015.1034436.
—. "La noción de comunalidad." Unpublished. Oaxaca, n.d.

Fry, Tony. *Becoming Human by Design*. Bloomsbury Publishing Plc, 2012. doi.org/10.5040/9781474294041.
—. "Design for/by 'The Global South.'" *Design Philosophy Papers* 15, no. 1 (January 2, 2017), 3–37. doi.org/10.1080/14487136.2017.1303242.
—. *Remaking Cities: An Introduction to Urban Metrofitting*. New York, NY: Bloomsbury Academic, 2017.
—, Clive Dilnot, and Susan C. Stewart. *Design and the Question of History*. Bloomsbury Publishing Plc, 2015. doi.org/10.5040/9781474245890.

Gutiérrez Borrero, Alfredo. "El sur del diseño y el diseño del sur." *International Colloquium Epistemologies of the South: South-South, South-North and North-South Global Learning Coimbra* (July 10, 2014).
—. "Resurgimientos: Sures Como Diseños y Diseños Otros." *Nómadas* no. 43 (2015), 113–29. doi.org/10.30578/nomadas.n43a7.

Harding, Sandra. "One Planet, Many Sciences." In *Constructing the Pluriverse: The Geopolitics of Knowledge*. Edited by Bernd Reiter. Durham, NC: Duke University Press, 2018. doi.org/10.1215/9781478002017-003.

Irwin, Terry, Gideon Kossoff, and Cameron Tonkinwise. "Transition Design Provocation." *Design Philosophy Papers* 13, no. 1 (January 2, 2015), 3–11. doi.org/10.1080/14487136.2015.1085688.

Kalantidou, Eleni, and Tony Fry, eds. *Design in the Borderlands*. New York, NY: Routledge, 2014.

Krippendorff, Klaus. "Redesigning Design: An Invitation to a Responsible Future." *Design: Pleasure or Responsibility*. Helsinki: University of Art and Design, 1995, 138–62.

López-Garay, Hernán, and Daniel Lopera Molano. "Alter Design: A Clearing Where Design Is Revealed as Coming Full Circle to Its Forgotten Origins and Dissolved into Nondesign." *Design Philosophy Papers* 15, no. 1 (January 2, 2017), 63–67. doi.org/10.1080/14487136.2017.1303974.

Lugones, María. "Toward a Decolonial Feminism." *Hypatia* 25, no. 4 (October 2010), 742–59. doi.org/10.1111/j.1527-2001.2010.01137.x.

Manzini, Ezio. *Design, When Everybody Designs: An Introduction to Design for Social Innovation* (Design Thinking, Design Theory). Cambridge, MA: The MIT Press, 2015.

Marenko, Betti, and Jamie Brassett, eds. *Deleuze and Design* (Deleuze Connections). Edinburgh: Edinburgh University Press, 2015.

Margolin, Victor, and Manzini, Ezio. "Democracy and Design: What Do You Think? DESIS Network." Accessed April 21, 2018. www.desisnet-work.org/2017/04/11/democracy-and-design-what-do-you-think.

Mignolo, Walter. *The Darker Side of Western Modernity: Global Futures, Decolonial Options*. (Durham, NC: Duke University Press, 2011). doi.org/10.1215/9780822394501.
—. *Local Histories/Global Designs: Coloniality, Subaltern Knowledges, and Border Thinking* (Princeton Studies in Culture/Power/History) Princeton, NJ: Princeton University Press, 2012.

Schultz, Tristan. "Design's Role in Transitioning to Futures of Cultures of Repair." In *Research into Design for Communities, Volume 2*. Edited by Amaresh Chakrabarti and Debkumar Chakrabarti. Singapore: Springer Singapore, 2017., 225–34. doi.org/10.1007/978-981-10-3521-0_19.— et al. "What Is at Stake with Decolonizing Design? A Roundtable." *Design and Culture* 10, no. 1 (January 2, 2018), 81–101. doi.org/10.1080/17547075.2018.1434368.

Tlostanova, Madina. "On Decolonizing Design." *Design Philosophy Papers* 15, no. 1 (January 2, 2017), 51–61. doi.org/10.1080/14487136.2017.1301017.

Tunstall, Elizabeth. *Ethical Know-How: Action, Wisdom, and Cognition*. (Writing Science) (Stanford, CA: Stanford University Press, 1999).
—. "Decolonizing Design Innovation: Design Anthropology Critical Anthropology, and Indigenous Knowledge." In *Design Anthropology. Theory and Practice*. Edited by Wendy Gunn, Ton Otto, and Rachel Charlotte Smith (London: Bloomsbury, 2013), 232–50.

Vazquez, Rolando. "Precedence, Earth and the Anthropocene: Decolonizing Design." *Design Philosophy Papers* 15, no. 1 (January 2, 2017), 77–91. doi.org/10.1080/14487136.2017.1303130.

Yelavich, Susan, and Barbara Adams, eds. *Design as Future-Making*. London: Bloomsbury Publishing Plc, 2014. doi.org/10.5040/9781474293907.

1
HISTORIES

MADE IN PATRIARCHY II Researching (or Re-Searching) Women and Design

Cheryl Buckley

1. By the late 1970s and through the 1980s, women design and architectural historians influenced by second-wave feminism and a handful of pioneering texts began to approach these questions armed with feminist theories. In this context, notions of design value, taste, and significance were seriously undermined; in fact, the basic premises of academic disciplines began to be questioned as the new discipline's failure to account for women as producers, designers, consumers, and users of design became clear. See, e.g., Anthea Callen, *The Angel in the Studio: Women in the Arts and Crafts Movement 1870–1914* (London: Astragal, 1979); Dolores Hayden, *The Grand Domestic Revolution: A History of Feminist Designs for American Homes, Neighborhoods, and Cities* (Cambridge, MA: MIT Press, 1981); Philippa Goodall, "Design and Gender," BLOCK 9 (1983), 50–61; Gillian Elinor et al., eds., *Women and Craft* (London: Virago, 1987); Judy Attfield and Pat Kirkham, eds., *A View from the Interior: Feminism, Women and Design* (London: The Women's Press, 1989); and Ellen Perry Berkeley, ed., *Architecture: A Place for Women* (Washington, DC: Smithsonian Institution Press, 1989).

2. Swiss Design Network Research Summit, "Beyond Change: Questioning the Role of Design in Times of Global Transformations," Basel, March 8–10, 2018, www.beyondchange.ch/font (accessed August 8, 2018).

3. Cheryl Buckley, "Made in Patriarchy: Toward a Feminist Analysis of Women and Design," *Design Issues* 3, no. 2 (1986), 3–14; and Cheryl Buckley, "Women Designers in the North Staffordshire Pottery Industry, 1914–1940" (Ph.D. thesis, University of East Anglia, 1991).

More than thirty years ago, women's relationship to design underwent a process of critical questioning by historians, practitioners, curators, and critics that continues today.[1] At the core was feminist politics, and as feminists began to look to all areas of women's lives, asserting that the "personal is political," design inevitably came under scrutiny. The Swiss Design Network research summit in 2018, titled "Beyond Change," invited a response to the provocation, "Design cannot change anything before it changes itself." This paper, developed from a keynote address delivered at the summit, argues that what is essential to effect change is a reconsideration of women's relationship to design.[2] This reconsideration is undertaken by reflecting on arguments made in the article, "Made in Patriarchy," published in *Design Issues* in 1986; it asks if the questions posed then are useful today.[3]

It begins by considering the changing nature of debates within feminism. It then revisits debates about the nature of design practice by examining definitions of design and the designer and the role of the historian in interpreting and understanding the connections between women and design. Insisting that design is a vital part of everyday life that has shaped our public personas and individual identities, it proposes that thinking about the innumerable ways in which design is produced, where it is produced, and by and for whom it is produced has the potential to prompt a changed understanding of design.

Situating Myself

4. Cheryl Buckley and Hazel Clark, *Fashion and Everyday Life: London and New York* (London: Bloomsbury, 2017).

5. See Cheryl Buckley, *Potters and Paintresses: Women Designers in the Pottery Industry 1870–1955* (London: The Women's Press, 1990).

As a design historian who has been working in the field since the late 1970s, my intellectual framework was fundamentally shaped by the dual, intersecting formations of social class and gender as I researched a diverse array of things that were produced and designed: domestic tableware, working-class housing, dress-making at home, and, most recently, fashion in everyday lives.[4] Importantly, this research was informed by my teaching, mainly of practice-based design students (i.e., fashion, industrial design, 3-D design), as well as my Ph.D. research. Although the latter was focused on the producers of design, an interest in the processes of representation and identity construction emerged, along with a growing concern for women users and consumers of design in the process of teaching practice-based design students.

Exploring the roles of women designers in the North Staffordshire ceramics industry, my doctoral research led to the discovery of numerous examples of ceramic designs in archives (e.g., the Josiah Wedgwood Archive) that had barely registered in design's histories. This recognition prompted several theoretical and methodological questions about the nature of design history. These ceramic designs – largely conventional, routine, and everyday – were predominantly domestic, neither technically nor visually innovative; they made only an occasional nod to modernity. However, these designs were fundamentally decorative and clearly shaped by the strong traditions inherent in the British ceramic industry. The "designers," and what was understood by the term "design" in this particular industry didn't conform to "accepted" definitions of design. In these definitions, a marked division, in design terms, was made between the production of shape and pattern design.[5] Some who "produced" these designs were called designers, while others were described as paintresses or production managers. The line between craft, machine, and new technologies was also blurred – although ceramics in North Staffordshire ostensibly were made by industrial methods, new technologies were not always what they seemed; certainly in the first half of the twentieth century, craft techniques were intrinsic to the whole production process.

Design Struggles

6. See Edward P. Thompson, *The Making of the English Working Class* (London: Pelican, 1963); and Sheila Rowbotham, *Hidden from History* (London: Pluto Press, 1980). See also Betty Friedan, *The Feminine Mystique* (1963; repr. London: Penguin Classics, 2010); Juliet Mitchell, *Psychoanalysis and Feminism* (Oxford: Pantheon, 1974); and Kate Millet, *Sexual Politics* (1970; repr. New York: Simon & Schuster, 1990).

7. Heidi Hartmann, "The Unhappy Marriage of Marxism and Feminism: Toward a More Progressive Union," in *Women and Revolution: The Unhappy Marriage of Marxism and Feminism*, ed. Lydia Sargent (London: Pluto Press, 1981); and Sheila Rowbotham, "The Trouble with Patriarchy," *New Statesman* 98 (December 1979), 970–71.

8. Rozsika Parker and Griselda Pollock, *Old Mistresses: Women, Art and Ideology* (London: Routledge & Kegan Paul, 1981).

9. See, e.g., Elizabeth Wilson, *Adorned in Dreams: Fashion and Modernity* (London: Virago, 1985); Jane Gaines and Charlotte Herzog, *Fabrications: Costume and the Female Body* (New York, NY: Routledge, 1990); and Daphne Spain, *Gendered Spaces* (Chapel Hill, NC: University of North Carolina Press, 1992).

Assessing these archives prompted further questions about what doing "design" actually meant, what being a "designer" involved, and crucially, who designed.

My approach and thinking, influenced in part by Marxist historians such as E. P. Thompson (author of *The Making of the Working Class*), were also shaped by immersion in second-wave feminist texts, including Sheila Rowbotham's *Hidden from History*.[6] The joint interest in Marxism and feminism led me to reconsider the meaning of patriarchy. The works of Heidi Hartmann and Sheila Rowbotham were especially useful in this regard, in particular their thoughtful conceptualizations of patriarchy as neither universal nor transhistorical concepts, but as situated in time and place.[7] Griselda Pollock and Rozsika Parker's critique of the ideological underpinnings of disciplines – in their case, art history – was also vital.[8] And working with colleagues who were interested in women and gender – not just design historians, but also those working in film studies, fashion history, and architectural history – also shaped my thinking.[9]

In the midst of my Ph.D. research, my article, "Made in Patriarchy: Towards a Feminist Analysis of Women and Design," was published. Its purpose was to provide theoretical and methodological tools for this empirical doctoral study of women's role in design in the ceramic industry. This theoretical questioning had four key propositions. First, women had interacted with design in numerous ways, but they largely had been ignored; when women's involvement with design *was* acknowledged, it was within the context of patriarchy. Second, patriarchy was reshaped and reconfigured depending on specific social, economic, and political circumstances, as well as geography and history. The consequences for women's roles in design were clear: women were categorized; they had sex-specific skills and attributes; they were deemed "feminine," "natural," "decorative," "instinctive." Third, although the various ideologies of patriarchy and its concrete and diverse manifestations were powerful, an array of assumptions about design, the designer, and the meaning of design compounded these views. In the language of writer and activist Rozsika Parker, the devices and tactics deployed by design historians were described as "the rules of the game."[10] The concept of the designer as the "auteur" – an omnipotent, god-like, heroic figure who took a place in the history of pioneering individuals (inevitably men) – was pivotal. Linked to this was the idea that the meaning of design resided in its "author's" intentions (i.e., in the designer's), and the historian's preference for the monograph as a means of writing history reiterated this. Fourth, the effects of other powerful ideologies were ingrained, particularly in the West, including the idea of design as a key element in progress (technological, social, and aesthetic), the concept of "good" design, and, linked to both of these, the commitment to modernism.

What this current article asks is whether these propositions have any validity and currency today or whether our preoccupations and needs have fundamentally changed. To address these questions, I return to the questions that were posed more than thirty years ago. First, with four areas of discussion in mind, I consider key debates in feminism, particularly the influence of third-wave feminism, the growing importance of intersectionality, and the complexities of an identity politics that recognizes a number of subject positions, including class, sexuality, race, ethnicity, and geography, as well as gender. Second, I look again at what we mean by design and the designer, as well as the continuing privileging of categories and sites of design, and types of roles and activities. I argue that perhaps we are still failing to recognize not only that design is polysemic, but also that the work of design makers, producers, and assemblers can be ordinary and everyday – part of routine, mundane lives – and that it is this capacity that makes design so potent. Third, I propose that we acknowledge the micro as well as the macro, considering the particular and the local, as well as the global. As Susan Stewart points out, "we cannot speak of … small, or miniature work independent of [the] social values expressed toward private space – particularly of the ways the domestic and the interior imply the social formation of an interior subject."[11] That the small-scale, domestic, intimate, and, perhaps, also the transitory and incidental remain on the periphery of designers' interests is indicative that this has yet to be done, I argue. Fourth, I want to propose that we take care with over-arching narratives and stay critically attuned to the

10. Quoted in Griselda Pollock, "Vision, Voice and Power: Feminist Art History and Marxism," *BLOCK* 6 (1982), 5.

11. Susan Stewart, *On Longing: Narratives of the Miniature, the Gigantic, the Souvenir, the Collection* (Durham, NC: Duke University Press, 1993), 95.

Design Struggles

12. Rowbotham, *Hidden from History*, 79.

13. News reports on each of these issues can be found online. For reporting on Carrie Gracie, see, e.g., www.radiotimes.com/news/tv/2018-01-08/carrie-gracie-bbc-news-unequal-pay/ and carriegracie.com/news.html; for the #MeToo movement, see, e.g., metoomvmt.org; for the Time's Up Now movement, see, e.g., www.timesupnow.com; for stories about women MPs in the United Kingdom, see, e.g., www.parliament.uk/business/committees/committees-a-z/commons-select/women-and-equalities-committee/news-parliament-2017/sexual-harassment-women-girls-public-evidence-17-19/; and for reporting on the restrictions on wearing the hijab in Europe, see, e.g., www.theguardian.com/world/2017/mar/14/headscarves-and-muslim-veil-ban-debate-timeline. All URLs above accessed January 8, 2018.

power of historians as they (we) attempt to make sense of the past – especially in accounting for women.

Reflections on Recent Debates within Feminism

Serendipity led me to write this section about women, gender, and feminism on February 6, 2018, the hundredth anniversary of the Representation of the People Act, which gave British property-owning women aged thirty and over the right to vote. Unquestionably a milestone for women's rights in Britain, the campaign for the vote underscored one of the ongoing criticisms of feminism in the West in the past 100 years – namely, that this and subsequent campaigns have been predominantly about gaining rights and power for middle-class white women. Indeed, even though in 1918 the Independent Labour Party and the Trade Union movement were involved in the campaign for the vote, the popular perception of the campaign was that "it was mainly middle-class."[12] The question of class is vital; and although it is important to note that economic power is just one aspect of class position, it is pivotal. On the same day – February 6, 1918 – that property-owning women aged thirty and over gained the vote in Britain, all men regardless of income and property ownership were enfranchised for the first time. British women had to wait until 1928 to be enfranchised on the same basis.

Women's issues are again at the fore for a number of reasons, highlighting yet again the complexities of the debate about women, gender, and feminism. A handful of examples help to make the point: the #MeToo and Time's Up Now campaigns in the United States; the debates about equal pay at the British Broadcasting Company (BBC) in the United Kingdom (typified by the resignation of the BBC's China correspondent, Carrie Gracie, over equal pay); the sexual harassment of women MPs and political assistants in the Houses of Parliament in the United Kingdom; the debates about wearing the hijab in Britain and in Europe[13] and the alternative stance taken by a hundred French celebrities and intellectuals whose letter, published in *Le Monde*, attracted a great deal of approbation in

Britain because it appeared to defend misogyny.[14] Certainly the history of the campaign for the vote in Britain shows that feminism in 1918 – a century ago – was complex, with many different voices that were not represented equally. This remains so today, although arguably the complexities have multiplied.

Feminism, in tackling questions of race, sexuality, ethnicity, and class, is many things. Taking bell hooks's proposition that feminism is "the movement to end sexism, sexual exploitation, and sexual oppression," Sara Ahmed, the British-Australian feminist theorist, concurs with hooks that feminism must be intersectional.[15] Situating herself as a British woman of color whose feminism came from East to West (i.e., from Lahore, Pakistan, to the United Kingdom, and then Australia) rather than the other way around, Ahmed acknowledges second-wave feminism's insistence that "the personal is political," but she also asserts that "the personal is theoretical."[16] The theoretical is Ahmed's stock-in-trade as an academic, but she sees its relevance as being close to home and the everyday. Seeking to expand the boundaries of feminism, she asks how can we "dismantle the world that is built to accommodate only some bodies."

> Sexism is one such accommodating system. Feminism requires supporting women in a struggle to exist in this world. What do I mean by *women* here? I am referring to all those who travel under the sign *women*. No feminism worthy of its name would use the sexist idea "women born women" to create the edges of feminist community, to render trans women into "not women," or "not born women," or into men.[17]

Ahmed's book is a call to be awkward, wilful, and disruptive. She identifies the destructiveness of heteronormativity, as well as the instability of location in a postcolonial world that, crucially, is shaped by multiple historical trajectories. In the discourse on feminism and women (rather than the wider discussion of gender), Ahmed's argument is pivotal: "[I]n a world in which human is still defined as *man*, we have to fight for women and as women."[18] This extends to design and design history, and while noting the

14. According to journalist Agnès Poirer, these women (who included writers, actresses, and academics) appeared to many younger feminists in France and abroad "as a retrograde bunch of over-privileged celebrities and intellectuals both totally unconcerned by the plight of all those anonymous victims of rape and sexual harassment and too preoccupied by their sexual freedom." (Agnès Poirer, *The Observer*, January 14, 2018, 32–33). Countering this perspective, the letter's initiator, Abnousse Shalmani, argued that "[w]e do not dismiss the many women who had the courage to speak up against Weinstein. We do not dismiss either the legitimacy of their fight. We do, however, add our voice, *a different voice*, to the debate." (Ibid.)

15. Sara Ahmed, *Living a Feminist Life* (Durham, NC: Duke University Press, 2017), 5.

16. Ahmed, 10.

17. Ahmed, 14.

18. Ahmed, 15.

19. Judy Attfield, *Wild Things: The Material Culture of Everyday Life* (Oxford: Berg, 2000).

20. Ahmed, *Living a Feminist Life*, 11.

21. Ahmed, *Living a Feminist Life*, 14.

22. Buckley and Clark, *Fashion and Everyday Life*.

23. Buckley and Clark, 7.

plethora of works in gender studies, a focus on women is a tactical priority right now. Indeed, one might argue that by approaching design through the prism of women, design is better illuminated. Revisiting feminism as advocated by Ahmed can provide some useful tools to expose design's ideological priorities and embedded value systems.

Re-Visioning Design through a Feminist Lens

In thinking about things and their design, the "made" things around us are the theoretical focus of this paper. These things include *Design*, or "things with attitude," as described by Judy Attfield, but mainly those "wild things" that constitute the bulk of material things – design in the lowercase.[19] More elusive and less easy to categorize, these "wild things" escape the boundaries of privileged *Design*. They defy categorization as a "special type of artifact"; instead, they are "just one type of 'thing' among other 'things' that make up the summation of the material world."[20] If *Design* is "things with attitude," then Attfield insists on "wild things" as the site of the sociality of design that "dislocate[s] it from the habitual aesthetic frame … to present it as just one of the many aspects of the material culture of the everyday."[21]

In *Fashion and Everyday Life*, Hazel Clark and I considered how fashion (in the lowercase) is part of everyday lives.[22] Keen to move beyond the analysis of fashion as intrinsic to modernity, indicative of change and innovation, we insisted on fashion as an ongoing element of people's lives. We argued that although the extraordinariness of "high fashion" has been clearly visible, "ordinary" fashion has been resolutely invisible. However, visual sources depicting everyday lives show how fashion's cycles have been "worked with" and adopted even if they do not always reveal the latest style or articulate a coherent "look." Such fashion is heterogeneous and represents a bringing together of familiar garments accumulated in closets and wardrobes over time. To these garments might be added something modern: a new coat or the latest hat; but most often, they would be ensembles of clothes acquired over years.[23] Here, we point to the ongoing participation by various people in the making, producing, assembling, or (might we even say?) designing, often routinely, of clothes or things. Part of our argument is that the spaces and places in which these processes of making and assembly occur are vital to how these "fashions" are perceived. By looking beyond fashion's familiar terrain – catwalk, boutique, department store, designer – a complementary trajectory can be traced. Indeed, fashion was embedded in and contingent on the practices of people's everyday lives, and it was located in some familiar spaces – on the street, although not only the major thoroughfares but also in its margins and back streets. It also took shape in some intimate places – the wardrobe or the sewing box – and in rituals and commonplace social interactions: going shopping, to work, out for dinner, or to collect the kids. We argued that the structures of power that designate meaning and, crucially, status are to be found in the places and spaces where "things" are made/produced/assembled – "designed." From this observation, we can reread Susan Stewart, noting that the grand and the gigantic speak to the values of the exterior life of the city (or nature), whereas the small or miniature expresses interiority, the domestic, and the social formation of the interior subject. The implications of this juxtaposition for design as it moves between the two – between the world of the city and the large scale on the one hand and the intimate and the particular on the other – are clear.

One of Attfield's tactics was to challenge the idea that design is the domain of the professional designer, residing only in formal design structures, design schools, and professional bodies. Instead, she reminds us that design is also an active verb that involves making/producing something – designing things:

> The experience of designing is not confined to professional designers, nor [to] amateur do-it-yourself activities, such as home decorating; it is something that most people do everyday when they put together a combination of clothes to wear or plan a meal.[24]

This position resonated with our thinking in *Fashion and Everyday Life*, allowing us to pursue the idea that fashion design is not only the province of the designer. Indeed, this position offered us the scope to question who the designer is; it provided an opportunity to challenge the privileging of certain types of design practice; and it enabled reconsideration of aspects of design that have slipped to the sidelines, or to the margins: the practices and making of stuff for everyday lives.

Home crafts, do-it-yourself (DIY) making and crafting, home dressmaking, sewing, knitting, the domestic making and assembling of things – shelves, tables, sheds, beds – as well as everyday ordering, arranging, and planning. This making – in the sense of constructing – can involve adaptation, reuse, and recycling, as well as the production of everyday devices in the home, garage, garden, workshop, and workplace. Reflecting on this, it is useful to return to this notion of the "making" or "producing" of things. Latterly, design historians have steered away from this as they explore the meaning of things: their use, exchange, circulation, and reuse. But perhaps to come to different understandings of women's relationship to design today means making a case for thinking more deeply about those who produce, make, and assemble things?

Striking here is the status and meaning of a design activity such as service design. What types of services do we mean? Primarily, we have meant exterior metastructures: transport systems, the processes of government, the organization of social services, the planning of public housing. However, we might also think of the mundane practices involved in the design or production of services in everyday lives – services that are undertaken on a routine and daily basis by, for example, parents raising children, or grown-up children supporting their elderly parents or relatives, or the planning of full-time work, being a parent, running a home. Indeed, individual acts of producing and assembling services are replicated in different ways across the globe. Crucially, these services are highly political but are a low priority for politicians today.

PATRIARCHAL STRUCTURES

Re-Visiting Women and Design History

The final section of this paper reflects on the power and influence of historians as they have tried to make sense of design's past through the prism of women and gender. Looking back at design history literature written predominantly in the United Kingdom, we see that some of the foundational texts of feminist design history were published thirty-five years ago. These texts typically focused on the home and on craft, and they were interdisciplinary in nature. Drawing on a range of early texts, scholars working in the field of design history in Britain in the 1970s also positioned themselves as *counter* to a number of dominant and established disciplines – notably art history and architectural history. But it was also allied to these – in particular the "New Art History," as it was termed in Britain in the 1980s – to initiate a process of critical questioning of art historical methods – firstly around class, and then around sex and gender.[25] Design history also enjoyed fruitful synergies with cultural studies, responding to some of the theoretical paradigms preoccupying scholars working in that field – especially in relation to poststructuralist theories. For example, the journal *BLOCK*, in which Philippa Goodall's key essay "Design and Gender" appeared, was at the intersection of art history, cultural studies, film studies, and design history.[26] Retrospectively, Pat Kirkham and Judy Attfield's edited volume of essays, *A View from the Interior: Feminism, Women and Design*, published in 1989, provided a microcosm of the thinking that was taking place in the field.[27]

Although important theoretical debates relating to broad conceptual themes (e.g., consumption, the body, space, and identity) were pivotal from the late 1980s through to the 2000s, a plethora of texts explicitly or implicitly drew on ideas that had emerged in the context of feminism and gender studies (probably more of the latter and fewer of the former).[28] In this context, ignoring questions of gender and women in the writing of design history was certainly less academically acceptable. Both historical and theoretical writing about fashion and dress provided some of the most interesting scholarship in which these debates were developed. Bringing sustained critical

25. Jonathan Harris, *The New Art History: A Critical Introduction* (London: Routledge, 2001).

26. Goodall, "Design and Gender." See, e.g., Jon Bird et al., eds., *The BLOCK Reader in Visual Culture* (Abingdon: Routledge, 1996). See also adri.mdx.ac.uk/block.

27. The work was a harbinger of things to come, and it also reprinted key early work. Its fifteen essays drew together a range of different scholars, setting up debate between feminist historians and encapsulating the variety of ways in which feminism and gender studies had influenced design history to date. It included discussions on menswear and masculinity, gender, community and postwar housing, domestic consumption in postwar Britain, and the meaning of the stiletto heel. *A View from the Interior* is an excellent example of the effect that feminism and gender studies had on a subject area, and it was especially important because it brought together some of the latest scholarship in this field. Attfield and Kirkham, *A View from the Interior*.

28. Examples include Beatriz Colomina, ed., *Sexuality and Space* (Princeton, NJ: Princeton Architectural Press, 1992); Doreen Massey, *Space, Place, and Gender* (Cambridge, UK: Polity Press, 1994); Elizabeth Grosz, *Space, Time and Perversion: Essays on the Politics of Bodies* (New York, NY: Routledge, 1995); and Frank Mort, *Cultures of Consumption: Masculinities and Social Space in Late Twentieth-Century Britain* (London: Routledge, 1996).

29. Examples include Barbara Burman, The Culture of Sewing: Gender, Consumption, and Home Dressmaking (Oxford and New York, NY: Berg, 1999); Christopher Breward, Fashioning London: Clothing the Modern Metropolis (Oxford and New York: Berg, 2004); Caroline Evans, Fashion at the Edge: Spectacle, Modernity, and Deathliness (New Haven, CT: Yale University Press, 2003); Carol Tulloch, Black Style (London: V&A Publications, 2004); Alys Eve Weinbaum et al., eds., The Modern Girl Around the World: Consumption, Modernity, and Globalization (Durham, NC: Duke University Press, 2008).

30. Joan W. Scott, Gender and the Politics of History (New York, NY: Colombia University Press, 1999), 16.

31. Scott, 17.

32. Scott, 17.

33. Buckley, "Made in Patriarchy," 4–7.

34. John Brewer, "Microhistory and the Histories of Everyday Life," Cultural and Social History 7, no. 1 (2010), 87–109.

35. Brewer, 89.

36. Brewer, 96.

engagement based on outstanding empirical research and theoretical reflection to design history, writers asked questions about women and fashion, dress and race, fashion and place/space, and modernity.[29] What we see in these works is the carrying through of earlier theoretical questioning that addressed subject identities to a range of disciplines.

In *Gender and the Politics of History*, published in 1999, Joan Scott noted the proliferation of historical writing about women, adding up to "the new knowledge about women."[30] She also proposed that "more than in many other areas of historical inquiry, women's history is characterized by extraordinary tensions: between practical politics and academic scholarship; between received disciplinary standards and interdisciplinary influences; between history's atheoretical stance and feminism's need for theory."[31] Underpinning these tensions, she observed, was a common aim "to make women a focus of inquiry, a subject of the story, an agent of the narrative."[32] Complicating this inquiry, as in all aspects of history, was a range of assumptions about the field under investigation – whether literature, film, art, architecture, or design.

Confronting some of these issues, historian John Brewer proposed some ways of thinking about the subjects of history that are extremely useful.[33] In "Microhistory and the Histories of Everyday Life," published in 2010, Brewer examines the different motivations for what he sees as two fundamentally different ways of viewing the world. He describes these views as prospect and refuge history.[34] Prospect history "is written from a single, superior point of view – a bird's-eye perspective or from a lofty peak… Because of height, size, and distance, what is observed and recorded is general, not specific."[35] This view produces narratives of history that "are univocal in their exclusion of voices that do not fit the uniform model of change, and univocal in that they do not recognize the contradictions and conflicts within the model."[36] Reflecting on the field of design history, it may be that the ways in which we, as historians, have thought about design is exclusionary and univocal as we sought to prioritize (for diverse reasons, whether social, political, cultural, or economic) what we saw as the important challenges and concerns of the age: modernization, progress, consumption, urbanization.

37. Brewer, 89.

38. Brewer, 92.

39. Brewer, 99.

40. Brewer, 96.

41. Fiona Hackney, "Quiet Activism and the New Amateur," *Design and Culture* 5, no. 2 (2013), 171.

In contrast, refuge history, which Brewer investigates and advocates, "is close-up and on the small scale. Its emphasis is on a singular place rather than space… The emphasis is on forms of interdependence, on interiority and intimacy rather than surface and distance."[37] He argues that a concern for the everyday and the intimate (characteristics of refuge history) is often interpreted as "part of the more general rejection and critique of grand narratives"; and although noting that this is true, he argues that it is important to understand "what is at stake here is not … the question of narration, but … the issue of scale and point of view."[38] Noting that refuge history is fundamentally heterogeneous, he observes that this heterogeneity constitutes both its greatest difficulty and its greatest potential.[39]

Brewer's article is worthy of further consideration – particularly when he proposes "that … only by shifting the perspective, scale, and point of view of historical analysis, creating variations on small-scale history, [can] the relationship between structure and agency … be properly understood."[40] I want to situate my own research on women and design upon this ground, asking that we begin to understand making/producing/assembling as part of a continuum *that is design*. This perspective can include the close-up, domestic, intimate, personal. For example, in her article, "Quiet Activism and the New Amateur," Fiona Hackney proposes the existence of

> new super-connected amateurs who, informed by the existence of on- and offline resources (citizen journalism, community broadband, online forums, and social media), as well as their individual life experiences and expertise, are quietly active as they open up new channels of value and exchange by engaging in alternative craft economies and harnessing assets in often surprising, productive ways.[41]

Reflecting on the historiography of design history, we can see that research and publishing on women's varied and complex relationships to design is uneven. For example, the discipline's primary journal, the *Journal of Design History*, has published articles that discussed the routine,

42. See, e.g., Jesse Adams Stein, "Making 'Foreign Orders': Australian Print-Workers and Clandestine Creative Production in the 1980s," *Journal of Design History* 28, 3 (2015), 275–92; Stephanie Bunn, "Who Designs Scottish Vernacular Baskets?," *Journal of Design History* 29, no. 1 (2016), 24–42; Patricia Zakreski, "The Victorian Christmas Card as Aesthetic Object: 'Very Interesting Ephemerae of a Very Interesting Period in English Art-Production,'" *Journal of Design History* 29, no. 2 (2016), 120–36; and Deirdre Pretorius, "Graphic Design in South Africa: A Post-Colonial Perspective," *Journal of Design History* 28, no. 3 (2015), 293–315.

43. This informal survey involved looking at the articles, images, keywords, and footnotes from the past ten years of the *Journal of Design History*, from volume 22 (2009) to volume 31 (2018), to identify the ones that addressed questions of women's relationships with design.

44. At the time of writing this paper, thirty-eight issues were examined, and each issue typically had at least four articles, thus there were c. 150 articles in total published in these ten volumes (2009–2018). Of these, nine articles *significantly* addressed women's relationships with design.

45. Cheryl Buckley, "Made in Patriarchy: Theories of Women and Design – a Reworking," in *Design and Feminism: Re-Visioning Spaces, Places, and Everyday Things*, ed. Joan Rothschild (New Brunswick, NJ: Rutgers University Press, 1999), 109–18.

the local and vernacular, the ordinary and transitory, and different geographies, and it has fundamentally challenged the prioritization of research into modernism and good design.[42] However, publishing about *women* as designers/producers/makers and as users/consumers/intermediaries is remarkably scant.[43] Although numerous articles have as their underpinning a concern with gender (probably 25%), the journal published few articles between 2009 and 2018 that directly addressed women.[44] As editorial chair of this journal between 2011 and 2016, I and the editorial board were extremely alert to questions of women and gender; but what I want to suggest is that, unlike gender, the question of women's relationship to design has slipped to the margins of scholarship and research.

Although I don't have clear answers as to why this marginalization has happened, I have written elsewhere about the consequences of the shift to gender studies away from women's studies.[45] I argued that, from the 1990s, the politics of feminism took a back seat to that of gender studies in part because of its failure to adequately respond to the complexities of global inequalities and the differential experiences of women. Perhaps another question to ask is the extent to which the uncoupling of design history from design practice has contributed to this marginalization and loss of activism? What has become apparent is that more and more frequently in the teaching of design practice at degree level in British universities, the study of design's histories has been squeezed and marginalized as pedagogic thinking has emphasized business, marketing, and promotion modules rather than historical, theoretical, and critical ones.

From the outset in the 1970s, design history in Britain had a close relationship to design practice, taught in the new polytechnic sector in which the Bachelor of Arts (B.A.) art and design degree programs predominated. As a result, it maintained an engaged, activist element that connected practice, history, and theory. A central aim and priority was to engage designers in critical debates about their practice – in part through historical examples, but also by drawing on critical theory. As a result, for those practicing as design historians in Britain, design history was never only a subbranch of the humanities; rather, it was intimately linked to practice with a concern for critical and theoretical discourses, as well as historical ones. Although design history emerged differently in the United States, an engagement with the history of design was increasingly articulated around the emerging field of design studies, which again addressed practice and theory, as well as history.[46] The consensus was that to understand contemporary practice one needed to understand its past; as Victor Margolin put it, "the challenge for those of us who study design at the end of the twentieth century is to establish a central place for it in contemporary life."[47]

Indeed, we might now contend that design has secured a place at the center of contemporary life, but is it a univocal and totalizing notion of design that has little space for routine, mundane, everyday practices? Further, as Brewer has pointed out, the fundamental difficulty of refuge history is dealing with its heterogeneity; but he also saw this heterogeneity as its greatest potential. Arguably as design historians, our responsibility is to recognize complexities and complications, to look for the awkward and disruptive, and not to settle for easy and comfortable narratives.

Looking back and forward, "Made in Patriarchy" in 1986 was didactic and provocative – the product of a particular point in an academic and intellectual life. Feminist theory and history provided essential critical tools that helped to challenge some of the embedded assumptions about design and the designer. Today's reinvigorated feminism can do this again. The title of my original article was "Made" in patriarchy, not "Designed" in patriarchy because then, as now, design was an ideologically loaded term that I wanted to question. With Ahmed's contention as the starting point – that "in a world in which human is still defined as *man*, we have to fight for women and as women" – we might return to the question of women's relationship to design, helping to prise open understandings and to change perceptions of what design means and who does it, so as to illuminate the possibilities of design as a vital component of everyday lives.[48]

46. See, e.g., this journal's special issue on design history and design studies, *Design Issues* 11, no. 1 (1995).

47. Victor Margolin, "Design History or Design Studies: Subject Matter and Methods," *Design Issues* 11, no. 1 (1995), 15.

48. Ahmed, *Living a Feminist Life*, 15.

Design Struggles

Acknowledgments

Cheryl Buckley's text is based on her keynote for "Beyond Change," and first appeared in *Design Issues* 36, no. 1 (2020): 19–29. The text is reproduced by permission of the MIT Press.

BREAKING CLASS Upward Climbers and the Swiss Nature of Design History

Paola De Martin

> ... when she thought it over afterwards, it occurred to her, that she ought to have wondered at this, but at the time it all seemed quite natural ...
> —Lewis Carroll, *Alice in Wonderland*

Introduction

Give us a Break! is the title of my ongoing Ph.D. research based on the biographies of designers with working-class backgrounds in Zurich during the neoliberal era (approximately 1970 to 2010). My oral sources include, first of all, extended narrative interviews with five upward climbers born between 1952 and 1992. One further interview was undertaken by a sociologist asking me to talk about my own social mobility. Shorter exchanges with an ever-growing number of class-passers enrich this corpus, and finally oral and written exchanges with half a dozen experts from the design field complete it. I combine this polyphony with photographs given to me by the interviewees and with visual references mentioned during our talks. I soon realized that my material was resistant to a single analytical approach. This is why, in this essay, which is based on my presentation at the 2018 Swiss Design Network (SDN) conference "Beyond Change," I will sketch out the combined approach that I've developed during the last six years of my research in order to do justice to the matter. In fact, I soon discovered, somehow unsurprisingly, that these biographies are a completely new content for design history, one that provides rich aesthetic and existential details of former proletarian lives, and by doing so says much about the aesthetics of social inequality. Beyond this, I found out – to my surprise – that these transformative paths open up a wholly new perspective on design history. I started to use them like special lenses that enlighten the sociohistorical spectrum of the design world. Before I can explain how and why this is so, I want to give a quantitative and qualitative overview of the Swiss context of class and neoliberalism and its connection to the creative industries.

The Swiss Design of Inequality – Facts and Figures

Most people around the world, I've noticed, do not think of Switzerland as a country with a strong working-class presence, but in fact, this was the reality when I grew up as the child of workers in Zurich. Born in 1965, I remember very well that until the late 1970s the city was still a major workers' capital, with a very vivid and diverse working-class culture. For example, from one of the major magazines in Zurich, my mum – a factory worker first and a cleaner later – would buy workers' trousers for my dad and the hard plastic tableware that we used every day and for many years before we could afford ceramics. My dad – he was a construction worker – would take his own food to the construction site in a tiffin box and play cards every Sunday morning in one of the many workers' bars. Living according to a typical gendered labor division – he constructs and she cleans – together they knew quite something about the architecture, the design, and the art of class-making, a knowledge they passed on to me performatively. But there was also a reflexive space and a shared language of sly adaptation and open resistance. The key figures I remember well: a workers' pastor, a workers' doctor, a workers' soccer tournament, a workers' bowling club, and a workers' alpine club. We would sing workers' pop songs, and also leftist intellectual songs, cite famous quotes from workers' plays and novels that made us feel proud (my favorite:

"The difference between a lady and a flower girl is not how she behaves, but how she is treated," from *My Fair Lady* by George Bernard Shaw). We would go to the workers' library, read workers' magazines, and some of us would even engage as photographers in the now perished Workers' Photography Association, the Swiss Arbeiterfotobund. The great majority of us would vote for the socialist party and sometimes for other workers' parties more on the extreme left. We would celebrate our immemorial parties on our memorial days all year round. This world was so self-evident and present then; who would ever have thought that it would completely disappear? I didn't think so much about it when I became a textile designer in the 1990s; at the time, I sensed the connection between my profession and industry. But this industry, too, has almost disappeared, and I went on to become a design historian questioning the social impositions of globalization. Only then did I begin to reflect on the speed and radicality of the downfall of working-class cultures, and I felt the need to exchange thoughts as a lecturer at the ZHdK, the Zurich University of the Arts.

I'm far from romanticizing this era. Proletarian life was a constant struggle. I have no sympathy for populist attitudes that mystify the "simple people," because I never thought of the milieu of my background as simple. It is a sense of unbelief that overcomes me when I'm at the ZHdK, again and again, and a critical distance towards innovative enthusiasm. It's also the new architecture of the school that triggers my reserve, again and again. Before it was repurposed as the ZHdK campus, the Toni Areal was a yogurt factory where some of my mother's best friends were employed. In their free time, she would perform an ostentatiously neat and decent lady, and he would perform an ostentatiously lean and modern, introverted smart-guy. As a child, I was fascinated by the overdetermination of their styles. Today I think that stripping off their working-class props and conforming to bourgeois gender norms was important for them, as for many other working-class people I knew, because inside the factory they were denied their gender and sex to an extent that dehumanized and transformed them into functional blue-collared tools serving the logic of material production. She would work

SOCIAL LOOKING GLASS

countless hours of her life on the assembly line, and he would endlessly drive the truck up and down the iconic ramp of the Toni factory.

1. Jan Jagodzinski, *Visual Art and Education in an Era of Designer Capitalism: Deconstructing the Oral Eye* (New York, NY: Palgrave MacMillan, 2010).

Today this ramp has become a media icon that stands for the successful transformation of the old, repetitive, and material labor into the new, creative, and immaterial one. Toni is one of the many former factories that have undergone this change. Where in earlier days the poorly educated could find jobs behind the discreet walls of soap, beer, turbine, textile, shoe, weapon, and engine factories, there are now restaurants and museums, galleries, libraries, and educational institutions. In the former industrial areas, you will also find design, art, and architectural studios, as well as advertising, music, and film production sites, and finally, close together, shops selling mass-produced goods, niche design articles, and second-season stuff alike. Over the last four decades Zurich has become a global capital of finance, higher education, insurance, raw material trading, IT – and the creative industries (CI). My own fashion brand Beige, the Freitag flagship store, Google, On running shoes, UBS and Credit Suisse, the expanding Swiss Federal Institute of Technology (ETH) and ZHdK, among other higher educational institutions – we are all part of this new reality, no less so than the annual Long Night of the Museums and the restaurants that are open all night long and all year round, the Street Parade, the Zurich Film Festival, the extension of the major art museum Kunsthaus Zurich, the Prime Tower skyscraper, the new Europaallee, the Theater Spektakel in summer and the Zurich Marathon in winter. The skin of the city today is the postmodernist, diverse, rich, sustainable, enjoyable – and remarkably red-green ruled – surface of neoliberalism, or what Jan Jagodzinski has aptly coined "designer capitalism."[1] Not surprisingly, Zurich regularly ranks as one of the cities with the highest quality of life worldwide. But quality always has, whatever capitalism rules, a price which not everybody can afford. Former workers' areas have been gentrified and the once-strong working class has lost its symbolic capital. While the number of working-poor families and homeless people grows at the margins of the city, white-trash-bashing has become socially and politically acceptable.

The changes in Zurich over the last few decades

2. Bundesamt für Statistik (BFS), *Statistisches Jahrbuch der Schweiz 2018* (Zurich: NZZ Libro, 2018), 106, 624.

3. Toni Ricciardi, *Breve storia dell'emigrazione italiana in Svizzera* (Rome: Donizelli, 2018), 122–32.

are representative of the structural changes that have taken place in Switzerland as a whole. For example, the agricultural or first sector employed 14.5% of the Swiss working population in 1960, and now employs just 3.3%. This small share is even more dramatic if we take into consideration that it is bolstered by notoriously high public subsidies for agricultural products and services. In contrast, the tertiary or services sector, which includes the creative industries, now employs two and a half times as many people as it did in 1960: 75.5% as opposed to 39%. The secondary, industrial and craft sector, employed 46.5% of the Swiss working population in 1960. This percentage has more than halved to just 21.1% today.[2] Who are these new workers now?

When I talk in public about Swiss working-class issues, the audience – be it in Zurich, Buenos Aires, Oslo, Ahmedabad, or Berlin – tend to assume two things. First, that in Switzerland, the super-rich country, there aren't any "real" workers anymore, and second, that I'm talking about migrants. It seems so unthinkable that there are workers in this country at all, and that not all of them are from abroad. But in fact, Swiss workers have always represented the majority of the working class. Between 1970 and today, the share of migrant and low-skilled employees in the first and secondary sectors fluctuated between 20% and 40%, depending on the region, the branch, and the economic situation. In the early 1970s, migrant workers numbered more than half a million and were almost all Italians. After the oil crises of the 1970s, almost two-thirds of the Italian community were instrumentalized as economic buffers and had to leave the country to save the Swiss economy. In the early 1980s, the country recovered from the oil price shocks and more and more small but significant groups of Spaniards, Portuguese, Yugoslavs, and others came with precarious regular permits to work in the agricultural and industrial sectors and the building, care, and cleaning branches.[3] Many illegal migrants came from non-European countries to seek better lives for themselves and their families. The estimated number of these "sans-papiers" lies in the six-digit range.

A new phenomenon since the late 1980s is the so-called working poor, which today numbers 145,000 people. Together with their non-working family members living in the same household, this adds up to more than 571,000 people living in relative poverty, equivalent to 14% of the 8.2 million inhabitants of Switzerland. Seven percent of children and teenagers in this country suffer from relative poverty. This means that they survive, of course, in the medium-term, but don't have the means to live a dignified life, which leads to stress-related illnesses and a lower life expectancy. Relative poverty puts a moral and economic pressure on people to enter – at a young age and without undertaking further education – the ever-shrinking labor market for poorly skilled professions, which typically leads to a life of low pay and diminished opportunities for themselves and their children. Shame at being poor is widespread, and the remarkable numbers of working poor who do not claim the state welfare to which they are entitled can be seen as a quantitative proxy of this social shame. Invisibility is what most characterizes poverty in this country.[4]

The middle class, in spite of all the pessimistic gloom, has not disappeared at all but has undergone a transformation resulting in new winners and losers in the financial, technical, knowledge-based, and creative economies.[5] Compared to the structure of the middle class some forty years ago, the middle class of today is on the whole more hierarchical, but less hierarchical on the micro-scale of everyday business. Status angst, passive-aggressive symptoms of depression, along with eager assimilation to a normative optimism are widespread among this diverse middle class.[6] To complete the picture, the new phenomenon of the neoliberal era must be mentioned at the other end of the social scale: the super-rich. The growing inequality in Switzerland can be traced back to the racing away of their incomes, and much more of their fortunes.[7]

In Zurich, besides these economic elites, the other winners of neoliberalism, the cultural capitalists, are also highly concentrated. The proportion of Zurich's population older than fifteen holding a degree in higher education was less than 10% in 1970 and is 47% in 2010. This is the highest of all Swiss cities (Geneva: 44%; Bern: 43%; Basel: 38%; St Gallen: 31%; Swiss average: 29%). Whereas the working-class migrants who arrived during the three decades of the post-War economic boom delayed the shift

4. BFS, *Statistisches Jahrbuch der Schweiz 2018*, 528; Christin Kehrli and Carlo Knöpfel, eds., *Handbuch Armut in der Schweiz* (Lucerne: Caritas-Verlag, 2006), 78–79; Claudia Schuwey and Carlo Knöpfel, eds., *Neues Handbuch Armut in der Schweiz* (Lucerne: Caritas-Verlag, 2014), 68. Margrit Stamm, "Arbeiterkinder an die Hochschulen! Hintergründe ihrer Aufstiegsangst," *Dossier* 16, no. 2 (2016), 25–27, margritstamm.ch/images/Arbeiterkinder%20an%20die%20Hochschulen!.pdf.

5. For an up-to-date insight into the debate around the erosion of middle class, see Daniel Oesch and Emily Murphy, "Keine Erosion, sondern Wachstum der Mittelklasse. Der Wandel der Schweizer Berufsstruktur seit 1970," *Social Change in Switzerland* no. 12 (2017), www.socialchangeswitzerland.ch/?p=1377.

6. For a very good sociohistorical summary of this aspect, see Oliver Nachtwey, *Die Abstiegsgesellschaft: Über das Aufbegehren in der regressiven Moderne* (Berlin: Suhrkamp, 2016).

7. For quantitative and qualitative survey of the Swiss super-rich, see Ueli Mäder, Ganga Jey Aratnam, and Sarah Schilliger, *Wie Reiche denken und lenken: Reichtum in der Schweiz: Geschichte, Fakten, Gespräche* (Zurich: Rotpunktverlag, 2010); Ueli Mäder, *Macht.ch: Geld und Macht in der Schweiz* (Zurich: Rotpunktverlag, 2015).

Design Struggles

8. Daniel Frizsche, "Zürich, die gebildete Stadt," *Neue Zürcher Zeitung*, February 1, 2017, 19.

9. Catrin Seefranz and Philippe Saner, *Making Differences: Schweizer Kunsthochschulen. Explorative Vorstudie* (Zurich: Zürcher Hochschule der Künste, 2012), 38–45, blog. zhdk.ch/artschooldifferences/ files/2013/11/Making_ Differences_Vorstudie_ Endversion.pdf; Philippe Saner, Sophie Vögele, and Pauline Vessely, *Schlussbericht. Art. School.Differences: Researching Inequality and Normativities in the Field of Higher Art Education* Zurich: Zürcher Hochschule der Künste, 2016), 150ff, blog. zhdk.ch/artschooldifferences/ files/2016/10/ASD_ Schlussbericht_final_web_ verlinkt.pdf.

from a manufacturing to a services economy for longer than other European countries, the new migrants accelerate it. In Zurich, the high concentration of cultural and economic elites is fed by international employees, of whom 80% hold a degree in higher education and 10% have a Ph.D. The share of Zurich's population with only nine years of compulsory schooling or less diminished from 33% in 1970 to 19% in 2010.[8]

Unfortunately, we lack long-term data on the social backgrounds of those working in Zurich's creative industries. We know that exclusion in the admission process exists for design studies at the ZHdK, and has increased since the implementation of the Bologna reforms in the first decade of the new millennium. It is less pronounced than in medical studies, for example, and comparable to exclusion rates in humanities at the Zurich University. At the ZHdK, the percentage of students whose parents hold only a mandatory school degree is 6% (compared to an average among the Swiss working population of 14%) and is mostly accounted for by poorly educated migrant workers, whose children are more likely than the offspring of poorly educated Swiss workers to grasp their chance in design education. The percentage of students at the ZHdK whose parents hold a secondary school degree is 28% (compared to an average among the Swiss working population of 42%). When it comes to higher education, the relation between ZHdK students and the general population reverses. The parents of approximately 60% of ZHdK students hold a degree in higher education – half of them a Swiss degree and the other half a foreign one (compared to an average among the Swiss working population of 29%). A majority of the growing number of international students who move to Zurich to study design are the relatively well-equipped heirs of cultural capital, mostly coming from Germany and other European countries.[9]

The most recent data on employees in the CI sector illustrate a remarkable growth of 8% in the period from 2005 to 2008 in Zurich's greater area. The growth of the CI sector is more dynamic than the economy as a whole and continues to be so after the crisis of 2008. This is especially true for the CI in Zurich, according to the creative industry reports of 2010 and 2016. But one has to take into consideration that in the 2010 report an employee is counted as such only if they've worked at least six hours weekly,[10] whereas in the 2016 report the threshold for being considered an "employee" is just one hour of work per week.[11] In other words, someone working for just 52 hours per year – an intense one-week project, say – would, in the 2016 report, be considered as employed in the sector and thus contribute to the creative industry's seemingly miraculous growth. Such quantitative enthusiasm disguises the precarity that all designers experience.[12] The market is highly competitive, the wages are notoriously low, permanent job contracts are extremely rare, and to make a living is almost impossible without public subsidies, cross-financing, and wealthy parents who can support their offspring through the many lean periods. Not surprisingly, when asked about their satisfaction a year or two after graduating, a consistently high share of former design students – approximately 40%; twice as many compared with other studies – would not choose the same field of study again.[13] However, the boom of design courses, design events, design museums, and design shops alike, attracts more and more students from social milieus who would not previously have been informed about the existence of such studies. As yet, we know little about the correlation between the social background of designers and the long-term rate of success. However, all scholarly literature agrees that we should keep on questioning "the mechanisms through which social class continues to have a sizeable effect beyond education."[14]

Give us a Break!, indeed. I use the exclamation mark in the title of my Ph.D. to demand a shared public pause, a break to think and reflect on our time of massive social transformation. Furthermore, I ask for the subaltern voices of my interviewees to be recognized, my own included. What does it mean for designers and the children of Zurich's workers to trespass the class boundaries of our society – the old one and the new one in the making? What does it mean to climb the ladder in a society whose inequalities one has become so accustomed to as to think they are "quite natural," to quote my epigraph from *Alice in Wonderland*?

What does meaning mean after all in the context of

10. Christoph Weckerle and Huber Theler, *Dritter Kreativwirtschaftsbericht Zürich: Die Bedeutung der Kultur- und Kreativwirtschaft für den Standort Zürich* (Zurich: Zürcher Hochschule der Künste 2010), 52, preview.tinyurl.com/yyovz5vn.

11. Christoph Weckerle, Roman Page, and Simon Grand, *Von der Kreativwirtschaft zu den Creative Economies: Kreativwirtschaftsbericht Schweiz 2016* (Zurich: Zürcher Hochschule der Künste, 2016), 83, www.creativeeconomies.com/downloads/creative-economy-report-2016.pdf.

12. For a short introduction to the historical making of precarity in the creative sector, see Franz Schultheis, "Kreativarbeit zwischen Beruf und Berufung," in *Kreativität als Beruf*, ed. Franz Schultheis, Christoph Henning, and Dieter Thomä (Bielefeld: transcript Verlag, 2019), 87–142.

13. Schweizer Dienstleistungszentrum Berufsbildung, Berufs-, Studien- und Laufbahnberatung (SDBB), *Die erste Stelle nach dem Studium: Die Beschäftigungssituation nach einem Studium an einer Fachhochschule* (Heft 4, 2009) (Bern: SDBB-Verlag, 2009), 16–20; SDBB, *Die erste Stelle nach dem Studium: Die Beschäftigungssituation nach einem Studium an einer Fachhochschule* (Heft 4, 2011) (Bern: SDBB-Verlag, 2011), 20–24; SDBB, *Die erste Stelle nach dem Studium: Die Beschäftigungssituation der Neuabsolventinnen und Neuabsolventen von Schweizer Hochschulen* (Bern: SDBB-Verlag, 2013), 86–91.

14. Francesco Laganà, "Inequalities in Returns to Education in Switzerland," in *Education, Occupation, and Social Origin: A Comparative Analysis of the Transmission of Socio-Economic Inequalities*, ed Fabrizio Bernardi and Gabriele Ballarino (Cheltenham, UK/ Northampton, MA: Edward Elgar Publishing, 2016), 211. For a general critique of neoliberal meritocracy, see Jo Littler, *Against Meritocracy: Culture, Power and Myths of Mobility* (London: Routledge, 2017).

15. Michel Foucault, *The Archeology of Knowledge* (London: Routledge, 2002), 9.

design and social inequality? In the following sections, I will describe how I engaged in the endeavor of this quest. First, I will explain how a *habitus break*, a concept coined by the sociologist Pierre Bourdieu, can be fruitfully deployed by design historians for the development of alternative meanings. I will set out how I conceptualize human bodies as *walking social archives* in general, and the symptoms of ease and unease of upward climbers who encounter institutional design settings in particular as *knowledge of the social history of design under seal*. Second, I will expose how I break this seal together with my interviewees, and then analyze the manifest articulation of this break. Finally, I will turn the concrete articulations of habitus breaks into concrete historical questions. This will bring to the surface a huge gap in social theory, which is also a huge social practitioner's trap. My call for new design historians, practitioners, and activists to cover this tricky void will conclude the picture.

Class-Passers Break the Seal of Social Nature

When we are in the modus of everyday action, we can't ask history why we are doing whatever we are doing. To be functional in our everyday actions, we constantly forget the making of society and transform social history into "social nature." If we want to know which history we forget, we must interrupt this naturalizing process. Biographical disruptions and transgressions like the ones my interviewees experience, therefore, are key narratives for historical knowledge production. As Michel Foucault noted: "One of the most essential features of the new history is probably this displacement of the discontinuous, its transference from the obstacle to the work itself."[15]

Social upward movers from the working classes that make it into the design field embody precious memories, because their trajectories cross more limits than many other paths. They move from the lowest classes to the hot spots of cultural production while trespassing the middle classes. They get in touch with poor and wealthy milieus, they learn from fields that focus on economic accumulation and those that focus on the accumulation of cultural capital, and they accustom themselves to very dependent and then also to very self-determined lifestyles. My interviewees don't just reproduce social status, nor do they completely internalize the common-sensical "social nature" that justifies inequalities, but rather break with its sense. By doing so they experience ruptures with the self-evident "nature" of society. These ruptures, again, produce continuous ruptures in their habitus.[16] This is the symptomatic moment when social nature points its finger to social history.

We all "know" a lot about this history, basically, but this knowledge is implicit and encapsulated in our bodies. Only when triggered by certain settings that are different from what we learned to be natural does this sedimented knowledge come to the surface. This is why, in an upper-middle-class-dominated field like the design field, only the class-passers feel the upper-middle-class norms. For designers with a middle-class and much more for those with an upper-middle-class background these norms are so natural, they cannot even think about it. This is what makes normativity so powerful as a tool of domination: the rulers cannot see its contingency like fish cannot feel water, and if the dominated dare to speak about it, it is easy for those in power to accuse them of being insane. Institutions cannot talk and think about power relations, but humans can, and I encourage my interviewees to "think over afterward" and "wonder about" this strange social wonderland of design. My interviewees describe the fascination for the design field and the general feeling of being very welcome initially, but also their unexpected unease and a thrilling pressure to adapt to it that follows up, as soon as they enter the culturally loaded spaces. They tell me about their sudden fast heartbeat and stutter when they try to explain this unease, about a dry mouth and a tension in their neck when they get overruled by somebody more accustomed to the legitimate habits of the design field, somebody who behaves in it like a fish in water, while they learn to breathe in this new atmosphere. Most of them express a feeling of social shame about their former tastes and preferences, a shame that is totally new to them. And some relate to me their indecipherable nightmares in which they try to be normal according to the rules of art and design, but regularly fail to do so.

16. For the context of habitus in design history, see my glossary and Pierre Bourdieu, "Introduction" and "The Sense of Distinction" (from *Distinction: A Social Critique of Taste*), in *The Design History Reader*, ed. Grace Lees-Maffei and Rebecca Houze (London: Bloomsbury Academic Publishing, 2010), 402–8.

Design Struggles

17. Pierre Bourdieu, *La misère du monde* (Paris: Editions du Seuil, 1993), 522; Andreas Bremer and Andrea Lange-Vester, eds., *Soziale Milieus und Wandel der Sozialstruktur: Die gesellschaftlichen Herausforderungen und die Strategien der sozialen Gruppen* (second updated edition) (Wiesbaden: Springer VS, 2014), 29; Eva Barlösius, *Pierre Bourdieu* (Frankfurt am Main: Campus Studium, 2016), 87–89.

Women experience similar bodily manifestations when entering a male-dominated space, people of color when entering a predominantly white space (remember the movie *Get Out!* by Jordan Peel), and LGBTQIA+ people when entering a heteronormative space where nonbinary sexes and genders are considered an impossible thing.

If a shared language to reflect on these difficulties isn't available, class-passers will get lonely like the prisoner at the reform school in Alan Sillitoe's novel *The Loneliness of the Long-Distance Runner*, and they will endure a lifelong estrangement. I remember the embarrassing encounter with a famous designer whom I wanted to interview, but couldn't win over to do so. He talked very disparagingly about working-class lifestyles, that of his parents included. When I met him by coincidence many years later sitting in the row in front of me at the theatre he couldn't take his eyes from me and at the same time pretended not to know me; his gaze was full of shame and at the same time full of desire to be recognized. Another one tells his colleagues that his father, a worker, died a long time ago, but this isn't true. I understand their behavior as a way of breaking contact with their working-class selves. Steep upward climbers from the underprivileged milieus never completely match the legitimate habitus and fight a constant inner fight between their former, primary and their adapted, secondary habitus. Speaking with Bourdieu, they experience a *clivage de l'habitus*, a "habitus divided against itself" – or just a "habitus break."[17] This inner division can be as painful and dizzying as severely injuring a part of your body, and the sociological literature mostly focuses on the hardships that all upward movers encounter and must be strong enough to bear if they want to resist the ousting forces of the so-called leaky pipeline – a metaphor for the increasingly unlikely survival of all degraded social groups during their moving up within a structurally discriminating system.

I certainly don't want to play down these hardships, for I have experienced them myself. But I have two additions to make.

First, representatives from lower classes tradition-ally lack the self-confident eloquence that the represent-atives of the educated bourgeoisie learn from childhood onwards. This deficiency draws working-class kids and petty-bourgeois agents not so much into high academic fields (such as philosophy, literature, theater, classical music, or architecture), but far more into fields where they imagine they will do a "real" job and can express symbolic sophistication through popular material rather than through powerful talk: fields like the design field. Within this field, where one becomes a professional symbolic producer of status objects, a habitus divided against itself is – paradoxically – the most fitting disposition, because the social tension caused by the division can be transformed and eased by designing distinctive objects. This leads to an ambiguous state of mind, one that is empowering and alienating at the same time, over and over again. But exactly for this reason upward movers are real experts of design, and the design field is the ideal field of activity for ambitious and skilled young representatives from the lower classes who are eager to become part of the upper-middle classes.

Second, following the call of the SDN conference "Beyond Change", I want to draw more attention to the fact that design historians can actually do something very insightful and of broader interest by starting with the impulses that come from habitus breaks, instead of just registering their impositions. I highlight the emancipatory potential of such breaks. Like Pierre Bourdieu, I stand up for social history and design sociology as a kind of

Illustration by John Tenniel, from Lewis Carroll, *Alice in Wonderland* (Harmondsworth: Penguin, 1998 [1865]), 33.

18. Pierre Bourdieu and Pierre Carle (director), *Soziologie ist ein Kampfsport: Pierre Bourdieu im Portrait* (DVD recording) (Frankfurt am Main: filmedition suhrkamp, 2009).

19. Sigmund Freud, "Fräulein Elisabeth von R.," in *Studies on Hysteria*, eds. Sigmund Freud and Joseph Breuer (London: Hogarth Press, 1975), 160.

intellectual martial art of knowledge production.[18] We can take the chance given by habitus breaks for an intellectual break. Which reflexive space opens up if we do so? Which common histories can be seen if we look outside the fissures that the habitus breaks of class-passers open up? Inspired by Alice's hand grasping outside the window in the illustration, I will point to the stories that connect our habitual dispositions with the yet-undiscovered sources in our design archives.

Design – a Clean Thing?

The first attempt at answering the above questions was made by collecting biographical anecdotes, which one by one added up to a more or less reflected overlook on the lifelong trials and errors of myself and my interviewees. Biographical anecdotes are connected through an existential weave, by a time- and space-specific psychological, historical, social, and sensual (or aesthetic) tie, and that is what "makes sense," a commonly shared sense, above all. Sigmund Freud once noted, somewhat surprised, that the stories his patients told him in psychoanalytical sessions were structured more like novels; yet they were of great scientific interest even though they did not look like scientific anamneses at first glance: "It still strikes me myself as strange that the case stories I write should read like short stories and that, as one might say, they lack the serious stamp of science."[19]

Bourdieu says quite the same thing according to the sociological analysis of anecdotes, be they biographical or literary:

> These representative and representational samples, exemplifying very concretely, like swatches of cloth, the reality described, thereby present themselves with all the appearances of the commonsense world, which is also inhabited by structures, but one dissimulated in the guise of contingent adventures, anecdotal accidents, particular events. This suggestive, allusive, elliptical form is what makes the literary text, like what is real, deliver up its

structure, by veiling it and by snatching it from our gaze.[20]

20. Pierre Bourdieu, *The Rules of Art: Genesis and Structure of the Literary Field* (Cambridge, UK: Polity, 1996), 336.

21. Diane Reay, *Class Work: Mothers' Involvement in Their Children's Primary Schooling* (London: UCL Press, 1998), 2.

And quite the same, again, can be stated about the single works of designers. Creative manifestations are "representative and representational samples" that contain social structures; they are somehow material and visual "anecdotal accidents." One of my interviewees highlighted this fact when he said that after he started thinking about the source of his imagination he realized that all his works had a deep connection to his social background. After all, and quite obviously, this can also be said of my research. As the sociologist Diane Reay says: "I have written extensively elsewhere on reflexivity and research methods. … I believe all research is in one way or another autobiographical or else the avoidance of autobiography."[21]

This said, we can go on asking: how exactly are the biographies and the designs of my interviewees connected? And to which concrete social structures? If one understands biographies of a certain social type as parts of a collective biography, then it is striking that class-passers from working-class milieus that make it into the design field systematically use similar concepts and metaphors to describe the loss of their habitual self-evidence. I condensed these concepts and metaphors as far as possible, and the following hierarchy and polarization emerged. First, the legitimate lifestyle of the design field appears to be one that is naturally superior to the lifestyle of the working-class milieus. Second, the superiority is described by the chain of terms *progressive-clean-civilized-right*, the inferiority by the chain of terms *backward-unclean-primitive-false*. The central concepts and metaphors are clean (and its connotations such as sterile, white, brilliant, hygienic, enlightened, healthy) v. *dirty* (and its connotations such as infected, trashy, dark, dull, stuffy, sick).

All my interviewees stated that this kind of hier-archical dichotomy was new to them, and that they didn't look down in this way on their own families and friends before getting accustomed to the legitimate tastes of the design field. Quite the opposite. Most of my interviewees have mothers who worked as cleaners in the wealthy areas of the city, while living in the poor ones. They were often

Design Struggles

22. Ricciardi, *Breve storia*, 37–39.

23. For a good overview on this with striking visual material, see Rea Brändle, *Wildfremd, hautnah: Zürcher Völkerschauen und ihre Schauplätze 1835–1964* (Zurich: Rotpunkt, 2013).

24. Richard Dyer, *White* (London: Routledge, 1997), 113.

25. James Baldwin, Raoul Peck (director), et al., *I Am Not Your Negro* (DVD recording) (Los Angeles: Magnolia Home Entertainment, 2017), 107 sec.

taken along to their mothers' workplaces when no one else could look after them. It is amazing how they describe their epistemic shock when they enter the same spaces many years later as designers, but of course through another door, not only metaphorically speaking. They know a lot about cleansing and erasing, they know what it means to be judged as negligible, invisible, and dirty, as their mothers were judged while cleaning.

The clean aesthetic of the design scene echoes certain painful biographical experiences of the sons and daughters of workers. For example, most of them have experienced the forces of gentrification, which have turned un-cool, neglected urban spaces into cool and shiny ones, but only after their families were displaced from these areas. Others tell me about their fear of being separated from their families by the authorities because they were judged as white trash or Black trash, no matter. I grew up for the first years of my life excluded from Switzerland, the clean country, because my parents, Italian migrant workers, were assigned a status that denied them to live in Switzerland with their children. The neighborhood where we lived in Zurich was called disparagingly *Negersdorf*, i.e., "Negro village," a racist designation dating back to the rise of xeno-phobia in the early twentieth century in Switzerland, when Italians were considered *una razza sfruttabile*, "an exploit-able 'race.'"[22] The othering of Italian migrant workers functioned in a similar way to the othering of freaks in the circus and of people of color displayed in the Zurich zoo and in many fairs in the city's center until the late 1960s.[23] I feared physical and verbal racist anti-Italian attacks, and one of the most common insults was that Italians were dirty and stinking and that their presence would spoil the country. The darkening (or blackening) of inferiorized and the brightening (or whitening) of superiorized social groups is a very common, implicitly racist epistemic bias. Richard Dyer noted in his critical book on normative whiteness: "Class as well as such criteria of proper whiteness as sanity and noncriminality are expressed in terms of degrees of translucence, with murkiness associated with poor, working-class, and immigrant white subjects."[24] As James Baldwin says, "white is a metaphor for power,"[25] and so an inferiorized person becoming whiter in the eyes of the

unconsciously sexist, racist, or classist beholder is a metaphor for becoming more powerful. Also compelling in this
context is Sigmund Freud, who coined the discriminatory
idea of women as a "dark continent." Keeping all of this
in mind, it is only one of the most extreme examples of
structural violence within a wide intersectional spectrum,
that the mother of one of my interviewees was sterilized for
reasons of racial hygiene in the late 1950s, against her will
and without her knowing. She had Swiss nationality, she
was white, but she was a very poor working-class woman.

      The anecdotal way in which my interviewees
connect their habitual breaks to their social experience
of racial discrimination is remarkable and disturbing.
Strangely, in all my interviews the perception of a real
social cleansing comes very close to the perception of working-class tastes, manners, and memories being symbolically
washed off the design field. As if symbolic hygiene would
echo social hygiene, they must first adapt their lifestyle
to a new cleansed color palette and sober patterns. But
that's just the beginning. After that, they must whitewash
themselves from deep habitual reflexes that are considered
dirty and rough and quickly train themselves to desire in a
distinctive, "clean" way. And last but not least, they must
erase their dirty memory from their soiled background,
for the stigma of bad taste seems also to be directed to
the lively details of one's own working-class background.
Annie Ernaux, who moved up from the French working
class and became a writer, describes in her socioanalytic
novel *La Place* her subjugation to the rules of good taste
that imposed her to remain silent about her working-class
background. But Ernaux, too, seems to stress the move
of sociology as a martial art when she highlights that it's
only thanks to this classist and humiliating silencing that
she remembers all the details of her proletarian life. A nice
paradox: the memories that she was supposed to break
away like bad tastes turn out to be the core of her literary
coming-out.[26]

      One could oppose at this point in my argument,
and in fact a lot of people argue against me as follows,
that these bourgeois, modernist exclusions no longer exist
in our diverse postmodern times, when everything seems
possible, from pastiche to high trash. But quite the opposite

26. Here I'm paraphrasing the
original quote, which reads: "Le
déchiffrement de ces details
s'impose à moi maintenant,
avec d'autant plus de necessité
que je les ai refoulé, sûre de
leur insignificance. Seule une
mémoire humiliée avait pu me
les faire conserver. Je me suis
pliée au désir du monde où je
vis, qui s'efforce de vous faire
oublier les suovenirs du monde
d'en bas comme si c'était
quelque chose de movais goût."
Annie Ernaux, *La Place* (Paris:
Gallimard, 1983), 72–73.

Design Struggles

27. Greg Tate, *Everything but the Burden: What White People Are Taking from Black Culture* (New York, NY: Broadway Books, 2003).

28. Zygmunt Bauman, *Postmodernity and its Discontents* (New York, NY: New York University Press, 1997), 14.

29. Gabriele Dietze, "Okzidentalismuskritik: Möglichkeiten und Grenzen einer Forschungsperspektivierung," in *Kritik des Okzidentalismus: Transdisziplinäre Beiträge zu (Neo-)Orientalismus und Geschlecht*, ed. Gabriele Dietze et al. (Bielefeld: transcript Verlag, 2009), 23–54.

is the case, for what makes this triple cleansing even more alienating and complex today is the fact that working-class lifestyles are considered a kind of cheap, "natural" resource for designers. One interviewee said that it's exactly these tastes and manners that designers eagerly look out and take without asking permission, use for their own purposes in their design work, make experiments with, and then forget and get rid of. What designers take from poor and underprivileged cultures as a resource to gain a sublime surplus is "everything but the burden," as Greg Tate aptly presents it in the context of the appropriation of Black culture by white cultures.[27] My interviewees express an ambivalent attitude toward this new edition of slumming practices. They must adopt them, but they can never identify completely – for very obvious reasons – with their sophisticated cynicism. This double play makes them lose speed and wit, which again leaves them behind, kind of uncool. The sociologist Zygmunt Bauman notes that those who cannot play these fast-changing, witty games quickly are considered the boring losers who do not pass the ultimate postmodern test, and are therefore "the 'dirt' of postmodern purity."[28] Everything is possible today in terms of trashy lifestyles, yes, but only if a socially cynical surplus whitewashes the dirt of social empathy away.

As already mentioned, class-passers are welcome in the design field at first and given the chance to become "pure" in this postmodernist sense, as well as to become "clean" in a more modernist sense. But it's an unfair chance. Those who cannot cut off that "dirty" part of themselves must either accept a lower status in the field or fall completely out of the leaky pipeline. These strange inclusive and exclusive rules of an unfair game strongly remind me of the context of the civilizing mission practice, where the colonized were given a Western bonus – or what Gabriele Dietze has coined the "occidental dividend"[29] – if they assimilated to the legitimate tastes and manners of the ruling power. This paternalism is often referred to as "positive racism," but in fact, racism is never positive. "Positive racism" is a symbolic game of trade, where the privileged systematically gets a higher share than the underprivileged.

Reloading History –
the Martial Art of Knowledge Production

30. For an up-to-date and general introduction, see Patricia Purtschert, Harald Fischer-Tiné, and ETH Zürich, eds., *Colonial Switzerland: Rethinking Colonialism from the Margins* (Basingstoke: Palgrave MacMillan, 2015). For the more detailed, intersectional connection between colonialism, classism, sexism, and racism in Switzerland, see Patricia Purtschert, *Kolonialität und Geschlecht im 20. Jahrhundert: Eine Geschichte der weissen Schweiz* (Bielefeld: transcript Verlag, 2019).

It might seem exaggerated to connect macro- and micro-perspectives to this extent, and to stress the connections between the present manifestations of habitus breaks of designers with working-class backgrounds with colonialism and racism in Swiss design history, especially in a country – Switzerland – that was never a colonial power. But at this point it's important to remember that the design field, also in Switzerland, emerged thanks to the reformers of the Arts and Crafts movement in the second half of the nineteenth century, i.e., the age of free trade imperialism, and it consolidated its professional and relatively autonomous position in the artistic field thanks to the modernist avant-gardes of the interwar period, i.e., the age of revolutions and the crises of liberalism. Switzerland was not an "innocent" colonial player but entangled through and through with these violent adventures.[30] It seems, therefore, that during these periods the unequal relationship between the working-class milieu and the design field was shaped in a way that continues to manifest its effects to this day. We just don't know much about it yet. Colonialism, racism, classism, sexism – and then formal, habitual, discursive, and finally aesthetic cleansing. It's as if inexplicable, subtle, and grueling ghosts of the past were triggered by the encounter between the former working-class selves and the design field. I'm always surprised that this is the case even in more technical or mechanical design studies where one wouldn't expect it, like industrial design or photography. The design space seems soaked as a whole with these ghosts of a strange racism of good and cool taste. And it's impossible to get rid of it on your own; we all seem to have been hijacked by a system we don't know the origins of.

What if we turn over the impositions of these ghosts and seriously ask if they are based on facts? What if we enter our design archives and ask history to what extent colonialism, racism, and social hygiene are constitutive components of the modernist mission, just as machine aesthetics, functionalism, reductionism, rationalism, and scientific management are? What if we, design historians, practitioners, and activists seriously ask ourselves why these

Design Struggles

31. Teju Cole, *Blind Spot*
(London: Faber & Faber, 2016),
110.

questions emerge now, in postmodern times?

Whatever the answers to these questions turn out to be, as long as we have not found them and mediated them broadly, the epistemic violence of a racism of cool and good taste – quite undisturbed by critical design history so far – remains a poison that in the long run wears its victims down. It is a hardship to survive the ousting effects of the leaky pipeline, fighting all alone against old ghosts kept secret from the dominant design discourse. And in my experience, it's a tangible relief to share with others the speculative indexes of our bodily manifestations, our habitus breaks – indexes that point to undiscovered sources that nourish these ghosts. This is why, at the end of this essay, I have placed some photos of my interviewees handed out to me in support of my work, showing them standing nearby pipelines and running water, a subject all of them choose without my input and independently of each other. Coincidence? I don't believe so.

Sometimes we can only wonder after a delay, like Alice in Wonderland, and then we might start to question what it's all about. Sometimes we understand immediately and wonder why we mirror from scratch things that are usually invisible. We can see these things if we stand in- and outside at the same time, as one of my interviewees put it. I want to encourage young researchers and practitioners to trust their eyes when they have these speculative moments. Stand in- and outside and you will see that we are all interlaced through meanings of which we lack the proof. Teju Cole calls the strong sense of a connection without a proof "poetry," which is "the secret channel that connects the work to other work."[31] It needn't be secret, it could be concrete. This channel – I learned during my research process – cuts through layers of deep history. I want to encourage young historians to follow the index given by the habitus breaks of the class-passers, to enter the design archives and make sense of all our blind spots, and finally banish the ghosts of the past with their research. I like to encourage new generations of design practitioners and activists to engage with these new historians. Be brave, connect all formulas of beauty without discrimination – the past, present, and future ones.

Photographs of the author and interviewees of her Ph.D. research, showing them nearby running water. From left to right: Paola De Martin, Giorgio von Arb, Alberto Vieceli, Natalie Pedetti.
Source: private family archives of the depicted individuals, published with their kind permission.

Glossary

Design field
Design can be replaced here by other historical terms, such as applied arts, handicrafts, decorative arts, industrial art, styling, or the German *Formgebung* and *Gestaltung*. *Field* is a sociological term that can also be replaced by the colloquial term *scene* in the context of this essay. By *design field* or *design scene* I mean the professional environment of teaching, practice, theory, media, market, conservation, exhibition, and promotion, which deals with the design of consumer goods from the smallest series to mass production. The design field is relatively autonomous, i.e., it both follows and distinguishes itself from other fields of cultural production, such as marketing, art, or architecture. The social history of the hierarchical differentiation between and within these fields has not been written yet.

Working-class milieus
Working-class milieus are all milieus just above, on, and below the line of respectability which represents the contested boundary to the large group of the middle-class milieus. According to the European ISCO- and ISEI-indices, workers have little cultural and economic capital and little access to profitable networks. They have at most a secondary school qualification and/or not more than compulsory education, and found occupations in industrial production, sales, and services with little social prestige. *Milieu* is a current sociological concept that differentiates the old class concept horizontally. Horizontal differentiation means that in each layer of a hierarchically structured class society further typological distinctions can be made on the vertical level of groups that are coherent in themselves. Since the 1970s, the most important horizontal differentiation in the social sciences has focused on the increase of professional self-determination, which varies greatly within all social strata, but is much less pronounced within the lower ones. The working-class milieus account for about 20% of the population in Switzerland.

Habitus

A habitus, as defined by the sociologist of taste and class, Pierre Bourdieu, is a model developed to understand systematic social behavior and social judgments. A habitus models the unconscious template of inner dispositions, a limited set of reflexes that one uses to make sense and act spontaneously according to one's place in society. Limitations make these dispositions useful and economic, because they reduce the complexity of social history and social future. A habitus also translates our selective historical projections into projections for our future and this gives coherence to all our present actions. Doing this or that, we believe quite naturally, is not/working well for working-class people, or is un/typical for well-educated people, or is un/natural for women, or who talks like this is/not truly a Black/white person, or is/not something you should desire if you hold a certain position. A habitus is creative in the sense that the concrete emanation on the surface of our "social nature" changes constantly, driven by the competitive dynamism of capitalism, and constantly needs to be designed anew. But what remains as a constant, if we do not resist it, is the existence of an exploitable difference between more or less valuable social groups.

Bibliography

Baldwin, James, and Raoul Peck. *I Am Not Your Negro: A Companion Edition to the Documentary Film directed by Raoul Peck.* London, etc.: Penguin Random House, 2017.

Barlösius, Eva. *Pierre Bourdieu.* Frankfurt a. M.: Campus Studium, 2016.

Bauman, Zygmunt. *Postmodernity and its Discontents.* New York, NY: New York University Press, 1997.

Bourdieu, Pierre. *La misère du monde.* Paris: Editions du Seuil, 1993.
—. *The Rules of Art: Genesis and Structure of the Literary Field.* Cambridge, UK: Polity, 1996.
—. *Soziologie ist ein Kampfsport: Pierre Bourdieu im Portrait.* Filmedition Suhrkamp, a film by Pierre Carle, 2009.
—. "Introduction and the Sense of Distinction. From: Distinction, a social critique of taste." In *The Design History Reader.* Edited by Grace Lees-Maffei and Rebecca Houze. London and New York, NY: Bloomsbury Academic Publishing, 2010, 402–8.

Bremer, Andreas, and Andreas Lange-Vester, eds. *Soziale Milieus und Wandel der Sozialstruktur: Die gesellschaftlichen Herausforderungen und die Strategien der sozialen Gruppen.* 2nd, updated edition. Wiesbaden: Springer VS, 2014.

Brändle, Rea. *Wildfremd, hautnah: Zürcher Völkerschauen und ihre Schauplätze 1835–1964.* Zurich: Rotpunkt, 2013.

BFS, Bundesamt für Statistik, ed. *Statistisches Jahrbuch der Schweiz 2018.* Zurich: NZZ Libro, 2018.

Carroll, Lewis. *Alice in Wonderland.* London: Penguin Classics, 1998.

Cole, Teju. *Blind Spot.* London: Faber & Faber, 2016.

Dietze, Gabriele. "Okzidentalismuskritik: Möglichkeiten und Grenzen einer Forschungsperspektivierung." In *Kritik des Okzidentalismus: Transdisziplinäre Beiträge zu (Neo-)Orientalismus und Geschlecht.* Edited by Gabriele Dietze et al. Bielefeld: transcript, 2009, 23–54.

Dyer, Richard. *White.* London: Routledge, 1997.

Ernaux, Annie. *La Place,* Paris: Gallimard, 1983.

Freud, Sigmund. "Fräulein Elisabeth von R." In Sigmund Freud and Joseph Breuer. *Studies on Hysteria.* London: Hogarth Press, 1975.

Foucault, Michel. *The Archeology of Knowledge.* London: Routledge, 2002.

Frizsche, Daniel. "Zürich, die gebildete Stadt." *Neue Zürcher Zeitung NZZ,* February 1, 2017, 19.

Jagodzinski, Jan. *Visual Art and Education in an Era of Designer Capitalism: Deconstructing the Oral Eye.* New York, NY: Palgrave MacMillan, 2010.

Kehrli, Christin, and Carlo Knöpfel, eds. *Handbuch Armut in der Schweiz.* Luzern: Caritas-Verlag, 2006.

Laganà, Francesco. "Inequalities in Returns to Education in Switzerland." In *Education, Occupation, and Social Origin: A Comparative Analysis of the Transmission of Socio-Economic Inequalities.* Edited by Fabrizio Bernardi and Gabriele Ballarino, 199–214. Cheltenham, UK/Northampton, MA: Edward Elgar Publishing, 2016.

Littler, Jo. *Against Meritocracy: Culture, Power and Myths of Mobility.* London and New York, NY: Routledge, 2017.

Mäder, Ueli, Ganga Jey Aratnam, and Sarah Schilliger. *Wie Reiche denken und lenken: Reichtum in der Schweiz: Geschichte, Fakten, Gespräche.* Zurich: Rotpunktverlag, 2010.
—. *Macht.ch: Geld und Macht in der Schweiz.* Zurich: Rotpunktverlag, 2015.

Nachtwey, Oliver. *Die Abstiegsgesellschaft: Über das Aufbegehren in der regressiven Moderne.* Berlin: Suhrkamp, 2016.

Oesch, Daniel, and Emily Murphy. *Keine Erosion, sondern Wachstum der Mittelklasse: Der Wandel der Schweizer Berufsstruktur seit 1970* (Social Change in Switzerland; 12), 2017. www.socialchangeswitzerland. ch/?p=1377.

Purtschert, Patricia, Harald Fischer-Tiné, and ETH Zürich, eds. *Colonial Switzerland: Rethinking Colonialism from the Margins.* Basingstoke: Palgrave MacMillan, 2015.
—. *Kolonialität und Geschlecht im 20. Jahrhundert: Eine Geschichte der weissen Schweiz.* Bielefeld: transcript, 2019.

Reay, Diane. *Class Work: Mothers' involvement in Their Children's Primary Schooling.* London: UCL Press, 1998.

Ricciardi, Toni. *Breve storia dell'emigrazione italiana in Svizzera.* Roma: Donizelli, 2018.

Saner, Philippe, Sophie Vögele, and Pauline Vessely. *Schlussbericht Art.School.Differences: Researching Inequality and Normativities in the Field of Higher Art Education.* blog.zhdk.ch/ artschooldifferences/files/2016/10/ ASD_Schlussbericht_final_web_verlinkt.pdf, 2016.

Seefranz, Catrin, Philippe Saner, and ZHdK, eds. *Making Differences: Schweizer Kunsthochschulen: Explorative Vorstudie,* 2012. blog.zhdk.ch/artschooldifferences/ files/2013/11/Making_Differences_ Vorstudie_Endversion.pdf.

Schuwey, Claudia, and Carlo Knöpfel, eds. *Neues Handbuch Armut in der Schweiz.* Luzern: Caritas-Verlag, 2014.

Schultheis, Franz. "Kreativarbeit zwischen Beruf und Berufung." In Franz Schultheis, Christoph Henning, and Dieter Thomä. *Kreativität als Beruf.* Bielefeld: transcript Verlag, 2019, 87–142.

SDBB, Schweizer Dienstleistungszentrum Berufsbildung, Berufs-, Studien- und Laufbahnberatung. *Die erste Stelle nach dem Studium: Die Beschäftigungssituation nach einem Studium an einer Fachhochschule* (Heft 4, 2009). Bern: SDBB-Verlag, 2009.
—. *Die erste Stelle nach dem Studium: Die Beschäftigungssituation nach einem Studium an einer Fachhochschule* (Heft 4, 2011). Bern: SDBB-Verlag, 2011.
—. *Die erste Stelle nach dem Studium: Die Beschäftigungssituation der Neuabsolventinnen und Neuabsolventen von Schweizer Hochschulen.* Bern: SDBB-Verlag, 2013.

Stamm, Margrit. "Arbeiterkinder an die Hochschulen! Hintergründe ihrer Aufstiegsangst." *Dossier* 16, no. 2 (2016). margritstamm.ch/images/Arbeiterkinder%20an%20die%20Hochschulen!.pdf

Tate, Greg. *Everything but the Burden: What White People Are Taking from Black Culture*. New York, NY: Broadway Books, 2003.

Weckerle, Christoph, Huber Theler, and ZHdK, eds. *Dritter Kreativwirtschaftsbericht Zürich: Die Bedeutung der Kultur- und Kreativwirtschaft für den Standort Zürich*. https://preview.tinyurl.com/yyovz5vn , 2010.
—, Roman Page, Simon Grand. *Von der Kreativwirtschaft zu den Creative Economies: Kreativwirtschaftsbericht Schweiz 2016*, 2016. www.creativeeconomies.com/downloads/creative-economy-report-2016.pdf.

Paola De Martin

DESIGN FOR THE REAL WORLD
Contesting the Origins of the Social in Design

Alison J. Clarke

1. Victor Papanek, preface to Design for the Real World: Human Ecology and Social Change (New York, NY: Pantheon, 1971), xxi.

There are professions more harmful than industrial design, but only a few of them. ... Never before in history have grown men sat down and seriously designed electric hairbrushes, rhinestone-covered file boxes, and mink carpeting for bathrooms, and then drawn up elaborate plans to make and sell these gadgets to millions of people. ... Today industrial design has put murder on a mass-production basis. By designing criminally unsafe automobiles that kill or maim nearly one million people around the world each year, by creating whole new species of permanent garbage to clutter up the landscape, and by choosing materials and processes that pollute the air we breathe, designers have become a dangerous breed.
—**Victor Papanek, *Design for the Real World*** [1]

In 1971, an obscure book focusing on design's social usefulness to humankind, penned by a previously unknown Austrian-American author, was translated from Swedish to English and published as *Design for the Real World: Human Ecology and Social Change*. Quickly emerging as a bestselling author, Victor Papanek, the design critic behind the 300-page, breathlessly delivered, hyperbolic treatise on the failings of the contemporary design profession, was invited to appear on a prime-time U.S. television chat show. Once installed in the broadcasting studio, cameras rolling, the maverick designer pulled out a prototype of one of his recent creations to demonstrate what socially responsible design might engender. Wielding a bright-blue concertinaed bedpan, designed to be pumped up with warm air beneath the hospital patient, the social designer elaborated on how his observations of the inhumanity of the conventional stainless steel contraption, during a recent visit to a clinic, had inspired its redesign:

2. Satesh Kumar, filmed interview with Victor Papanek, Schumacher College, 1991 (Victor Papanek Foundation, University of Applied Arts Vienna).

> I began to realize there was something inherently wrong with bedpans; because they are noisy, they clutter, they're difficult to move around, disgusting to wash out and clean – and they are unbelievably chilly, and they're expensive; they need a small room in each hospital floor just to be stored, and they cause back injuries.[2]

The flimsy inflatable plastic bedpan, one of a limited number of designs prototyped by Papanek, failed to reach production despite its showcasing on prime-time American TV. And yet, that was never really the intention behind his designs. Rather, the unlikely (and impractical) medical appliance formed part of a repertoire of product designs, from portable play environments for disabled children to dung-powered tin can radios for nonliterate communities, devised to contest the assumptions of Western corporate capitalism: agitprop interventions in a social design revolution whose legacy endures today.

The Origins of the Social in Design

Victor Papanek is commonly considered the pioneer of social design, and several decades on *Design for the Real World* (which has never fallen out of print) remains one of the most widely read critiques of design practice to this day. As social design, humanitarian design, design anthropology, transition design, and movements in decolonizing design take on increasing contemporary prescience, the work of iconic figures such as Papanek, still regularly referred to for

Victor Papanek with George Seegers, *Tin Can Radio*, customized by users. Courtesy University of Applied Arts Vienna, Victor J. Papanek Foundation.

Victor Papanek

with an
introduction by
R. Buckminster Fuller

DESIGN FOR THE REAL WORLD

Human Ecology
and Social Change

Victor Papanek, with an introduction by R. Buckminster Fuller, *Design for the Real World: Human Ecology and Social Change* (New York: Pantheon Books, 1971).

3. Papanek, *Design for the Real World*, xxvi.

its challenging of Western, corporate, patriarchal design paradigms, demands further critical scrutiny. Papanek himself emphasized to his students and reading public that: "As socially and morally involved designers, we must address ourselves to the needs of a world with its back to the wall while the hands on the clock point perpetually to one minute before twelve."[3] *Design for the Real World*, although peppered with eccentric, hyperbolic statements and anachronistic observations (such as the prediction that video gaming will never "catch on"), remains, nearly half a century later, unerringly foresighted in its identification of design culture as an undertheorized mechanism of environmental and social destruction and a key terrain of political action.

Much present design discourse upholds a polarized model of design hatched in the broadly neo-Marxist 1970s paradigm that buoyed Papanek's vitriolic critique: rehearsing a rhetoric that pits a morally and ethically virtuous design practice (sustainable, socially embedded, community-based, codesigned, etc.) against a model of designers as the handmaidens of a profit-driven corporate culture. Within this paradigm, figures such as Papanek emerge as the romanticized pioneers of a socially inculcated vision of design; an idyll lost to the globalized hegemony of twenty-first-century neoliberalism in which designers act merely as mediators of large-scale gentrification, the digital and analogue colonizers of previously authentic local settings, objects, practices, and social relations. Yet, this precariously ahistorical rendering of designers as "good" or "bad" downplays the complexity of design's role within the political and moral economies that drive social change. In tracing and deconstructing the origins of social design through an examination of Papanek's biography, design, and design criticism, this essay argues for the vital role of historical analysis, and historiographic understanding, in complexifying the past and future potentialities of design as a culture and practice.

Alison J. Clarke

Formations

4. Papanek, 44, 45.

5. Papanek, 46.

A young Jewish refugee who launched his own design practice, Design Clinic, in New York shortly after World War II, Papanek was soon confronted by what he described as the "narrow market dialectics" that dictated the ethics of industrial design.[4] After escaping the horrors of Nazi Vienna and meeting with the Futurama dreamscape of the New York World's Fair in 1939, design at first proffered an overwhelming vision of optimistic progressivism and democracy. Paradoxically, Papanek soon discovered that its principal role lay in fuelling the all-consuming, undiscerning cacophony of American commercial culture, and with it, some of the more destructive aspects of humanity's seemingly insatiable desire for stuff. And so began his search, as an outsider, for an alternative model of design that might heal society's ills, remedy social inequality, and empower its users: "The designer bears a responsibility for the way the products he designs are received at the marketplace. But," he reflected on considering his earliest forays into low-cost furnishing design in the 1940s,

> this is still a narrow and parochial view. The designer's responsibility must go far beyond these considerations. His social and moral judgment must be brought into play long *before* he begins to design, since he has to make a judgment as to whether the products he is asked to design or redesign merit his attention at all. In other words, will his design be on the side of the social good or not?[5]

What began as a critique of the frivolities of a design culture ramped up to meet the demands of unbridled postwar consumer culture had, by the 1960s, culminated in a full-blown global campaign against a profession that wreaked irreversible ecological damage, endorsed neocolonial development, and perpetuated social inequality: with *Design for the Real World* its erstwhile manifesto.

Translated into over twenty languages, and taken up by a generation of designers and design students desperately seeking an alternative politics of design, Papanek's work took on a life of its own – its clarion call weaponized

6. Victor Papanek, "What is Contemporary?," *La Mer* 2 (August 1950), 25.

7. See Peter Lang and William Menking, eds., *Superstudio: Life Without Objects* (Milan: Skira, 2003).

in the dismantling of the beaux-arts hierarchies and modernist teachings of European design schools, and the opening out of design beyond the reductionist dualities of Western and non-Western.

As a designer and critic of international renown, Papanek consciously pitted himself against the ideologies of his modernist émigré forebears, who had viewed mass-produced, standardized industrial design through the lens of Western rationalism. Describing the Bauhaus style, in one of his earliest pieces of design criticism, as a "fascist negation of living that is now proven a lie," he proposed in its place a humane, indigenized design approach imbued with anthropological sensitivity to the local, the vernacular, and an understanding of the broader cultural nuances of design's power in undermining or solidifying social inclusion.[6] In challenging design's assumed role as the originator of frivolous fripperies in an age of overabundance, his ideas pivoted on the overarching theory that design was the key agent of social change, not merely a tool for stylization, aestheticization, or a driver for increased consumption. As an integral part of the social design agenda, he advocated non-Western tropes of design – from the material cultures of the Inuit to the Suku Bali – as holistic models of design whereby things are understood as inseparable from the social relations, customs, rituals, and histories in which they are embedded. The politics of design, in other words, relied on understanding the practice as a cultural rather than rational, problem-solving phenomenon.

Contexts

Design for the Real World, and the social remit it engendered, did not, of course, operate in a vacuum. In Europe, the radical Italian design group, Superstudio, which famously advocated "life without objects" as part of a self-consciously disaffected stance towards late capitalism, exercised a similar contemporary fascination with the vernacular and indigenous object.[7] "Objects and tools represent a particular field of investigation; they lend themselves much better to being used as keys in the interpretation of complex relationships: objects are the direct

Alison J. Clarke

witnesses of the creative drive," recounted Superstudio designer Alessandro Poli, in describing the group's "Extra-Urban Material Culture" initiative of 1973: a project aimed at collecting, recording, and analyzing handmade peasant tools prior to their disappearance through technological advance.[8] Yet, unlike the Italian design radicals whose work was famously showcased in the 1972 MoMA exhibition *Italy: The New Domestic Landscape*, with a number of their catalogue contributions renouncing the practice of architecture and design altogether in faux flourishes of avant-gardist gestures,[9] Papanek stood by an unerringly (and often unfashionably) pragmatic stance that earned him praise and criticism in equal measure. "In an environment that is screwed up visually, physically, and chemically, the best and simplest thing that architects, industrial designers, planners, etc., could do for humanity would be to stop working entirely," he wrote several years before Superstudio's high-profile rejection of architectural and design practice.[10]

Design for the Real World, which Papanek dedicated to his students "for what they have taught me," was deliberately conceived as an antidote to inaction and what Papanek would later describe as the "romantic bourgeois Marxism" that had spread like an epidemic through design schools.[11] "In all pollution designers are implicated at least partially," he wrote towards the end of its preface, "but in this book I take a more affirmative view: it seems to me that we can go beyond not working at all, and work positively. Design can and must become a way in which young people can participate in changing society."[12] Papanek harnessed the ideals of a new generation of designers, advocating the cross-fertilization of ideas through a hands-on pedagogic approach. Yet he was adept at borrowing from, as much as facilitating, his students – harnessing the social ambitions of student designers from a diversity of institutions, regions, and geopolitical contexts, ranging from the U.S. and Scandinavia through to Indonesia. Notably the curricula he devised included women as a specific social group excluded from mainstream design culture, with female students initiating projects such as contraceptive pill packaging for illiterate women. Despite these gestures, attuned to a newly feminist cohort, Papanek actively sought and maintained a patriarchal profile equivalent to

8. Alessandro Poli, cited in Lang and Menking, *Superstudio* 226. See Alison J. Clarke, "The Indigenous and the Autochthon," in *Global Tools: When Education Coincides with Life, 1973–1975*, ed. Valerio Borgonuovo and Silvia Franceschini (Istanbul: Salt, 2019).

9. See Ross Elfine, "Superstudio and the 'Refusal to Work,'" *Design and Culture* 8, no. 1 (2016), 55–77. Elfine suggests that the radical Italians transformed the reality of mass-unemployment among 1970s Italian architects and planners into an avant-gardist politicized stance of the "refusal to work" in a postindustrial, late-capitalist economy.

10. Papanek, *Design for the Real World*, xxvi.

11. See Chapter 9, "Pragmatism before Politics: Social Design Turns Nomadic," in this volume.

12. "Pragmatism before Politics."

13. See Alison J. Clarke, Design and the New Environment: From Styrofoam Domes to the Volita Project," in *Victor Papanek: Designer for the Real World* (Cambridge, MA: MIT Press, forthcoming 2021).

14. Barbara Ward and René Dubois, *Only One World: The Care and Maintenance of a Small Planet* (London: Andre Deutsch, 1972).

the "heroic" male corporate designers he condemned in public. The inclusion of a spoof design job, dubbed the "Volita Project" – which involved the commissioning of a life-size animated plastic woman (in various finishes from snake-skin to leather) – in the first edition of *Design for the Real World*, was condemned by women readers and, much to his bemusement, removed by the publisher from future editions.[13]

Yet publication of the groundbreaking volume perfectly preempted, or coincided with, a maelstrom of interconnected events, interventions, and political crises that led to the foregrounding of environmentalism, postindustrial futures, postcolonial thinking, and degrowth economics: all of which threw into relief the politics of industrial design and its intertwined relation with Western capitalist, expansionist, and development politics.

In 1972, in *Only One Earth* (an unofficial report commissioned by the Secretary-General of the UN Conference on the Human Environment, as a precursor to the 1972 Stockholm Congress), British economist Barbara Ward and French-born American environmentalist René Dubois, identified the postwar consumer revolution – described as "a twenty-five-year boom … among the industrialized nations after 1945" – as the key environmental hazard of the twentieth century, "gobbling up resources and increasing requirements of materials and energy at an unprecedented rate."[14] This publication was one of many that emerged from a newly forming canon of environmental critique. But its specific mention of consumerism, and its conduit advertising, helped formalize Western consumer culture as a central tenet of environmental discourse. This critique highlighted the vicissitudes of an industrial development agenda, which simultaneously promoted manufacturing and consumer economies whilst bemoaning their deleterious impact on environmental and social structures.

This critique was further buoyed by the countercultural rhetoric and alternative economic theories of the late 1960s and early 1970s. For example, Wolfgang Haug's neo-Marxist *Critique of Commodity Aesthetics* (1971), identified design as a key driver of capitalism, accusing it of complicity in generating an insatiable desire for commodities which in turn resulted in the dissolution of authentic social relations. The publication of Haug's book coincided with that of *Design for the Real World*, and though they addressed very different audiences, they both pointed to design as a central object for critical examination in sketching out alternative postindustrial economies and social life.

Most significantly, the UN Conference on the Human Environment held in Stockholm in 1972, served as a springboard from which emerged a broader discourse around design for development, one that sought to remedy the political dilemma over the local-global dichotomies of industrialization and its environmental consequences. Papanek had striven to address this same dilemma since the early 1960s, in his codesigns for so-called developing countries and communities, which included prototypes for an African TV set and even a low-cost, self-assembly revolver (for vermin control) for poor rural communities in the U.S. More specifically, the 1972 Stockholm conference laid the groundwork for future initiatives that purported to address the unchecked force of consumer desire: namely the collaboration of the International Council of Societies of Industrial Design (ICSID) and the United Nations Industrial Development Organization (UNIDO), and the signing of the Ahmedabad Declaration on Industrial Design for Development in 1979. Both organizations were represented at the 1972 conference, and their collaboration five years later, in which Papanek played a critical role, would mark a turning point in the formalization of the design profession's role in development policy, impacting on small-scale manufacture and craft economies in countries ranging from India to Mexico. Despite his involvement in these policy schemes, he was also an avid critic – engaging early on in the 1970s debate around decolonizing design, challenging top-down solutions to local conditions, and the use of copyright and patents.[15]

15. See Alison J. Clarke, "Design for Development, ICSID and UNIDO: The Anthropological Turn in 1970s Design," *Journal of Design History* 29, no. 1 (2016), 43–57.

Trajectories

Design for the Real World quickly emerged as a classic of alternative culture. On the radical student bookshelf it was positioned between tomes such as Rachel Carson's warning of imminent ecological disaster, *Silent Spring* (1962), and Teresa Hayter's critique of the mechanisms of neocolonialism, *Aid as Imperialism* (1971). Papanek's iconoclastic designs, provocative journalism, and unique pedagogic projects rattled a complacent corporate design establishment and the design avant-garde alike. His "real world" paradigm posited a model of design that served humanity – culturally and practically addressing the needs of the socially excluded rather than oiling the lucrative wheels of consumer corporations or stoking the egotism of individual designers. "Design and production talent have been wasted," bemoaned Papanek in a typically acerbic think-piece in the design press, "on the concocting of such inane trivia as mink-covered toilet seats, electronic finger-nail polish dryers, and baroque fly-swatters."

Yet despite being adopted as part of the burgeoning politics of environmentalism, underpinned by the groundswell of countercultural activity, much of Papanek's pioneering social design derived directly from the funding and policies of Cold War U.S. military design experimentation. His celebrated "Big Character" diagram, devised in a student workshop of 1968 that explored the role of design in forging environmental politics and social inclusivity, is a case in point. Although it shared the countercultural graphic aesthetics seen, for example, in Marshall Henrichs radical design for the poster box set *Blueprint for Counter Education* (1970), Papanek's diagram – presented as a fold-out in *Design for the Real World* – sketched a model of design transdisciplinarity that had its origins in a bionics laboratory bankrolled in part by the U.S. military during Papanek's tenure at Purdue University, Indiana, in the mid-1960s. During this same period, immediately prior to the publication of his groundbreaking social design treatise, he combined, seemingly without hesitation, his international lecturing as a design activist addressing students who opposed the Vietnam War and the complicity of U.S. chemical corporations, with stints as a design consultant for both Dow Chemicals and the U.S. military. The humanitarian design he promoted in the pages of *Design for the Real World*, such as the "TV for Africa," was born of the politics of U.S. intervention in the "Third World," reimagined and repackaged as a grassroots form of empowerment and social inclusion.[16]

Despite the canonization of *Design for the Real World* as an exemplar of social design thinking, even during the time of its first release the book and its message were met with some skepticism outside design circles. While it received acclaim in Europe, U.S. journalists were decidedly less enthralled by the designer's airy intellectualizing. "We're deep in the heart of Survivalsville," began a profile article in the *L. A. Times*, "the consumer-advocate country where the world's clock is always at 10 minutes to 12 and time is running out."[17] Refusing to take Papanek's earnestness too seriously, the piece featured the "elegant, crisp man with the Austrian accent – looking like a fashion designer in his tailored knit shirt-suit" posing in an ergonomic recliner of his own design, one photo showing him sitting upright, the other slightly less dignified, fully reclined with feet pointing to the ceiling. The *L. A. Times* journalist cast aside the reverence Papanek was accustomed to, adopting instead a playful mockery toward the designer's unerring social conviction and borderline pretentiousness:

> You find him seated in his gray, Madison Avenue-come-to-college office surrounded by Marimekko bags ("In Finland it's just a workers" hangout. But here they think it's chic'), and black-and-white photos of Robert Kennedy and children of the Third World ghettos.[18]

Under the title "Down with Designers?," America's premier mainstream journal, *Time*, published a review of Papanek's anti-consumer polemic. The review focused on the idealistic naivety of the author's rhetoric, which, the reporter explained, "is so extreme at times that he calls corporation executives 'criminals.'"[19] Some critics, the review concluded, might indeed argue that it was Papanek himself, with his utopian vision of design, who had "lost contact with the real world."[20]

One of Papanek's iconic designs from this period, the "Tin Can Radio" – a DIY-assembly, dung-powered audio player made for distribution in rural Indonesian communities – epitomized a shift in design thinking,

16. See Alison J. Clarke, "Bionics and Creative Problem-Solving: The Making of a Post-War Designer," in *Victor Papanek: Designer for the Real World*.

17. Alan Cartnal, "Dean's Aim to Clean Up L.A.," *Los Angeles Times*, March 5, 1972.

18. Cartnal, "Dean's Aim to Clean Up L.A."

19. Unknown author, "Down with Designers?," *Time*, February 21, 1972, 47.

20. "Down with Designers?"

21. Gui Bonsiepe, "Design e ottosviluppo," *Casabella* 385 January 1974), 42–45.

22. This trajectory from Second World War experimentation in cybernetic science, military, and information technologies, and its merger with the 1960s counterculture movement was established in the 1990s with essays such as Richard Barbrook and Andy Cameron's widely cited "The California Ideology" (*Science as Culture* 6, no. 1 [January 1996], 44–72) and is now an established historical tenet of the period. Where Barbrook and Cameron's essay traced the politics of the long-predicted convergence of the media, computing, and telecommunications into hypermedia" back to a loose network driven by the notion of romantic individualism on the West Coast of the United States, director Adam Curtis's critical film series of 2011, *All Watched over by Machines of loving Grace*, further traces the "cult" of the belief in humanity's liberation through computers back through early colonializing theories of racial divide, and the brand of libertarianism embraced by Silicon Valley, inspired by Ayn Rand's Objectivist ideas. U.S. historians, including Felicity D. Scott, Fred Turner, and Orit Halpern, have written extensively on the intertwining of counterculture and Cold War design and technology, and the exhibition *Hippie Modernism: The Struggle for Utopia* (Walker Art Center, 2016) curated by Andrew Blauvelt, traced the countercultural fascination with technologies born of World War II experimentation, from plastics through to computing technologies.

23. Orit Halpern, "The Planetary Test," in *Victor Papanek: The Politics of Design*, ed. Mateo Kries, Amelie Klein, and Alison J. Clarke (Rhein m Weil: Vitra Design Museum, 2018), 288–99, 290 cited here.

24. Halpern, "The Planetary Test," 290.

and has regularly been included in social design exhibitions as an early example of innovation within the genre. But even in the early 1970s, such artifacts and inventions were identified by some figures within design, including the Ulm School of Design alumnus Gui Bonsiepe, as a thinly disguised form of neocolonialism. In a full-blown critique published in the Italian design journal *Casabella*, Bonsiepe accused Papanek outright of collusion with the U.S. military, which, he argued, would appropriate the device as a cheap means of disseminating pro-American propaganda in largely nonliterate countries.[21]

Contradictions of the "Real World" Manifesto

The innate contradictions of Papanek's "real world" manifesto were born from the merger of Second World War experimentation with 1960s countercultural tropes – a phenomenon that historians, curators, and critical filmmakers over the last two decades have identified as underpinning the broader phenomenon of the so-called "Californian Ideology": the neoliberal, techno-social utopianism enshrined in the Silicon Valley concept of inno-vation.[22] As a self-proclaimed socially responsible designer, Papanek's pedagogic style centered on an expanded idea of design as part-anthropological observation, part-humanitarian intervention. Design, according to Papanek, was far removed from the practice of merely stylizing and devising individual products and, as such, lent itself to a politically liberal agenda. Yet this seemingly progressive attack on the conservative, corporatized profession of industrial design actually relied on what U.S. historian Orit Halpern has described as a "growing ecological understanding that emerged from a history of experiments which transformed life itself during and after the Second World War."[23] It was this Cold War context, rather than the burgeoning countercultural ecological movement that led to Papanek, in Halpern's words, "signpost[ing] this new-found epistemology of design by noting the future at stake in the mundane everyday decisions of industrial design [as] nothing short of survival of the species."[24]

Set against the backdrop of rising disquiet over

U.S. consumer culture's role in promulgating a postwar culture of obsolescence, as popularized by social commentator Vance Packard in *The Waste Makers* (1960), Papanek's condemnation of mainstream designers as creators of a "whole new species of permanent garbage" crucially placed design practice at the center rather than periphery of social change. Much of his "real world" design manifesto, including his famed "Copenhagen Map" plotting the politics of design, arose directly from the ideologies and experiments funded by the U.S. government and military in the 1960s. Yet that same manifesto undeniably came to exert an agency of its own in the rewriting of the potentialities of a social agenda for design's future; a trajectory that continues to be fraught with political ambiguities, as the "social" increasingly comes to stand in for "real world" politics in contemporary design.

SUSTAINABLE DESIGN ON THE WORLD STAGE
The International Council of Societies of Industrial Design and Environmental Concerns, 1970–1990

Tania Messell

1. Wolfram Kaiser and Jan-Henrik Meyer, eds., *International Organizations and Environmental Protection: Conservation and Globalization in the Twentieth Century* (New York, NY: Berghahn Books, 2019).

2. Jonathan M. Woodham and Michael Thomson, "Cultural Diplomacy and Design in the Late Twentieth and Twenty-First Centuries: Rhetoric or Reality?" *Design and Culture* 9, no. 2 (2017), 237.

At a time when climate change is commonly regarded as a global challenge, and environmental concerns have been put forward on the agenda of international organizations more forcibly than ever,[1] international design organizations have increasingly included sustainability as part of their policies and programs. The World Design Organization (WDO, formerly the International Council of Societies of Industrial Design) and the International Council of Design (ico-D, formerly the International Council of Graphic Design Associations) have for instance become fierce advocators of design practices respectful of the environment.

By the 1980s and 1990s, these organizations, initially formed to strengthen the profession and promote its status to governments, industry, commerce, and the general public, had set out to play a more powerful role in the shared concerns of humanity, such as food, clean energy, health, and sustainability.[2] Notably, the WDO aligned its aims with the United Nations Sustainable Development Goals (SDGs) – drafted by 169 member states in 2015 – to help advance the SDGs and bolster sustainable design practices.[3] On the other hand, whilst sustainability has become a central concern in contemporary design practices, a gap remains between environmental realities and the practices advanced by design education and the design industry.[4] The profession has also been criticized for a lack of engagement with the underlying causes of environmental crisis, including its role in reproducing such conditions. This situation has extended to professional fora: in 2002 Victor Margolin suggested that "in those areas in which designers do have the autonomy for free discussion, notably conferences, journals, and in the college and university classroom, the proposals for change have been all too modest and have rarely come out strongly against the expansion model of economic growth."[5]

Furthermore, the rhetoric of sustainability, sustainable design, and sustainable development has been condemned for preserving consumer capitalism and market imperatives. Advocates of eco-tech agenda such as dematerialization have been described as favoring a status quo economic approach to society, whilst ignoring the social and political dimensions of the problem.[6] Concepts such as sustainable design in particular have been criticized for failing to recognize "the Western/globalized hegemonic being-in-the-world as inherently defuturing,"[7] a structural injustice "inscribed within the world's financial system, transnational politics, the international labor market, the global system of production, and the exchange of raw and manufactured commodities."[8] In this context, it is not surprising that, as Alice Twemlow writes, "most professional design organizations … strike an uneasy balance between design's relationship to commerce and its role as provocateur and social conscience."[9] This chapter inquires into how international design organizations, branding themselves as global agents of betterment and promoting cross-border professional interests, have navigated such imperatives historically.

Whilst there is an increased interest in environmental histories of design,[10] the position of international design organizations towards this topic remains relatively unexplored. Professional organizations have helped establish design as a fully-fledged profession through monitored membership,

3. WDO, "World Design Agenda 2017–2019," wdo.org/resources/world-design-agenda/ (accessed January 6, 2019).

4. Alastair Fuad-Luke, *Design Activism: Beautiful Strangeness for a Sustainable World* (London: Earthscan Routledge, 2009), 49; Joanna Boehnert, *Design, Ecology, Politics: Towards the Ecocene* (London and New York, NY: Bloomsbury, 2018), 8.

5. Victor Margolin, *The Politics of the Artificial: Essays on Design and Design Studies* (Chicago, IL: University of Chicago Press, 2002), 95.

6. Damon Taylor, "A Brief History of (Un)Sustainable Design," in *The Routledge Handbook of Sustainable Product Design*, ed. Jonathan Chapman (Abingdon: Routledge, 2017), 21.

7. Helder Pereira and Coral Gillett, "Africa: Designing as Existence," in *Design in the Borderlands*, ed. Eleni Kalantidou and Tony Fry (Abingdon: Routledge, 2014), 125. "Defuturing" has been described by Tony Fry as "a condition of mind and action that materially erodes (un-measurably) planetary finite time, thus it gathers and designates the negation of 'the being of time,' which is equally the taking away of our future." Tony Fry, *Design as Politics* (Oxford: Berg Publishers, 2011), 21.

8. Tony Fry, *Design Futuring: Sustainability, Ethics and New Practice* (London: Bloomsbury Academic, 2008), 42.

9. Alice Twemlow, "I Can't Talk to You if You Say That: An Ideological Collision at the International Design Conference at Aspen, 1970," *Design and Culture* 1, no. 1 (2009), 25–26.

10. The Design History Society's annual conference of 2017, held at the University of Oslo, was on the theme of "Making and Unmaking the Environment." See also Kjetil Fallan and Finn Arne Jørgensen, "Environmental Histories of Design: Towards a New Research Agenda," *Journal of Design History* 30, no. 2 (2017) and Kjetil Fallan, ed., *The Culture of Nature in the History of Design* (Abingdon: Routledge, 2019).

11. Jill Seddon, "Mentioned, but Denied Significance: Women Designers and the Professionalization' of Design in Britain, c. 1920–1951," *Gender & History* 12, no. 2 2000), 427, 428; Grace Lees-Maffei, "Introduction: Professionalization as a Focus in Interior Design History," *Journal of Design History* 21, no. 1 (2008), 5.

12. Jonathan Woodham, "Local, National and Global: Redrawing the Design Historical Map," *Journal of Design History* 18, no. 3 (2005), 263.

13. This phrase will be used throughout this text since it was the term used by ICSID to describe nations on their way to industrialization and highlights the binary understanding that ICSID nurtured towards these nations at the time.

14. The ICSID's Executive Boards nevertheless remained constituted by mostly Western designers during the period studied. This situation was replicated in the organization's working groups, whilst the ICSID secretariat has consistently been located in Western countries. Tania Messell, "Constructing a 'United Nations of Industrial Design': ICSID and the Professionalization of Design on the World Stage, 1957–1980," (doctoral thesis, University of Brighton, 2018).

15. Messell. "Constructing a 'United Nations of Industrial Design.'"

16. Pauline Madge, "Design, Ecology, Technology: A Historiographical Review," *Journal of Design History* 6, no. 3 (1993), 149.

the formulation of professional standards of practice and codes of conduct, information exchange and promotional activities, amongst other undertakings.[11] Their often extensive membership makes cross-border professional networks especially worth examining. As Jonathan Woodham notes: "Concerned with the furtherance of the professional status of designers around the world, the potential outreach of these organizations in terms of members and influence is enormous."[12] Drawing from these perspectives, this chapter will examine the environmental discourse and initiatives of the International Council of Societies of Industrial Design (ICSID) in the 1970s and how they evolved subsequently. Established by designers from Europe and the United States in 1957 to raise the professional status of designers and establish international standards for the profession and design education, ICSID experienced a drastic geographical expansion from the 1960s onwards, when members from both fronts of the Cold War, alongside so-called "developing countries,"[13] joined the organization.[14] This growth took place alongside the diversification of the organization's activities, which increasingly set out to reposition design amongst complex problems such as user rights, technological change, and pollution.[15] But, as this chapter argues, whilst ICSID became interested in the responsibility of the designer towards the environment, the tension between professional concerns on the one hand and the aspiration of designers to contribute to a sustainable future on the other persisted throughout the following decades, due to the prevalence of industrial, economic, and professional imperatives.

Becoming a "United Nations" of Industrial Design

ICSID's interest in ecology developed in the late 1960s and 1970s, when "the first great wave of environmentalism … emerged as a distinct social, political – and design – movement."[16] This period witnessed landmarks such as the first Earth Day celebration in 1970, the United Nations summit in 1972, and the publication of Paul Ehrlich's *The Population Bomb* and the Club of Rome's *Limits to Growth* reports (1968 and 1972 respectively), which, by underlining

ICSID'75
MOSCOW

ИНФОРМАЦИОННЫЙ
БЮЛЛЕТЕНЬ 2
INFORMATION
BULLETIN 2

ДИЗАЙН ДЛЯ ЧЕЛОВЕКА
И ОБЩЕСТВА
DESIGN FOR MAN
AND SOCIETY

Promotional material for ICSID's Congress in Moscow, 1975. ICSID Archive, University of Brighton Design Archives, ICD/02/7/1.

the planet's limited capacity to sustain the rate of growth, caused far-reaching debates on the consequences of industrial societies and ways of avoiding global ecological disaster.[17] As stated above, ICSID had already set out to promote socially-engaged approaches through a wide

17. Peder Anker, *From Bauhaus to Ecohouse: A History of Ecological Design* (Baton Rouge, LA: LSU Press, 2010), 101.

18. Alison Clarke, "Design for Development, ICSID and UNIDO: The Anthropological Turn in 1970s Design," *Journal of Design History* 29, no. 1 (2016).

19. ICSID, "Congresses" boxes, ICD/2, ICSID Archive, University of Brighton Design Archives, Brighton. Throughout the chapter, all references preceded by the initials "ICD" indicate materials that are held at the ICSID Archive, University of Brighton Design Archives, Brighton.

20. Madge, "Design, Ecology, Technology," 158.

21. Messell, "Constructing a 'United Nations of Industrial Design,'" 191.

22. Tania Messell, "Contested Development: ICSID's Design Aid and Environmental Policy in the 1970s," in *The Culture of Nature in the History of Design*, ed. Kjetil Fallan (Abingdon: Routledge, 2019).

program of philanthropic initiatives aimed at the aid and health sectors. These efforts, which from the early 1970s were often initiated in close collaboration with governmental and non-governmental agencies, took place alongside the rise of an anthropological discourse within the design profession, as ICSID turned away from a discourse steeped in scientific operationalism to a more user-centered and grassroots understanding of human needs.[18] As part of this shift, environmental concerns became increasingly heard within the organization. Several of ICSID's council members were active in environmental issues in the 1970s, an interest which in turn was reflected in ICSID's international congresses, which were organized by member societies in collaboration with ICSID's Executive Boards. ICSID congresses held in London in 1969, in Kyoto in 1973, in Moscow in 1975, and in Dublin in 1977, touched upon the designer's position towards environmental degradation in their overall themes and panels.[19] ICSID had also given its support to the landmark symposium and exhibition "Design for Need: The Social Contribution of Design," which was held at the Royal College of Art in London in 1976, where an international roster of designers, architects, representatives of non-governmental organizations, and alternative technology groups discussed design solutions for projects of social value, including resource preservation.[20] In terms of alliances, from 1974 onwards ICSID also set out to grow closer to the United Nations Environment Program (UNEP), and closely collaborated with Victor Papanek, author of the bestselling book *Design for the Real World: Human Ecology and Social Change* (1971), who throughout the 1970s advocated for socially and environmentally sound design practices within ICSID's Working Group Developing Countries IV.[21]

However, an ambiguous understanding of environmental practices prevailed amongst ICSID's development initiatives. Mostly overseen by Western designers, these activities advocated the use of local practices and foreign innovation, but pressed for technology transfers whilst often overseeing local attempts to coordinate institutional and professional responses to environmental degradation.[22] As will be examined next, this ambiguity tainted ICSID's other undertakings during this period. Although ICSID's

Executive Board was on numerous occasions admonished by UNEP and council members to develop activities concerning the designer's role towards the protection of the natural environment, and to establish a working group on the latter,[23] the organization failed to take on the topic further and to radically challenge the profession from within. The following sections will examine the reasons for this deep-seated ambivalence.

Antagonist Interests: Ties to Industry

As Woodham notes, the increase in the number of design organizations from the 1940s onwards reflected "the growing number of professionals in the field as well as their perceived need to campaign collectively for greater recognition of their value to business, commerce, and society."[24] The profession's economic reliance on business and the manufacturing and retail sectors coexisted with a necessity to answer the commercial agendas of such employers, which subsequently tempered any social, environmental, and moral preoccupations.[25] ICSID's ambivalent vision of the designer's role towards the environment could similarly have been the result of the organization's repeated attempts to tie closer bonds with industry. Since its establishment, ICSID regarded the latter as a central source of recognition and funds, a situation that continued throughout the 1970s. Established in 1964, ICSID's Working Group Professional Practice, which in 1973 included designers from France, Finland, Holland, Australia, Japan, Israel, and Poland, for instance, strove to promote the profession, strengthen design education, and forge closer links primarily with industry, by the 1970s.[26] On the other hand, many of the organization's promotional members had close-knit relations with industry, which often financed their activities. The introduction of a new kind of membership wed ICSID to industry in a more direct manner. In 1971 ICSID created the associate membership, to which government departments, research centers, universities, and companies could subscribe. This membership, which cost an annual fee of $1000 and which ICSID planned to offer to industrial concerns in capitalist, socialist, Western, and non-Western

23. In 1971, Martin Kelm at the Zentralinstitut für Gestaltung in the GDR proposed that ICSID's 1973 congress theme would be "Environment Protection and Design." In 1972, Henri Viénot shared with Josine des Cressonnières the belief that ICSID needed to pursue activities on design and the natural environment, whilst Frank Dudas proposed in 1974 that several Interdesign workshops were to treat environmental issues. The same year Gui Bonsiepe proposed the creation of a working group on these topics. Correspondence from Martin Kelm to Henri Viénot, 1971, ICD/10/10/1; correspondence from Henri Viénot to Josine des Cressonnières, June 5, 1972, ICD/08/9/1; correspondence from Frank Dudas to ICSID, May 1974, ICD/08/4/1; correspondence from Gui Bonsiepe to Josine des Cressonnières, March 4, 1974, ICD/08/3/2.

24. Jonathan Woodham, *Twentieth-Century Design* (Oxford and New York: Oxford University Press, 1997), 175.

25. Woodham, 231.

26. ICSID, minutes general assembly, Tokyo, 1973, ICD/03/7/8, 71.

Design Struggles

27. ICSID, minutes executive board meeting, Brussels, November 17–18, 1971, CD/04/2, 12.

28. ICSID, "Why Become an ICSID Associate Member," 1976, ICD/10/28/2; ICSID, 'Application Form for Associate Membership," 1973, CD/10/28/3.

29. ICSID, "General Assemblies," 1980–89 boxes, CD/3.

30. ICSID, "Aim of the ICSID-Industry Commission," 1970s, CD/06/11.

nations,[27] allowed the latter to be informed of new trends and increase the visibility of their products through design awards.[28] By the 1980s, this policy had led to the inclusion of companies such as Hewlett Packard, Sharp Corporation, and the Finnish state-owned oil company Neste Oyj,[29] whose financial contributions constituted a precious support for ICSID.

Conversely, when ICSID set out to influence industry, little resulted from such initiatives, a situation which further prevented the implementation of environmentally friendly practices. In 1974, ICSID set up ICSID Industry Commission to better involve industry in the drafting of ICSID's goals and to assist its campaign for funds, which ICSID continuously lacked. Presided over by Count René Boël, a Belgian industrialist and diplomat who acted as Patron of ICSID, the group aimed to establish a dialogue between designers and business concerns at the level of decision-making; reflect on the potential of design to solve problems of industrial production, user-needs, and pollution; and disseminate the findings within wider industrial spheres.[30] Its first meeting, held in 1975, was attended by leading figures in industry such as Umberto Agnelli, managing director of Fiat; Renaud Gillet, managing director of Rhône-Poulenc; and Renzo Zori, Olivetti's Director of the Division of Industrial Design. Aiming to

First meeting of ICSID's Industry Commission, 1975. ICSID, Message, May/June 1975. ICSID Archive, University of Brighton Design Archives, ICD/09/1/3.

develop pilot projects that were "good for society,"[31] the specters of professional recognition and profit remained. Moreover, when two pilot studies were instigated for the Italian automobile manufacturer Fiat and the French chemical and pharmaceutical company Rhône-Poulenc, the propositions only touched the redesign of working spaces, and the experience ended due to a lack of follow-up by both companies.[32]

As noted above, this ambivalence between social and environmental welfare and economic interests, alongside ICSID's difficulty affecting industrial concerns, took place once again within the organization's development activities. Whilst the promotion of ecologically sound practices and technology constituted a cornerstone of ICSID's policies towards developing countries,[33] and ICSID's longstanding relation with UNIDO was grounded in a discourse based on cultural and technological diversity, the rhetoric of industrial development remained.[34] This positioning reflected a wider interest in answering "basic need" in international development discourses, which at the time put the former at the forefront of industrial policies.[35] Such changes, however, did not erase the development paradigm, which, having originated in North America and Europe, had by then, as Arturo Escobar notes, increasingly colonized "social reality."[36]

Controlled versus Uncontrolled Growth

In line with the above discussion, a tension also prevailed between ICSID's human-centered discourse on the one hand and the rhetoric of unchallenged economic growth on the other. As ICSID's secretary-general, Belgian design promoter Josine des Cressonnières, stated in 1977, industry "is compelled to profit." Drawing upon the Club of Rome's reports and the endorsement of the New International Economic Order by the United Nations in 1974, she underlined that ICSID could nevertheless reveal that it would be possible to "work simultaneously for the common good <u>and</u> for the productive society [underlining in original]."[37] Some individuals, however, had favored more radical alternatives.

31. ICSID, minutes Executive Board meeting, Brussels, December 11–12, 1971, ICD/04/2, 10.

32. ICSID, "ICSID-Industry Commission," ICD/06/11.

33. Messell, "Contested Development," 132.

34. Tania Messell, "Globalization and Design Institutionalization: ICSID's XIth Congress and the Formation of ALADI, 1979," *Journal of Design History* 32, no. 1 (2019), 91–93; Victor Papanek, "For the Southern Half of the Globe," *Design Studies* 4, no. 1 (1983).

35. Matthias Schmeltzer, "A Club of the Rich to Help the Poor? The OECD, 'Development,' and the Hegemony of Donor Countries" in *International Organizations and Development, 1945 to 1990*, ed. Marc Frey et al. (Basingstoke: Palgrave Macmillan, 2014).

36. Arturo Escobar, *Encountering Development: The Making and Unmaking of the Third World* (Princeton: Princeton University Press, 1995), 5.

37. Josine des Cressonnières, "Statement of Intent," 1977, ICD/04/4, 2.

For instance, during ICSID's Third Seminar on Industrial Design Education in 1967, ICSID's then-president, Argentinian designer and Ulm rector Tomás Maldonado, advanced the necessity of controlling industrial and economic growth, a statement which received the approval of practitioners from the US, UK, India, and Brazil. As he suggested:

> We must think how it is possible to develop design for control. There is resistance in capitalistic Western countries to control, but in today's reality

Tomás Maldonado speaking at ICSID's General Assembly in London, 1969. Design Council Archive, University of Brighton Design Archives, DCA/O8/8.

chaotic growth is aided by designers to increase all populations, population of people, objects, information, etc. It is clear that this kind of growth does not have a very brilliant future.[38]

Maldonado was subsequently invited to orchestrate the contents of ICSID's 1969 congress in London, "Design, Society, and the Future," through which he advocated the need to reduce unbridled production and consumption. However, the rest of ICSID's Executive Board and British

38. ICSID, Third Seminar on Industrial Design Education, Syracuse University, September 7–10, 1967, session 8, ICD/13/1/3, 3.

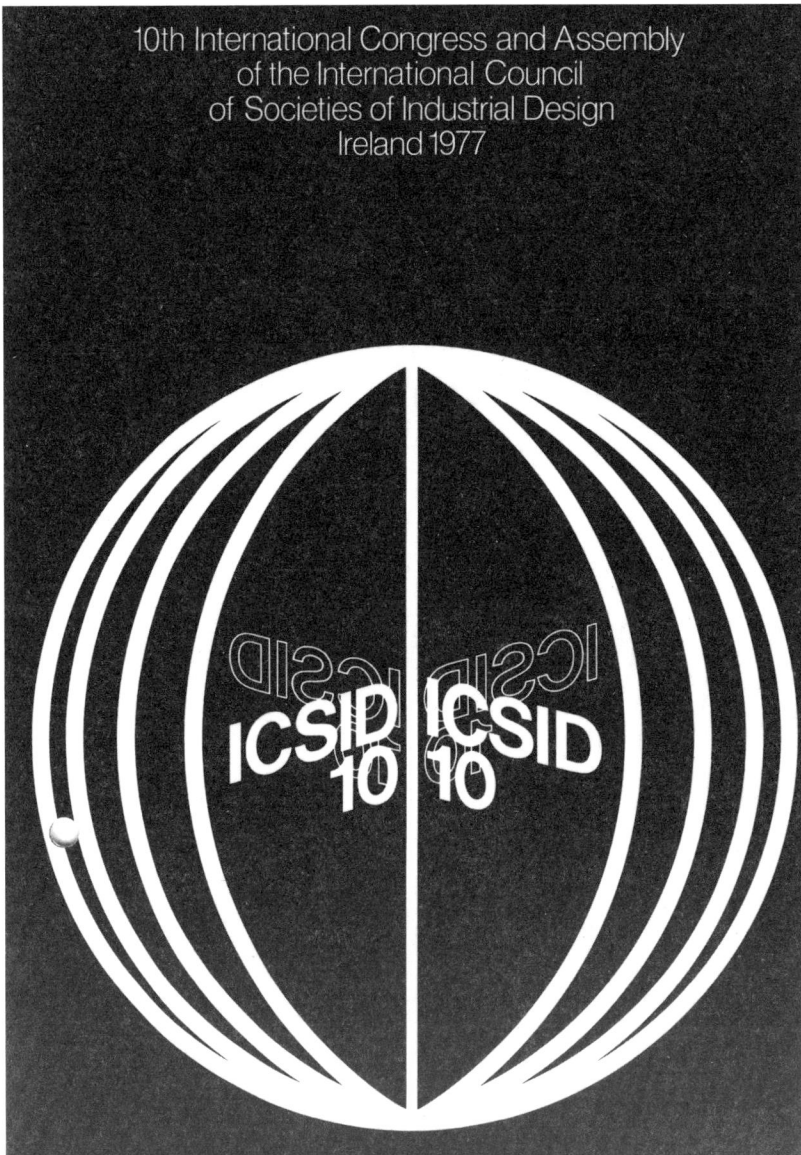

10th International Congress and Assembly of the International Council of Societies of Industrial Design
Ireland 1977

Raymond Kyne and Brendan Matthews, brochure for ICSID's Congress in Dublin, 1977. ICSID Archive, University of Brighton Design Archives, ICD/02/8/1.

39. Messell, "Constructing a 'United Nations of Industrial Design.'"

40. ICSID, "Hernstein's Seminar (Austria, 1977)" file, ICD/07/6/2.

41. International Trade Centre UNCTAD/GATT, "Provisional Outline of the Trade Promotion Handbook: Product Design and Packaging for Export," 1973, ICD/12/34.

42. ICSID, transcription of tapes, general assembly in Dublin, tape one, ICD/03/9/13, 4.

organizers did not share this stance, and as with most of ICSID's past and future congresses, the event saw the promotion of design as a flexible and innovative profession at the service of economic growth, which in this context took place parallel to debates tackling the designer's social and environmental responsibilities.[39]

The contribution of design to financial prosperity also took shape in the council's other initiatives. For instance, this discourse pervaded a seminar held at the Hernstein Management Centre of the Vienna Chamber of Commerce in 1977, titled "Group Dynamics Seminar for Top Managers and Designers." Whilst the event aimed to gather designers and industrialists to discuss ways of developing products that answered social and environmental needs, it also focused on the benefits of design understanding to spur marketability and ultimately profit.[40] This vision similarly prevailed in ICSID's collaboration with the International Trade Centre (ITC) in 1973, when the council assisted the ITC in conceiving a guidebook aimed at developing countries, titled "Product Design and Packaging for Export," which advised the former on how to increase sales.[41] Thus, whilst the council did acknowledge the need to answer human and environmental needs, it also continuously promoted the capacity of design to spur competitiveness and economic growth.

Professional Imperatives

As shown in the following, ICSID's ambivalence towards environmental responsibility also stemmed from the grassroots professional interests of a large section of its membership. Growing dissatisfaction over ICSID's engagement with world issues had developed amongst its members, a tension which appeared most clearly during the council's general assembly in Dublin in 1977. During this event, twenty-four council members, all of them professional bodies and representing half of ICSID's membership, presented a "Seven-point Manifesto."[42] The text advocated ICSID to concentrate its efforts on alleviating the everyday problems of industrial designers by answering the longstanding lack of recognition by manufacturers and users

ICSID Executive Board Members at the General Assembly in Dublin, 1977. ICSID Archive, University of Brighton Design Archives, ICD/02/8/3.

and by developing design education through collaborative efforts between council members.[43] The congress, "ICSID 10," which marked ICSID's tenth edition and twentieth anniversary, aimed to address the topics of development and identity "in a kaleidoscopic world."[44] However, in stark contrast to the event's humanistic aims, the manifesto urged designers to develop products that favored efficiency and profitability in order to strengthen their relationship with industry, which they regarded as the profession's main challenge.[45] As one of the signatories stated, industry needed to be defended – "because whether we like it or not, we have to work for it. Industry produces products we all use. It is the way our society works."[46]

The manifesto underlined how industry and public authorities could only be convinced of the value of industrial design if designers produced products that would sell better and that could be produced more efficiently. Most importantly, the signatories stated that whilst

43. ICSID, minutes general assembly, Dublin, September 23–24, 1977, ICD/03/9/16, 8.

44. Kenji Ekuan, "ICSID 10 Congress (Closing Speech)," September 1977, ICD/02/3/5.

45. Franco Raggi, "ICSID Dublino: Il designer va dallo psicanalista," MODO no. 6 (January–February 1978), 25.

46. ICSID, transcription of tapes, general assembly in Dublin, September 23–24, 1977, ICD/03/9/13.

47. ICSID, minutes 10th general assembly in Dublin, September 23–24, 1977, ICD/03/9/16, 8–9.

48. Ibid., 13.

49. ICSID, *ICSID News*, 1977–85, ICD/09/1/5; ICSID, ICSID News, 1986–89, ICD/09/1/6.

50. Madge, "Design, Ecology, Technology," 159.

51. ICSID, "ICSID Seeks Deeper Cooperation," *ICSID News*, no. 5 (1989), ICD/09/1/6, 3.

the recreation of harmony between man and nature … may be a goal in general, the creation of harmony between man and his tools or means, reproduced through <u>industrial processes</u>, is the goal and only justification of industrial design [underlining in original].[47]

The manifesto and its demands were ratified with a total of 111 votes, twenty-four against and with nine abstentions, reflecting its overwhelming support.[48] As a result, ICSID's Executive Board adopted the proposed redirection of ICSID policies towards a greater emphasis on practicing designers as opposed to social and environmental issues. The "Seven-point Manifesto" ushered in a new era within the organization in the 1980s, when it tended to focus on professional and commercial imperatives.

Conclusion: Post-1980

This chapter has revealed ICSID's ambivalent stance towards the environment in the 1970s, which as it argues resulted from professional, promotional, and economic interests. In this context, the internationalization of design was accompanied by an alliance with a globalizing corporate nexus, which at times overshadowed environmental initiatives. In the following decades, ICSID's engagement with sustainability was maintained in varying degrees. Whilst ICSID did attempt to include sustainability amongst its activities in the 1970s, these efforts slowed down in the 1980s, when its congresses became overtly concerned with the profession's contribution to business, marketing, and design strategies for global markets[49] – reflecting a wider turn towards "design for profit" in the mainstream design profession.[50] This lack of interest resulted in a meeting of representatives of ICSID societies in 1989, where thirty participants from fifteen countries summoned ICSID to question the kind of design it was promoting and the designer's responsibilities towards "humanity, society, and nature."[51] ICSID's engagement with wider issues subsequently resumed in the 1990s and the 2000s. In 1998, ICSID participated in founding the "Design for the World" organization with the International Council of Graphic Design Associations (Icograda) and the International Federation of Interior Architects/Designers (IFI), with the support of the Barcelona Design Center, a collaboration which set out to spur the use of design in human-centered initiatives.[52] In 2003, ICSID and Icograda in turn founded the International Design Alliance (IDA) to promote the design professions and "working together for a world that is balanced, inclusive, and sustainable."[53] This rhetoric persisted throughout the 2010s, when ICSID, renamed the World Design Organization (WDO), renewed its vows to contribute to a sustainable future. Grounded in a discourse of sustainable development, which has been criticized as preserving the status quo,[54] the extent to which these initiatives have balanced environmentally responsible practices with diverse professional, cultural, and socioeconomic contexts, as well as recognized the structural and ecological inequalities underpinning the environmental crisis, would however warrant further examination.

52. Jonathan Woodham, "Design for the World," *A Dictionary of Modern Design*, 2nd ed. (Oxford: Oxford University Press, 2016), 220-21.

53. Jonathan Woodham, "International Design Alliance (IDA)," *A Dictionary of Modern Design*, 2nd ed. (Oxford: Oxford University Press, 2016), 356.

54. Julie Davidson, "Sustainable Development: Business as Usual or a New Way of Living?," *Environmental Ethics* 22, no. 1 (March 2000), 25–42; Arturo Escobar, *Encountering Development: The Making and Unmaking of the Third World* (Princeton: Princeton University Press, 1995); Mark R. Kramer, Rishi Agarwal, Aditi Srinivas, "Business as Usual Will Not Save the Planet," *Harvard Business Review*, June 12, 2019, hbr.org/2019/06/business-as-usual-will-not-save-the-planet (accessed July 22, 2019).

GREEN PROMISES

Design Struggles

Bibliography

Anker, Peder. *From Bauhaus to Ecohouse: A History of Ecological Design*. Baton Rouge, LA: LSU Press, 2010.

Boehnert, Joanna. *Design, Ecology, Politics: Towards the Ecocene*. London and New York, NY: Bloomsbury, 2018.

Clarke, Alison. "Design for Development, ICSID and UNIDO: The Anthropological Turn in 1970s Design." *Journal of History of Design* 29, no. 1 (2015), 43–57.

Davidson, Julie. "Sustainable Development: Business as Usual or a New Way of Living?" *Environmental Ethics* 22, no. 1 (March 2000), 25–42.

Escobar, Arturo. *Encountering Development: The Making and Unmaking of the Third World*. Princeton, NJ: Princeton University Press, 1995.

Fallan, Kjetil, ed. *The Culture of Nature in the History of Design*. Abingdon: Routledge, 2019.
—, and Finn Arne Jørgensen. "Environmental Histories of Design: Towards a New Research Agenda." Special Issue: Environmental Histories of Design. *Journal of Design History* 30, no. 2 (2017), 103–21.

Fry, Tony. *Design Futuring: Sustainability, Ethics and New Practice*. London: Bloomsbury Academic, 2008.
—. *Design as Politics*. Oxford: Berg Publishers, 2011.

Fuad-Luke, Alastair. *Design Activism: Beautiful Strangeness for a Sustainable World*. London: Earthscan Routledge, 2009.

ICSID Archives. University of Brighton Design Archives, Brighton.

Kaiser, Wolfram, and Jan-Henrik Meyer, eds. *International Organizations and Environmental Protection: Conservation and Globalization in the Twentieth Century*. New York, NY: Berghahn Books, 2019.

Kramer, Mark R., Rishi Agarwal, and Aditi Srinivas. "Business as Usual Will Not Save the Planet," *Harvard Business Review*, June 12, 2019. hbr.org/2019/06/business-as-usual-will-not-save-the-planet (accessed July 22, 2019).

Lees-Maffei, Grace. "Introduction: Professionalization as a Focus in Interior Design History." *Journal of Design History* 21, no. 1 (2008), 1–18.

Madge, Pauline. "Design, Ecology, Technology: A Historiographical Review." *Journal of Design History* 6, no. 3 (1993), 149–66.

Margolin, *The Politics of the Artificial: Essays on Design and Design Studies*. Chicago, IL: University of Chicago Press, 2002.
—. "Design for Development: Towards a History." *Design Studies* 28, no. 2 (2007), 111–15.

Messell, Tania. "Constructing a 'United Nations of Industrial Design': ICSID and the Professionalization of Design on the World Stage, 1957–1980." Doctoral Thesis, University of Brighton, 2018.
—. "Globalization and Design Institutional-ization: ICSID's XIth Congress and the Formation of ALADI, 1979." *Journal of Design History* 32, no. 1 (2019), 88–104.
—. "Contested Development: ICSID's Design Aid and Environmental Policy in the 1970s." In *The Culture of Nature in the History of Design*. Edited by Kjetil Fallan, 131–46. Abingdon: Routledge, 2019.

Papanek, Victor. "For the Southern Half of the Globe." *Design Studies* 4, no. 1 (1983), 61–64.

Pereira, Helder, and Coral Gillett. "Africa: Designing as Existence." *Design in the Borderlands*. Edited by Eleni Kalantidou and Tony Fry, 109–31. Abingdon: Routledge, 2014.

Raggi, Franco. "ICSID Dublino: Il designer va dallo psicanalista." *MODO* no. 6 (January-February 1978), 21–24.

Seddon, Jill. "Mentioned, but Denied Significance: Women Designers and the "Professionalization" of Design in Britain, c. 1920–1951." *Gender & History* 12, no. 2 (2000), 425–47.

Taylor, Damon. "A Brief History of (Un) Sustainable Design." *The Routledge Handbook of Sustainable Product Design*. Edited by Jonathan Chapman. Abingdon: Routledge, 2017.

Twemlow, Alice. "I Can't Talk to You if You Say That: An Ideological Collision at the International Design Conference at Aspen, 1970." *Design and Culture* 1, no. 1 (2009), 23–49.

WDO. "World Design Agenda 2017–2019." wdo.org/resources/world-design-agenda/ (accessed January 6, 2019).

Woodham, Jonathan M. *Twentieth-Century Design*. Oxford and New York, NY: Oxford University Press, 1997.
—. "Local, National and Global: Redrawing the Design Historical Map." *Journal of Design History* 18, no. 3 (2005), 257–67.
—. *A Dictionary of Modern Design*. 2nd ed. Oxford: Oxford University Press, 2016.
—, and Michael Thomson. "Cultural Diplomacy and Design in the Late Twentieth and Twenty-First Centuries: Rhetoric or Reality?" *Design and Culture* 9, no. 2 (2017), 225–41.

NORWEGIAN WOOD
Trails to Ecological Design

Kjetil Fallan

Made famous by the Beatles' 1965 hit song, and subsequently catalyzed by Haruki Murakami's 1987 novel, the term "Norwegian wood" has taken on a mythical allure in international popular culture. Its commercial appropriations today include a rock festival, a best-selling book about firewood, a craft beer, as well as a purportedly ethical and sustainable fashion and homewares brand – all favoring the phrase for its allusions to something genuine, wholesome, and natural. Whereas the appropriateness of many of these appropriations certainly could be questioned, the term's universal familiarity and distinct connotations make it an apt point of departure for exploring some of the less-trodden trails to ecological design. Judging by today's discourse – whether scholarly, professional, or popular – one might get the impression that ecological design is a recent or flat-out ahistorical phenomenon, the result of a new and immaculate imperative. Only by retracing key historical trajectories, however, can we hope to arrive at a fuller understanding of its complexities and contemporary significance.

Just like the song and the novel, the emerging discourse on ecological design traced in the following bridged the local and the global, inserting the national in the international – and vice versa. The rise of popular environmentalism and the migration of basic ecological ideas from the life sciences to general and professional media in the latter half of the 1960s helped change the meaning of internationalization in design discourse. If hitherto primarily gauged by the local export of exquisite objects and the rising fame of national design heroes, internationalization now also came to signify a new concern for how local communities were affected by the border-defying nature of environmental problems and a growing awareness of the global connections underpinning our material culture and natural ecosystem alike. In this chapter, I will trace one of the many trajectories through the emergence of this new understanding of design's environmental entanglements by following the writings and actions of the Canadian-Norwegian architect Robert Esdaile and his quest for an ecologically founded design education and practice. Shifting to a more literal understanding of "Norwegian wood," the final section examines the morality of materials in the marked shift in the 1960s from teak to pine as the dominant material in Norwegian furniture design.

Although Nordic design in general tends to be associated with nature and the natural, at least when mediated internationally,[1] the trope of "nature" has been particularly pronounced in Norway. During the heyday of "Scandinavian Design" in the 1950s, nature was portrayed as a sublime presence, a majestic force – a source both of material resources and creative inspiration. The growing acknowledgment that the serenity and purity of nature hitherto taken for granted was now under threat, and that design and designers were implicit in this environmental destruction, significantly changed how nature was perceived and invoked in design discourse. The concept of ecology, at this very time spilling over into the public realm from the narrower confines of the life sciences, quickly became a favored tool amongst design professionals for rethinking human-nature relations. Making it his life's mission to reform design practice and education according to ecological principles, Robert Esdaile and his concern for what comes "after us" represents one of the first sustained efforts to bring an ecological, or ecologically informed, critique to bear on design and its practices and ideologies in a Norwegian context. Tracing Esdaile's work leads us along one of many trails through the extensive and dense Norwegian wood(s), exemplifying how ecological design grew from many different roots, and that one of its main characteristics is the dual attention to the local and the global.

1. Niels Peter Skou and Anders V. Munch, "New Nordic and Scandinavian Retro: Reassessment of Values and Aesthetics in Contemporary Nordic Design," *Journal of Aesthetics & Culture* 8, no. 1 (2016), 6–8.

2. Letter to Robert Esdaile
from secretary Armand
Halvorsen of the National
College of Applied Art
and Craft/Oslo School of
Architecture, dated January
18, 1964. Robert Esdailes
arkiv, NAM1995:23 Serie
D Korrespondanse, NTNU
University Library, Trondheim.

3. Arne Gunnarsjaa,
Arkitekturleksikon (Oslo:
Abstrakt forlag, 1999), 224.

Finding Ecology

At the exact same time as the Beatles released "Norwegian Wood," in December 1965, Robert Esdaile launched a targeted and comprehensive criticism of designers' lack of concern for environmental problems on the pages of the Norwegian architectural magazine *Arkitektnytt*. His acutely titled essay, "The Environmental Crisis," was published in five installments from 1965 to 1967, setting the tone for the budding debate on ecology and design in Norway. Canadian-born Esdaile trained at McGill University, Montreal, and at the University of Cambridge. After marrying Elin Høst, a Norwegian, he moved to Norway in 1948, where he first worked as a planner before setting up an architectural practice in 1955. Collaborating with key figures such as Odd Brochmann, Dag Rognlien (editor of *Arkitektnytt* from 1966), and Christian Norberg-Schulz, Esdaile remained a steadfast modernist, a member of the International Congresses of Modern Architecture (CIAM) to the very end, and a key promoter of Le Corbusier's ideas in Norway. From 1964, initially filling in for Sverre Fehn, he taught at the Oslo School of Architecture,[2] until being appointed professor at the Norwegian Institute of Technology in 1971.[3] Esdaile was as radical a citizen as he was a design theorist and educator. After he attended the

Robert Esdaile, apartment building at Bjørnekollen, Oslo (1956). Photo: Bjørn Winsnæs (1959).
Courtesy of the National Museum of Art, Architecture, and Design. CC-BY-NC.

seventh congress of the International Union of Architects (IUA) in Havana, Cuba, in 1963, where both Fidel Castro and Ernesto "Che" Guevara addressed the delegates, he took to signing private letters "Venceremos" and "Hasta la victoria siempre." Deeply inspired by his experience in Cuba, he would later cite from Fidel's and Che's IUA talks in his teaching as a way of convincing his students that they and their profession could make a difference in – and to – the world.[4]

With a background in planning, in his essay on the environmental crisis Esdaile homed in on perhaps the most obvious target: the car and its implications for the organization of transport systems and settlement patterns. Esdaile argued that this quintessential symbol of modern society and personal liberation had become a massive paradox, paralyzed by its own success: "The dream of 'living freely' murders the freedom of living."[5] The car was both a societal and an environmental problem:

> the privately owned automobile … creates chaos, pollution, an alarming number of deaths [*sic*] and wounded. It distorts civic life and will in time congest and pollute the most exquisite countryside, our last reserve of inspiration and human dignity. This is not a fantasy, but a pure statement of facts.[6]

He did not oppose the car as such, but believed that its production, distribution, and use had to be brought under strict regulation to keep it from suffocating our airways and highways alike.

The car was just a convenient example, though, and Esdaile cast the entirety of human history as "a career which gradually freed him [Man] from the inhibiting discipline of nature. The acquired knowledge of this last millennia [*sic*] of his existence on earth is like a bulldozer out of control. All the 'signs' and warnings which nature gently confronts us with are being trodden upon in a gigantic stampede. This planless stampede leaves behind it an environmental crisis."[7] Stopping the bulldozer required coordinated planning and a holistic, or at least systemic, approach to design. Over-specialization resulted in tunnel vision and the pulverization of responsibility, he argued.

4. Robert Esdailes arkiv, NAM1995:23 Serie D Korrespondanse, Nasjonalmuseet for kunst, arkitektur og design; Nils Werenskiold, "Den radikale arkitekt-professor," *Aktuell*, no. 8 (February 20, 1971), 28, 29; anon., "Miljøvokteren," *Dagbladet*, May 30, 1970, p. 5.

5. Robert Esdaile, "Our Environmental Crisis II," *Arkitektnytt* no. 3 (1966), 42.

6. Esdaile, 42.

7. Robert Esdaile, "Our Environmental Crisis," *Arkitektnytt* no. 20 (1965), 376.

Design Struggles

8. Esdaile, 376.

9. Richard Buckminster Fuller, *Operating Manual for Spaceship Earth* (Carbondale: Southern Illinois University Press, 1968).

10. Andrew G. Kirk, *The Whole Earth Catalog and American Environmentalism* (Lawrence: University Press of Kansas, 2007), 56–64; Peder Anker, *From Bauhaus to Ecohouse: A History of Ecological Design* (Baton Rouge, LA: Louisiana State University Press, 2010), 68–82.

11. Robert P. McIntosh, *The Background of Ecology: Concept and Theory* (Cambridge, UK: Cambridge University Press, 1985).

12. Robert Esdaile, "Our Environmental Crisis III," *Arkitektnytt* no. 14 (1966), 254.

13. Finis Dunaway, *Seeing Green: The Use and Abuse of American Environmental Images* (Chicago, IL: University of Chicago Press, 2015), 66.

However, it is in Esdaile's prescription for curing this illness that his intervention becomes particularly perceptive. Addressing the environmental crisis, he suggests, requires that design engages with "ecological issues, because this exact and beautifully broad science coordinates mans [*sic*] behavior with the laws and habits of nature."[8] Esdaile's trumpeting of ecology in a mainstream design context stands out, three years before the arrival of Buckminster Fuller's *Operating Manual for Spaceship Earth*[9] and the first *Whole Earth Catalog* – publications that were key in popularizing ecology and promoting the idea of "whole systems" thinking in design discourse.[10] Although ecological thought has a long history, there is broad consensus that as a distinct discipline ecology emerged in the early twentieth century. It was only in the 1960s, however, that it gained public prominence, as a consequence of increased concern for the state of the environment.[11]

Esdaile was an architect, not a biologist, and there is nothing in his article that indicates any profound scientific knowledge of ecology. His interest in the concept seems to have been as an inspiration or tool with which designers could learn to think more holistically about their interventions in the world and the environmental impact of their practice. The time was ripe, he claimed, for the human species to put its creative capacities to better use:

> The success of people to adapt themselves has been at times astonishing and admirable, at other times they have wasted the land depleting both their energies and reserves. Never before has the power of man to waste and ravage been so decisive. Final destruction lies in his own hands.[12]

This latter observation on the prospect of human-originated obliteration is clearly colored by the Cold War climate in the wake of the Cuba crisis. In an environmentalist context, Esdaile's comment recalls a tagline later made instantly famous: "We have met the enemy and he is us," which cartoonist Walt Kelly originally applied to a poster he created for the first Earth Day in 1970.[13] It also preempts a very similar remark made by György Kepes in the context of the vastly ambitious "Universitas Project" at New York's

Museum of Modern Art in 1972: "At this historical junction, the real beasts are man-created: we face ourselves as the enemy."[14] Kepes, an artist, designer, and scholar teaching at MIT, then went on to say that this new awareness of our precarious situation had made us begin

> to see that our extended body, our social and man-transformed environment must develop its own self-regulating mechanisms to eliminate the poisons injected into it and to recycle useful matter. Environmental homeostasis on a global scale is now necessary to survival.[15]

Like Kepes, Esdaile saw in ecology a conceptual model for thinking across scales and along relations. Only by adopting an ecological mindset, he argued, could designers help to reinstate the equilibrium they have contributed to upset by, in the words of Victor Papanek, "creating whole new species of permanent garbage to clutter up the landscape, and by choosing materials and processes that pollute the air we breathe."[16] To pull back from the brink of Armageddon and set spaceship earth on a more sustainable course, Esdaile reasoned, we needed an entirely new approach to planning the human environment. Recalling its publication date – 1966 – his suggested strategy remains an early articulation of key principles of ecological design:

> What resources can we now call upon to face this new situation? Certainly not new weapons: certainly not a new invention. No, a conscientious ability to see with microscopic clarity and macroscopic breadth the interwoven and complex unity of man and nature. The science is called ECOLOGY. If we could apply it in its generous wholeness which is its supreme justification, we might have time to regain a balance. But the application of Ecology demands a changed state of mind: an *I-Thou* relationship instead of an *I-it* relationship. This has *nothing* to do with the sentimentality of a "back to nature" attitude which is the prestige of the well-to-do urban dweller. It embodies rather humility and collaboration, expressing the balance in biological

14. György Kepes, "Art and Ecological Consciousness," in *The Universitas Project: Solutions for a Post-Technological Society*, ed. Emilio Ambaszed (New York, NY: MoMA Publications, 2006), 152.

15. Kepes, 154.

16. Victor Papanek, *Design for the Real World: Human Ecology and Social Change* (New York, NY: Pantheon Books, 1971), xi.

Design Struggles

17. Esdaile, "Our Environmental Crisis III," 254.

18. "Bilag til søknad fra Prof. Robert Esdaile," dated August 21, 1978. Robert Esdailes arkiv, NAM1995:23 Serie D Korrespondanse, Nasjonalmuseet for kunst, arkitektur og design.

19. "Protokoll fört vid förberedande samträde mellan interesserade i utställningsprojektet ÄN SEN DÅ... den 18 dec. 1968," Robert Esdailes arkiv, NAM1995:23 Serie Gc Manuskripter til foredrag, artikler og andre ekster, Nasjonalmuseet for kunst, arkitektur og design.

sciences. Most important to the architect, it gives a very clear picture of environmental factors and their interplay.[17]

Exhibiting Doom and Gloom

"The Environmental Crisis" was just the beginning of Esdaile's passionate and long-lasting efforts in the name of ecological design, most of which he would channel through his teaching and campaigns for educational reform. An alternative way of communicating the message, though, was the medium of exhibitions. In 1968, marking the occasion of his employer, the Oslo School of Architecture, moving out of the premises of its parent institution, the National College of Applied Art and Craft, he organized an exhibition about urban environmental problems. According to him, this event was the "precursor" to another exhibition shown the following year in Oslo "on [his] initiative" called *And after us…*[18] This claim is slightly misleading, though, as the latter exhibition was a local adaptation of a concept developed by architecture students at Chalmers Institute of Technology in Gothenburg and shown at a dozen venues in Sweden since May 1968, generating considerable media coverage and public attention. A delegation from the Oslo School of Architecture, led by Esdaile, along with representatives from the Norwegian Society for the Conservation of Nature and the United Nations Association of Norway, met with one of the original curators, Ivar Fernemo from Chalmers, and others in December 1968 to plan a Norwegian version of the show.[19] The basic message of the exhibition – that the future of the world and humanity alike was threatened by our maltreatment of the environment – was carried over from the Swedish edition, including excerpts from research by leading Swedish environmentalist-scholars underpinning this view, such as biologist-cum-geographer Georg Borgström and biochemist Hans Palmstierna. As agreed, though, Esdaile added to this Norwegian material, sampling from, for example, zoology professor Rolf Vik's popular writings on the environmental crisis, a Rachel Carson-derived exposé of DDT by Ragnhild Sundby (professor of zoology at the Norwegian College of

Agriculture and, from 1972, president of the Norwegian Society for the Conservation of Nature), historian Tore Linné Eriksen's work on developmental aid, and Esdaile's own crusade against the private car.[20]

Through the medium of a pop-up exhibition structure designed for ease of assembly and transport accompanied by a comparatively comprehensive catalog, Esdaile and his architecture students – assisted by design students from the National College of Applied Art and Craft – then organized and presented this broad swath of scholarship using visually striking infographics and photomontages accompanied by succinct texts. Neatly indicating the pertinent yet precarious nature of the project's main message, the catalog's cover featured an illustration composed of an ultrasound image of a six-week-old fetus rendered in red superimposed on a black-and-white image of Earth seen from space. Rendering an unborn child in this context makes it an extreme example of the trope of "children as emotional emblems of the future" identified by Finis Dunaway as key in the visual culture of environmentalism: "Within the context of popular environmentalism, children's bodies provide a way to visualize the largely invisible threats of radiation, toxicity, and other environmental dangers."[21] A forceful symbol of Mother Earth, this illustration, paired with the distressing title, *And after us…*, efficiently communicated the sense of fragility and

20. Anon., ed., *og etter oss…* (Oslo: Norges naturvernforbund, 1970).

21. Dunaway, *Seeing Green*, 3.

Spread from the exhibition catalog *And after us…* illustrating "today" (left) and "tomorrow?" (right).

og etter oss...

Front cover of the catalog for the exhibition *And after us*... featuring an image of a fetus superimposed on a "blue marble" photo of the earth.

urgency which the exhibition sought to instill in the public. And the message hit home. Not only was the exhibition met with great public interest, drawing eighty thousand visitors in Oslo alone before moving on to Bergen, Trondheim, and other venues[22] – it even pushed back at the academic community, becoming "important in triggering a call to action amongst the environmentally concerned at the University [of Oslo]," especially for the emerging ecophilosophers.[23] Sigmund Kvaløy Setreng, a research fellow and former student of professor Arne Næss and prime mover in the formation of the Ecophilosophy Group,

> was greatly impressed by the exhibition, and invited the architects to join hands with students of ecology, philosophers, and technical climbers from the Alpine Club, to create a Co-working Group for the Protection of Nature and the Environment at the University.[24]

Their subsequent correspondence reveals that Esdaile was clearly flattered and motivated by Kvaløy's gesture, as it meant bringing design discourse to the epicenter of environmental scholarship and activism.[25]

Decentralizing Design

In June 1966, Esdaile wrote to Håkon Stenstadvold, rector of the National College of Applied Art and Craft, regarding an exhibition planned for the institution's 150th anniversary two years later. At this point, at least until its relocation in 1968, the Oslo School of Architecture had a rather symbiotic relationship with the National College of Applied Art and Craft, from which it had spawned in 1962.[26] Exactly what his role was in these plans is unclear, but Esdaile's involvement is testimony to his commitment to the reform of design in general, across professional specializations. Turning again to ecology, he advised that the exhibition should showcase

> a new attitude towards the idea of dwelling, showing that it is possible to make a fundamental

22. Anon., "Og etter oss…," *Norsk natur*, no. 5 (June 1969), 34–39.

23. Peder Anker, "Science as a Vacation: A History of Ecology in Norway," *History of Science* 45, no. 4 (2007), 463.

24. Anker, 463.

25. Letters from Robert Esdaile to Sigmund Kvåløy, dated July 8, 1969, August 31, 1969, and October 1, 1969, Robert Esdailes arkiv, NAM1995:23 Serie Gc Manuskripter til foredrag, artikler og andre tekster, Nasjonalmuseet for kunst, arkitektur og design.

26. Gunnarsjaa, *Arkitekturleksikon*, 729.

27. Robert Esdaile, letter to Håkon Stenstadvold, June 24, 1966. Statsarkivet i Oslo, A-10583, 02/Da-0170.

28. Esdaile, letter to Håkon Stenstadvold.

29. Most famously articulated in Christian Norberg-Schulz, *Genius Loci: Towards a Phenomenology of Architecture* (New York, NY: Rizzoli, 1980).

30. Letter from Robert Esdaile to professor Knut Knutsen. Undated [1966–1969]. Robert Esdailes arkiv, NAM1995:23 Serie Gc Manuskripter til foredrag, artikler og andre tekster, Nasjonalmuseet for kunst, arkitektur og design.

improvement in the urban structure, in the dwelling structure, or an integration of both which would combine to solve a large number of pressing ecological problems.[27]

Furthermore – and perhaps somewhat surprisingly coming from a Canadian immigrant – he lamented the fact that our material culture was being transformed through "a steadily increasing number of mass-production articles of foreign design and origin," making it all the more "imperative that Norway makes an effort to express the material and regional quality of its products – especially those products which form our own environment."[28] It is not unlikely that Esdaile's interest in design's local context and environment was informed by his collaborator and colleague Christian Norberg-Schulz, who at this time had just begun developing his theories of place in architecture which later would become massively influential.[29] Crucially, though, Esdaile's interest in locally distinct design solutions was paired with his appreciation of the global perspective fostered by ecological thinking in response to the environmental crisis. This juxtaposition of scales inspired by ecology and regionalism effectively preempted the idiom "think globally, act locally," which some years later would become the slogan of the Friends of the Earth (established in 1969) and emblematic of the environmentalist movement in general.

This insistence on acting locally for the greater (global) good would become a staple of Esdaile's teaching practice and his steadfast drive for educational reform. Not long after he started teaching at the Oslo School of Architecture he wrote a letter to the head of the school, professor Knut Knutsen, complaining that "two scientific subjects that concern relations between humans and nature, ecology and ethnology … are utterly neglected in the school's curriculum."[30] Knutsen was known for his renewal of Norwegian timber architecture and his gentle treatment of the natural surroundings, especially following his cabin in Portør (1949), so Esdaile presumably expected his superior to take favorably to his ideas for teaching ecological design. Writing again to the school's management in April 1968, he presented a "draft program for socio-ecological studies." The purpose was to increase the students' knowledge about the most pressing of "current problems," emphasizing the consequences of the environmental crisis for the design professions.[31] "Failing to address these questions," he claimed, "is tantamount to denying our descendants the right to live, or to accept the aggravation of the misery of the world."[32] His proposed reading list included works by scholars represented in *And after us…*, such as Borgström, Palmstierna, and Vik.[33]

For Esdaile, however, introducing courses on ecology and related topics would only go some way towards the required educational reform. Dismissing what he dubbed "the 98% adoption of a technical scientific approach to Ecology for training of architects," Esdaile argued that "for architects the important thing is to UNDERSTAND, see, smell, feel, and diagnose in this way, respecting with an almost religious awe the beautiful synthesis of all nature from the cosmic to microcosmic."[34] Therefore, merely revamping the curriculum would not do – the very structure of architectural education had to change, from large, centrally located academic institutions to small, geographically dispersed nodes of practical learning. This type of distributed learning was required because "students need more intimate working knowledge of environmental issues, and it is questionable if this can be achieved from an institutional mileau [sic]."[35] The first public presentation of his ideas for a decentralized architectural education appeared on the pages of *Arkitektnytt* in 1969. What he suggested was that a central institution – a "mother-school" – could serve as a central hub for, say, sixty "outposts" located in small communities around the country. Each outpost would consist of a dozen or so students conducting locally specific, real-life projects supervised by one or a few teachers. The local context was crucial to the new type of design and planning expertise he envisaged: "Here the group is confronted with the people, the resources, the traditions, and the future prospects of the place. Here is the architect's laboratory."[36] Moving to a new outpost every semester, interspersed by brief visits to the mother-school for theoretical teaching components as well as project presentations and appraisals, the students would thus in the course of the program receive solid, yet varied hands-on and in situ experience with planning and design work. "An

31. Robert Esdaile, memo titled "Til S.A.O.," dated April 1968. Robert Esdailes arkiv, NAM1995:23 Serie D Korrespondanse, Nasjonalmuseet for kunst, arkitektur og design.

32. Robert Esdaile, memo titled "Planlegging ved SAO," undated. Robert Esdailes arkiv, NAM1995:23 Serie Ga Manuskripter til forelesninger og annet undervisningsmateriell, Nasjonalmuseet for kunst, arkitektur og design.

33. Ibid.

34. Letter from Robert Esdaile to "Tore" [no last name provided], October 24, 1969. Robert Esdailes arkiv, NAM1995:23 Serie D Korrespondanse, Nasjonalmuseet for kunst, arkitektur og design.

35. Robert Esdaile, "Perspektives [sic] of architectural education," manuscript dated 1974. Robert Esdailes arkiv, NAM1995:23 Serie Gb Materiale knyttet til undervisning ved NTH, Nasjonalmuseet for kunst, arkitektur og design.

36. Robert Esdaile, "Desentralisering av arkitektutdannelsen," *Arkitektnytt* no. 9 (1969), unpaged.

Design Struggles

37. Robert Esdaile, "Undervisningens dilemma," *Arkitektnytt* no. 19 (1969), unpaged.

38. Letter from Robert Esdaile to Øystein Dalland, dated August 22, 1969. Robert Esdailes arkiv, NAM1995:23 Serie D Korrespondanse, Nasjonalmuseet for kunst, arkitektur og design.

39. Letter from Robert Esdaile to Sigmund Kvaløy, dated July 8, 1969. Robert Esdailes arkiv, NAM1995:23 Serie Gc Manuskripter til foredrag, artikler og andre tekster, Nasjonalmuseet for kunst, arkitektur og design.

40. Letter from Arne Næss to Robert Esdaile, undated (1975). Robert Esdailes arkiv, NAM1995:23 Serie D Korrespondanse, Nasjonalmuseet for kunst, arkitektur og design.

41. Minutes from meeting on the decentralization of architecture, dated March 6, 1970. Robert Esdailes arkiv, NAM1995:23 Serie D Korrespondanse, Nasjonalmuseet for kunst, arkitektur og design.

42. Robert Esdaile, "The decentralized school of architecture: A new response to our environmental crisis," unpublished manuscript, January 9, 1975. Robert Esdailes arkiv, NAM1995:23 Serie Gc Manuskripter til foredrag, artikler og andre tekster, Nasjonalmuseet for kunst, arkitektur og design.

43. Letter from Robert Esdaile to *Architectural Design* (att: editorial Assistant Barbara Goldstein), dated February 20, 1975. Robert Esdailes arkiv, NAM1995:23 Serie Hb Materiale knyttet til undervisning ved NTH, Nasjonalmuseet for kunst, arkitektur og design.

outpost," he explained, "is perhaps best likened to F. L. Wright's Taliesin, but the purpose is entirely different. We are to serve society's needs under its organic development, not a subjective formalism."[37]

Writing to an acquaintance he hoped could help set up an outpost in Alta, a small town in the far north of Norway, the geographer Øystein Dalland (who would later become professor of environmental planning at Telemark University College), Esdaile was confident that "in a very near future we could count on creating a miniature school of architecture in Alta, a school complete with an ecologist, sociologist, and an architect-planner."[38] Not surprisingly, Esdaile's radical proposal proved hard to realize. Hoping to secure broader academic support for the idea, he wrote to Kvaløy suggesting they could discuss the matter in the Co-working Group for the Protection of Nature and the Environment at the University of Oslo.[39] Even though the latter had little to offer beyond moral support, he kept in touch – also with their "godfather," Arne Næss.[40] His own institution's management was not entirely dismissive of the decentralization idea, agreeing to establish a committee tasked with exploring its feasibility.[41] Except for a couple of ad hoc trial projects more akin to summer excursions, though, the scheme would remain at the proposal stage. That did not deter Esdaile from persistently promoting the idea, even long after he moved to Trondheim in 1971 to take up his professorship at the Norwegian Institute of Technology. His new institution does not seem to have been any more enthusiastic about it than was the Oslo school, but as late as 1975 he described the scheme as "a new educational response to our environmental crisis."[42] He also sought to publish the idea internationally, writing to *Architectural Design* magazine that "we can't count on initial Govm't support nor on students who primarily want qualifying semesters. We have to count on the appeal that the idea has for the few and the appeal of Norways [*sic*] dramatic landscape."[43]

Norway's dramatic landscape clearly held significant appeal to Esdaile himself. For the cover of the first issue of 1976, *Byggekunst* chose an image of Esdaile's own DIY cabin – a repurposed coastal artillery emplacement on top of a cliff above the Jøssingfjord in south-western

BYGGEKUNST

arkitektur, form og miljö

1·76

Norske Arkitekters Landsforbund
Nr. 1 — 1976 — 58. årgang

INNHOLD:
Kulturlandskapets historie
Hytte ved Jøssingfjord
Småbruk i Vågåmo og Lindås
Forskningsbiblioteket på Ullandhaug
Kunstnerverksted
EYC-bygget, Strasbourg
Høvik Verk Stål
Møbler - innredning
Houens Fond. 8 premierte bygg
Bøker
Produktnytt

Front cover of *Byggekunst* (no. 1, 1976) featuring Robert Esdaile's DIY cabin on top of a cliff above the Jøssingfjord in south-western Norway. Courtesy of *Arkitektur N*.

Norway. The simple, un-intrusive structure consisted of a low wooden roof raised on top of the artillery emplacement, which was built in 1942 as part of Hitler's Atlantic Wall. Reclaiming a remote, spectacular site from the destructive forces of military technology and, by the smallest means possible, turning it into a sanctuary for the appreciation of the natural landscape, the project constitutes a highly symbolic gesture – a three-dimensional manifesto of ecological design. The location of the site made

44. Letter from Robert Esdaile to the Norwegian Pollution Control Authority, dated February, 17, 1979. Robert Esdailes arkiv, NAM1995:23 Serie Gc Manuskripter til foredrag, artikler og andre tekster, Nasjonalmuseet for kunst, arkitektur og design.

45. Robert Esdaile, "'Jansholet': Hytte ved Jøssingfjord," Byggekunst 58, no. 1 (1976), 6–7.

the project doubly symbolic, as the Jøssingfjord featured prominently in environmentalist discourse at the time, due to the heavy pollution of the fjord caused by waste from the Titania company's ilmenite mines nearby (the world's biggest bearing of that mineral). As a concerned citizen Esdaile contributed to this attention by complaining to the newly established (1974) Norwegian Pollution Control Authority, accusing it of being too lenient towards the company's practices.[44] The power of the double symbolism inherent to his cabin project was naturally not lost on Esdaile, who presented it to the readers of *Byggekunst* explicitly as a commentary on the combined ills of society and an intervention in the name of more sustainable modes of interaction with nature.[45]

Moral Materials

What's in a chair? The rise of the environmentalist movement and the emerging ecological sensitivity of design professionals discussed above coincided with a marked shift in furniture design: the sudden abandoning of tropical woods in favor of indigenous ones. The Norwegian furniture industry had enjoyed considerable commercial success and critical acclaim from the mid-1950s as part of the wider international interest in Scandinavian design. Paradoxically, though, this furniture, which to international audiences apparently expressed something inherently Scandinavian, was predominantly made from woods nowhere to be found in the region, but which had to be imported from far corners of the globe – most notably teak, but also mahogany, rosewood, etc. Always fearing a fad, design critics grew skeptical of the fashion for tropical woods in the 1960s, but their arguments soon moved beyond the usual warnings against herd mentality and lack of originality. The tropical materials which had contributed to the international fame of Scandinavian design were now cast as alien, false, and extravagant; as inappropriate for Norwegian furniture. Alf Midtbust, director of the National Federation of Furniture Manufacturers, put it succinctly: "The Danes conquered the world with teak from Siam… We Norwegians have the opportunity to conquer the world using pine and birch."[46] In stark contrast to Denmark, Norway (and Sweden) has vast forests ripe with resources readily available to local designers and manufacturers, and utilizing these rather than tropical imports became a moral imperative.[47]

The design magazine *Bonytt* led the way, propagating quite intensely for the use of indigenous woods, especially birch and pine, in the name of functional appropriateness, national traits, ethics, and resource management alike. Leisure cabins became a stepping stone in this campaign, on the assumption that these spaces required furniture which was simpler, sturdier, and cheaper than in permanent homes – and pine, especially, was considered optimally suited for such designs.[48] In 1965, a spate of design competitions, organized by the National Federation of Furniture Manufacturers, the Norwegian Home Craft Association, and the Furniture Industry's Trade Council, resulted in a wide range of innovative furniture, much of which was made from pine. The same year, the Norwegian Furniture Fair in Stavanger dedicated an exhibition to new designs in pine, which generated considerable attention.

Pine, of course, has many applications other than furniture, and was the basis for many small businesses and industries in towns and rural districts across the country. Designing furniture in pine to be manufactured by such enterprises rather than by traditional cabinetmakers or furniture factories had a double effect: firstly, it allowed these enterprises to move into the production of finished goods with a higher profit margin, thus potentially generating economic growth in local communities threatened by depopulation. Secondly, designing for simple, rational production without relying on specialized craft expertise, and using an inexpensive and abundant material, resulted in affordable products. Such design projects could thus also contribute to social sustainability, a feature considered inseparable from design for environmental sustainability by key thinkers from William Morris to Arne Næss, and intricately intertwined also in other, contemporary efforts to revitalize local communities by design.[49]

The work of designer Edvin Helseth becomes particularly interesting in this context. Throughout the 1960s he developed several furniture systems – all in

46. Alf Midtbust, "Frem for furua," *Bonytt* no. 5 (1965), 126.

47. Kjetil Fallan, "'The "Designer": The 11th Plague': Design Discourse from Consumer Activism to Environmentalism in 1960s Norway," *Design Issues* 27, no. 4 (2011), 34.

48. See, e.g., Alf Midtbust, "Frem for furua," *Bonytt*, no. 5 (1965), 126–27; Marianne Gullowsen, "Efterlyses...," *Bonytt* no. 5 (1965), 139–40; Arne Remlov, "Det lyktes – så langt," *Bonytt* no. 7/8 (1965), 221–24; Arne Remlov, "Vår mann i Stavanger," *Bonytt* no. 9 (1965), 252–58; Arne Remlov, "Fra det ene til det annet...," *Bonytt* no. 9 (1966), 242.

49. Malin K. Graesse, "The Weaving World of Deep Ecology and Textile Design: Locating Principles of Sustainability at Austvatn Craft Central" (master's thesis, University of Oslo, 2017).

pine – for small, local industries based in the heavily forested regions around Norway's largest lake, Mjøsa. In 1961 Helseth designed the modular storage system 5-15 for Systemtre A/L in Hamar (the town was also home to Helseth's design practice) and redesigned the flexible bookshelf system BBB for the rake manufacturer Eidsvoll Rivefabrikk. None of these companies had any experience with furniture production but extensive knowledge about wood processing, so the choice of material, the unconventional know-how, and the constraints and affordances of the production process, were key factors in the design process. Helseth brought these experiences to the table when he designed the furniture series Trybo, launched in 1965. Manufactured by the local sawmill Stange Bruk, the various pieces in the series were designed using pine in standard dimensions, assembled in only right angles and straight lines, requiring as little finishing as possible.

Designer Edvin Helseth (left) and the General Manager of Trysil Municipal Forest Administration, Jostein Bjørnersen (right), demonstrates a Trybo chair for the Minister of Industry, Sverre Walter Rostoft, on the occasion of receiving the Norwegian Design Award in 1967. Courtesy of DOGA – Design and Architecture Norway. CC-BY-NC.

The joints were pine plugs rather than nails or screws.[50]
To be assembled by the customer (or retailer), the furniture
was shipped flat-packed for more economical (and thus
more environmentally-friendly) transport – a concept later
made world-famous by IKEA. Trybo was favorably received
in design circles, and it was precisely its social design ambitions and attention to resource use which was highlighted.
The jury of the Norwegian Design Award, which it received
in 1967, hailed it as "an exceptionally good example of
product development based on strictly limited raw materials
and production facilities."[51]

As mentioned above, whole system thinking was
essential in formulating theories of ecological design.
Helseth's design practice can be seen as a real-world manifestation of this mode of thinking. His systemic approach
to design made apparent – and thus consequential – the
many material, social, economic, and ecological connections extending from his pine furniture. Fully in line with
his systemic design philosophy, the Trybo furniture was
originally developed as an integral part of a new, modular,
prefabricated leisure cabin model, the Trysil cabin, commissioned by Trysil Municipal Forest District. When the
project was presented in the British Council of Industrial
Design's *Design* magazine, it was again as an example of
environmentally sensible social design:

> [the cabin] was designed in response to two needs.
> The first was to create more work in an area of
> depopulation. The other was to produce a holiday
> house which was easy to erect and would fit into the
> landscape, as part of a plan to develop tourism in
> the region.[52]

The cabin itself, naturally also made from pine, was
designed by Helseth's colleague in the architectural office
Arkitim, Hans Østerhaug. Trybo was thus part of the new,
morally acceptable material culture of leisure, but also a
paradigmatic example both of the systemic thinking and
the attention to regional specificities integral to the development of ecological design.

50. Harriet Clayhills, "Hytter med system," *Bonytt* no. 9 (1965), 240–43; Liv Schjødt, "Vi trenger hyttemøbler også!," *Bonytt* no. 1 (1966), 12–13.

51. Alf Bøe, *Den norske Designpris, de syv første år/The Norwegian Design Award, its first seven years* (Oslo: Norsk Designcentrum, 1969), 52.

52. Alf Bøe, "Designed for Leisure Living," *Design* no. 248 (1969), 32–34.

Conclusion

Just as the Beatles established "Norwegian Wood" as an instant enigma in popular culture, from the mid-1960s Norwegian wood took on a new meaning in design culture – both literally and figuratively. The growing awareness of and attention to the precarious state of the natural environment and the harm inflicted on it by industry and consumer society made designers and architects recalibrate their professional ethics. Inspired by models and ideals culled from the life sciences, and particularly from ecology, radically-minded and eloquent educators and practitioners called for new approaches to design, to manufacturing, and to consumption – ultimately, to life itself. Conceptually and ideologically, Norwegian wood represented a reaction both to the refined but elitist niceties of 1950s Scandinavian design and to the rampant consumerism symbolized by jukeboxes and Juicy Fruit. Simultaneously a model ecosystem, a material and economic resource, and a setting for a natural and healthy leisure life, Norwegian wood is a shorthand for the broad scope of professional and societal changes deemed necessary to design a more sustainable future.

"Isn't it good, Norwegian wood?"

RETHINKING MIDCENTURY MODERN
A View from Postcolonial India

Sria Chatterjee

1. Jawaharlal Nehru, *Jawaharlal Nehru's Speeches* (New Delhi: Publications Division, Ministry of Information and Broadcasting, Government of India, 1983), 25. It was in his stirring "Tryst with Destiny" speech that Nehru made this proclamation.

2. For an excellent account of the fine balance between state power and democracy and the adoption of a strong central state, see Gyan Prakash, "A Fine Balance," in *Emergency Chronicles: Indira Gandhi and Democracy's Turning Point* (Princeton, NJ: Princeton University Press, 2019), 38–75.

When, at the stroke of midnight on August 15, 1947, India woke "to life and freedom"[1] and was inaugurated as a sovereign nation-state after two centuries of colonial rule, hopes for a new postcolonial India were both feverishly optimistic and deeply troubled. The carnage of the Partition of India that followed this inauguration, and the unsettled aftermath of World War II that formed the background to it, meant that the founders of the new nation-state did not have an easy task on their hands. While nationalist rhetoric claimed that this was indeed a new period of history, this claim was not founded on any real revolutionary defeat of the old colonial structures, especially in the realms of social order, economy, law, and bureaucracy. What emerged for the founding figures and constitution-makers of new India (a constitutional republic and a democracy) as the utterly vital component in the reconfiguration of a colony into a nation-state was a strong, centralized state, and its requisite: a sturdy, unified national identity. This was not an easy task for a country so diverse.[2]

The National Institute of Design (NID) – officially established in Ahmedabad in India in 1961 and spearheaded by Gautam Sarabhai and his sister Gira – was, among other things, a product of newly independent India's attempt to create both a centralized national identity and a democratic public. After independence in 1947, the first Prime Minister, Jawaharlal Nehru, had an optimistic and socialist vision to transform the country from a rural society to an urban state. His Industrial Policy Resolution of 1953 aimed to establish training and development programs that would accelerate the growth of small industries, which in turn would lead to a broader improvement in working and living conditions for the masses. It was in this context that the first steps towards the NID were drafted. It was funded and supported by the Indian government and the largest private US philanthropic foundation of the Cold War era, the Ford Foundation. In the first two decades, the Foundation supported governmental programs and initiated a stream of institutional recommendations researched and written by technical experts from the United States and Europe. Among these was Charles and Ray Eames's 1958 report on Indian design, which would become the basis and blueprint for the foundation of the NID.[3]

3. The suggestion that an Indian higher education Institute might "serve as a center for creative studies in design and fashion" was first floated in 1954 in an earlier Ford Foundation report, which was chaired by Sven Hagberg of Stockholm's vocational craft school and which sought to evaluate the potential of village and small industries in India. Douglas Ensminger, unpublished report, "Planning Team on Small Industry Makes Its Report, India, Report No. 40," quoted in Claire Wintle, "Diplomacy and the Design School: The Ford Foundation and India's National Institute of Design," *Design and Culture* 9, no. 2 (May 4, 2017), 208, doi.org/10.1080/17547075.2017.1322876.

4. Charles Eames, *The India Report* (Ahmedabad: National Institute of Design, 2004), iii.

Towards a New School of Design

In 1956, Charles Eames was invited on behalf of the Ford Foundation by Monroe Wheeler, Director of Exhibitions and Publications at the Museum of Modern Art (MoMA) in New York, to tour the country with the aim of recommending a design training program that would aid small-scale industries, and "that would resist the present rapid deterioration in design and quality of consumer goods."[4] The Ford Foundation worked closely with MoMA, drawing

Charles Eames at the National Institute of Design in Ahmedabad, 1960s.
Photo: Dashrath Patel.

5. "What Was Good Design? MoMA's Message, 1944–56" (Department of Communications, Museum of Modern Art, May 2009).

6. Wintle, "Diplomacy and the Design School."

7. Eames, *The India Report*, 2.

8. Pupul Jayakar, "Extract from Tribute to Charles Eames," in Eames, *The India Report*, 16.

9. Jawaharlal Nehru, *The Discovery of India* (Calcutta: Signet Press, 1946), 39, 43, 46.

10. "I approached her [India]," Nehru wrote, "almost as an alien critic full of dislike for the present as well as for many of the relics of the past that I saw… I was eager and anxious to change her outlook and appearance and give her the garb of modernity… There was a great deal to be scrapped, that must be scrapped." Nehru, 30–31.

11. Van Wyck Brooks, "On Creating a Usable Past," *The Dial*, April 11, 1918, 337–41.

especially on their Good Design exhibitions of the 1950s, which defined and disseminated so-called good design in an attempt to shape postwar consumer culture through exhibitions at home and abroad.[5] This resonated with the Foundation's India representative Douglas Ensminger's claim that one of the principal problems of midcentury Indian industry was its lack of "competence in design."[6] The Eameses spent five months traveling in India, photographing widely, to arrive at a sense of "those values and those qualities that Indians hold important to a good life."[7]

The outcome of this tour, the Eameses' *India Report*, which started with a passage from the Bhagavad Gita, stressed that the role of design should lie in defining and elevating "standards of living" through everyday objects and services rather than through a focus on "industrial standardization." The report, as Pupul Jayakar reiterates, "focuses on India's tradition and philosophy that is familiar with the meaning of creative destruction and stresses the need to appraise and solve the problems of our times with tremendous service, dignity, and love."[8] It is useful here to turn briefly to Jawaharlal Nehru's *Discovery of India*. Written in 1946, a year before independence, this book brought an almost outsider view on the country's people and places and is a text with which the Eameses would no doubt have had some familiarity. It presents "Indian culture" as emerging out of a conflict between what Nehru terms India's *usable past* and *disposable past*. For Nehru, the usable past comprised aesthetic or cultural products (i.e., "heritage") expunged from their "value context" and made usable for the present prerogatives of modernity, national unity, development, etc. The disposable past, therefore, consisted of ways of life, value systems, or hierarchical social structures (located particularly in the Indian village and the figure of the peasant).[9] To build the "house of India's future, strong and secure and beautiful," as Nehru sought, required cutting away these entrenched social systems that might constrain the path to a cleaner, fairer, more efficient modernity.[10] The concept of the usable past was first introduced by American cultural critic Van Wyck Brooks in his widely read 1918 essay, "On Creating a Usable Past." "What is important for us?" Brooks asks in his quest for a national usable past.[11] If Brook's quest was

Pupul Jayakar in conversation with others at the NID campus, 1960s.
Photo: Dashrath Patel.

12. Brooks.

13. Lauren Kroiz, *Creative Composites: Modernism, Race, and the Stieglitz Circle* (Berkeley, CA: University of California Press, 2012). Art historian Lauren Kroiz explores how US-born painters such as Arthur Dove and Georgia O'Keeffe used the techniques of collage to assemble a "usable past" from the regionalized cultures of African, Hispanic, and Native Americans. See also Preston Thayer and Alexandra Lange, eds., *Modern Design/Folk Art, Exhibition Catalogue* (New Mexico: University Art Gallery, New Mexico State University, 2011).

14. The Department of Science and Art (DSA), for example, was set up by the British Government as early as the 1850s to introduce superior design and artisanal sensibility to industrial workers. See Arindam Dutta, *The Bureaucracy of Beauty* (New York, NY: Routledge, 2006) for how the DSA exerted a powerful influence on the growth of museums, design schools, and architecture throughout the British Empire.

15. In the early 1900s, Rabindranath Tagore started a school for young children that grew into an educational experiment and an artistic and intellectual hub in rural Bengal. An exchange with the Bauhaus in 1922 has been well documented in Regina Bittner and Kathrin Rhomberg, eds., *The Bauhaus in Calcutta: An Encounter of Comsopolitan Avant-Gardes* (Ostfildern: Hatje Cantz, 2013).

that of the modernist literary critic hoping to clear away the useless aspects of the past to find "the desire, the aspiration, the struggle, the tentative endeavor, and the appalling obstacles"[12] that would give a deeper significance to the spiritual history of America, then Nehru, writing as both alien observer and invested politician, looked to symbols to do part of the work of recuperating and reinnovating India's usable past. While Brooks's call united American critics, artists, and designers of the 1930s such as Lewis Mumford, Arthur Dove, Alexander Girard, and Alfred Stieglitz (with the help of his friend and curator of the Museum of Fine Arts in Boston, Ananda Coomaraswamy) in seeking linkages with earlier folk forms to guide contemporary practice, Nehru's devising of a usable past brings us back full circle to the Eameses in India in the late 1950s.[13]

The NID was not only a product of the surge in institution building in India at the time, but also drew on a long history of debates and initiatives around industrial design initiated by the British in colonial India more than a century prior to independence. The NID was enlisted under the Ministry of Commerce and Industry, which in many ways followed the conception of industrial design in relation to rural reform already set up by the British.[14] The first Five Year Plan (launched by Jawaharlal Nehru in 1951), following up on the Report of the Committee for Art Education (1947), called for the setting up of Regional Design Centres in Bombay, Bangalore, and New Delhi. Modeled loosely on Rabindranath Tagore's Santiniketan school's craft and design unit, Silpa Bhavan, these centers, led by artists such as Pran Nath Mago in Delhi, were seen as training centers for artisans.[15] Soon after independence, the Ministry of Industry and Commerce established two bodies that would provide financial and technical subsidies and otherwise promote India's textile industry and crafts heritage: the All-India Handicrafts Board (which oversaw all crafts except weaving) and the All-India Handloom Board (which oversaw weaving).

Kamaladevi Chattopadhyaya, a UK-educated nationalist and feminist Gandhian, headed the All-India Handicrafts Board, while Pupul Jayakar, a feisty theosophist and cultural advisor to a generation of Prime Ministers (Jawaharlal Nehru and Indira Gandhi), led the

All-India Handloom Board. Jayakar's political career began when she was appointed assistant to the Indian National Congress activist Mridula Sarabhai in the Kasturba Trust in 1940.[16] This was also the beginning of Jayakar's long association with the Sarabhai family and their industrial and cultural stakes in the promotion of Indian textiles. In the 1950s, both Kamaladevi Chattopadhyaya and Pupul Jayakar were apprehensive about the introduction of factory-based mass production in India as a part of Nehru's vision for Indian development, of which they formed a crucial part. Although worried about how Western mass production techniques might affect the artisan groups, they looked, odd as it may seem at first sight, to the United States for a practical and theoretical approach to contemporary material culture.[17]

Based in Ahmedabad, a city dubbed the "Manchester of India" for its proliferating textile mills, and home to Mahatma Gandhi's Sabarmati ashram, the NID was spearheaded by brother and sister Gautam and Gira Sarabhai, heirs to the wealthy mill-owning Sarabhai family. Gautam had a Ph.D. in mathematics and was, at the time, chairman of Calico Textile Mills, while Gira had lived in New York and trained at Frank Lloyd Wright's studio in Arizona. In 1951, it was agreed with the Ford Foundation's newly appointed representative in India, Douglas Ensminger, that the Foundation would provide funds and expert assistance to expand and improve the new Community Development Program, upon which the government of India placed high hopes for village-level social and economic development.

Objects and Exhibitions

As critical writing on the Eameses' India photographs has shown, the American designers relied on a superabundance of images, just as they would go on to do in their exhibitions and installations, where sensory overload acted as the necessary stimulus for processing certain threads of information.[18] For Charles, the possibility of finding patterns and making connections between "apparently dissimilar phenomena" became essential to this photographic excess.

16. See Reena Nanda, *Kamaladevi Chattopadhyaya: A Biography* (New Delhi: Oxford University Press, 2002); and Elise Hodson, "Pupul Jayakar's 'Great Conversation': The Roles of Design, Craft, and the United States in Transforming Indian Identity and Industry, 1952–1965" (master's thesis, Bard Graduate Center, 2009).

17. Kamaladevi Chattopadhyaya, *At the Cross-Roads* (Bombay: National Information and Publications, 1947); Kamaladevi Chattopadhyaya, *America: The Land of Superlatives* (Bombay: Phoenix Publications, 1946); Nico Slate, *Colored Cosmopolitanism: The Shared Struggle for Freedom in the United States and India* (Cambridge, MA: Harvard University Press, 2012). This is particularly evident in the two books published by Chattopadhyaya in the 1940s. Also, in terms of US-India relations, Nico Slate argues that Cedric Dover worked to fulfill Nehru's promise of India as a "bulwark for the rising colored world" through his use of history and culture. If Cold War politics provided the potential for a push for equality in the United States among "colored cosmopolitans," Kamaladevi Chattopadhyaya played a similar role with her 1946 book on America as a land of superlatives.

18. See Sria Chatterjee, "Postindustrialism and the Long Arts and Crafts Movement: Between Britain, India, and the United States of America," *British Art Studies* no. 15, doi.org/10.17658/issn.2058-5462/issue-15/schatterjee.

19. Pat Kirkham, *Charles and Ray Eames: Designers of the Twentieth Century* (Cambridge, MA: MIT Press, 1995), 184.

20. Nehru, *The Discovery of India*, 9.

While in India they focused on the form and function of objects of daily use and processes of craft and textile making, and their approach to cultural specificity was embedded in a larger midcentury American notion of democratic cultures and a celebration of folk objects. The Eameses, like their friend and collaborator Alexander Girard, foraged other cultures for objects to use both as decoration and as sources for film and exhibition projects, where objects were stripped of their cultural contexts and meaning-making capacities and were redefined to make meaning in a different context.[19] For example, the Eameses' 1969 film *Tops*, almost a decade in planning, features 123 tops spinning through the length of the film (accompanied by a score by Elmer Bernstein). These tops were sourced from all over the world – India, China, Japan, the United States, France, and England. While it functions at one level as a celebration of the physics of motion, this unifying physics runs through the culturally and visually diverse objects, producing an ideological crescendo in the universalism of science and a celebration of liberal humanism in the difference and similarity of all cultures. The Eameses' film counted, therefore, on the ability of the human eye and mind to make the intellectual leap between cultural symbols (here, tops) and the ability to both distinguish them and regard them in a longer continuum of human experience and design.

The universalizing tendencies of the Eameses were directly valuable for India's coming of age. Nehru's copious writings about the country's underlying unity despite the existence of widespread ethnoreligious, linguistic, and regional diversity often placed the dream of unity in "the mind of India" at "the dawn of civilization." This unity "was something deeper, and within the fold, the widest tolerance of belief and custom was practiced and every variety acknowledged and even encouraged."[20] The striving for a unified national identity is central to the debates and decisions around art, design and nation-making in this period., nature, and nation that have run and continued to run throughout this entire thesis. The overall effect of US-based international networks (which operated across international boundaries) was to consolidate US hegemony in economically or strategically important areas of the world through the nurturing of pro-US "modernizing elites," of whom the Sarabhais were a key example.

In the newly independent India, the currency of the utilitarian object was rapidly accruing value. In the closing years of colonial rule, the Indian National Congress pushed for a Committee for Art Education and investment in the transformed realities of contemporary India, which included both ideological and practical realities (i.e., the forging of a holistic national culture through a common aesthetic vocabulary, and the domestic and lived experience of the new Indian citizen who would inhabit this national consciousness).[21] The possibilities that the Indian government and the network of international elites that it mobilized saw in American design overlapped with US interests in India. "Soft-power" initiatives such as foreign aid and so-called knowledge transfers for economic and social "modernization" were among the diplomatic strategies applied by the US to win over nonaligned countries; in particular, the US sought to cultivate newly independent India as a democratic counterweight to China.[22] As Greg Castillo writes in his study of the cultural diplomatic politics of Cold War midcentury design, "[f]rom World War II through the 1960s, what US foreign policy analysts found problematic was not the rapid pace of worldwide Americanization but the lack thereof. In response, they called for aggressive overseas propaganda programs."[23] In addition to familiarizing American audiences with Indian design and vice versa, exhibitions played an important role in establishing cultural ties and collaborative programs between countries. For example, the 1955 *Textiles and Ornamental Arts of India* exhibition at MoMA, curated by Alexander Girard and Edgar Kaufmann Jr., then Director of MoMA's Good Design exhibitions, collected a vast number of textiles, crafts, and decorative objects from India and Indian collections around the world.[24] As Mary Staniszewski has insightfully noted, "fine art's other – popular culture, advertising and the mass media – was supplying the universal language of international communities."[25] Both Girard and Kaufmann were well known as collectors of folk arts, and the show was preceded in the fall of 1954 by a six-week tour of India by Girard, meant as a survey and collecting trip. The purpose of the

21. *Report of the Committee for Art Education, 1947* (Bombay: Government Central Press, 1948), 4.

22. For example, Inderjeet Parmar shows how Carnegie, Rockefeller, and Ford Foundations were key to the "elite dominance of U.S. foreign affairs" and to "creating national and global networks of intellectuals committed to a Progressive-era state-building project for globalist ends." See Inderjeet Parmar, *Foundations of the American Century: The Ford, Carnegie, and Rockefeller Foundations in the Rise of American Power* (New York: Columbia University Press, 2012). David Engerman shows how foreign aid as a Cold War tool for the superpowers unravelled domestic politics and policies in India; see David C. Engerman, *The Price of Aid: The Economic Cold War in India* (Cambridge, MA: Harvard University Press, 2018). See also Olivier Zunz, *Philanthropy in America: A History*, rev. ed. (Princeton, NJ: Princeton University Press, 2014); and Michael E. Latham, *The Right Kind of Revolution: Modernization, Development, and U.S. Foreign Policy from the Cold War to the Present* (Ithaca, NY: Cornell University Press, 2010).

23. Greg Castillo, *Cold War on the Home Front: The Soft Power of Midcentury Design* (Minneapolis, MN: University of Minnesota Press, 2010), xiv.

24. Saloni Mathur describes the exhibition as an "imaginary bazar" and provides a fuller account of its conception and reception and the role of the Eameses in it. See Saloni Mathur, "Charles and Ray Eames in India," *Art Journal* 70, no. 1 (2011), 40–42.

25. Mary Anne Staniszewski, *The Power of Display: A History of Exhibition Installations at the Museum of Modern Art* (Cambridge, MA: MIT Press, 1998), 257.

26. Quoted from the Museum of Modern Art Archives, Record Citation ICE-D-5-54 (1/5). "Preliminary Report on the Indian Voyage from Edgar Kaufmann, Jr. to Porter Mcray, Nov 30 1954," in Donald Albrecht, ed., *The Work of Charles and Ray Eames: A Legacy of Invention* (New York, NY: Harry N. Abrams in association with the Library of Congress and the Vitra Design Museum, 1997), 33.

27. For other instances of this, see Gay McDonald, The 'Advance' of American Postwar Design in Europe: MoMA and the Design for Use, USA Exhibition 1951–1953," *Design Issues* 24, no. 2 (March 1, 2008), 15–27; Takuya Kida, Japanese Crafts and Cultural Exchange with the USA in the 1950s: Soft Power and John D. Rockefeller III during the Cold War," *Journal of Design History* 25, no. 4 (November 1, 2012), 379–99, doi.org/10.1093/jdh/eps033.

28. The USIA used Fuller's domes for erecting exhibition pavilions within short periods of time and they became symbols of US engineering marvels. See "A Splendid Pleasure Dome," in Jack Masey, *Cold War Confrontations: US Exhibitions and Their Role in the Cultural Cold War* (Baden, Switzerland: Lars Muller Publishers, 2008), 58–67.

exhibition was to improve Indian-American relations by arousing enthusiasm in the US for the splendor of Indian achievements. This goal, Kaufmann reported,

> was part and parcel of the museum's program of international artistic exchange … and took its point from the urgency with which India today, independent and industrially burgeoning, was being courted by both parties in the cold war contest of world influence – the US and Russia.[26]

Charles and Ray Eames were invited to make a film at the exhibition. They used 35 mm slides in film form, a technique they had recently developed. In the film, the objects of the exhibition become the central figures and nodes of the moving slides as the camera glides and pulses in rhythm to Ustad Ali Akbar Khan's "Morning Raga." The film opens with a meditation on color in Indian fabrics by Alexander Girard and continues with Pupul Jayakar narrating off-screen a prose poem on the symbolism of color in India. The importance of the object as at once a commercial entity and tool of soft diplomacy can be seen in the collaborative work of Alexander Girard, Charles Eames, and George Nelson in the Herman Miller firm (e.g., the Textiles & Objects shop that opened in New York in 1961) and the exhibitions they designed, especially for the Good Design series. For MoMA, the shift of focus from painting to object, all for the dissemination of "good design" in the mid-twentieth century, founded on the modernist precepts of functionalism, simplicity, and truth to materials, urgently promoted a modernism of everyday things, an astute and coordinated effort at creating consumer taste.[27]

In 1959, following the *Textiles and Ornamental Arts* exhibition, *Design Today in India and America*, an exhibition of exemplary design objects housed in a Buckminster Fuller geodesic dome, opened in New Delhi.[28] On entering the dome, the viewer was met with an Indian-style brick courtyard with variously shaped matted platforms leading towards the center on which objects were placed, each tagged with a number. The exhibition included chairs, lamps, china, glassware, kitchen utensils, textiles, and tools from thirteen countries, and would stay on as a permanent design collection at the National Institute of Design, then still in its incubatory planning stages.[29] Speaking of the exhibition, Pupul Jayakar claimed that the "purpose of her government's invitation was to focus attention on the vital problem of product design in terms of rapidly developing small-scale industry."[30] While MoMA selected 350 objects for the show, it was the architect and designer George Nelson (and his New York-based firm) that designed the installation and catalog.[31] Citing socioeconomic transformations, Jayakar continued to say that

> improved communications, the breakdown of caste barriers, the carrying of an urban civilization through radio and cinema to the small town and distant village, the availability of power, the introduction of new machines, new materials, new tools, and new techniques, have led to a breakdown of the traditional pattern of production, altered the relationship between producer and consumer, and pose a challenge to the forms that underlie production and distribution in this country.

However, she was adamant that the exhibition should serve not as an invitation for the imitation of the outward appearance of its objects, but only to "stimulate inquiry and to focus attention on the urgent problem of product design and the comprehension of the nature and place of materials, tools, functions and disciplines, in the creation of objects of daily use."[32]

At the NID

In their *India Report*, the Eameses stressed the need for rural India to develop an "alert and impatient national conscience – a conscience concerned with the quality and ultimate values of the environment."[33] "NID's concern is with the quality of the physical environment and its relevance to human needs," Gautam Sarabhai claimed. "The endeavor is not only to respond to existing demands with discrimination and without preconceptions, but to create an

29. "MoMA Press Release No. 77" (MoMA Press Archives, October 24, 1958).

30. "MoMA Press Release No. 31," 1.

31. United States Congress House Committee on Un-American Activities, *The American National Exhibition, Moscow, July 1959: The Record of Certain Artists and an Appraisal of Their Works Selected for Display. Hearings* (U.S. Government Printing Office, 1959). The same year, George Nelson and his office mounted the massive American National Exhibition in Moscow.

32. "MoMA Press Release No. 31."

33. Eames, *The India Report*, 10.

A design discussion in progress at the NID, 1960s.
Photo: Dashrath Patel.

34. "National Institute of Design: Internal Organisation, Structure and Culture" Ahmedabad: National Institute of Design, 1972).

awareness of problems of contemporary significance that are as yet generally unrecognized."[34] Gautam Sarabhai's emphasis on the professionalization of design was in part beholden to his interest in psychology, organizational behavior, and education (the Sarabhais collaborated with and hosted the educator Maria Montessori, the psycho-analyst Erik Erikson, and A. K. Rice of the Tavistock Institute for Human Relations in Bloomsbury, London). Over the first nine years, the Governing Council of the NID included the craft revivalist Pupul Jayakar and members from government organizations and private companies such as New Delhi Cloth & General Mills, the Ministry of Industrial Development, the Government of Gujarat, the Gujarat State Fertilizer Corporation in Baroda, Ambica Mills, Tata Industries Private Limited, Tata Oil Mills, Bombay, and so on. This diversity of industrial and state interest in the administration was to be reflected in the kinds of projects the early NID faculty and students would take up. There were, therefore, competing approaches to the environment, human needs, agency and social composition, industry and technoscience in the mid-twentieth century.

The central interlocutors of Guatam and Gira at this time included their brother, the physicist Vikram

Sarabhai; Shona Ray of Calico Mills; Dashrath Patel; the London-educated Indian expat from Uganda, H. Kumar Vyas, who joined NID as faculty in 1962; Douglas Ensminger from the Ford Foundation; and James Prestini, the visiting consultant from the University of California, Berkeley. At the same time, Gautam maintained close correspondence with his European expat designer friends in the US, such as Walter Gropius and George Nelson from Harvard and MIT.[35] While a portion of the sizeable Ford Foundation funds given to the NID was to be used for materials, equipment, and books, a larger portion of the funds was mandated for the "employment by the Institute of three foreign design experts," each of whom would serve as a teacher-consultant for two years, and four more foreign experts, each of whom would serve for one year as front-line supervisors as well as short-term consultants.[36]

As is well known, Louis Kahn, who was invited to design another Sarabhai-led institution, the Indian Institute of Management in Ahmedabad, ran seminars at the NID for faculty and students. His 1962 architecture lecture "Form and Design" was followed by training courses, the first of which, Basic Design, began in April 1963.[37] Kahn, Prestini, and Frei Otto remained regular consultants and visitors. In the early days, the Swiss-born photographer Christian Staub came for three years, while longer- and shorter-term visitors to the graphic arts section included the Swiss Armin Hofmann, Peter Teubner, and Hans-Christian Pulver from Basel. Through these networks, young faculty members I. B. Patel, Mahendra Patel, and Vikas Satwalekar were sent to Basel for training. Hans Gugelot and E. Reichl from Ulm visited the product design department and established a way for senior NID staff such as H. K. Vyas and M. R. Date to work with Diener and Lindigner in Ulm and continue their collaborations after they returned to India.[38] The efforts of the Hochschule für Gestaltung Ulm (Ulm Design School) in Germany towards postfascist cultural regeneration and political reformation struck a particular chord with the young democratic Indian republic. Contrary to the belief that India served as a passive recipient for knowledge transfers from the US in its Cold War cultural diplomatic schemes, Saloni Mathur has shown how India framed Charles Eames within its postcolonial effort to

35. National Institute of Design, 50 Years of the National Institute of Design, 1961–2011, 30, 31; "MoMA Press Release No. 85" (MoMA Press Archives, December 17, 1958). Others included the architect and city planner Dean J. Luis Sert; the Philadelphia-based artist and filmmaker Leo Lionni, who in that period worked in advertising; and in New York the Danish architect Erik Herlow, who was responsible for the 1958 MoMA exhibition, 20th Century Design from the Museum Collection, which was the first of its kind entirely devoted to "useful objects."

36. "Letter from Douglas Ensminger to Gautam Sarabhai," February 27, 1962, Ford Foundation Grants Reel 3022, Ford Foundation Archives, New York. There was also a large sum set aside for foreign travel and study fellowships for Indian members of the Institute staff. In February 1962, the Ford Foundation granted the NID $550,000 to supplement an initial grant of $200,000 that they had given in October 1961. The Ford Foundation supplemented these funds again in the late 1960s and the Institute received further assistance from the Government of India.

37. National Institute of Design, 50 Years of the National Institute of Design, 1961–2011, 37.

38. "Letter from Prabhakar B. Bhagwat (Dean of Studies, NID) to Samuel E. Bunker (Assistant Representative, Ford Foundation)," December 13, 1966, Ford Foundation Grants Reel 3022, Ford Foundation Archives, New York.

Design Struggles

39. Mathur, "Charles and Ray Eames in India," 34–53.

40. Farhan Sirajul Karim, "MoMA, Ulm and Design Pedagogy in India," in *Western Artists and India: Creative Inspirations in Art and Design*, ed. Shanay Jhaveri (London: Thames and Hudson, 2013), 122–39.

establish design institutes and reform small-scale industry. She makes visible a set of interconnections between a postwar modernism and a postcolonial one.[39] Farhan Sirajul Karim similarly frames the NID's connection with the Hochschule für Gestaltung Ulm as less of an institutional collaboration and more of a permeation of ideas back and forth through Indian academics and designers such as H. K. Vyas and Sudha Nadkarni.[40] The NID in many ways embodied both the national and international fronts of the newly independent country. Despite the apparent emphasis on cultural specificity and the vernacular on which the institute was built, the nature of its commissions and collaborations often proved much more internationalized and mechanized.

The filmmaker Mani Kaul's 1968 documentary *Forms and Designs*, co-scripted with the artist and designer Akbar Padamsee and commissioned by the Films Division of India sets up an opposition between functional forms of industrial design and decorative arts in India. Making no secret of the fact that Kaul did not think that the future of design lay in the integration of form and function, the film served as a critique of the NID's role in reconceptualizing craft and village industries. By visualizing the strange and surreal transformations of products of everyday use into sleek electric gadgets, the camera enters the courtyard and studios of the NID: "For the younger generation," it says, "responds to the call of modern professions which concede

Charles Eames, Vikas Satwalekar and others at work in NID. 1960s.
Photo: Dashrath Patel.

to a universal system … where mass production over-
shadows art. Where function is sacred and form secondary."[41] Kaul's film coincided with Douglas Ensminger's
lament that the NID was perhaps not "evolving as an
indigenous Indian institution," to rectify which he invited
the American Eameses back to do a follow-up report.

The early, heady years of the NID as an alliance
of governmental, elite, and US technocratic impulses was
resisted by Indian intellectuals even before the institute's
inception. Concerns about a top-down designed environment arose early on within the political and cultural sphere.
As Mulk Raj Anand pointed out in the June 1967 issue of
Marg magazine:

> In the year 1952, the first Prime Minister of India,
> Jawaharlal Nehru, accepted a memorandum from
> the *Marg* group about the formation of an All
> India Council of Design. He was aware of the
> fundamental problems of our agro-industrial
> civilization, which is in transformation from the
> agriculture to industry through the introduction of
> the machine as an important part of our develop-
> ment. He believed that the machine is dangerous if
> it is not controlled, adjusted, and made a tool for
> progress towards economy, precision, and refine-
> ment in our lives.[42]

This council was never formed; but by the late 1950s steps
towards the establishment of the National Institute of
Design were well underway.

Conclusion

What followed for the NID in the late 1960s and 1970s was
not a story of singular success but rather a complicated
story. This is perhaps unsurprising if we go back to the
design school's well-intentioned but paradoxical beginnings
(between tradition and modernism) that this essay started
with. Over the course of the 1960s, the NID would, in many
ways, move away from the original investment in vernacular
cultures and objects and move towards a curriculum that

41. Mani Kaul, *Forms and Designs* (India, 1968), 1:32–1:38 min.

42. Mulk Raj Anand, "Design for Living," *Marg: A Magazine of the Arts* 20, no. 3 (June 1967).

43. Report by J. S. Sandhu, sent to Charles and Ray Eames, September 16, 1970, 1:44, Folder 2, The Papers of Charles and Ray Eames, Manuscript Division, Library of Congress, Washington, D.C.

mirrored the program at the Hochschule für Gestaltung Ulm. In 1970, J. S. Sandhu, a designer and teacher at the Royal College of Art in London, wrote a follow-up to the Eameses' *India Report*, which in no uncertain terms claimed that the Eames report had been cast aside and that the impetus towards raising standards of living and supporting and improving village industries, as the Eameses had suggested, had been entirely lost. In Sandhu's opinion, the NID had spiraled instead into producing knock-offs of Western designs, and the heavy borrowing or copying of the Bauhaus and Ulm models was not only "injudicious" and "ill-considered" but would in fact hinder rather than promote development.[43] While Sandhu's report prompted a change of guard at the NID in the following years, it is important for this essay because it highlights the underlying tensions that characterized India's modernizing ambitions, its commitment to India's "usable past" and its international relations during the Cold War.

iNTERNATiONALiSM

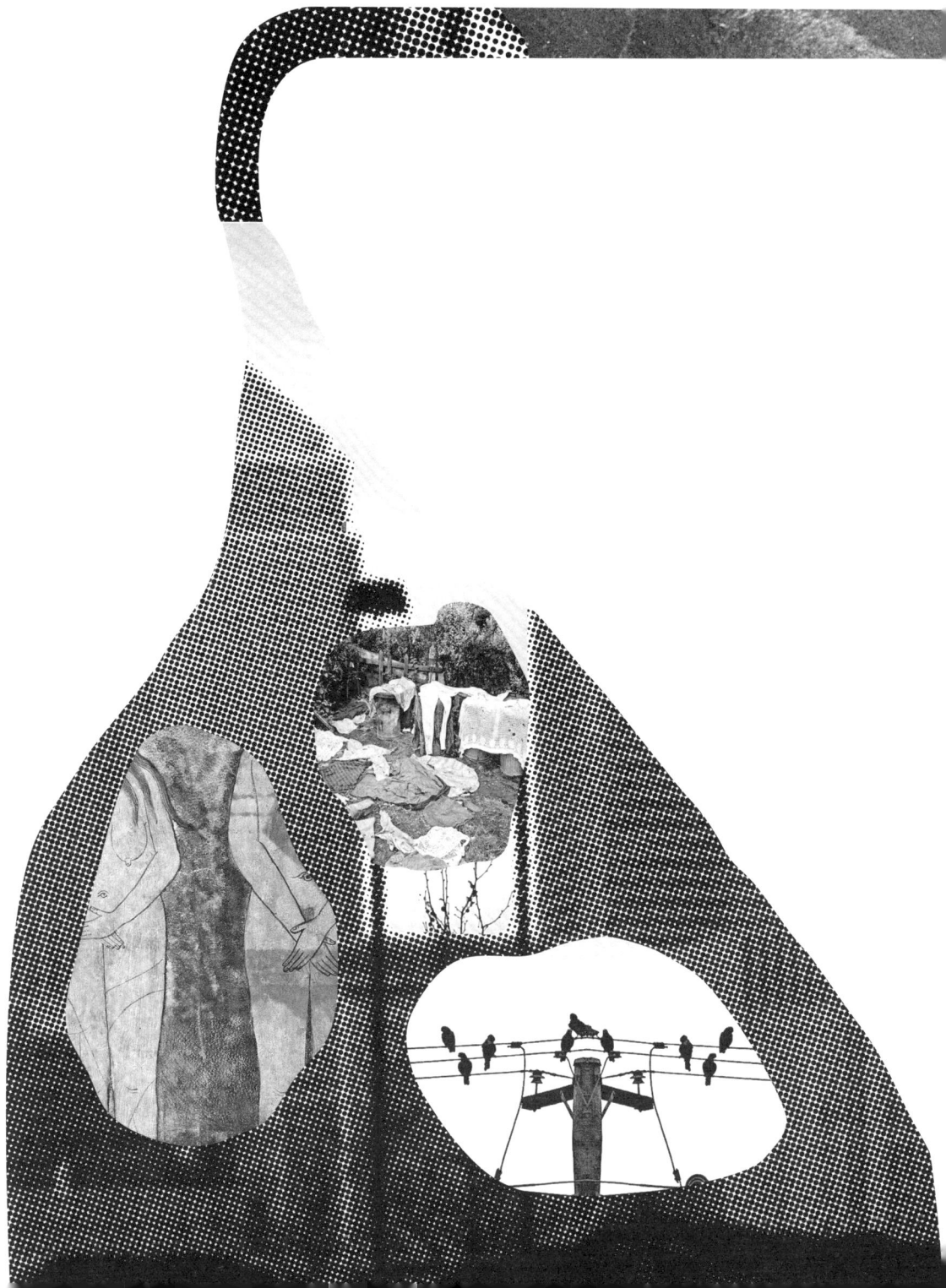

II
PEDAGOGIES

WHAT IS NEEDED FOR CHANGE? Two Perspectives on Decolonization and the Academy

Ahmed Ansari and Matthew Kiem / Decolonising Design

1. Norman W. Sheehan, "Indigenous Knowledge and Higher Education: Instigating Relational Education in a Neocolonial Context" (Ph.D., 2004), espace.library.uq.edu. au/view/UQ:187777; Norman W. Sheehan, "Indigenous Knowledge and Respectful Design: An Evidence-Based Approach," *Design Issues* 27, no. 4 (October 1, 2011), 68–80, doi.org/10.1162/ DESI_a_00106; Eleni Kalantidou and Tony Fry, *Design in the Borderlands* (Abingdon and New York, NY: Routledge, 2014); Tristan Schultz et al., "What Is at Stake with Decolonizing Design? A Roundtable," *Design and Culture* 10, no. 1 (January 2, 2018), 81–101, doi.org/10.1 080/17547075.2018.1434 368; Arturo Escobar, *Designs for the Pluriverse: Radical Interdependence, Autonomy, and the Making of Worlds* (Durham, NC: Duke University Press, 2018); Andrea Botero, Chiara Del Gaudio, and Alfredo Gutiérrez Borrero, "Editorial. Special Issue: Autonomía – Design Strategies for Enabling Design Process," *Strategic Design Research Journal* 11, no. 2 (2018); Yoko Akama and Joyce Yee, "Special Issue: Embracing Plurality in Designing Social Innovation Practices," *Design and Culture* 11, no. 1 (2019), 1–11; Tony Fry. "Design for/by 'The Global South,'" *Design Philosophy Papers* 15, no. 1 (2017), 3–37.

Introduction

In recent years there has been a clear and growing interest across the humanities in the ideas and methodologies of decolonial movements. We and our colleagues in the Decolonising Design group, along with a significantly growing number of fellow researchers and theorists, have played various roles in supporting this interest in the field of design studies, building upon previous but often marginal and neglected precedents within the field.[1] While such interest is a welcome development, it is one that comes with its own set of problems, namely, the question of to what extent the acceptance of decolonial theory is a function of efforts to tame its meaning and neutralize its political force. A key aspect of this problem lies in the brute but unavoidable fact that universities, particularly those situated in the Global North, are not, and never have been, places that favor structural decolonization, and in fact, as we address in this conversation, universities and academic circuits are key sites for the concentration and reproduction of colonial power outside of the academy.[2]

Research agendas based on the concept of decolonizing design inevitably confront the problem of liberal pluralistic inclusion, a mode of false or limited concession that works to immunize colonial power against the possibility of its own dissolution.[3] The challenge in this respect is to understand and respond to what Angela Mitropoulos has described as a form of "change that does not change."[4] If, as Eve Tuck and K. Wayne Yang have cogently argued, decolonization is not, and ought not be treated as a metaphor, it seems clear that a critical analysis of the use of decolonial theory within design studies is as important a task as the application of decolonial theory as such.[5] Indeed, each of these moments is best understood as two modes of the same basic imperative, an imperative that vastly exceeds the core "descriptive statement" that defines the basic function of universities within established networks of colonial power.[6]

The following readings of this situation with respect to design studies represent two brief, provisional, and necessarily partial perspectives. While our responses address the limitations that we perceive within the field of design studies, the analyses that we undertake are orientated towards understanding the place of design theory within a colonial context, a context that is more often than not externalized for the sake of defining the specific "field" or "discipline" of design as such. Our goal is to understand what must change in how we understand design in order to be able to speak more coherently of design as a means of, specifically, decolonizing processes of change. Inevitably we must approach the question of whether this goal is itself consistent with the aims of decolonization as such.

Putting Design on the Line – Matthew Kiem

A critical factor in the strength of interest that academics are presently giving to decolonial ideas and methodologies has been the actions of decolonizing movements, movements that have asserted the need for change not simply in the curricula of higher education programs, but in the overall conditions faced by students, teachers, and other

2. Walter Mignolo, "Globalization and the Geopolitics of Knowledge: The Role of the Humanities in the Corporate University," *Nepantla: Views from South* 4, no. 1 (2003), 97–119, muse. jhu.edu/article/40206.

3. Ellen Rooney, *Seductive Reasoning: Pluralism as the Problematic of Contemporary Literary Theory* (Ithaca, NY: Cornell University Press, 1989) Angela Mitropoulos, "Precari-Us?" *Mute* 1, no. 29 (2006), www.metamute.org/editorial/ articles/precari-us.

4. Angela Mitropoulos, "Art of Life, Art of War: Movement, Un/Common Forms, and Infrastructure," *E-Flux*, no. 90 (April 2018), www.e-flux.com/ journal/90/191676/art-of-life-art-of-war-movement-un-common-forms-and-infrastructure/.

5. Eve Tuck and K. Wayne Yang, "Decolonization Is Not a Metaphor," *Decolonization* 1 (September 8, 2012).

6. Gregory Bateson, *Steps to an Ecology of Mind: Collected Essays in Anthropology, Psychiatry, Evolution, and Epistemology* (Chicago, IL: University of Chicago Press, 2000); Sylvia Wynter, "Unsettling the Coloniality of Being/Power/Truth/Freedom: Towards the Human, after Man, Its Overrepresentation – An Argument," *CR: The New Centennial Review* 3, no. 3 (2003), 257–337, muse.jhu.edu/journals/ncr/ summary/v003/3.3wynter. html; Sylvia Wynter, in *The Ceremony Found: Towards the Autopoetic Turn/Overturn, its Autonomy of Human Agency and Extraterritoriality of (Self-)Cognition1* (Liverpool: Liverpool University Press, 2015), 184–252, liverpool. universitypressscholarship. com/view/10.5949/ liverpool/9781781381724. 001.0001upso-97817813817 24-chapter-008.

Removal of the statue of Cecil Rhodes (sculptor: Marion Walgate) from the campus of the University of Cape Town, April 9, 2015. Photo: Desmond Bowles.

7. Malcolm Harris, "Against Everyone with Conner Habib 49: Malcolm Harris or Why All Millennials Should Be Marxists," interview by Conner Habib, November 27, 2018, www.youtube.com/watch?v=q5u-LmR_QI8.

8. Aníbal Quijano, "Coloniality of Power, Eurocentrism, and Latin America," trans. Michael Ennis, *Nepantla: Views from South* 1, no. 3 (2000), 533–80, muse.jhu.edu/article/23906; Walter Mignolo, *The Darker Side of Western Modernity: Global Futures, Decolonial Options* (Durham, NC: Duke University Press, 2011), 8. Walter Mignolo describes the colonial matrix of power as "four interrelated domains: control of the economy, of authority, of gender and sexuality, and of knowledge and subjectivity."

9. Amit Chaudhuri, "The Real Meaning of Rhodes Must Fall," *The Guardian*, March 16, 2016, www.theguardian.com/uk-news/2016/mar/16/the-real-meaning-of-rhodes-must-fall.

staff within the university. As Malcolm Harris has argued, the former is best recognized as a subset of the latter: a curriculum is a dimension of the working conditions of a university.[7] The desire for a different curriculum is a desire to have one's interests as a minority subject realized in ways that majority subjects take for granted. As such, friction and conflict over what is to be taught, how, and for the sake of whose particular needs or comfort are the result of contested material interests within what decolonial theorists call the colonial matrix of power.[8]

A case in point is the 2015 Rhodes Must Fall movement.[9] While it initially began as a protest against a memorial statue for British colonizer Cecil Rhodes at the University of Cape Town, the movement quickly grew into calls for the decolonization of tertiary education across universities both within South Africa and around the world. Even as a contested and nonhomogenous movement, Rhodes Must Fall stands as a clear example of how processes and conditions of knowledge production are intimately connected to processes and conditions of power. Rhodes Must Fall calls attention to how universities continue to embody colonial power even as they attempt to incorporate the ideas and practices of decolonial movements. At the same time, Rhodes Must Fall demonstrates how institutions can be forced into concessions by the kinds of movements that embody a desire for change beyond the control and determination of colonial interests.

A useful point to draw from the way that Rhodes Must Fall expressed its demands for curriculum change is that theoretical practice is immanent to and not distinct from material interests and social conflict. As Walter Mignolo helps us to understand, these terms are neither reducible nor inseparable: we are where we think and we think where we are, even as that sense of location is contested or on the move.[10] The work of Angela Mitropoulos demonstrates how change, conflict, and movement are not external to theoretical practice but are part of it.[11] The same can be said of design.[12] This is why certain theoretical oppositions are irresolvable; sticking points exist not simply at the level of ideas but reflect conflicting interests and ambitions. As Frantz Fanon put it,

> The need for [decolonization] exists in its crude state, impetuous and compelling, in the consciousness and in the lives of the men and women who are colonized. But the possibility of this change is equally experienced in the form of a terrifying future in the consciousness of another "species" of men and women: the colonizers.[13]

The case for decolonization is therefore not one that we can expect to be recognized and conceded to in the mode of a disinterested rational discourse. At some level – whether at the scale of micro- or macroaggression – colonizing subjects experience decolonization as an affront to both reason and reasonability. Coloniality is the control and exploitation of other peoples' land and labor, a fact that holds even in cases of "tolerance" or enlightened humanitarianism.[14] Rationality in this case amounts to the rationalization of a specifically colonial interest.[15]

Versions of this idea are well established within humanities research and decolonizing literature. The extent to which this is materialized in practice, however, is an entirely different question. On this front, the connections that exist between materiality, power, interest, conflict, and ideas is something that I think is important for design theorists to think about, particularly as we observe the ways in which the field of design studies incorporates the

10. Mignolo, *The Darker Side of Western Modernity*.

11. Angela Mitropoulos, "Autonomy, Recognition, Movement," *The Commoner* no. 11 (2006), 5–14, www.commoner.org. uk/11mitropoulos.pdf.

12. Angela Mitropoulos, "Archipelago of Risk: Uncertainty, Borders, and Migration Detention Systems," *New Formations: A Journal of Culture/Theory/Politics* 84/85 (Winter 2014/Summer 2015), 163–83, muse.jhu.edu/ journals/new_formations/ v084/84.mitropoulos.html.

13. Frantz Fanon, *The Wretched of the Earth*, trans. Constance Farrington (Harmondsworth: Penguin Books, 1970), 27.

14. Ghassan Hage, *White Nation: Fantasies of White Supremacy in a Multicultural Society* (New York, NY: Routledge, 2000); Elizabeth A. Povinelli, *The Cunning of Recognition: Indigenous Alterities and the Making of Australian Multiculturalism* (Durham, NY and London: Duke University Press, 2002); Tuck and Wayne Yang, "Decolonization Is Not a Metaphor"; Aileen Moreton-Robinson, *The White Possessive: Property, Power, and Indigenous Sovereignty* (Minneapolis: University of Minnesota Press, 2015); Laurer Michele Jackson, "'White Fragility' Has a Whiteness Problem," *Slate Magazine*, September 5, 2019, slate.com/ human-interest/2019/09/ white-fragility-robin-diangelo-workshop.html.

15. Aníbal Quijano, "Coloniality and Modernity/Rationality," *Cultural Studies* 21, no. 2–3 (March 1, 2007), 168–78, doi.org/10.1080/09502380 601164353; Enrique Dussel, "Anti-Cartesian Meditations: On the Origin of the Philosophical Anti-Discourse of Modernity," trans. George Ciccariello-Maher, *Journal for Cultural and Religious Theory* 13, no. 1 (2014), 11–53; Mitropoulos, "Archipelago of Risk."

16. Nadine Botha, "The Portable Flush Toilet: From Camping Accessory to Protest Totem," *Design and Culture* 10, no. 1 (January 2, 2018), 17–31, doi.org/10.1080/17547075.2018.1430985.

17. Samer Akkach, "Modernity and Design in the Arab World," in *Design in the Borderlands*, ed. Eleni Kalantidou and Tony Fry (Abingdon and New York, NY: Routledge, 2014), 61–75.

18. Fanon, *The Wretched of the Earth*, 27.

concepts and methods of decolonial theory. The concern that I have in mind here is the extent to which design theorists assume that design can be decolonized on the cheap, that is to say, within a prescribed and minimally disruptive set of parameters. While some are openly hostile to the idea of decolonizing design, a significant part of the problem is that the design field as a whole – insofar as it is governed by colonizing subjects and institutions – still believes that it can do the right thing by colonized subjects whilst continuing to maintain control over the directions and outcomes of decolonization.

I would suggest that the question of design and decolonization has at least two dimensions of significance. Firstly, design theory is of critical importance to understanding the role of design in social conflicts, as both means and agent.[16] Secondly, decolonial theory is of critical importance in analyzing the concept of design as something that is itself immanent to history and social conflict.[17] This second point matters because a position that views the existence of ideas as immanent to interests and material processes must also understand that none of these terms escape the processes and implications of social change. We are right to believe that design is a critical and necessary factor of social transformation. It would be a mistake, however, to expect that design can be decolonized without radical and contentious forms of social transformation. Fanon is, again, very clear on this point: "Decolonization, which sets out to change the order of the world" is not a question of managed transition but, rather, "a program of complete disorder."[18] Decolonizing design thus implies something far more challenging than a call to supplement or reform design as we presently understand it. I would suggest that it is more appropriate to view decolonizing design as a subset of the notion of decolonization in general rather than primarily as a subset of design. This is because, notwithstanding some overlap, the constituency of interest and accountability for decolonizing design is something other than what the field of design studies is configured to serve. Taken to the limit, decolonizing design implies a transformation of the very conditions – political, economic, institutional, etc. – by which design theorists make sense of what design is. As such, if the notion of decolonizing design is to match the imperatives of decolonial movements, at some level this must imply a willingness to put the very coherence of design (as "we" know it) at stake. This implies that, as theorists of design, we must be willing to look at a concept that we believe is critical to our ability to affect transformation and understand that it too must be subject to serious critique and radical transformation. On this reading, decolonizing design is a movement for disordering the interests, desires, and assumptions that design holds in place. It is not meant to be appealing to everyone.

These arguments are not meant to imply that design or design studies as we know it is coherent in the sense of having a simple, singular, or uncontested meaning. Design has always been a term of struggle, misunderstanding, and debate over issues that themselves reflect conflicting interests and ambitions.[19] What is less deniable, however, is that, despite its relative indeterminacy, the idea of design in practice still encompasses a cluster of meanings that are sufficiently stable and continuous enough to act as a function within the reproduction of capitalist economics. Few people may see exactly eye-to-eye on what design is, but no one can reasonably deny the levels of support that industries and governments have invested in promoting design as an object of research, practice, and learning. The coherence that design has obtained is not reflected in the ideas that people have of it alone. It exists in the sum of resources that colonial power has invested in it, both in its historical and contemporary forms.[20] The question of design's coherence is a question of the power relations that it helps to hold in place, even as such relations may be contested or in tension. It is not to say that there is only one meaning of design; it is to say that the meaning of design is as much a political and economic question as it is a theoretical one. On this basis, decolonizing design cannot but imply divergence and disruption. Contesting the coherence of colonial power is precisely the point.

Design's elevation as a matter of concern to the academy is reflective of its value to the colonial matrix of power. This is why design has the status that it does within the field of tertiary education – it plays a role in the reproduction of colonial relations. The terms of this value

19. Arindam Dutta, *The Bureaucracy of Beauty: Design in the Age of Its Global Reproducibility* (New York, NY: Routledge, 2007); Lara Kriegel, *Grand Designs: Labor, Empire, and the Museum in Victorian Culture* (Durham, NC: Duke University Press, 2007).

20. Dutta, *The Bureaucracy of Beauty*; Lilly Irani, "'Design Thinking': Defending Silicon Valley at the Apex of Global Labor Hierarchies," *Catalyst: Feminism, Theory, Technoscience* 4, no. 1 (May 7, 2018), doi.org/10.28968/cftt.v4i1.243.g322.

Design Struggles

21. Akkach, "Modernity and Design in the Arab World," 62.

22. Sheehan, "Indigenous Knowledge and Higher Education"; Uncle Charles Moran, Uncle Greg Harrington, and Norm Sheehan, "On Country Learning," *Design and Culture* 10, no. 1 (January 2, 2018), 71–79, doi.org/10.1080 /17547075.2018.1430996.

23. Roberto Mangabeira Unger, *Knowledge and Politics* (New York, NY: Simon and Schuster, 1976). With regards to a "decolonial turn" in design scholarship ("transition design," design for social innovation," the just transition"), see: Terry Irwin, "Transition Design: A Proposal for a New Area of Design Practice, Study, and Research," *Design and Culture* 7, no. 2 (2015), 229–46; Pelle Ehn et al., *Making Futures: Marginal Notes on Innovation, Design, and Democracy* (Cambridge, MA: MIT Press, 2014); Ezio Manzini, *Design, When Everybody Designs: An Introduction to Design for Social Innovation* (Cambridge, MA: MIT Press, 2015); Damian White, "Just Transitions/ Design for Transitions: Preliminary Notes on a Design Politics for a Green New Deal," *Capitalism Nature Socialism* 22, no. 3 (2019), 1–20.

need not be stable for such a power relation to be a critical factor in how workers within the academy are incentivized to produce design theory. This is why decolonizing design requires a willingness to put the coherence of design and design studies at stake; as Samer Akkach describes it, "design" has an "unrecognised social structure inscribed in its very constitution."[21] It is this question of constitution that needs to be addressed.

To take decolonization seriously we must contend seriously with the scope of change and the relations of accountability that this implies. As Rhodes Must Fall demonstrates, the academy is an institution in which contests of interest, desire, and accountability unfold. The good news is that this means that the interests of the colonial matrix of power are not fully determinant of any particular theoretical practice. Such a notion would ignore the complexity of the world we live in, a complexity that encompasses the alternative forms of value that colonized subjects have found in their own, differently configured conceptions of design.[22] What it does imply, however, is the need to analyze the production of design theory as reflective of social movements and political contestation. A key point in all of this is that, as a political concept, decolonizing design means taking sides, and doing so amid processes that you are unlikely to be in control of.

A Project Doomed to Fail? – Ahmed Ansari

What does it mean to decolonize designerly knowledge within the context of today's rapidly changing design landscapes, especially from within the confines of the Anglo-European academy? Despite (growing) attention in recent years to various approaches or movements that seek to institute radical programmatic changes within key institutions in modern Anglo-European societies, as well as effect deeper and broader programmatic and paradigmatic – i.e., institutional and structural – change in societies and cultures,[23] little in how the Anglo-European academy produces knowledge appears to have changed.

Certainly, all current indications seem to point to the opposite: the term "decolonization" seems to have been mainstreamed, subsumed under longstanding liberal Anglo-European approaches to social justice for underrepresented groups that emphasize "inclusivity," "diversity," and "pluralization." What we are now seeing is that the mainstreaming of decolonization has meant its interpellation into "business-as-usual" – as given in a recent essay on decolonizing design practice on the website of the American Institute of Graphic Arts (AIGA):

> There are ways to integrate a process of decoloni-ality into your everyday practice… [I]t's not just *who* you work with, but also *how* you collaborate. For studios, agencies, and any others hiring for a project, make sure to not only pay your freelancers' worth but also that the culture of your company is welcoming to them.[24]

I would say that this is not where our imperative to decol-onize should stop. Society is the product of imagination combined with materialized political will.[25] There is nothing natural about how our present social systems are organized and structured: they are the unfinished products of history. Given the speed at which technological change is driving social and cultural restructuring in the twenty-first century, there is much to consider about the role that design, as a significant activity in determining the nature of these structural changes, can play in imagining and materializing radically different institutions and other social structures, *especially* those that are not modern derivatives of colonial histories.

Simply put, it is *not good enough* to aim merely for redistributive or egalitarian justice based on systems that themselves remain unchanged. Paying immigrant or independent laborers a fairer wage, while certainly a goal to which designers in a position to influence institutional policies and paradigms should orient themselves, does not in itself, in my opinion, constitute a move towards undoing the very institutional structures that depend on maintaining other forms of inequality at other scales and in other contexts, and in fact rely on inequality as a vital component of their organization. We should, especially as educators, ask ourselves whether the constitution of

24. Anoushka Khandwala, "What Does It Mean to Decolonize Design?" *AIGA Eye on Design*, June 5, 2019, eyeondesign.aiga.org/what-does-it-mean-to-decolonize-design/.

25. Cornelius Castoriadis, *The Imaginary Institution of Society* (Cambridge, MA: MIT Press, 1997).

Design Struggles

26. Anne-Marie Willis, "Ontological Designing," *Design Philosophy Papers* 4, no. 2 (2006), 69.

MATRIX OF POWER

the typical design agency or consultancy, so much of the culture of which revolves around hierarchies dominated by white, male designers who move in elite social circles, and where the work that is done is itself often in the service of reproducing unsustainable practices and lifestyles, is not worth undoing.

In other words, what decolonizing design should *not* be founded upon is the assumption that we can decolonize design practice without significantly altering or transforming its prefigurative conditions, i.e., the nature of practice itself, the nature of the sites within which practice unfolds, and the systemic or structural conditions (of which material or technical conditions are but one aspect) within which its practices and institutions reside, and to which these practices are oriented towards reifying.

Thus, the decolonial turn in design, if there ever was one, has, by and large, both within the academy and without, failed. Despite the growing participation of hitherto marginal groups in both mainstream and fringe scholarly discourse and political activism and a growing concern with the ethics of not only the practical aspects of design, but larger systems of technical production and distribution, it is doubtful as to whether this has lead to a similar proliferation in the kinds of programmatic, struc-tural, and paradigmatic arrangements that pose as serious counters to, on the one hand, the liberal totalitarianisms of neoliberalization, modernization, and globalization, often performed under the guise of programs of development in the Global South, and on the other, the resurgent totalitar-ianisms and various (racio-ethno-religious) fascisms of the political right. In other words, if decolonization does not lead to genuinely different social and cultural arrangements through systemic technical reconfigurations, if it does not lead to radically different kinds of technical systems unlike any we experience today under global(izing) neoliberal capitalism, what is it good for?

If we believe that design is not simply a matter of changing politics and political will, or even of creating artifacts with political and ethical imperatives coded into them, but ontological, i.e., constitutive of the human condition,[26] then it behooves us to inquire and pay closer attention to the kinds of ontologies that have led to our present condition. To ask what design can be other than the socio-technical recreation and reification of our present unsustainability and the oppressiveness of the modern world-system,[27] both in a political and existential sense, is to ask what *other* modes of human existence can be possible on this planet that we share with a rapidly diminishing panoply of other forms of life. In this sense, decolonizing design – i.e., designerly practices that aim towards a decolonization of the modern world-system and the forms of human existence *it* enables and designs – means designing towards, transitioning towards, a *pluriverse*,[28] a "world where many worlds fit."[29] To design to decolonize means to design the material conditions of human existence so that new ontologies of the human can emerge that can counter our present condition.

I would argue that in the interests of continued human and nonhuman sustainment,[30] such a project of decolonizing design that maintains its radical force in speculating upon and reconceiving plural human ontologies needs to take into account three things: firstly, a new conception of what design and designing has been through human histories, as the continuous adaptation of human communities to their lived environments leading to distinct, localized forms of life – social, economic, political, and, of course, material or technical, i.e., cosmo-technics;[31] secondly, and connected, a commitment to the reinvigoration of the local, i.e., the development of designing and designs that emerge from within the historically contingent cosmo-ontologies and epistemologies of communities; and, thirdly, in concordance with Matthew's arguments above, the constitution of the sites of political action through which these cosmo-technical designs will come to fruition as functional, active projects of social change.

What role can the Anglo-European academy play in this project of cosmo-technical designing towards a pluriverse, founded as it is on Anglo-European knowledge systems, but also committed to a project of the transformation of "Other" knowledges into forms palatable to its own (produced) subjects and to sustaining its existence as the exemplary institutional form of knowledge capture, dissemination, and production in the modern world-system? In the Global South, projects of academic reform aimed

27. Immanuel Wallerstein, *The Modern World-System: Capitalist Agriculture and the Origins of the European World-Economy in the Sixteenth Century* (New York, NY: Academic Press, 1974).

28. Subcomandante Marcos, "Fourth Declaration of the Lacandon Jungle," *The Speed of Dreams: Selected Writings* (San Francisco, CA: City Lights Books, 1996), 80.

29. Arturo Escobar, *Designs for the Pluriverse: Radical Interdependence, Autonomy, and the Making of Worlds* (Durham, NC: Duke University Press, 2018).

30. Tony Fry, *Design as Politics* (Oxford: Berg, 2010).

31. Watsuji Tetsuro, *Climate and Culture: A Philosophical Study*, trans. Geoffrey Bownas (Westport, CT: Greenwood Press, 1961); Yuk Hui, *The Question Concerning Technology in China: An Essay in Cosmotechnics* (Falmouth: Urbanomics, 2016).

32. Masooda Bano, ed., *Modern Islamic Authority and Social Change, Volume 1: Evolving Debates in Muslim Majority Countries* (Edinburgh: Edinburgh University Press, 2017); B. Mwesigire, "Decolonising Makerere: On Mamdani's Failed Experiment," *African Arguments* 1 (2016).

33. Partha Chatterjee, "The Curious Career of Liberalism in India," *Modern Intellectual History* 8, no. 3 (2011), 687–96.

34. Arturo Escobar, "Worlds and Knowledges Otherwise: The Latin American Modernity/Coloniality Research Program," *Cultural Studies* 21, nos. 2–3 (2007), 179–210; Escobar, *Designs for the Pluriverse.*

at decolonizing the university have had many notable failures,[32] primarily because of the near-monopoly of local elites, educated largely in Western institutions, on both the administrative and pedagogical functions of the universities of the Global South.[33] In the universities of the Global North, the sites of both knowledge and structural hegemony, the project to successfully produce radical socio-technical alternatives seems doomed to failure. Teaching white and nonwhite elites to incorporate non-Anglo-Eurocentric aesthetics or even design concepts or principles in order to create yet more artifacts for Western markets eager for novel goods is a travesty of the radical promise that decolonization, as a political project that seeks to undermine the very structures of neoliberal capitalism and modernization, embodies.

In this, I agree with Matthew that the project of decolonizing design knowledge and the production of cosmologically local alternatives does not seem to be a project that can unfold inside the academy as it stands today. Design academia would have to embark upon the unlikely project of not only including the presence and voices of scholars from outside of it, but, more importantly, perspectives and alternatives that have the potential to destabilize and undermine its very presence: it would mean foreclosing on the conservatory, the design studio, the academic conference, etc., as the site of presumably radical speculation on futural possibilities. In the present time, this seems highly unlikely: hence, my assertion that the challenge to Western academic hegemony can only come from outside it.

In this context, Arturo Escobar's call for a "struggle towards autonomy" can be interpreted as the political struggle of scholars within and without the Anglo-European academy towards realizing their agency as the kinds of subjects that gather together and activate local knowledges and knowledges otherwise in the service of speculating upon other worlds and their possibilities,[34] in tandem with, and connected to the terrains of everyday life where unfold the political engagements of communities seeking to realize futures other than that which the modern world-system seeks to impose on them. What this would mean for designers is to forge a tighter connection between projects of decolonizing knowledge, projects of radical programmatic and structural reimagination, and projects of social and cultural transformation through active political struggle: between decolonial design, ontological design, and autonomous design.

Protest at Black Lives Matter rally in Belmore Park, Sydney, June 6, 2020.
Photo: Matthew Kiem.

Bibliography

Akama, Yoko, and Joyce Yee. "Special Issue: Embracing Plurality in Designing Social Innovation Practices." *Design and Culture* 11, no. 1 (2019), 1–11.

Akkach, Samer. "Modernity and Design in the Arab World." In *Design in the Borderlands*. Edited by Eleni Kalantidou and Tony Fry, 61–75. Abingdon and New York, NY: Routledge, 2014.

Bano, Masooda, ed. *Modern Islamic Authority and Social Change, Volume 1: Evolving Debates in Muslim Majority Countries*. Edinburgh: Edinburgh University Press, 2017.

Bateson, Gregory. *Steps to an Ecology of Mind: Collected Essays in Anthropology, Psychiatry, Evolution, and Epistemology*. Chicago, IL: University of Chicago Press, 2000.

Botero, Andrea, Chiara Del Gaudio, and Alfredo Gutiérrez Borrero. "Editorial. Special Issue: Autonomía: Design Strategies for Enabling Design Process," *Strategic Design Research Journal* 11, no. 2 (2018).

Botha, Nadine. "The Portable Flush Toilet: From Camping Accessory to Protest Totem." *Design and Culture* 10, no. 1 (January 2, 2018), 17–31. doi.org/10.1080/17547075. 2018.1430985.

Castoriadis, Cornelius. "The Imaginary Institution of Society." Cambridge, MA: MIT Press, 1997.

Chatterjee, Partha. "The Curious Career of Liberalism in India." *Modern Intellectual History* 8, no. 3 (2011), 687–96.

Chaudhuri, Amit. "The Real Meaning of Rhodes Must Fall." *The Guardian*, March 16, 2016. www.theguardian. com/uk-news/2016/mar/16/ the-real-meaning-of-rhodes-must-fall.

Dussel, Enrique. "Anti-Cartesian Meditations: On the Origin of the Philosophical Anti-Discourse of Modernity." Translated by George Ciccariello-Maher. *Journal for Cultural and Religious Theory* 13, no. 1 (2014), 11–53.

Dutta, Arindam. *The Bureaucracy of Beauty: Design in the Age of Its Global Reproducibility*. New York, NY: Routledge, 2007.

Ehn, Pelle, Elisabet M. Nilsson, and Richard Topgaard. *Making Futures: Marginal Notes on Innovation, Design, and Democracy*. Cambridge, MA: MIT Press, 2014.

Escobar, Arturo. "Worlds and Knowledges Otherwise: The Latin American Modernity/ Coloniality Research Program." *Cultural Studies* 21, no. 2–3 (2007), 179–210.
—. *Designs for the Pluriverse: Radical Interdependence, Autonomy, and the Making of Worlds*. Durham, NC: Duke University Press Books, 2018.
—. "Autonomous Design and the Emergent Transnational Critical Design Studies Field." *Strategic Design Research Journal* 11, no. 2 (2018), 139–146.

Fanon, Frantz. *The Wretched of the Earth*. Translated by Constance Farrington. Harmondsworth: Penguin Books, 1970.

Fry, Tony. *Design as Politics*. Oxford and New York, NY: Berg, 2010.

Hage, Ghassan. *White Nation: Fantasies of White Supremacy in a Multicultural Society*. New York, NY: Routledge, 2000.

Harris, Malcolm. "Against Everyone With Conner Habib 49: Malcolm Harris or Why All Millennials Should Be Marxists: Interview by Conner Habib," November 27, 2018. www. youtube.com/watch?v=q5u-LmR_QI8.

Hui, Yuk. *The Question Concerning Technology in China: An Essay in Cosmotechnics*. Falmouth: Urbanomics, 2016.

Irani, Lilly. "'Design Thinking': Defending Silicon Valley at the Apex of Global Labor Hierarchies." *Catalyst: Feminism, Theory, Technoscience* 4, no. 1 (May 7, 2018). doi.org/10.28968/cftt.v4i1.243.g322.

Irwin, Terry. "Transition Design: A Proposal for a New Area of Design Practice, Study, and Research." *Design and Culture* 7, no. 2 (2015), 229–46.

Jackson, Lauren Michele. "'White Fragility' Has a Whiteness Problem." *Slate Magazine*, September 5, 2019. slate.com/human-interest/2019/09/white-fragility-robin-diangelo-workshop.html.

Kalantidou, Eleni, and Tony Fry, eds. *Design in the Borderlands*. Abingdon and New York, NY: Routledge, 2014.

Khandwala, Anoushka. "What Does It Mean to Decolonize Design?" *AIGA Eye on Design*. eyeondesign.aiga.org/what-does-it-mean-to-decolonize-design/ (Published June 5, 2019).

Kriegel, Lara. *Grand Designs: Labor, Empire, and the Museum in Victorian Culture*. Durham, NC: Duke University Press, 2007.

Manzini, Ezio. *Design, When Everybody Designs: An Introduction to Design for Social Innovation*. Cambridge, MA: MIT Press, 2015.

Marcos, Subcomandante. "Fourth Declaration of the Lacandon Jungle." *The Speed of Dreams* (1996), 80.

Mignolo, Walter. "Globalization and the Geopolitics of Knowledge: The Role of the Humanities in the Corporate University." *Nepantla: Views from South* 4, no. 1 (2003), 97–119. muse.jhu.edu/article/40206.
—. *The Darker Side of Western Modernity: Global Futures, Decolonial Options*. Durham, NC and London: Duke University Press, 2011.

Mitropoulos, Angela. "Autonomy, Recognition, Movement." *The Commoner* no. 11 (2006), 5–14. www.commoner.org. uk/11mitropoulos.pdf.
—. "Precari-Us?" *Mute* 1, no. 29 (2006). www.metamute.org/editorial/articles/ precari-us.
—. "Archipelago of Risk: Uncertainty, Borders and Migration Detention Systems." *New Formations: A Journal of Culture/Theory/ Politics* 84/85 (Winter 2014/Summer 2015), 163–83. muse.jhu.edu/journals/ new_formations/v084/84.mitropoulos.html.
—. "Art of Life, Art at War: Movement, Un/Common Forms, and Infrastructure." *E-Flux* 90 (April 2018). www.e-flux.com/ journal/90/191676/art-of-life-art-of-war-movement-un-common-forms-and-infrastructure/.

Moran, Uncle Charles, Uncle Greg Harrington, and Norm Sheehan. "On Country Learning." *Design and Culture* 10, no. 1 (January 2, 2018), 71–79. doi.org/10.1080/17547075. 2018.1430996.

Moreton-Robinson, Aileen. *The White Possessive: Property, Power, and Indigenous Sovereignty*. Minneapolis, MN: University of Minnesota Press, 2015.

Mwesigire, B. "Decolonising Makerere: On Mamdani's Failed Experiment." *African Arguments* 1 (2016).

Povinelli, Elizabeth A. *The Cunning of Recognition: Indigenous Alterities and the Making of Australian Multiculturalism*. Durham, NC, and London: Duke University Press, 2002.

Quijano, Aníbal. "Coloniality of Power, Eurocentrism, and Latin America." Translated by Michael Ennis. *Nepantla: Views from South* 1, no. 3 (2000), 533–80. muse.jhu.edu/ article/23906.
—. "Coloniality and Modernity/Rationality." *Cultural Studies* 21, no. 2–3 (March 1, 2007), 168–78. doi.org/10.1080/ 09502380601164353.

Rooney, Ellen. *Seductive Reasoning: Pluralism As the Problematic of Contemporary Literary Theory*. Ithaca, NY: Cornell University Press, 1989.

Schultz, Tristan, et al. "What Is at Stake with Decolonizing Design? A Roundtable." *Design and Culture* 10, no. 1 (January 2, 2018): 81–101. doi.org/10.1080/17547075.2018 .1434368.

Sheehan, Norman W. "Indigenous Knowledge and Higher Education: Instigating Relational Education in a Neocolonial Context." 2004. espace.library.uq.edu.au/view/UQ:187777.
—. "Indigenous Knowledge and Respectful Design: An Evidence-Based Approach." *Design Issues* 27, no. 4 (October 1, 2011), 68–80. doi.org/10.1162/DESI_a_00106.

Tetsuro, Watsuji, trans. Geoffrey Bownas. *Climate and Culture: A Philosophical Study*. Westport, CT: Greenwood Press, 1961.

Tuck, Eve, and K. Wayne Yang. "Decolonization Is Not a Metaphor." *Decolonization* 1 (September 8, 2012).

Unger, Roberto Mangabeira. *Knowledge and Politics*. New York, NY: Simon and Schuster, 1976.

Wallerstein, Immanuel. *The Modern World-system: Capitalist Agriculture and the Origins of the European World-economy in the Sixteenth Centenary*. New York, NY: Academic Press, 1974.

White, Damian. "Just Transitions/Design for Transitions: Preliminary Notes on a Design Politics for a Green New Deal." *Capitalism Nature Socialism* (2019), 1–20.

Willis, Anne-Marie. "Ontological Designing." *Design Philosophy Papers* 4, no. 2 (2006), 69.

Wynter, Sylvia. "Unsettling the Coloniality of Being/Power/Truth/Freedom: Towards the Human, after Man, Its Overrepresentation – An Argument." *CR: The New Centennial Review* 3, no. 3 (2003), 257–337.
—. In *The Ceremony Found: Towards the Autopoetic Turn/Overturn, Its Autonomy of Human Agency and Extraterritoriality of (Self-)Cognition*1, 184–252. Liverpool: Liverpool University Press, 2015.

REDESIGNING DESIGN IN THE PLURIVERSE
Speculative Fabulations from a School in the Borderlands

Zoy Anastassakis

1. According to the notion of "affect" proposed by Jeanne Favret-Saada and discussed by Márcio Goldman, to be affected by the situations one comes across has nothing to do with belief or emotions that elude reason, but with affect as the result of a process of allowing oneself to be affected by the same forces that affect others, thus enabling a certain type of relation to establish itself. These are affects that are aroused or revealed within a lived experience of alterity. This is not an automatic identification with the perspectives of others, but, rather, the result of gambling on the possibility that, by taking part and allowing oneself to be affected, one's own knowledge project is put to the test. See Jeanne Favret-Saada, "Ser afetado," *Cadernos de Campo* no. 13 (2005), 154–61; and Márcio Goldman, "Jeanne Favret-Saada, os afetos e a etnografia," ibid., 149–53.

2. Paulo Freire, *Pedagogia do oprimido* (Rio de Janeiro: Paz e Terra), 2005. bell hooks, *Teaching to Transgress: Education as the Practice of Freedom* (New York, NY: Routledge, 1994).

3. ESDI was founded in 1962 as an independent design school run by the state of Rio de Janeiro. In 1975 it was incorporated into the Rio de Janeiro State University (Universidade do Estado do Rio de Janeiro, UERJ). It was the first design school in Brazil to offer a bachelor's degree in industrial design. Currently, it provides undergraduate degrees in design and architecture/urbanism, and masters and doctorate degrees in design. It has approximately 400 undergraduate and 100 graduate students. Since 2003,

WARNING! Instead of an Introduction

Warning! If you expect to find neutrality, coherence, and impartiality in an academic text, cease reading right now! It seems to me that a situated perspective is a fundamental component of an academic engagement guided by an ethic of affects.[1] In this paper, I intend to take this commitment seriously, bringing to the debate what has affected me during the last three decades in which I have participated in the academic community of a design school situated in Rio de Janeiro, Brazil.

One should not expect to find here a report of successes or results. First and foremost, this paper is an effort to think through attempts and rehearsals on "education as a practice of freedom."[2] Nor will my attention be restricted to a distinct group of specific people. What interests me is the quality of affects and relations in play in the situations described. Later, in dialogue with the anthropologists Arturo Escobar and Tim Ingold, I will characterize this as "pluriversal agencings."

Confabulating with these affects, I return to some situations I came across in the Superior School of Industrial Design, at Rio de Janeiro State University (ESDI/UERJ),[3] to create a speculative fabulation[4] from some encounters with "Amerindians, Blacks, and the Poor"[5] which took place there. Telling these stories, I look for descriptive tools that allow me to both convey and be conveyed by the affects, thus protecting and caring for the "matters of concern"[6] at play in the situations in which, together, redesigning design,[7] we carve pathways toward the "pluriverse."[8]

By "together" I refer to all of those with whom I shared experiences; that is, those with whom I experienced the stories I now tell. However, more than the facts, what interests me is the quality of the relations and affects. Written as a political act, this paper comes from a combination of these affects and the reflections on them developed with Professor Marcos Martins while preparing a book about our experiences as ESDI's directors between 2016 and 2018.

Once upon a Time in a Brazilian Design School

Once upon a time there was a school where I was often annoyed. I had been annoyed in other schools before. So, nothing new. But in this one my annoyance was different, perhaps more dramatic, because everyone said that it was the best school for that subject in that place. I don't know how, but I survived the course and my affliction, and seven years later, right there, graduated as an industrial designer.

Nine years after that, in 2008, I began a doctoral degree in anthropology, in which I questioned the origin myths of design in Brazil.[9] During the degree, I returned to that school as an apprentice teacher under the same professor that, in 1999, had supervised my undergraduate project. In 2008, there was a different buzz on campus compared to my time as a student. This had to do with the presence of "Black" and "Poor" students there. As part of the UERJ, as of 2000 ESDI had to adhere to the policies of social and racial quotas, in which this university was a pioneer.[10]

Since its implementation, however, the quotas have been contested by certain segments within the university. Matters were not – and are not – any different at ESDI. Some professors never hid their discomfort with the

35 percent of undergraduate students are admitted based on social and racial quotas.

4. Speculative fabulations can be defined as the making of anthropological fictions sufficiently vivid and intense to open space to the imagination of transformative futures, as to be capable of intervening in and reshaping reality. It can be cultivated by means of experimentations on correspondence and participant observation, where the one who observes acts with response-ability and engagement. Cultivating the signs of a change in a situation, speculative fabulations maximize the friction with experience in order to imagine poissible futures. In this sense, these are experiments in anthropological imagination that aim to intervene in and modify reality, challenging the existing order to transform the future. A form of activist storytelling that deals with real stories where multiple players are enmeshed in partial translations and liminal transformations across difference.

5. Here, I adopt the expression used by the samba school Estação Primeira de Mangueira, winner of the 2019 Rio Carnival, in place of the dictum "Order and Progress" which is written at the center of the Brazilian flag. It is important to note that the adoption of the terms "Índios, Negros e Pobres," or, in English, "Amerindians, Blacks, and the Poor," is not casual but rather politically oriented. Identified with the Native and People of Color movements, the samba school mobilizes these categories to discuss the violence imposed by "progressive" policies in the lives of these populations. Thus with this motto, the Mangueira denounces the racism still in force in Brazil.

6. Bruno Latour, "Why Has Critique Run Out of Steam? From Matters of Fact to Matters of Concern," *Critical Inquiry* 30, no. 2 (Winter 2004), 25–248.

7. The Colombian anthropologist Arturo Escobar proposes "redesigning design from within and from without." Arturo Escobar, *Designs for the Pluriverse: Radical Interdependence, Autonomy, and the Making of Worlds* (Durham, NC: Duke University Press, 2017). To this proposal he links the expression "design for the pluriverse," which is the title of the book in which he puts forward the notion of ontological design. "In this context, designs for the pluriverse becomes a tool for reimagining and reconstructing local worlds" (ibid., 4). Promoting an "autonomous design" that distances itself from commercial and lucrative ends towards more collaborative and situated approaches, Escobar reclaims

Design Struggles

the decolonial debate and the notion of the pluriverse, with its relation to the Zapatista idea of a world in which many worlds would coexist.

8. Walter Mignolo, an Argentinian semiologist and one of the exponents of Latin American decolonial thought, proposes "pluriverse" not as a world of independent units, but as a way of thinking and understanding that dwells in the entanglements, in the borders. It is thus not concerned with studying borders by dwelling within a fixed territorial epistemology, which would mean that we accept a pluriverse that exists somewhere out there, and which can be observed from the outside. According to Mignolo, to access such a mode of thought we must, on the contrary, dwell within the border. Not to cross it, so as to observe or describe it, but to remain within it. See Walter Mignolo, "On Pluriversality," posted on October 20, 2013 waltermignolo.com/on-pluriversality/ (accessed on April 16, 2019). For Escobar, "the borderlands are strategically important spaces for the reconstruction of an ethics and praxis of care in relation to what ought to be designed, and how" (Designs for the Pluriverse, 207). Quoting Tony Fry, Escobar proposes that "this would be an ontology of repair of the broken beings and broken worlds that have resulted from centuries of defuturing designing and their alleged accumulated outcome, the anthropocene." In his view, "herein lies the possibility of, and ground for, the reconstitution of design in, for, and from the South, not as a total rejection of design but as 'critical selection and local innovation' involving the creation of structures of care toward the Sustainment" (ibid.).

9. Zoy Anastassakis, Triunfos e impasses: Lina Bo Bardi, Aloisio Magalhães e o design no Brasil Rio de Janeiro: Lamparina Editora, 2014).

10. In 2000, the Legislative Assembly of Rio de Janeiro passed a law that reserves half of all places at state-run universities to students from public schools. In the following year, a new law was passed, stipulating that 40 percent of all available places should be reserved for Black people, based on a principle of self-designation. Two years later, the selection process was modified: 20 percent of the available places were reserved for Black students, 20 percent for students from public schools, and 5 percent for ethnic minorities and people with physical disabilities. Data on the family income was also required of these candidates, and those whose families had an income of over R$300 per capita were excluded from the process. In 2007, the

presence of the beneficiaries of these policies at the school, and a variety of arguments have been evoked to disqualify them and their academic performance. However, much like the abuse hurled at Afro-Brazilian religions discussed by Goldman and Flaksman, I have noticed that, at ESDI, too, "as usually happens in the Brazilian case, this prejudice and this racism never self-styles itself and functions without reference to colors and races, which are always substituted by pseudo-universals."[11]

A former student who had benefited from the system of quotas mentioned an episode in which a professor, in class, confessed that she found it difficult to teach students who did not have art books at home, and who, despite being over eighteen, had never been to the Museum of Modern Art in New York. The student felt that situations like this were evidence that, even now, more than ten years after the implementation of a system of quotas, some professors did not yet have the sensibility to deal with "Black and the Poor" students from the *favelas*, such as himself.

What this former student sees as a deficiency in the professor – that is, the lack of sensibility to deal with students like him – is the converse of the accusation that the professor aimed at the class, which, in her view, reflected a deficiency in students who benefited from social and racial quotas. What distinguishes them is that she feels authorized to speak, without constraint or discomfiture, and without any interest in the repertoire that the student bears. From the student, in contrast, the expected response is silence, a resigned recognition of his own deficiency, and the requisite effort to overcome it through study.

In many other situations like this one, it is note-worthy that the values of universality and equality, taken to be the ends and means of formal education, are called upon not to congregate, but to repel those who do not or will not conform to the elitist standards that inform the university. This applies to the very law[12] that empowered "Black and the Poor" young people to obtain places in the public universities of Rio de Janeiro, which were upheld by these principles. In many cases, instead of ensuring access, they ultimately serve as arguments for policies that, in practice, inhibit or even prevent quota students from accessing or remaining in university.

In 2011, after finishing my doctoral degree, I was hired as an associate professor at ESDI. The system of quotas at UERJ was already over ten years old. Without a doubt, at that time, the place was altogether different, much more interesting for being less homogenous in what pertains to the student body,[13] most of whom had been white children from middle-class families with access to high-quality education, as was my case.

On coming back to that place, I did not see myself returning to the same school in a different role: previously a student, now a professor. Being myself someone else already, I also returned to somewhere else, a place now transformed. It was this feeling that compelled me to return. It was as if, collaborating in the transformation of the academic life of that place, I could transmute my own experience as a student resentful of the elitism that never ceased to be exalted by much of the academic staff, who seemed to believe that they were educating an intellectual elite that would redeem the nation, and would be responsible for making viable, through design, a pathway for development. Far from these developmentalist dreams, it was with joy[14] and hope that I came back. After all, it seemed to me that things could no longer remain the same. Not just there, but in Brazil as a whole.

Living Together in Difference: Stories of Opposition and Reinvention

In 2002, a man who was born into poverty was elected president of the Republic. Hailing from the Northeast, migrating with his family from the backlands of Pernambuco to industrial São Paulo, lacking higher education, molded in the trade unions of the car industry, founder of the Workers' Party (Partido dos Trabalhadores, or PT). During his government, Luiz Inácio Lula da Silva invested in a set of policies aimed at repairing the social inequality that is a constitutive characteristic of Brazil.

With Lula and later with Dilma Rousseff, the PT remained in power from 2002 to 2016, when President Rousseff was deposed in a coup. Two years later, on April

law was changed yet again, incorporating, alongside the 5 percent of places reserved for ethnic minorities, places for people with disabilities, the children of police officers, firemen, and penitentiary agents killed or incapacitated during work. Two years later, the ceiling for per capita family income was raised to one and a half times minimum wage. UERJ had no say in the formulation of these measures, having only to put them into practice.

11. In the original: "como costuma acontecer com frequência no caso brasileiro, esse racismo não se autonomeiam e funcionam sem mencionar cores e raças, sempre substituídas por pseudo universais." Marcio Goldman and Clara Flaksman, "Tentativa de criminalizar práticas de sacrifício religioso é preconceituosa," *Época*, April 17, 2019, epoca. globo.com/tentativa-de-criminalizar-praticas-de-sacrificio-religioso-preconceituosa-artigo-23606318/.

12. To view the current law of quotas in the state of Rio de Janeiro, see alerjln1.alerj.rj.gov.br/contlei.nsf/c8aa0900025feef6032564ec0060dfff/1b96527e90c0548083257520005c15df?OpenDocument (accessed April 18, 2019).

13. Regarding the faculty, until 2019 ESDI had just one Black teacher. Therefore, while among the students we found much more diversity than before the quotas, among the faculty the situation was almost the same.

14. Isabelle Stengers, *Au temps des catastrophes: Résister à la barbarie qui vient* (Paris: La Découverte, 2013).

15. Marielle Franco (1979–2018) was like many of our students at ESDI and UERJ. A generation of Black and Poor young people who, for the first time, had access to higher education and who, in parallel with their academic background, engaged in political struggles and social movements. From another place, these Poor and Black youth now combined political militancy with higher education, graduating as masters and doctors, and thus becoming able to compete in a number of places of speech and performance that were, hitherto, restricted to a mostly white elite. Marielle was born and raised in one of the favelas of Complexo da Maré, in the northern suburbs of Rio de Janeiro. In 2016, she was elected city councilor of the city, with more than 46,000 votes, and was then the fifth most voted candidate in Rio and the second most voted woman for the position of city councilor in the country. As a councilwoman, she worked in collecting data on violence against women, ensuring abortion, and increasing female participation in politics. In her first year in office, she organized and presented sixteen bills, two of which were approved: the first dealt with the regulation of mototaxi services, and the second pointed to the construction of spaces for natural childbirths. In August 2017, the House rejected, by nineteen votes to seventeen, her proposal to include Lesbian Visibility Day in the city's calendar. Her murder took place at the beginning of her second year as a councilwoman. On the night of March 14, 2018, in the central region of the city, the criminals matched their car with hers and fired several shots, which also killed the driver. Even after the arrest of two suspects for these murders, the investigation points to political motivations. In 2018, Marielle was preparing to run for the post of Senator of the Republic for the State of Rio de Janeiro, a position that was filled by Flávio Bolsonaro, one of the sons of Jair Bolsonaro, elected president of the country in the same year.

16. "É importante lembrar que em apenas doze anos nós colocamos na universidade a mesma quantidade de alunos que eles levaram quase cem anos para colocar, nesse país. ... uma bobagem eles acharem que, me tirando do jogo, está resolvido o problema deles. O problema deles não sou eu. O problema deles são vocês, que não querem mais ser tratados como gado. Vocês querem ser tratados como gente, vocês não querem mais permanecer apanhando, não querem mais ser coadjuvantes, mas, sim, sujeitos da história." Luiz Inácio Lula da Silva, "Fala no no ato em homenagem a Marielle Franco no Circo Voador," Rio de Janeiro, April 2, 2018, video published by Rádio Rio West FM,

7, 2018, Lula was sentenced to prison, where he stayed for 580 days. Some days before his arrest, in an act in honor of Marielle Franco,[15] a councilwoman assassinated on March 14, he declared:

> It is important to remember that in only twelve years we put in universities almost the same number of students that they took over one hundred years to place, in this country... It is foolish that they think that, by taking me out of the game, their problem is solved. I'm not their problem. You're their problem, you who don't want to be treated like cattle anymore. You want to be treated like people, you don't want to be beat down, you no longer want to play a supporting role, but rather be subjects of history.[16]

A while later, Lula admitted he was convinced that "the difference" would come from the generation of poor people who had access to university because of education policies put into effect during his government. It was this "difference" that I felt when I returned to ESDI in 2008.

In 2015, at UERJ, we had elections for deans and direction boards. In this university, the whole academic community has the right to vote, including professors, staff, and students. I was on maternity leave when I received an email from the outgoing director, calling on the teachers to organize a ticket for ESDI's directorship. After all, the deadline for registering had already passed, and no one had put forward a candidacy.

We met during the following days to discuss our options. I proposed that we evaluate our chances for decentralizing administrative tasks and sharing responsibility for directing the school. Some colleagues offered to contribute toward this idea, but no one had, yet, proposed a candidacy.

Finally, I and Marcos Martins, who was coordinating a curricular revision that was about to be implemented, decided to run. Otherwise the implementation of the new pedagogical curriculum would be compromised. Not restricted to pedagogical aspects, the reformulation was also oriented by political issues directly related to the adequacy of the course to the diverse realities of the students who entered the university through the quota system.

The curricular revision was based on the understanding that the school could no longer ignore the diversity of perspectives for the professional practice of contemporary design, nor could it neglect the challenges faced by the students to conclude their degrees and to enter the job market. At last, we felt that the course needed to be updated, not in terms of ideals or universal values, but, on the contrary, in search of situated, possible, and viable alterations that could attend to the demands of that academic community, at that time, and in that place.

This was not a peaceful, consensual process, nor was it organized around ideas. It resulted from tense debates and plenty of negotiating with students, staff, and the university's Department of Pedagogic Orientation and Supervision. By opening the process up to the participation of all, through a work dynamic involving small, alternating groups, as proposed by Marcos, we finally concluded the process, which had dragged on for more than ten years.

We took office as the new directorship on March 1, 2016, as a team sharing all responsibilities. A strike started on the same day and lasted for six months, after which we faced a year and a half of profound crisis that began when the state of Rio de Janeiro, UERJ's sole benefactor, started to delay the funding necessary for paying wages and scholarships, and for the upkeep of installations and academic activities. The ensuing instability affected not only the university, but many other segments of the public sector, including the payment of retirees. Responding to the situation, at ESDI we began a series of experiments to avoid closing the school.[17]

Meanwhile, we invited students to work with us, sharing managerial activities. Responding to an open call, eight students offered to be part of what we called Esdilab. Organized into two groups, they acted on behalf of the school, drawing up proposals for occupying and using its facilities and equipment, and reformulating its institutional communication.

From this collaborative effort, which brought together directors and students, a series of initiatives emerged which transformed important aspects of life in the school, including the realization of large-scale projects developed with other students, alumni, professors, staff,

www.youtube.com/watch?v=KMC7Luy5HUI (accessed on April 11, 2019).

17. On the experiences at ESDI between 2016 and 2018, see my articles "Remaking Everything: The Clash between Bigfoot, the Termites and Other Strange Miasmic Emanations in an Old Industrial Design School," *Vibrant* 16 (2019); "É na luta que a gente se encontra: o encontro de estudantes de design com os pluriversos indígenas na Escola Superior de Desenho Industrial e no Museu do Índio," *Lugar Comum* no. 54 (Rio de Janeiro: UFRJ, 2019); "How Can We Correspond to a Time of Ruins, from within the University? Openings, Occupations and Resurgences on a Brazilian Design School," *Society and Space*, August 7, 2018, www.societyandspace.org/articles/how-can-we-correspond-to-a-time-of-ruins-from-within-the-university-openings-occupations-and-resurgences-on-a-brazilian-design-school; with Marcos Martins, "Smoke signals from Brazil," *Eye Magazine* 24, no. 95 (Winter 2018), www.eyemagazine.com/feature/article/smoke-signals-from-brazil; and with Jilly Traganou et al., "Temporarily Open: A Brazilian Design School's Experimental Approaches Against the Dismantling of Public Education," *Design and Culture* 11, no. 2 (2019), 157–72. To consult the chronology of the movements in the school during this period, see ESDIaberta2017.wixsite.com/linhadotempo, which publishes the results of the master research developed by Juliana Paolucci, supervised by Marcos Martins and myself in the Graduate Programme in Design at ESDI (Juliana Paolucci, "Esdi Aberta: Design e (r)existência na Escola Superior de Desenho Industrial," 2017).

18. I take the notion of the "pluriverse" from Walter Mignolo, as "a way of thinking and understanding that dwells in the entanglement" (Mignolo, "On Pluriversality"). I call "pluriversal agencings" the processes of interstitial differentiation put into effect not by individuals or hermetic groups, but by entanglements formed at the borderlands, what could be characterized, in Ingold's terms, as "the meshwork of knotted and entangled lines." Tim Ingold, "On Human Correspondence," *Journal of the Royal Anthropological Institute* 23, no. 1 (2016), 9, 18.

19. Along with habit and attentionality, agencing is one of the principles that informs the notion of "correspondence," formulated by the British anthropologist Tim Ingold. While correspondence "is the process by which beings or things literally answer to one another over time," "habit" (rather than volition), "agencing" (rather than agency), and "attentionality" (rather than intentionality) are defined as follows: "habit as 'doing undergoing,' agencing as a process in which the 'I' emerges as a question, and attention as a resonant coupling of concurrent movements." And, Ingold proceeds: "In the correspondence of agencing, then, there are no volitional subjects, no 'I's or 'you's to place before any action. ... The agent is inside the process of his or her action, inside the verb, not separate from it... A becoming [that] is neither one nor two, nor the relation of the two, it is the in-between." He calls this experience of the interval "interstitial differentiation." Ingold, "On Human Correspondence," 9, 17, 18.

20. Ingold.

21. Freire, *Pedagogia do oprimido.*

22. Grada Kilomba, *Plantation Memories: Episodes of Everyday Racism* (Münster: Unrast Verlag, 2018).

23. Mignolo, "On Pluriversality."

and institutional partnerships. These projects – the building of a new entrance to the school, a renewed visual communication, and a website – called into question notions of hierarchy, authorship, and project, because they resulted from "pluriversal"[18] "agencings,"[19] open and negotiated by many, in which there was no definition of individuals and groups responsible for actions, but, rather, an increasing effort to assume the entangled character of achievements, widening the borderlands until it made little sense to try to identify who was who in the "meshwork of knotted and entangled lines."[20]

This is a fundamental character of the transformations we experienced at ESDI between 2016 and 2018: we were fully committed to breaking the barriers between the established roles that distinguish staff, professors, and students. What we went through with these initiatives did not transform the existing hierarchical structures. However, through them we reinstituted the school's ecology of life, since our way of acting called for a change of attitude, inviting everyone to break free of the banking concept of education[21] that puts teachers and staff as providers and students as consumers of an educational "service."

Transgressing this logic, we were inviting everybody to act as inhabitants of the place – which made all of us co-responsible for what happened there. In dialogue with bell hooks, Grada Kilomba relates opposition and reinvention.[22] At ESDI, we were not just opposing the government or the banking concept of education. We were also trying to reinvent the ecology of life in the school. As nobody wanted to assume the directorship, we were faced with the need to become collectively responsible.

Not everyone agreed or took part. Many times we were few; and some of our colleagues made a point of manifesting their discomfort at seeing the school being run cooperatively. In the meanwhile, we sought to be transparent and open, always in contact with the academic community and the university's central administration.

To this end, we put out open calls, offering to collaborate with all who answered them. Not without difficulty, we invested in producing a common place where many worlds could coexist.[23] This place was not at all the result of an encounter between people who think and act in the same way. On the contrary, it was the difficult, but possible, and above all necessary, result of a collective production of spaces for living together in difference.[24]

Let us return to the "difference" instituted by the policy of quotas at UERJ, which, from a broader perspective, was thematized by Lula in the aforementioned quote: if it widens the spectrum of "difference" in the university, my understanding is that, as part of academic communities, it is our responsibility to increasingly expand spaces for the coexistence of difference. The university thereby becomes a fruitful environment for experimenting with "commoning"[25] and freedom, constituted by way of "pluriversal agencings."

Nothing is certain in processes such as these. Nor can we promote structural changes in universities and design schools overnight, for these are rigid institutions born of an ongoing modern and Eurocentric endeavor to disseminate a Western monoculture. But, as the Mangueira samba song goes: "Brasil, my *nego*, let me tell you the story that history won't tell, the underside of the same place. It is in the struggle that we meet."[26]

It seems to me that this struggle concerns claims and experiments on "commoning"[27] and freedom in the pluriverse. Pluriverse not as a place where one wants to arrive, but as an entangled way of thinking and understanding,[28] resulting from processes of correspondence,[29] which thrusts us toward a world where many worlds coexist, living together in difference.[30]

Redesigning Design in the Pluriverse

I now propose a detour to confabulate on some other encounters that deeply affected me. They once again widen the borderlands where diverse worlds coexist in difference, multiplying the pluriversity of knowledge in transit at ESDI. This time, I narrate some encounters between some students (many of them Black and Poor) and Black and Amerindian researchers and artists.

In early 2017, I was approached by two graduate students that used to work as designers at the Museum of the Indian:[31] Simone Melo, responsible for many of the museum's exhibitions and publications; and Priscilla Alves

24. Donna Haraway, *Staying with the Trouble: Making Kin in the Chthulucene* (Durham, NC: Duke University Press, 2016).

25. Tim Ingold, *Anthropology and/as Education* (New York, NY: Routledge, 2018).

26. G.R.E.S. Estação Primeira de Mangueira, 2019. "Brasil, meu nego/ Deixa eu te contar/ A história que a história não conta/ O avesso do mesmo lugar/ Na luta é que a gente se encontra/ Brasil, meu dengo/ A Mangueira chegou/ Com versos que o livro apagou/ Desde 1500/ Tem mais invasão do que descobrimento/ Tem sangue retinto pisado/ Atrás do herói emoldurado/ Mulheres, tamoios, mulatos/ Eu quero um país que não tá no retrato/ Brasil, o teu nome é Dandara/ Tua cara é de cariri/ Não veio do céu/ Nem das mãos de Isabel/ A liberdade é um dragão no mar de Aracati/ Salve os caboclos de julho/ Quem foi de aço nos anos de chumbo/ Brasil, chegou a vez/ De ouvir as Marias, Mahins, Marielles, malês/ Mangueira, tira a poeira dos porões/ Ô, abre alas pros teus heróis de barracões/ Dos brasis que se faz um país de Lecis, Jamelões/ São verde e rosa as multidões."

27. Ingold, *Anthropology and/as Education*.

28. Mignolo, "On Pluriversality."

29. Ingold, "On Human Correspondence."

30. Haraway, *Staying with the Trouble*.

31. The Museum of the Indian (Museu do Índio) is the only official institution in Brazil exclusively dedicated to Amerindian cultures. Until 2018, it was linked to the National Indian Agency (FUNAI) and the Ministry of Justice. It carries out research and public projects geared towards the documentation and exhibition of the diversity of the hundreds of Native Brazilians. Created in 1953 by the anthropologist Darcy Ribeiro, it contains an extensive ethnographic and documentary archive. As well as organizing exhibitions, the museum publishes teaching material, documents Native Brazilian languages, and promotes Native Brazilian cultures among school students and teachers. These tasks led the museum to work with designers, including, among them, ESDI's students and alumni.

Design Struggles

32. ladaesdi.com.br/.

33. With this expression, I refer to ways of thinking and understanding of Amerindian peoples, which, according to Mignolo's formulation, can be defined as the "entanglement of several cosmologies connected today in a power differential." Mignolo, "On Pluriversality."

34. Tim Ingold, *Making: Anthropology, Archaeology, Art and Architecture* (London: Routledge, 2013), in reference to Vilém Flusser.

35. Escobar, *Designs for the Pluriverse.*

de Moura, who was then working as a graphic designer for a series of publications for Amerindian schools.

From our conversations, we organized a series of seminars at the Laboratório de Design e Antropologia[32] that aimed to explore alternative approaches for collaborations between students and Amerindian researchers, designers, artists, and activists. This resulted in a university extension project that seeks to foster these collaborations.

Alongside the "Correspondences" project, with Professor Ricardo Artur Carvalho, we reached out to the museum, which was interested in expanding its collaborations with designers. It led us to propose a design course there. Lasting for two academic semesters, it involved forty-six undergraduate and graduate students.

The first stage of this course took place during fifteen weeks between August and December 2017, with two weekly meetings of four hours each. Initially, we aimed to bring together ESDI students and the museum's team, but also to familiarize students with issues concerning Native Brazilians. We thus spoke not only to the museum staff, but also with some Amerindian researchers, designers, artists, and activists who were not necessarily linked to it.

The students also came into contact with publications and researches made by anthropologists, and explored the archives of the museum. As a result, they produced drawings, infographics, papers, and research reports speculating on design processes that could be developed in the next academic semester.

With these proposals, we did not aim to satisfy the demands of the museum (which always remained a possibility), but to design alternatives, or even to contest, thus pointing to other possible paths for communicating with, in, and through the institution. So, we set ourselves the challenge of acting in, with, beyond, and even, if needed, against the museum.

In this paper, I will not present the results or the processes developed at that time. Instead, starting from our encounters with Amerindian pluriverses[33] during that period, I want to confabulate on the possible paths of escape from the traps of design,[34] making way for a debate on a "transition design."[35]

Design is here taken to be a medium in which

Indigenous artist and architect Wally Kamayurá and student Yasmin Amparo da Glória at ESDI, 2017.

Zoy Anastassakis

177

relations are produced and affects shared. It is thus the quality of the affects and the relations that we should discuss. To this end, I return to Escobar's debate: "how to design without instrumentalizing relations (especially without pushing these relations further into an objectifying and individualized mode of hierarchy and control)?"[36]

36. Escobar, 214, 215.

Confabulating with "Amerindians, Blacks, and the Poor" in the Pluriversity

From these confabulations, the following questions emerge:
1. Like many of us, the students who took part in the course at the Museum of the Indian were not fully aware of the existence of Native people in contemporaneity. After all, official "history" insists on erasing the (hi)stories of these peoples who, ever since the start of European colonization in the Americas, have been constantly massacred, rendered invisible, and silenced.

When we noticed that our students were "astonished" to realize the contemporaneity of the Amerindian presence in Brazil, we decided to invest our time presenting material that would support their approximation to the museum and to our Amerindian interlocutors. This led us to spend more time discussing texts and talking than thinking specifically in terms of design.

ESDI students' classroom at the Indian Museum, 2017.

37. Eduardo Viveiros de Castro, "Os Involuntários da Pátria," *Chão da Feira* 65 (2017), chaodafeira. com/cadernos/ os-involuntarios-da-patria/.

After each of our meetings and readings, we invited the students to provide visual yields, such as drawings, collages, diagrams, and infographics, from their appreciations of the themes we addressed. It was hence by promoting debate around images that, together, we came closer not only to the Amerindian pluriverses, but also to anthropological ways of knowing.

2. On becoming aware of the existence of Native Brazilians and the violence that affects them, the students came to question their own realities, perceiving themselves as diverse and distinctly situated within the student body. On some occasions, this process assumed a cathartic quality: by discussing the impasses and violations of rights that target "Amerindians, Blacks, and the Poor" people in our country, we allow ourselves to become emotional, ultimately bringing to the debates our own life stories.

On one of these days, gathered around the large table upon which the students placed self-portraits produced after reading a paper by Brazilian anthropologist Eduardo Viveiros de Castro,[37] some students shared stories of times when they felt themselves to be victims of discrimination and socio-racial prejudice. On telling and listening to those stories, many of us cried copiously. I tried to bring the session to a close, and, even though I was profoundly moved, I did my best to support the students that had opened up in a way that I had never before witnessed in a classroom.

At that precise moment, in a classroom in front of ours, a professor was morally harassing quota students, questioning their academic capacity, claiming that they did not apply themselves, did not make an effort, and were unable to hand in high-quality work. That week, two student representatives sought out the professor, asking that such episodes not occur again.

Consulting with the university's Department of Pedagogic Orientation and Supervision we were informed that, to make a case against the professor, the students who felt they had been harassed had to make a formal complaint. Student representatives gathered various statements on discrimination and moral harassment against quota students, but also against women and LGBTQIA+ students, involving that professor and others. However, no student entered a formal complaint, which prevented the case from moving forward.

   To expand the debate on this clash, we invited the historian Ynaê Lopes dos Santos, a specialist on the history of slavery in the Americas who also researches African history and ethno-racial relations in Brazil, to give a lecture in the inaugural class of the academic year. She taught us other ways of perceiving Rio de Janeiro through the asymmetric ethno-racial relations forged in the economy of the slave market, which defined a segregationist way of producing spaces and sociabilities in the city, which until 1960 was the nation's capital.

   At the end of her lecture, after a sustained ovation, students asked questions on the most varied themes, such as racism and prejudice, the silencings and invisibilities that they produce, whether in relation to fundamental figures in the history of the arts and architecture in Brazil, or in more contemporary aspects, which led us to talk about Barack Obama and the film *Black Panther*. At that moment, Marielle Franco had not yet been murdered.

   3. Realizing that they differed from each other, and, above all, that they diverge from the ideal design student

PLURIVERSE

ESDI student Andrea Marroquin at Museu de Arte do Rio, 2017.

Indigenous curator and anthropologist Sandra Benites presenting to ESDI's students the exhibition *Dja Guata Porã* at the Museu de Arte do Rio, 2017.

38. Ingold, "On Human Correspondence."

39. Favret-Saada, "Ser afetado."

40. Latour, "Why Has Critique Run Out of Steam?"

41. Escobar, *Designs for the Pluriverse.*

historically fashioned in that school, these students came to debate the need to find other ways of acting professionally, as designers that correspond[38] to the issues that affect[39] them and those for whom and with whom they interact.

In this interim, in the aftermath of the coup d'etat that deposed President Dilma Rousseff, the Museum of the Indian, much like UERJ, found itself in a state of heightened vulnerability. With the end of a series of social policies in the country, and the political strengthening of groups tied to agribusiness and predatory extraction of natural resources – a phenomenon which was already occurring long before the coup – the protection of Native Brazilians and their cultures came increasingly under threat. The same was true for the public institutions related to indigenous issues, such as this museum.

Thus, at that time, working in the museum with the ESDI students also implied an alliance with the resistance movement of these two institutions. But I must stress that, as we were aware, working in the museum is not the same thing as working with or for Amerindians. Any design project considered in that situation also elicits critical evaluations of the conditions, limits, and possibilities of working with design in an engaged and committed way, not only with and to institutions, but, above all, with "matters of concern"[40] that affect those for or with whom projects are devised.

By not seeking to respond to demands, or to practice design in commercial terms, we approximate the notion of "ontological design" formulated by Escobar,[41]

Ibã Sales Huni Kuin in one of the workshops he gave at ESDI, 2017.

who understands design as a means for thinking of the transition from the hcgemony of the modern, universalist ontology to a pluriverse of socionatural configurations. In this way, a tool for reimagining and reconstructing other possible worlds.

Considering the design possibilities in the museum, we realized that there was no escaping from the debate on the ethical and political implications of the practice of design. To whom and to what do designers answer with the alternatives that they raise? To whom and to what is each of them corresponding when they opt for a particular project? Should we still think in terms of design when it comes to facing the "struggles for autonomy by communities and collectives"?[42]

4. By setting aside space and time to debate these questions, we sort of suspended the expectations of the museum, which had hoped to receive more design solutions, not demands. By allowing ourselves to suspend the need for answers in the form of design projects, raising new questions at every encounter with the museum staff, we carved a space for the possibility of transforming our ways of acting as designers and, complementarily, for an alteration in the perception of design in that institution.

For the museum staff, who were used to the presence of designers in their midst, we extended other invitations; not so much to act as providers of material and orientation for our design work, but above all for us, together, to speculate on what a group of designers can do in a museum such as that. By forcing this displacement, we were all experimenting with design at the borders,[43] at the limits, transgressing barriers and norms that keep apart research, engagement, affect, and project. Seeking to dodge the traps set by design, we questioned the modern and Eurocentric belief in design as a redeemer, to assume a pluriversal approach in which "design does not transform the world, it is rather part of the world transforming itself."[44]

In the midst of this process of so many transformations, we established relations with some Amerindian film-makers, designers, anthropologists, architects, artists, and teachers, such as Alberto Álvares, Daiara Tukano, Denilson Baniwa, Francy Fontes, Ibã Sales Huni Kuin, Inê Kuikuro,

42. Escobar, 213.

43. Tony Fry and Eleni Kalantidou, *Design in the Borderlands* (Abingdon and New York, NY: Routledge, 2015).

44. Caroline Gatt and Tim Ingold, "From Description to Correspondence: Anthropology in Real Time," in *Design Anthropology: Theory and Practice*, ed. Wendy Gunn, Ton Otto, and Rachel Charlotte Smith (London: Bloomsbury, 2013), 146.

Design Struggles

45. Ilana Paterman Brasil and Zoy Anastassakis, "Il faut danser, en dansant: Essai de fabulation speculative," *Multitudes* 70 (Spring 2018), 202–9.

46. G.R.E.S. Estação Primeira de Mangueira, *Samba enredo 2019: Histórias para ninar gente grande*, www.mangueira.com.br/carnaval-2019/enredo.

47. hooks, *Teaching to Transgress* (accessed April 15, 2019).

Jaider Esbell, Sandra Benites, and Wally Kamayurá.

Also during 2018, we welcomed at ESDI Maria Eni Moreira, Makota Arrungindala, and her partner, Luiz Ângelo da Silva, Ogã Bangbala, with whom the doctoral student Ilana Paterman Brasil made several movies. At that time, Ilana presented her latest collaboration,[45] an animated film using video recordings of the dance of Orixás performed by Arrungindala, who not only danced to the sound of the *atabaque* drums played by Bangbala, but also narrated her difficult life story. In an unprecedented occurrence in ESDI's history, the auditorium was packed with an audience that included students, teachers and the Candomblé's practitioners, who had come to honor these two important figures of the religion in Rio. At the end of the session, the *atabaques* filled the hall with music, before going out into the open and joining in procession with the percussion collective Baque Mulher.

A few months earlier, it was Professor Ibã Sales Huni Kuin who invited us to sing and dance in the school's grounds. On three different occasions between 2016 and 2017 the founder of the Movement of Huni Kuin Artists (MAHKU) was responsible for workshops on song, drawing, and painting, leading us into the depths of Huni Kuin cosmology, in which the production of images through song is an ancestral knowledge transmitted by the Anaconda (*yube*). Carried by Ibã's songs, many of the participants entered a state of *miração*, as the Huni Kuin say, glimpsing, through the music, the pathways that lead to the pluriverse.

Dreaming in the Borderland

If I must end here, I will set out my own dream. Confabulating by means of affects and alliances with "Amerindians, Blacks, and the Poor"[46] students, teachers, artists, and researchers that happened at ESDI, I reclaim "education as a practice of freedom."[47] Digging pathways to the pluriverse, we can transform the university into a pluriversity, and design into a tool for transitioning from the hegemony of Western universalist ontology to the pluriverse of the socionatural configurations. Entangled in the pluriverse, together in difference, we can design other worlds that, as Mangueira's samba tells us, do not fit into the portrait.

Acknowledgments

This text is dedicated to Jonathan Nunes de Souza, who, ever since I returned to ESDI, opened my eyes and grabbed me by the hand; and to Bruna Fernandes Farias Pereira, who, with tenderness and courage, manages to open pathways in the densest forests. I thank Marcos Martins for the partnership; Alberto Álvares, Daiara Tukano, Denilson Baniwa, Francy Fontes, Ibã Sales Huni Kuin, Inê Kuikuro, Jaider Esbell, Sandra Benites, and Wally Kamayurá, with whom I learned so much; Idjahure Kadiwel, who blew in my ears: "Native people, not anthropologists, has to be invited to be here, to interchange with the students;" Simone Melo and Priscilla Alves de Moura, for approaching ESDI and the Museum of the Indian; Carlos Levinho, Ione Couto, and Elena Guimarães, for opening the Museum to ESDI's students; Ricardo Artur Carvalho, partner of many adventures in the school and in the museum; Els Lagrou, for the conversations about design, art, anthropology, and the Huni Kuin people; Amilton Matos, for the effort that enabled the collaboration with Professor Ibã Sales Huni Kuin; the researchers of the Laboratory of Design and Anthropology (LaDA), especially Giulia Cezini, Ilana Paterman Brasil, Juliá Sá

Indigenous artist and teacher Ibã Sales Huni Kuin presenting his work to ESDI students, 2017.

Earp, Marina Sirito, and Samia Batista, who made the "Correspondences" project happen; the organizers of the seminar "Indigenous Struggles, Good Living, and the Crisis of the Notion of Development" for the exchanges and for giving us the opportunity to receive, at ESDI, the leaders of the Nasa people, from Colombia, who presented us with their gigantic force! Encounters like these are worth a life! Finally, I would like to thank Tim Ingold, who invited me as a visiting researcher in the project "Knowing from the Inside: Anthropology, Art, Architecture, and Design," coordinated by him in the Department of Anthropology, University of Aberdeen, Scotland. It was during this time that I prepared a preliminary version of this text, which resulted in a paper presented at the "Art, Materiality and Representation" conference, organized by the Royal Anthropological Institute in the British Museum, London, in May 2018. Some months later, I presented a second version of this work in the international seminar "Indigenous Struggles, Good Living, and the Crisis of the Notion of Development," held at ESDI. These presentations were unfolded in a paper published by the journal *Lugar Comum*, in June 2019, and as part of the book *Refazendo Tudo: Confabulações em meio aos cupins na universidade*, published by Zazie Edições in 2020.

Bibliography

Anastassakis, Zoy. "Remaking everything: the clash between Bigfoot, the Termites and other strange miasmic emanations in an old industrial design school," *Vibrant* 16 (2019). www.scielo.br/scielo.php?script=sci_abstract&pid=S1809-43412019000100202&lng=en&nrm=iso&tlng=pt.
—. "É na luta que a gente se encontra: O encontro de estudantes de design com os pluriversos indígenas na Escola Superior de Desenho Industrial e no Museu do Índio." In *Lugar Comum* 54. Rio de Janeiro: UFRJ, 2019b. uninomade.net.
—. "How can we correspond to a time of ruins, from within the university? Openings, occupations and resurgences on a Brazilian design school." *Society Space*, August 7, 2018. societyandspace.org.
—. *Triunfos e Impasses: Lina Bo Bardi, Aloisio Magalhães e o design no Brasil*. Rio de Janeiro: Lamparina Editora, 2014.
—, and Marcos Martins. "Smoke Signals from Brazil." *Eye Magazine* 24, no. 95 (Winter 2018). www.eyemagazine.com/feature/article/smoke-signals-from-brazil

Brasil, Ilana Paterman, and Zoy Anastassakis. "Il faut danser, en dansant: Essai de fabulation speculative." *Multitudes* 70 (Spring 2018), 202–9.

Escobar, Arturo. *Designs for the Pluriverse: Radical Interdependence, Autonomy and the Making of Worlds*. Durham, NC, and London: Duke University Press, 2017.

ESDI Aberta 2017. ESDIaberta2017.wixsite.com/linhadotempo (accessed on March 29, 2019).

Favret-Saada, Jeanne. "Ser afetado." *Cadernos de Campo* no. 13 (2005), 154–61.

Freire, Paulo. *Pedagogia do oprimido*. Rio de Janeiro: Paz e Terra, 2005.

Fry, Tony, and Eleni Kalantidou. *Design in the Borderlands*. Abingdon and New York, NY: Routledge, 2015.

Gatt, Caroline, and Tim Ingold. "From Description to Correspondence: Anthropology in Real Time." In *Design Anthropology: Theory and Practice*. Edited by Wendy Gunn, Ton Otto and Rachel Charlotte Smith, 139–58. London: Bloomsbury, 2013.

G.R.E.S. Estação Primeira de Mangueira. *Samba enredo 2019: Histórias para ninar gente grande*. www.mangueira.com.br/carnaval-2019/enredo (accessed on April 15, 2019).

Goldman, Marcio. "Jeanne Favret-Saada, os afetos e a etnografia." *Cadernos de Campo* no. 13 (2005), 149–53.
—, and Clara Flaksman. "Tentativa de criminalizar práticas de sacrifício religioso é preconceituosa." *Época*, April 17, 2019. epoca.globo.com/tentativa-de-criminalizar-praticas-de-sacrificio-religioso-preconceituosa-artigo-23606318?utm_source=Facebook&utm_medium=Social&utm_campaign=compartilhar (accessed on April 18, 2019).

Haraway, Donna. *Staying with the Trouble: Making Kin in the Chthulucene*. Durham, NC and London: Duke University Press, 2016.

hooks, bell. *Teaching to Transgress: Education as the Practice of Freedom*. New York, NY: Routledge, 1994.

Ingold, Tim. *Anthropology and/as Education*. New York, NY: Routledge, 2018.
—. "On Human Correspondence." *Journal of the Royal Anthropological Institute* (N.S.) 23, no. 1 (2016), 9–27.
—. *Making: Anthropology, Archaeology, Art and Architecture*. London and New York, NY: Routledge, 2013.

Kilomba, Grada. *Plantation Memories: Episodes of Everyday Racism*. Münster: Unrast Verlag, 2019.

Latour, Bruno. "Why Has Critique Run Out of Steam? From Matters of Fact to Matters of Concern." *Critical Inquiry: Special issue on the Future of Critique* 30, no. 2 (Winter 2004), 25–248.

Mignolo, Walter. "On Pluriversality." waltermignolo.com/on-pluriversality/, posted on October 20, 2013 (accessed on April 16, 2019).

Museu do Índio. www.museudoindio.gov.br/. (accessed on April 15, 2019).

Paolucci, Juliana. *Esdi Aberta: Design e (r)existência na Escola Superior de Desenho Industrial*. Master's thesis. Design Post-Graduation Program, Superior School of Industrial Design, State University of Rio de Janeiro. Rio de Janeiro, 2017.

Silva, Luiz Inácio Lula da. *Fala no no ato em homenagem a Marielle Franco no Circo Voador*. Rio de Janeiro, April 2, 2018. Vídeo publicado pela Rádio Rio West FM. www.youtube.com/watch?v=KMC7Luy5HUI. Visited at 11/04/2019.

Stengers, Isabelle. "Reclaiming Animism." *E-flux* no. 36, 2012. www.e-flux.com/journal/36/61245/reclaiming-animism/ (accessed March 27, 2019).
—. *Au temps des catastrophes: Résister à la barbarie qui vient*. Paris: La Découverte, 2013.

Universidade do Estado do Rio de Janeiro. "Sistema de cotas." www.uerj.br/a-uerj/a-universidade/sistema-de-cotas/ (accessed on April 12, 2019).

Viveiros de Castro, Eduardo. "Os Involuntários da Pátria." *Chão da Feira* 65 (2017). chaodafeira.com/cadernos/os-involuntarios-da-patria/.

ANTIRACIST DESIGN A Decolonial Feminist Approach to Fashion Pedagogy

Tanveer Ahmed

There is a large body of literature that shows how fashion design can often "Other" marginalized and non-Western groups through stereotyping, exoticization, and orientalism. Academic studies in fashion design have identified how certain design approaches that borrow in a decontextualized and ahistorical way result in the privileging of Anglo-European cultures. In the context of globalization and rapidly diversifying undergraduate fashion design student cohorts, it is becoming increasingly necessary to teach students to think critically about how they draw inspiration from different cultures. However, there is currently no empirical research in fashion design education that helps educators understand how these processes work in practice. This gap in the current literature needs to be addressed for at least two key reasons. Firstly, to understand how the fashion ideation process may contribute to the reproducing of cultural hierarchies; and secondly, to consider the role that education systems can play in countering racial inequalities and thereby helping to create a more just society.

This chapter outlines a decolonial, feminist, practice-based approach used to develop an antiracist and anticapitalist fashion design pedagogy. It will show the value of Black feminist scholarship that calls for the decolonization of pedagogy through the application of nondualist conceptions of design. I will suggest how academic Chandra Mohanty's idea of the local as a relationally constructed site, rather than a bounded and fixed one, could be taken up by fashion educators to help encourage students to explore points of connection and disconnection between different cultures and histories. Mohanty's notion of the relational space could also be utilized to foster students' active awareness of how local and global cultures and histories might be more creatively interwoven to create a design process that resists stereotyping, appropriation, and racist forms of representation, and so contribute to developing new strategies and resources for fashion educators that can help challenge racial inequalities.

Introduction

Having taught fashion design in the UK for the last fifteen years, I have seen firsthand the exponential growth of this sector. This expansion has resulted in increasing numbers of students of color, both local and international, enrolling in undergraduate fashion programs. However, current undergraduate fashion design studies in the UK tend to underplay issues related to cultural diversity[1] and, worse, their largely Eurocentric curricula, dominated by expert-driven, market-centered, and industry-led capitalist models, can foster – and even encourage – racist and sexist forms of fashion design. Therefore, the question of how to educate fashion design students in this complex environment is a pressing one that remains both under-theorized and under-researched.

Integrating and foregrounding neglected and marginalized fashion perspectives into fashion design education is one approach that could help students rethink and relink the dichotomies between Western/non-Western, male/female, and body/mind. This chapter outlines such an approach that I piloted with undergraduate fashion design students in the UK. The class foregrounded nondualist and noncolonialist[2] concepts to develop "contra-Western understandings of design."[3]

This chapter begins by examining how racist currents are constructed in fashion design to illustrate how structures of Eurocentrism have, over many years, been maintained and embedded through cultural hierarchies

1. See "All Walks Beyond the Catwalk," www.allwalks.org.

2. Val Plumwood, Environmental Culture: The Ecological Crisis of Reason (New York: Routledge, 2002).

3. Tony Fry and Eleni Kalantidou, Design in the Borderlands (London: Routledge, 2015).

4. Linda Tuhiwai-Smith, *Decolonizing Methodologies* (London: Zed Books, 1999), 2.

5. Tansy Hoskins, Chapter 20 in *Stitched-Up: The Anti-Capitalist Book of Fashion* (London: Pluto, 2014).

6. Sandra Niessen, Ann Marie Leshkowich, and Carla Jones, *Re-Orienting Fashion: The Globalization of Asian Dress* (Oxford: Berg, 2003).

7. Richard Fung, "Working Through Appropriation," *Fuse* 16, nos. 5–6 (Summer 1993), 16–24, www.richardfung.ca/index.php?/articles/working-through-appropriation-1993/ (accessed March 1, 2015); Julia aka Garçonnière, "the critical fashion lover's (basic) guide to cultural appropriation," *à l'allure garçonnière* (blog), April 15, 2010, alagarconniere.blogspot.co.uk/2010/04/critical-fashion-lovers-basic-guide-to.html (accessed March 30, 2015).

8. Sarah Cheang, "To the Ends of the Earth: Fashion and Ethnicity in the Vogue Fashion Shoot," in Djurdja Bartlett, Shaun Cole, and Agnes Rocamora, eds., *Fashion Media Past and Present* (London: Bloomsbury, 2013), 46–58.

9. Elke Gaugele, ed., *Aesthetic Politics in Fashion* (Berlin: Sternberg Press, 2014); Ruby Sircar, "Dressing the Tiger: Decolonization and Style Racism in South-Asian Fashion," in Gaugele.

in fashion design cultures. I then outline how rethinking fashion *away* from industry and *toward* people's lived experiences can encourage a more relational approach: designing *with* difference to subvert the conventional fashion design process (a process that usually begins with fantasy narratives and experimentation on mannequins). This decolonial feminist approach offers, I will argue, the potential for resisting dominant Eurocentric and racist thinking in fashion design by exposing the "struggle between the interests and ways of knowing of the West and the interests and ways of resisting of the Other."[4]

Identifying Racist Currents in Fashion Design

Racism in fashion design is a topic that can raise unsettling feelings. However, it is also a topic that is gaining more and more attention, particularly in magazines and on social media.[5] In academia, there is increasing recognition of the problematic nature of dominant fashion narratives that maintain that the West has fashion and the non-West does not.[6] This has resulted in a greater focus on how fashion produces racism – for example, through designs that culturally appropriate different cultures; through the exclusion of nonwhite bodies from the fashion media and catwalk shows; and through the global dominance of European and Anglo-American fashion designs.[7]

Fashion scholars have specifically analyzed contemporary structures of race and racism in fashion.[8] Further studies analyzing the academic discipline of fashion history itself have linked key writings on fashion by early scholars to colonial and racist thinking.[9] Elke Gaugele and Monica Titton, for example, argue that some of the early influential work on fashion by Georg Simmel from 1904 is dominated by a "colonial-racist theorization" which has established a

> colonially biased, modern fashion theory in which, for example, Georg Simmel's understanding of fashion had at that point been limited to a "higher civilization." Based on a colonial-racist theorization, Simmel wrote about "savages," "primitive races," or "primitive conditions of life" who would

be afraid of "anything new" that they could "not understand" or "not assign to a familiar category."[10]

10. Elke Gaugele and Monica Titton, "Aesthetic Politics in Fashion: An Introduction," in Gaugele, *Aesthetic Politics in Fashion*, 10–17.

11. Sandra Niessen, afterword to Niessen, Leshkowich, and Jones, *Re-Orienting Fashion*.

12. Lisa Skov, "Fashion-Nation: A Japanese Globalization Experience and a Hong Kong Dilemma," in Niessen, Leshkowich, and Jones, *Re-Orienting Fashion*.

13. See, for example, the *International Journal of Fashion Design, Technology and Education*.

Simmel's writing, from over a century ago, establishes fashion as a subject linked with modernity, progress, and the West. Gaugele and Titton argue that this problematic foundation of fashion history needs to be exposed and that one way to do this could be by expanding alternative histories of fashion, such as those from India, and thus challenging hegemonic Global North narratives.

The fashion academic Sandra Niessen adds to this debate through an in-depth analysis of fashion from Asia.[11] Niessen claims that non-Anglo-European fashion and clothing styles have been subject to colonialist thinking which continues to affect designers in both the Global North and the Global South. She suggests that deeply entrenched ideas of what does and does not constitute fashion represent the dilemmas in fashion design cultures today: the way hegemonic Anglo-European fashion attempts to claim legitimate participation in the field and how it appropriates different cultural signs and symbols. This claim is supported by the findings of a series of interviews conducted by Lisa Skov with fashion designers based in Hong Kong, which highlight the tensions experienced by fashion designers who feel that to be successful they need to produce designs that draw on "traditional Chinese" motifs instead of developing their own signature styles.[12]

This dominant conception of fashion as an Anglo-European construct raises several important issues and challenges for contemporary fashion design education. There is a need, for example, to identify how Anglo-European narratives dominate in fashion design project briefs; to examine how cultural differences are used in the fashion design process; and how fashion design students reproduce forms of Othering in their work. However, existing academic studies on fashion design education tend to focus on other areas, such as the role of technology.[13]

Racism is an ongoing global issue that continues to be challenged through the work of social movements and legislation. However, racism remains pervasive in contemporary popular culture – including in fashion and in how the fashion industry works. For this reason, it is imperative

14. bell hooks, *Teaching to Transgress* (London: Routledge, 1994).

15. Frantz Fanon, *Black Skin White Masks* (London: Pluto Press, 2008 [1952]).

16. Chinua Achebe, *Things Fall Apart* (London: Penguin, 2006 [1958]).

17. Edward Said, *Orientalism* (London: Penguin, 2003 [1978]).

18. hooks, *Teaching to Transgress*, 202.

19. Chandra Talpade Mohanty, *Feminism Without Borders: Decolonizing Theory, Practicing Solidarity* (Durham, NC: Duke University Press, 2003), 241.

to expose and challenge asymmetrical power dynamics in the fashion design education process and to seek new ways of addressing racial inequities. The next section of this chapter will discuss a class I ran with undergraduate students that proposed an alternative approach to fashion design: decolonial fashion.

Decolonial Fashion

One approach to challenging racial inequality that has been taken up by a number of Black feminists including bell hooks, Chandra Talpade Mohanty, Heidi Safia Mirza, and others, calls for the decolonization of "our minds and our imaginations."[14] Theories of decolonization emerged from critiques of colonialism written by scholars including Frantz Fanon,[15] Chinua Achebe,[16] and Edward Said.[17] These theories problematize and interrogate the different ways in which Western colonialism exerts its global power both today and in the past. By exposing historical power structures, processes of decolonization attempt to revive and expose hidden epistemologies. hooks argues that a decolonial approach has the potential to establish "a politics of representation which could both critique and integrate ideals of personal beauty and desirability informed by racist standards, a system of valuation that would embrace a diversity of black looks."[18]

Fashion's reliance on aesthetics underpinned by racist currents means that a decolonial approach to thinking about fashion design potentially offers a broader agenda that exposes structural inequalities and also ways of resisting them.

Chandra Talpade Mohanty, drawing on the seminal work on Frantz Fanon, details the decolonization project as involving "profound transformations of the self, community and governance structures."[19] Mohanty calls on those practicing decolonization to actively withdraw and resist structures of "psychic and social domination" through "self-reflexive collective practice." Is this what decolonial fashion might look like? Mohanty proposes a pedagogical strategy called "the feminist solidarity or comparative studies model." This strategy, I suggest, has the potential

Tanveer Ahmed

20. Mohanty, 242.

21. Mohanty, 242.

to be taken up by fashion educators to help encourage students to explore points of connection and disconnection between different cultures and histories. This approach could, for example, help educators challenge the uncritical spaces currently being produced as a result of the disengagement of fashion design education from socio-cultural contexts. Mohanty elaborates:

> This curricular strategy is based on the premise that the local and the global are not defined in terms of physical geography or territory but exist simultaneously and constitute each other. It is then the links between the local and the global that are foregrounded, and these links are conceptual, material, temporal, contextual, and so on.[20]

Mohanty's notion of the relational also has the potential to be utilized to foster students' active awareness of how local and global cultures and histories might be more creatively interwoven, to create a design process that resists stereotyping, appropriation, and racist forms of representation. Mohanty argues that this pedagogical model "moves away from the 'separate but equal' (or different) perspective to the co-implication/solidarity one. ... Thus it suggests organizing syllabi around social and economic processes and histories of various communities of women."[21]

Adopting this approach in fashion design education, instead of abstract ahistorical approaches, orients educational experiences on historical and biographical specificities and differences. Mohanty emphasizes how this approach looks for points of disconnection between communities, as well as connections, in order to locate points of struggle and resistance.

Drawing on theories of decolonization, such as the one outlined by Mohanty, has the potential to encourage an alternative design process. The aim is to enable fashion educators and students to understand that fashion is not a politically neutral process. In what further ways might "the feminist solidarity or comparative studies model" be translated into the context of fashion design education?

22. Arturo Escobar, *Designs for the Pluriverse* (Durham, NC: Duke University Press, 2017).

23. Angela McRobbie, *British Fashion Design: Rag Trade or Image Industry?* (London: Routledge, 1998), 52.

24. Tibor Kalman and Maria Kalman, *(Un)Fashion* (London: Booth-Clibborn Editions, 2007).

25. See Mukulika Bannerjee and Daniel Miller, *The Sari* (Oxford: Berg, 2008).

26. See "Jean Paul Gaultier's latest collection reimagines sarees as 'winter sports wear,' because why not?," *Inuth* (website), November 16, 2017, www.inuth.com/lifestyle/fashion/jean-paul-gaultiers-latest-collection-reimagines-sarees-as-winter-sports-wear-because-why-not/ (accessed June 10, 2019).

Recentering Global Perspectives in Fashion: Running a Sari Workshop

In an attempt to recenter subaltern forms of knowledge in fashion design education, I used the sari as a starting point – firstly, because it is a garment I have grown up with, my parents having been born in India; and secondly, because I wanted to stress how fashion design is "pluriversal,"[22] comprising multiple ways of dressing bodies. Adopting a decolonial, feminist pedagogical methodology resulted in me drawing on my own biography as a strategy for contextualizing the sari and for opening debates about the racialized and gendered hierarchies in fashion design curricula that dictate what is and is not considered fashion. In addition, this strategy resulted in sharing with the class not just any saris, but saris belonging to my mother. This approach would, I hoped, have two results: firstly, to disrupt "fantasy" discourses in fashion design education through the physical presence of real garments;[23] and secondly, to enable students to experience, through wearing and "embodying" my mother's saris, a connection to everyday fashion cultures.[24]

A key question for me was whether the scope of a workshop activity had the potential to disrupt and resist some of the dominant ideologies of fashion that can promote racial inequalities.

Choosing this precolonial garment provided an example of a vernacular form of fashion in the form of unstitched cloth. Originating from the Global South, the sari remains marginalized in hegemonic fashion design epistemologies and practices as well as in fashion design education in the UK. Although knowledge about the sari can be found in most fashion design Higher Education Institutions (HEIs), and although the libraries of these institutions will usually have books on the topic,[25] the sari tends to be used as a form of inspiration in explicitly antihistoricist terms.[26]

Instead, this class aimed to re-present and challenge the problematic stereotypes in which the sari is steeped, especially concerning notions of the "primitive," cultural traditions, and gendered passivity. The class drew inspiration from many sources, including the London-based campaign group Sari Squad, a group of women, mainly of South Asian origin, who wore saris as a form of visible protest against far-right racist groups in the UK in the 1980s;[27] and the fashion label Not Sari, set up by the Canada-based designer Pranavi Suthagar.[28]

To give agency to a garment from the Global South in the fashion design process also involved experimentation with alternative ways to devise and initiate a fashion design process. To do this, a counter-hegemonic fashion narrative to dominant "fantasy scenarios" was adopted to develop a ideation process that centered on praxis (working with garments), collaboration (between students), participation (between educator and student), and experiential learning (working directly on the human body). Furthermore, the ideation process with saris inverted the usual fashion ideation process that sees fashion designers "take" inspiration from non-European sources.

To begin the class, I opened a large bag that contained thirty of my mother's neatly folded saris. The group gathered around, and I instructed them to pick up and feel the saris and ask any questions they might have. Students asked about the age of the saris, what material they were made from, and from what area of the world they originated. I noticed how tactile the students were, curious to unfold the saris and cautiously requesting permission to open them out. As students continued to ask questions, such as the length of the sari, I noticed how one student of Indian heritage (student 1) began to explain to others in the group that the *pallu* is the most decorated part of the sari, which can be draped in various ways according to taste and custom. As student 1 continued speaking she spontaneously gave a demonstration of how a *pallu* might be worn, and a subgroup of students formed around her as she interacted with the garment. Within this subgroup other students began to hold the saris against themselves and mimic the actions of student 1, using the *pallu* to cover their heads and shoulders too.

I gathered the students back to their chairs, leaving the saris in a disheveled heap on a table, and asked the whole group a direct question: "Is the sari fashion?" I wanted to find out how students articulated the West/non-West binary in relation to their role as fashion designers. A silence followed. I purposefully acknowledged

27. Alice Welton, "Sari Squad: The Afia Begum Campaign," *The Spectacle Blog*, July 29, 2016, www.spectacle.co.uk/spectacleblog/despite-tv/sari-squad-the-afia-begum-campaign/ (accessed February 15, 2019).

28. See www.notsari.com/about.

the silence and waited for students to respond, rather than help facilitate a group discussion by using prompts and further questions. Most striking in the silence was that I sensed a feeling of unease with my questioning and discomfort with the lack of responses. I knew that my asking this question as a South Asian tutor with Indian heritage would further compound the complexities of how to answer: what might be my response if a student were to say "no"? Finally, the lengthy pause was interrupted when another student of Indian heritage (student 2) raised her hand and replied "yes"; she added that she wore saris in India and she thought saris were fashionable. However, she then added that several of her peers in India think of the sari as something that their grandmother wore and wanted to disassociate themselves from that. Significantly, nobody else contributed to this discussion, so next I asked the students to raise their hands if they had ever worn a sari. Student 1 and student 2 raised their hands, two further South Asian students also replied that they had worn saris to religious festivals and weddings, and one white British student said she had worn a sari to an Indian wedding.

This last admission was not a surprise to me. Indeed, interracial marriage within the diasporic UK Indian community that I come from means that it is not uncommon to see white women wearing saris at community gatherings. Furthermore, the media often shows British politicians and international dignitaries wearing saris on official occasions, such as on tours of India or when visiting a religious site or Indian community in the UK. However, as the student observed, when white women wear saris it tends only to happen on occasions such as weddings, not in everyday settings.

The next series of PowerPoint slides I showed the class presented various ways in which a sari can be worn:

> photographs showing saris worn by my mother in the UK during the 1970s;
> photographs showing saris worn by my great grandmother in India during the 1960s;
> images of regional variations in India, such as the sari worn with pleats towards the back of the body, rather than the more common form of front

pleating;
images of saris transformed into other garments
such as the *sarini* (bikini sari), *sarong sari, gown sari,*
and *divided trouser sari*;
images of saris worn by *hijras*, members of the
third-sex community in India;
and YouTube instructional videos demonstrating
different ways to put on a sari.

I also spent some time offering personal anecdotes about
the types of saris my mother had worn, using the saris that
I had brought along. I highlighted one sari: it originates
from the 1960s, is made of nylon and adorned with bold
pink, purple, and blue swirling abstract colors and could be
described as looking "psychedelic." Although my mother
wore this sari through the 1960s and early 1970s and it can
be seen in many family photographs from that time, I have
never seen her wear this sari in my adult life. I asked her
about this before I brought the saris along to the class and
she told me that this sari's nylon fabric felt "modern" when
she had bought it in the late 1960s, but today it looked
cheap and "old-fashioned" to her. She also added that she
felt that the pattern on the sari was for someone younger
than her and consequently she felt "too old" to wear the
sari today.
    Following this PowerPoint presentation and general
discussion about my mother's saris, students were asked to
self-organize into groups of three or four and work together
to test out variations of how the sari could be worn using
either their own bodies or working on each other's bodies.
Inspired by some of the examples they had been shown,
students began to cocreate different possibilities from my
mother's saris (a selection of both evening and work sari's
made of a variety of materials, from silk and cotton to
nylon and polyester).
    Each group was asked to use their mobile phone
to photograph each of their experiments throughout this
process of experimentation. As they captured the variety of
outcomes, I asked the students to upload the photographs
onto Facebook, directly onto a page that had been set
up by their course leader specifically for this student year
group. The Facebook page was shown in real-time on the

projection screen so that all students could see what each group was posting, thus enabling a process of transparency within the classroom. I noticed that this process was enthusiastically welcomed because students laughed and watched the screen with interest as they saw each other's magnified images appear on the projection screen. There was also concentrated interest in each other's experiments.

As students began to unravel my mother's saris and explore draping, pleating, tying, knotting, and other forms of fabric manipulation around each other's bodies, there were two groups whose experiments stood out to me.

Group 1: The first group was noticeable because they were the only group disrupting the gender binary by using a male student as a model and tying the sari around his body; however, to put this in context, within the class of forty-seven students there were only two male students. I noticed that the other male student in the class did not experiment with trying on the sari. This male student, in contrast, appeared extroverted and was comfortable gaining attention from four other female students who were enveloping him in several saris at once. While this male student appeared to enjoy the attention he received from being the model, there was a sense of laughter from all the members of the groups as this happened and I wondered whether the male student was being mocked during this exercise or not. In response to the group's increasing laughter, it seemed to me, he began to "perform" each time his photograph was taken, playfully covering his face with the *pallu* in a dramatic way.

Group 2: A second group began to show an especially sophisticated approach to the task, working with specific pleating techniques. This was developed by one member of the group who told me she came from Thailand. This student said that she was experienced in tying a *sarong* – a length of fabric wrapped around the waist, worn in Southeast Asia and many other parts of the Global South – and she began to show the rest of the group the different ways a sarong can be tied. As I came over to speak, the student included me in this tutorial and showed that there were multiple ways of working a pleat into the fabric. I did not know these methods and tried them out myself using a sari, while other members of the group did the same.

As I walked around the room, a further two key issues were raised by several of the student groups. The first issue centered on the relationship between pattern cutting – the process of making and cutting patterns, usually from paper or card, for tracing a design onto fabric – and unstitched cloth: one group asked me how a paper pattern could be developed from this experiment with unstitched cloth, and how such a design could be further developed and reproduced for different sizes? This question made me realize how the experiment reversed the conventional fashion ideation process, in which paper patterns are developed *before* being constructed in fabric. These questions appeared to stem from the students' main fashion practice classes, which demand technical illustrations and a file of paper patterns for each final garment idea.

29. Peter McClaren, "Unthinking Whiteness, Rearticulating Diasporic Practice," in Peter Pericles Trifonas, ed., *Revolutionary Pedagogies: Cultural Politics, Instituting Education, and the Discourse of Theory* (London: Routledge, 2000), 167–84.

The second issue raised by many of the students was that they would never have considered designing a sari at undergraduate level because in terms of fashion technique a sari is just a length of fabric – this despite our discussion that a sari is constituted of different elements such as the *pallu*. This led to further questioning about whether unstitched cloth could warrant the status of afashion design because it was a garment lacking in technical precision or mastery. This point was raised by every group I spoke to and highlighted the complexity of the original question: "Is the sari fashion?"

The pilot workshop aimed to open debates about both Eurocentrism and market-driven short-termist fashion. Reflecting on how capitalist structures in education support racism,[29] I wanted to expose fashion design's constant drive for new garment designs and profit. This contrasts with a sari, which can be reconfigured in multiple ways and so is arguably more sustainable. Not only did this workshop successfully highlight certain tensions in dominant Anglo-Eurocentric approaches to fashion design, but it also sparked an alternative fashion ideation process, one rooted in decolonial approaches to design praxis.

The next stage of this phase of research will be to assess to what extent a decolonial approach to fashion design can be further implemented in fashion education. Evaluating this pilot class will be necessary for understanding how a class using collaborative exercises can

Design Struggles

30. Reena Bhavnani, Heidi Safia Mirza, and Veena Meetoo, *Tackling the Roots of Racism: Lessons for Success* (Bristol: Policy Press, 2005).

31. Gayatri Chakravorty Spivak, *The Post-Colonial Critic: Interviews, Strategies, Dialogues* (London: Routledge, 1990), 2.

operate within neoliberal structures based on individual assessment; and how fashion design classes can assess open-ended practices that do not produce a final garment outcome. Thus, such interventions raise questions about what pedagogical strategies will be most effective when it comes to disrupting dominant fashion cultures.

Conclusion

This chapter has set out to explore the potential of adopting a decolonial approach to teaching fashion design in the UK and the extent to which this approach could offer opportunities to challenge racist currents in fashion design education. Despite the limitations of the research undertaken so far, the study shows the value of cultural interventions which expose structural, social, and economic issues.[30] These classes were theory-based but also incorporated a fashion practice element and thus respond to calls to bring theory and practice together.[31]

The class showed how centering a garment from the Global South with undergraduate fashion students in the UK is not enough on its own; the fashion ideation process also needs to shift from a market-led capitalist logic and subvert the conventional fashion ideation process to expose how Eurocentrism is uncritically reproduced. Such a process requires less focus on individual student experimentation to enable more space for collaboration between students as well as between the students and their tutor. The role of technology is important here in empowering students to share their experimentation amongst themselves and make the ideation process more inclusive. Thus, adopting a decolonial feminist approach that emphasizes the role of personal everyday experience provides a valuable contribution to countering dominant Eurocentric narratives.

The urgent need for more a social-justice-oriented and pluralistic fashion design education has precedents. In her most recent book, *Be Creative*, Angela McRobbie asserts that through the postwar years, fashion design education in the UK was underpinned by social democratic and radical values, for example through "radical political perspectives such as antiracism, multiculturalism, feminism, antipoverty issues, etc."[32] Drawing inspiration from these contexts, the next step in this research will now be to experiment further with Mohanty's framework and to continue to develop strategies for more inclusive and antiracist forms of fashion design education.

32. Angela McRobbie, *Be Creative: Making a Living in the New Culture Industries* (Cambridge, UK: Polity Press, 2016), 161.

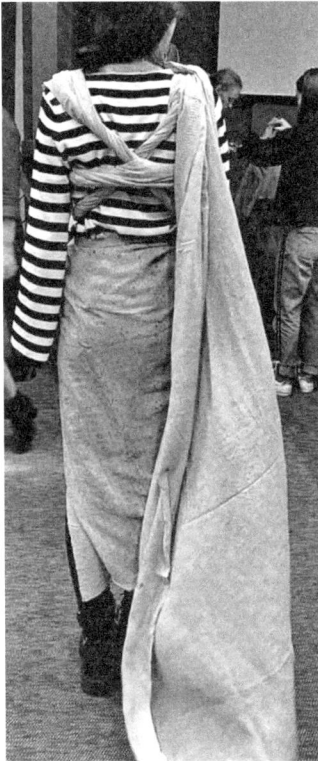

Class experimentation with draping and knotting my mother's sari around a student's body.
Photo: Irati Fonseca (student).

Bibliography

Achebe, Chinua. *Things Fall Apart*. Harmondsworth: Penguin, 2006 (1958).

Bannerjee, Mukulika, and Daniel Miller. *The Sari*. Oxford: Berg, 2008

Bhavnani, Reena, Heidi Safia Mirza, and Veena Meetoo. *Tackling the Roots of Racism: Lessons for Success*. Bristol: Policy Press, 2005.

Cheang, Sarah. "'To the Ends of the Earth': Fashion and Ethnicity in the Vogue Fashion Shoot." In *Fashion Media Past and Present*. Edited by Djurdja Bartlett, Shaun Cole, and Agnès Rocamora, 35–45. London: Bloomsbury, 2013.

Escobar, Arturo. *Designs for the Pluriverse: Radical Interdependence, the Making of Worlds*. Durham, NC: Duke University Press, 2017.

Fanon, Frantz. *Black Skins, White Mask*. London: Pluto Press, 2008 (1952).

Fry, Tony, and Eleni Kalantidou, eds. *Design in the Borderlands*. Abingdon and New York, NY: Routledge, 2015.

Gaugele, Elke, and Monica Titton. "Alternative Aesthetic Politics: An Introduction." In *Aesthetic Politics in Fashion*. Edited by Elke Gaugele, 164–73. Berlin: Sternberg Press; Vienna: Akademie der bildenden Künste, 2014.

hooks, bell. *Teaching to Transgress: Education as the Practice of Freedom*. New York, NY: Routledge, 1994.

Hoskins, Tansy E. *Stitched Up: The Anti-Capitalist Book of Fashion*. London: Pluto Press, 2014.

Kalman, Tibor, and Maira Kalman. *(Un)Fashion*. London: Booth-Clibborn Editions, 2007.

McClaren, Peter. "Unthinking Whiteness, Rearticulating Diasporic Practice." In *Revolutionary Pedagogies: Cultural Politics, Instituting Education, and the Discourse of Theory*. Edited by Peter Trifonas, 140–73. New York, NY: Routledge 2000.

McRobbie, Angela. *British Fashion Design, Rag Trade or Image Industry?* London: Routledge, 1998.
—. *Be Creative: Making a Living in the New Culture Industries*. Cambridge, UK; Maden, MA: Polity Press, 2016.

Mohanty, Chandra Talpade. *Feminism Without Borders, Decolonizing Theory, Practicing Solidarity*. Durham, NC, and London: Duke University Press, 2003.

Niessen, S. A. "Afterword." In *Re-orienting Fashion: The Globalization of Asian Dress Re-Orienting Fashion*. Edited by S. A. Niessen, Ann Marie Leshkowich, and Carla Jones. Oxford: Berg, 2003.

Plumwood, Val. *Environmental Culture: The Ecological Crisis of Reason*. New York, NY: Routledge, 2002.

Said, Edward W. *Orientalism*. London: Penguin, 2003 (1978).

Sircar, Ruby. "Dressing the Tiger: Decolonization and Style Racism in South-Asian Fashion." In *Aesthetic Politics in Fashion*. Edited by Elke Gaugele, 174–84. Berlin: Sternberg Press; Vienna: Akademie der bildenden Künste, 2014.

Skov, Lisa. "Fashion-Nation: A Japanese Globalization Experience and a Hong Kong Dilemma." In *Re-orienting Fashion: The Globalization of Asian Dress Re-Orienting Fashion*. Edited by S. A. Niessen, Ann Marie Leshkowich, and Carla Jones, 215–43. Oxford: Berg, 2003.

Spivak, Gayatri. *The Post-Colonial Critic: Interviews, Strategies, Dialogues*. New York, NY, and London: Routledge, 1990.

Tuhiwai-Smith, Linda. *Decolonizing Methodologies: Research and Indigenous Peoples*. London: Zed Books, 1999.

WEBSITES ACCESSED
Fung, Richard. "Working Through Appropriation." *Fuse*, 1993. www.richardfung.ca/index.php?/articles/working-through-appropriation-1993/ (accessed March 1, 2015).
Julia aka Garçonnière, "The Critical Fashion Lover's (Basic) Guide to Cultural Appropriation." *À l'allure garçonnière* (blog), April 15, 2010. alagarconniere.blogspot.co.uk/2010/04/critical-fashion-lovers-basic-guide-to.html (accessed March 30, 2015).
www.allwalks.org (accessed September 20, 2016).

NOT A TOOLKIT
A Conversation on the Discomfort of Feminist Design Pedagogy

Griselda Flesler
in Conversation
with Anja Neidhardt and Maya Ober / depatriarchise design

1. bell hooks, "Choosing the Margin as a Space of Radical Openness," *Framework: The Journal of Cinema and Media* 36 (1989), 15–23.

Questioning our assumptions and privileges, be that in a design classroom or any classroom, is not easy. Discussing how interlinked structures of oppression affect our bodies, lives, and practices often brings up emotions of fear, anger, and resistance. As educator Megan Boler puts it in her book *Feeling Power*, the effort of critically examining our values and cherished beliefs may lead to "discomforting" experiences for both educators and students. This process of moving out of one's location[1] defined by oppressive boundaries of race, gender, or class is difficult, often painful, but opens up a space of potential for change – as expressed by feminist activist and writer bell hooks – "a space where there is unlimited access to the pleasure and power of knowing, where transformation is possible."

Since its creation in 2017, the Chair of Design and Gender Studies at the Faculty of Architecture and Design (FADU) at the University of Buenos Aires, led by Professor Griselda Flesler, has been creating this transformative space, applying what Bolers names a "pedagogy of discomfort."

FADU's Design and Gender Studies is built on the belief that a profound change in design towards a more socially just and sustainable practice needs to start with design education. A crucial step in the process of transformation is to understand that the ways we see ourselves, the world, and the design discipline have been shaped by the dominant culture (which is patriarchal, Eurocentric, white, and heteronormative, to name just a few aspects). As we "engage in a collective self-reflection and develop accountability for how we see ourselves," as Boler puts it, discomfort can provide the first step towards change.

Acknowledging that the Eurocentric discourse dominates the discussion on design education, we take a political decision to focus on voices from the margins, disrupting the dominant models, challenging the established canons and norms. We see margins as places of resistance,[2] but also places of hope, kindness, and generosity. This text is the result of such hopeful resistance and generosity. Created in a collaborative process that included Skype calls, writing sessions in shared online documents, translations, and much more, it has grown out of many informal

2. hooks.

3. Sharlene Nagy Hesse-Biber, *The Handbook of Feminist Research: Theory and Praxis* (Thousand Oaks, CA: SAGE Publications, 2012), 12–13.

4. Hesse-Biber, 13.

5. Pierre Bourdieu, "La escuela como fuerza conservadora: desigualdades escolares y culturales," in *La nueva sociología de la educación*, ed. Patricia de Leonardo (Mexico: Ediciones El Caballito, 1986), 103–29.

Gabriela Gugliottella, lecturer at the Chair of Design and Gender Studies, discusses the projects of the students during the final presentation. Photo: Maya Ober.

The FADU building follows the paradigm of the modernist movement. The design of the campus as a whole was entrusted to the architects Caminos, Catalano, Sacriste, and Picarel. This rectilinear building with its almost unbroken symmetry fits within the most orthodox streams of the modern movement. Repetitive lines of reinforced concrete and cantilevers form the exterior. They are separated by rows of rectangular glass windows framed with thin steel, creating a rigorous structure. The whole construction celebrates glass and concrete and lacks any ornamentation or color. Photo: Maya Ober.

Design Struggles

conversations, text messages, and discussions. In the end feminism is extremely time-consuming.

In the conversation that you are about to read we reflect on how design education can be transformed and how this process can look like. Our intention is neither to offer rules for "good" design, nor to present a manual for a "feminist design education" – as this would demand the creation of new norms, a new hegemonic system, or a new canon. Instead of opening up alternatives to established hierarchical forms of teaching, it would situate the educational practice in direct relation to the static, rigid practices informed by patriarchy. We see a link between the need for manuals, toolkits, and answers and the dominant solutionist paradigm of design education. Instead of aiming to find quick and universally applicable solutions (which might help with some problems, but unintentionally also create new ones) we focus on asking questions, starting from the standpoint of the Other, the one who differs from the dominant norm. In doing so, we too are constantly unlearning the impulse of making that we acquired through our modern-driven design educations. Within this process of unlearning we stay uncomfortable, constantly trying to proceed with small steps and small gestures, *getting to* – as an ongoing process of imagining and realizing this transformation through design education practice, moving closer towards a more just future.

depatriarchise design: We would like to start by discussing the positivist model of knowledge construction, which in our view still prevails in design. Positivism is based on the belief that only those who are "objective" and "value-neutral" can gain "universal truths."[3] Postmodern and feminist critique of positivism has pointed out that women have been excluded from most mainstream research, and emphasizes that their perspectives and lived experiences bring crucial aspects to the process of knowledge building.[4] However, in our daily practices as designers and educators mainly in Switzerland, Germany, and Sweden we experience the persistence of that positivist thinking, often resulting in the belief that not only design as a discipline is neutral, but that design schools and academia are neutral spaces. How do you refer to this idea of a "neutral" university space when you interact with students?

Griselda Flesler: The first thing we say to the students in the first class is that there is no neutral university space, and that the relationships that occur in the classroom or workshop are not egalitarian or equal. Here I would like to refer to sociologist Pierre Bourdieu[5] to reflect on how the educational institution fulfills its ideological function and legitimizes the reproduction of social inequalities, constituted by class, race, age, and gender. Our public and free university can act as an example of that. At the University of Buenos Aires, everyone can study for "free," but the fact that there is no tuition fee doesn't mean that there are no costs linked to studying. (For example: next to going to university students cannot, or only to a limited extent, earn money to cover their own living costs, let alone those of other family members.) As a result, meritocratic logic – so deeply embedded in our society – predominates and inequalities are constantly reproduced. Tokenization of these different categories helps to maintain this status quo. Therefore, we so often hear about "the poor child who entered the university and has got great grades" or "the woman who succeeded in running a laboratory" as justifications that the existing system actually works. The prevailing thought is that if someone only "works hard enough" they can succeed, so nothing has to change.

Since educational institutions are not gender-neutral, gender studics, from an intersectional perspective,[6] offers us useful tools to approach our experiences as women within universities, to reflect on equity and the extension of rights. Universities are spaces for the construction, reproduction, and articulation of gender norms and regulations, and of sociosexual relations.[7] Within design education, my colleagues and I believe that using a gender-critical lens does not limit our focus only to female practitioners and their work, trying to rewrite them into the existing canon. An intersectional feminist approach goes beyond mere leveling with patriarchal structures, since it proposes a way of thinking about the conditions in which projects are being formulated and the manner in which design works. This implies that we understand design

The building of the FADU from outside. Photo: Paco Zea Garcia.

6. Kimberlé W. Crenshaw, "Mapping the Margins: Intersectionality, Identity Politics, and Violence against Women of Color," *Stanford Law Review* 43, no. 6 (1991), 1241–99.

7. Rafael Blanco, *Universidad íntima y sexualidades públicas: La gestión de la identidad en la experiencia estudiantil* (Buenos Aires: Miño y Dávila, 2014), 13.

8. Nelly Perazzo, *El arte concreto en la Argentina* (Buenos Aires: Gaglianone, 1983), 10.

9. Verónica Devalle, *La travesía de la forma: Emergencia y consolidación del Diseño Gráfico (1948–1984)* (Buenos Aires: Paidós, 2009), 249.

10. *nueva visión*, 1951, quoted in Griselda Flesler, "Nueva Visión (1951–1957), Volver a ver," *tipoGráfica* 59 (2004), 44, 45.

as a significant cultural practice, capable of producing meanings and spaces.

dd: In Argentina, design education mostly happens at universities. Starting with the specific case of FADU, let us have a look at the university as a physical and ideological place. The university space often conveys the narratives of rationality, functionality, and progress rooted in modernism and interwoven with colonial structures. Griselda, from your point of view, to what extent has modernism influenced design education in Argentina?

GF: The hegemony of the modern design movement has impacted a vast number of programs around the world, and Argentina is no exception. The bases of design programs at different national universities in Argentina were influenced by some members of the Arte Concreto Invención movement. This artistic avant-garde group emerged in the mid-1940s in Argentina, introducing – for the first time at the local level – a debate already started in Europe at the beginning of the twentieth century regarding the "Gute Form" and its relationship with technology.[8]

Many of the members of this movement constitute the generation of architects and designers who in the 1980s conceptualized the bases of the design programs of different national universities. One of them was Tomás Maldonado, a leading figure in the Argentine as well as the international design scene.[9] His contacts with European counterparts such as Max Bill were the key to the introduction of the ideas of the modern movement in Argentina.

In this context, some magazines acquired relevance as advocates of the architectural culture and the design model proposed by the modern movement. Among these journals – formed by professors and students of architecture at the University of Buenos Aires – were *nueva visión* (1951–57) edited by Maldonado, and *Summa*, directed by Carlos and Lala Méndez Mosquera.

The first issue of the *nueva visión* magazine was published in 1951 and designed by Alfredo Hlito, Tomás Maldonado, and Carlos Méndez Mosquera. It followed Bauhasian parameters: from its very beginnings, this magazine proposed a strong commitment to the foundations established by the modern movement: rationality, methodology, and readability. In its editorial, it presented the aim of "promoting the synthesis of all visual arts in a sense of objectivity and functionality."[10]

The modernist paradigm was perhaps useful for the creation of an unexplored field in the middle of the twentieth century in Argentina, but also became a model of exclusion and neutralization of other local traditions and ways of designing. Now, I think it is important to question why it still impacts the teaching programs and the common understanding of design within the academic community. Especially considering that the ideal of universal design has been created in a time and place very distant from the lived reality of our students. Gender and decolonial studies are necessary to provide tools that enable us to answer these questions and to understand the influence of the Global North in our practices.

dd: Let us come back to the modern movement and its role in laying the foundations of design education in Europe and formerly colonized countries like Argentina. We can already see its influence looking at the very architecture of the FADU building.

GF: The faculty of Architecture, Design, and Urbanism and the faculty of Exact and Natural Sciences are located in two adjacent buildings specifically designed to be used as faculties, under a modernization plan that implied the creation of the University City in the sixties of the last century.

After an international background contest, the design of the campus as a whole was entrusted to the architects Caminos, Catalano, Sacriste, and Picarel.[11] This rectilinear building with its almost unbroken symmetry fit within the most orthodox streams

11. Gabriel Sazbon et al., *Historia urbana y arquitectónica de la Universidad de Buenos Aires* (Buenos Aires: Eudeba, 2019).

12. Joan Scott, "El género: Una categoría útil para el análisis histórico," in *Sexualidad, género y roles sexuales*, ed. Marysa Navarro and Catharine R. Stimpson (Buenos Aires: FCE, 1999), 37–75.

of the modern movement. Repetitive lines of reinforced concrete and cantilevers form the exterior. They are separated by rows of rectangular glass windows framed with thin steel, creating a rigorous structure. The whole construction celebrates glass and concrete and lacks any ornamentation or color. On entering, we find ourselves in a central open courtyard (patio), characteristic of the International Style (for example, the Mies van der Rohe campus in the USA), going three floors high and covered with a grid of concrete beams forming a network of skylights, letting daylight in. The patio in particular (which is sixteen meters high) emphasizes the immense scale of the interior, compared to which a person is very small.

dd: So, modernist norms are reflected in the content of mainstream design education while they also define the physical space of the campus. In this way, the physical structure is the direct manifestation of the contents and norms transmitted in design curricula, which, as you pointed out earlier, are based on models created by the Bauhaus and the Ulm School of Design, and which are disconnected

Design Struggles

from the local Argentinian context. This can be observed by not only looking at what and who is present, in design history books for instance, but what or who is missing. When we look at design history and design education it becomes clear that women, indigenous people, and many other groups have been excluded. In which ways do you think intersectional feminist pedagogy can help to unmask not only patriarchal but also colonial power systems present in design?

GF: I believe that the logic of feminist pedagogy is fundamental to design education. In that sense, our work in the Chair of Design and Gender Studies is based on the concept of "gender" as a category of analysis proposed by historian Joan W. Scott,[12]

who argues that this is a crucial element in how power relations are established. Her approach uses the category of gender as a relational one, definitely disregarding the cultural interpretation of "woman" as a construct still tied to sex or to sexual differentiation. The reconfiguration of gender as a social relation means a new and radical problematization of the category "woman." It is necessary from my point of view to understand that a feminist pedagogy should discourage the epistemological need to think about the history of one essential identity. Subsequently, the questions should be about the meaning of a practice by which a certain identity is constituted, and not about the attributes traditionally associated with the subjects of the practice itself.

Wall of Pavilion III of the Faculty of Architecture, Design and Urbanism at the University of Buenos Aires. The presence of this graffiti shows how the feminist movement is spreading around the university campus. Photo: Maya Ober.

dd: Which processes had occurred outside of the university that permitted the opening of your chair?

GF: In recent years, Argentina has passed exemplary laws that recognize the particularity of violence against women, adolescents, and girls, extended the recognition for historically marginalized groups in society (the Equal Marriage Law, the Gender Identity Law, the Humanized Labour Law, etc.), and incorporated sexual education as a human right. Argentinian public universities have been subject to renewed attention for the last five years due to the emerging process of making sexist violence visible in this space, which includes both situations of harassment and complaints of discrimination based on sexual orientation, identity, and gender expression. This process gained greater visibility from 2015, with the mobilization of the Ni una menos collective, the growth of the women's movement, the incorporation into feminist youth groups, and the public drafting of a "feminist agenda" and of sexual dissent.[13] The increasing demands and claims around gender issues have had a huge impact on academia.

In the universities the demand for education with a gender perspective has spread, particularly in the social and human sciences and in an incipient way in the design disciplines.[14,15] This demand conveys a critique of higher education, programs, curricula, and of the teaching body, as well as the allegedly neutral status of university knowledge. And it demands a perspective that fosters a critique of universalism and a review of existing pedagogical devices.

Due to these transformations, it's become relevant to also investigate the changes that are taking place on the "inhabited" scale of the university space itself,[16,17] which advocates hospitality of different expressions of gender and sexuality. In recent years, gender, queer, and sexuality studies have begun to be interested in the role that architecture and geography play in the experience of bodies. Subsequently they have developed an attentive perspective on the projectual logic of space based on heteronormative systems and started to question the anonymous and "neutral" institutionalized architectural approach. It's become necessary to develop an analysis that takes the design of space into account and that pays attention to the voices, forms of agency, and subjectivities of different actors and how they use these spaces.

dd: You've just spoken about recent developments. But you were interested in looking at design from a gender perspective much earlier. What did you experience when you started sharing your thoughts in the context of the university and the design field in particular?

GF: When fifteen years ago I started thinking about design from a gender perspective, I encountered many prejudices and objections regarding the relevance of revealing these issues

13. Silvia Elizalde, "Hijas, hermanas, nietas: Genealogías políticas en el activismo de género de las jóvenes," *Revista Ensambles en sociedad, política y cultura* 4, no. 8 (2019), 86–93.

14. Griselda Flesler, Valeria Durán, and Gabriela Gugliottella, "Inclusión de la perspectiva de género en el campo proyectual," *Ciencia, Técnica y Mainstreaming Social* 2 (April 2018), 43–51.

15. Griselda Flesler, "Queering fadu: Perspectivas de género para desbordar las disciplinas de diseño," in *Actas de las XXXII Jornadas de Investigación XIV Encuentro Regional* (FADU-UBA, 2019).

16. Henri Lefebvre, *La producción del espacio* (Madrid: Capitán, 1974).

17. Doreen Massey, *Space, Place, and Gender* (Minneapolis, MN: University of Minnesota Press, 1994).

18. Elizabeth Kamarack Minnich, *Transforming Knowledge* (Philadelphia, PA: Temple University Press, 1990), 145–75.

in the design field. Generally during lectures at my faculty, "gender" was associated with a common understanding of the term "feminism," in other words, it was interpreted in an essentialist way, by assuming that the focus would be on discussing exclusively female architects and designers while disadvantaging their male counterparts. This binary and reductionist perspective was constructed as a reinforced concrete wall. And then came the challenge of creating some cracks in this wall.

dd: How did the transformation of the curricula from within the institution look like? And how is the relationship of your chair with the world outside of the university building?

GF: In 2014, after having taught a theoretical class on the subject every year as part of our Graphic Design Department's curriculum, I presented the idea of this chair. At first, I was asked to start teaching an elective course for graduate students, which I have been doing ever since. However, it seemed crucial to me that these subjects would already be taught at the undergraduate level, and finally, in 2016, with the support of a board of directors, the unit was unanimously approved for all students enrolled at FADU.

Currently, many of the processes taking place in Argentina regarding the struggle of women and LGBTIQA+ people directly impact the way we think about the content of our design curricula. It is significant that requests to deal with these topics today come from young students, and lecturers themselves often realize that they lack training in a gender perspective and begin to look for spaces where they can acquire it. This is something that did not happen a few years ago.

dd: Following philosopher Elizabeth Kamarck Minnich, the university is a place where "partial knowledge" is produced, pretending to be general and universal[18] – partial because many groups have been systematically excluded from its creation. This situation fosters and values certain epistemologies and traditions, and marks everything and everyone outside, in-between, and beyond the narrow understanding of the "universal" norms as "other" or "non." "Non" has also become a strong denominator within the design discipline. Many buildings for example are not accessible for wheelchair users and people pushing prams. And gendered bathrooms following the male-female binary and the absence of facilities for changing diapers are constraints that make clear that these buildings, among them university buildings, are created for certain bodies, excluding all those who deviate from the "norm" of a white, male, healthy, able-bodied person and exposing them to continuous stress.[19] Forms of so-called minority stress occur for instance when a breastfeeding mother is expected to plan her day meticulously in order to navigate an environment that was not designed for her, spending time and energy that she could otherwise invest in, for example, her actual work.[20, 21] This issue also concerns the question of who feels legitimated to learn and work within these buildings (and thus in academia). In your view, to what extent does the very structure of buildings reaffirm who is entitled to study or work there, and who does "not belong"? And how do you deal with this in your chair?

GF: We already know that the hegemonic modes of production of urban space linked to the modern movement have delineated for decades the symbolic boundaries of permissiveness and exclusion in defining those who deserve to inhabit the public space in a city and those who do not. In *Bodies That Matter*,[22] philosopher Judith Butler introduces the concept of "abject bodies" and states that pointing out the abject is essential for the normative and normal scope to be established. Butler discusses how regulatory schemes produce not only the terrain of

intelligible bodies but also a domain of unthinkable, abject, unliveable bodies. When design contributes to building this "normality," it hides the privilege of some subjects and establishes marks of visibility in those bodies that escape the norm. That's how privilege works: privilege is invisible to those who have it.

In our teaching, we work on projects that question this "universal subject" that only represents the privileged. In addition to the interesting projects that students develop within the course, one of the things that gives me the most satisfaction is to see how students transfer this discourse to other courses and question the ways in which they are taught design, and, out of that, develop successful proposals that improve and complexify the ways we are designing.

dd: It seems that only a radical rethinking of these norms will enable us to open curricula to new forms of knowledge production.[23] In what ways can the incorporation of a gender studies perspective transform design curricula and enable us to revisit the dominant paradigms within design? And how do you in your chair apply these thoughts in practice?

GF: When starting the Chair of Design and Gender Studies at FADU,[24] I wanted to merge the practice of design with the debates already initiated a few decades ago in Argentina by gender studies scholars, discussing the ways of building knowledge in various

Design Struggles

19. Jane Darke, "Women, Architects and Feminism," in *Making Space: Women and the Man-Made Environment*, ed. Matrix (London: Pluto Press, 1984), 11–25.

20. Alison Kafer, *Feminist, Queer, Crip* (Bloomington, IN: Indiana University Press, 2013).

21. Katheryn H. Anthony, and Megan Dufersne, "Potty Parity in Perspective: Gender and Family Issues in Planning and Designing Public Restrooms," *Journal of Planning Literature* 21, no. 2 (2007), 267–94, doi.org/10.1177/0885412206295846.

22. Judith Butler, *Bodies That Matter: On the Discursive Limits of "Sex"* (New York, NY: Routledge, 1993).

23. Marilyn Jacoby Boxer, "Challenging the Traditional Curriculum," in *Women in American Higher Education: A Feminist Perspective*, ed. Becky Ropers-Huilman, Barbara Townsend, and Judith Glazer-Raymo (Needham Heights, MA: Ginn Press, 1998), 493.

24. The Chair of Design and Gender Studies at FADU-UBA was founded in 2017 and was the first chair of its kind in South America. Since its creation, over a thousand students have completed the program.

25. bell hooks, *Teaching to Transgress: Education as the Practice of Freedom* (New York, NY: Routledge, 1994).

Poster of support for the 2019 mass protests in Chile in the foyer of the FADU building. Photo: Maya Ober.

disciplines. This union of theory and practice[25] has scarcely been present, neither in teaching and practice nor in the historical accounts and discourses regarding the legitimation of architecture and design.

Integrating a gender lens into the skills-oriented field of design education allows us to establish adequate theoretical tools for, on the one hand, understanding the sociocultural formation of gender stereotypes, and on the other, developing situated and nonstandardized designs. This leads to a design process that considers social differences and structural inequalities.

What does it mean to design with a gender perspective? Does it mean designing spaces, products, and signs exclusively for women, as is often implied? Or is it rather concerned with reflecting the diversity that characterizes society, in all its complexities and circumstances, to generate proposals for greater inclusion and emancipation?

At the Chair of Design and Gender Studies we also use a feminist perspective to transcend disciplinary divisions. This is why we work as a multidisciplinary group of teachers (sociologists, architects, artists, industrial and graphic designers, etc.), and also practice what we call the "open door" class to which we invite guests, including specialists in cultural and gender studies.

It is our policy to promote the participation of specialists, researchers, and invited lecturers so that they can present the topics in which they specialize and that are part of the curriculum. On the other hand, this "open-door" approach also means intervening in the space outside the classroom, to reclaim public space by defining what it is and who has access to it. Our work does not end within the assigned classroom; on the contrary, it invades other spaces in the university building. This implies admitting that depending on the context in which we find ourselves as students or teachers, our privileges may or may not be valid and validated.

For example, my authority as a teacher is not the same within the class as in a student assembly in the hall. In the same way, my corporality feels comfortable in class but not when I walk through the campus at night to take the bus. It is important not to essentialize discomfort only in

bodies that do not conform to generic regulations. We all feel at some point that discomfort, and the "pedagogy of discomfort" that we encourage is precisely to sensitize the community that what some people feel only at one time of day, others feel at all times in university life. In that sense, design from this perspective participates in the deconstruction of an essentialist thought and invites us to look from different perspectives at the objects of everyday life, our bodies, and the spaces in which we move. We aim to create a temporary experience of discomfort in order to explore how the embodied "Otherness" is mobile and located.

dd: To see the world through the perspective of someone who is

The mural reflecting on lived experiences of gender violence, created in a performative way by 200 students and lecturers of the FADU together with Onaire Graphic Collective.

26. Sandra Harding, "Feminist Standpoints," in *The Handbook of Feminist Research*.

27. Onaire is an Argentinian graphic design collective formed by five designers, Mariana Campo Lagorio, Gabriel M. Lopatín, Gabriel Mahia, Sebastián Puy, and Natalia Volpe. The group has developed a working method called "graphic stew," which serves as a tool for their collective work. This method encourages the participation of all members and subsumes in a single composition the views of each of them, thus transcending individual expression to achieve a collective statement.

28. Between 1976 and 1983, the most sinister military dictatorship in history took place in Argentina. A brief description of this epoch inevitably involves looting, abductions, torture, and disappearances – "a word that has made us tragically famous in the civilized world" (the National Commission on the Disappearance of Persons [CONADEP], 1983). A search and campaign for the disappeared people organized by the Madres y Abuelas de Plaza de Mayo (the Mothers of the Plaza de Mayo), who demonstrated in front of Government House to demand information on the whereabouts of their children. Thus the associations Mothers of Plaza de Mayo and Grandmothers of Plaza de Mayo were created during the dictatorship. Still today they meet every Thursday on the plaza and demand memory, truth, and justice. The persistent presence of these women for more than forty years in public space is undoubtedly an example and unavoidable reference for today's feminist movements.

rendered "different" and thus excluded for reasons of gender, skin color, and/or (dis)ability, to name but a few, and therefore experiences discrimination and oppression, can have the power to challenge one's worldview.[26] And of course, as a member of a marginalized group, reclaiming public space can have an emancipatory effect as well as a transformative one. What can this process look like? And where can it lead to?

GF: This process of *unlearning* can take the form of reclaiming space through a collective design act informed by students' perspectives and positionalities. For example, there were a few photographs of modernist designs hanging at the main entrance to our faculty, the major artery of this part of the campus, with thousands of students passing each day. Our chair teamed up with Onaire Graphic Collective[27] to initiate a performative creation of a mural in order to reclaim the space in which we learn and work on a daily basis. Around two-hundred students and lecturers participated in this physical and at the same time symbolic creation. The Onaire Collective proposed that we generate a "great graphic stew" – a term that tries to think in a more autochthonous way than the much-discussed French "collage." During two intense days of work, reflection, and learning, a graphic stew on gender violence and discrimination based on sexual orientation was created. The participants used their own perspectives, reflected on gender-based violence, and reclaimed the space and agency to decide about the visual language of the campus. In doing so, they covered the modernist works. In the context of a university policy of expanding rights, this large mural is now on the wall of the main entrance of the faculty and establishes a performative dialogue with another mural dedicated to the students and teachers who disappeared during the last military dictatorship in Argentina (from 1976 to 1983). We find these performative and conversational aspects very striking, since, in Latin America, there have always been historical links between academic feminism and political struggles. In Argentina, the case of the Madres y Abuelas de Plaza de Mayo is a good example of the political role of women in public space.[28] There are many

Griselda Flesler,
Anja Neidhardt and Maya Ober /
depatriarchise design

studies from feminist perspectives on the resignification of the public space, which implied, and still implies, the struggle of these women in the search for memory, truth, and justice.

dd: The lived experiences of oppressed people play a crucial role when it comes to feminist knowledge-building[29] and can form a useful reference for design. In the case of the collaborative mural creation, each person brought in their own experience and knowledge. To what extent do you think this can be seen as an act of collaborative knowledge-building? And could we argue that, by involving design and visual expression, a new or alternative method, other than solely writing, is being put to use?

GF: Certainly the creation of the collaborative mural was an act of collaborative knowledge-building, because for two days we exchanged points of view about very complex concepts such as identity, symbolic violence, and gender. It was necessary to discuss the approach in order to decide what we wanted to highlight in a mural within the privileged context of a university (since it is not a mural for public roads). Many of these responses arose at the time of assembling the individual pieces in the overall design, in the decisions that were taken together to arrange the final design. I think that, as Austin puts it,[30] language is performative and that the act of designing is performative in itself and is therefore

Pictures of the disappeared and killed students and members of the faculty during the last military dictatorship (1976–1983) in Argentina. Photo: Maya Ober.

29. Hesse-Biber, *The Handbook of Feminist Research*; Kamarack Minnich, *Transforming Knowledge*.

30. J. L. Austin, "Lecture IX," in *How to Do Things with Words* (London: Oxford University Press, 1962), 108–19.

31. bell hooks, *Teaching Community: A Pedagogy of Hope* (New York, NY: Routledge, 2003).

32. Paulo Freire, *Pedagogy of the Oppressed* (New York, NY: Seabury Press, 1968), 44–60.

33. Freire, 60–98.

34. Freire, 61.

35. Rafael Blanco, *Escenas militantes: Lenguajes, identidades políticas y nuevas agendas del activismo estudiantil universitario* (Buenos Aires: Clacso, 2017), 11.

an excellent methodological tool. We are not the same and we do not think the same after that wonderful meeting of designers, and nor is the faculty the same. Although I don't think design will change the world, it is a visibility tool and can be disturbing, in the sense of mobilizing the status quo. On the other hand it is attractive for the youngest and this cannot be overlooked if we want to legitimize the extension of rights from the base and not by imposing them.

dd: The conversational aspect of this project is also very interesting, especially since there seems to be a huge lack of conversation within hierarchical spaces. There is always the danger of a classroom becoming a space of domination, not only between teacher and student but also among students themselves.[31] Discrimination, harassment, and assault make schools and universities unsafe spaces. Philosopher Michel Foucault says that power circulates, and Paulo Freire speaks of a narrative of the traditional student-teacher relationship.[32] The question is, how can we break this cycle or narrative? How can we avoid the reproduction of domination in our educational practices? And how can we create more horizontal relationships based on dialogue and love as Freire suggests?[33]

GF: We have to facilitate dialogue by reclaiming the right to speak, so that we can achieve what Freire proposes. The University of Buenos Aires is public, free, and based on a cogoverning system, which means professors, graduates, and students take part in the main decision-making processes, hence they can equally participate in "the united reflection and action."[34] The student body is politically active, which creates interesting tensions and exchanges within the academic dynamics. According to social scientist Rafael Blanco, "the political is constitutive of the student experience in the public university, both for those who are more or less continuously engaged in an organization and for those who participate sporadically or not at all."[35] Blanco also sustains that the intimate and ordinary problems have impacted and redefined both the political agenda of the student organizations and the forms of politicization of university actors. Within this context, spaces are resignified (for example an all-gender bathroom on our campus) as well as the very content of what is taught. And once these doors are open, one can not close them again. Even though changes are at times slow, the debate culture is vivid and present within the university. Therefore, I find it interesting to think of design as a tool for those changes. I like to believe that

Griselda Flesler,
Anja Neidhardt and Maya Ober /
depatriarchise design

we have the possibility to redefine the university space.

dd: This is a powerful thought, especially since buildings like those of universities actively participate in the construction of our own sexual subjectivity. Since our experiences as students or educators within the campus are directly connected with our body and the bodies of others existing within the same space, the meaning of the space crosses through our subjectivity and our experiences. Design often participates in the policing of our sexual subjectivity and gender identity, reinforcing the binary. This is definitely the case with bathrooms. Studies reveal that conventional public toilet design, for instance, creates dangerous spaces for transgender and gender-nonconforming people.[36] You mentioned the all-gender bathroom on your campus that challenges the status quo of male-female restrooms in your university. How did this bathroom come into being and what role did a gender studies and design perspective play in it?

GF: In order to create conditions in which students feel belonging, we proposed in 2017 to the university government the creation of an all-gender bathroom, rejecting certain universalist and essentialist conceptions about identity and gender. For the past years, the gender narrative has been growing as part of activist agendas by students, increasing the number of demands directed at the

36. Jody L. Herman, "Gendered Restrooms and Minority Stress: The Public Regulation of Gender and Its Impact on Transgender People's Lives," *Journal of Public Management and Social Policy* 19, no. 1 (2013), 65–80.

37. Marissa Renee Campos, *Queering Architecture: Appropriating Space and Process* (master's thesis, School of Architecture and Interior Design at the College of Design, Architecture, Art, and Planning, Cincinnati, 2017), 85–96.

All-gender toilet sign designed by the students of the Chair of Design and Gender Studies. Photo: Maya Ober.

Design Struggles

university authorities.

Within this process, design can be an efficient tool to create a graphic identity signage that reaffirms a political position. However, at the same time design can reproduce the fantasy that visual identities can be homogeneously and statically defined, answering the needs of rigidly determined "target groups" and promising their functionality and effectiveness. Designing the signage of the all-gender bathroom was, therefore, a challenge, since the objective was to escape from the stereotyped and binary typologies of the traditional pictographic systems. Here the queering approach was helpful, moving beyond the static understanding of signage towards a fluid and digital one.

As a response to the creation of the bathroom, an interesting phenomenon happened: the walls of the newly reclaimed space got covered with "Thank you" graffiti. Usually used to express discontent, graffiti here became an affirmation of the space.

dd: So, the queering approach in design thanks to its fluidity allows us as designers to operate outside of restrictive binaries.[37] Therefore it directly influences the design process, shifting it from the traditional, static one, confined by a specific set of norms and parameters, to a fluid, hybrid one, enabling flexibility and multiple readings. This happened in the case of the bathroom signage, which is an animation and moves beyond traditional static infographics.

GF: Exactly. This approach enables us not only to deal with women and their production, but allows us to think about the conditions surrounding the development of projects and how the design of objects and spaces functions as a signifier process. Studying the fall of the old polarities in which Western culture used to oscillate – active/passive, inside/outside, master/slave, true/false, animate/inanimate, man/woman, among many others – allows us to rethink the way we design. Rejecting static categories enabled the students to create this infographic that defies accepted design norms and challenges the universalist paradigm of design.

dd: How does the fact that your university is public and free influence the transformation of the curricula and commitment to social justice?

GF: It implies that the whole society supports through taxes the structure of the public university. This means that there is a strong commitment from the entire academic community to contemporary social problems, and also that relations with spaces and movements outside of academia are constantly promoted.

Within this structure, we have developed a project based on some local and national laws that challenge us from a gender perspective. Approximately two hundred twenty students participate in this class. For the final project, they work in interdisciplinary groups of five (from different departments: architecture, graphic design, industrial design, fashion, and cinema).

dd: What are the laws that you work with?

GF: We work with the following laws:
1. Protocol of Institutional Action for the Prevention and Intervention in Situations of Violence or Gender Discrimination or Sexual Orientation (Resol. CD no. 4043/2015) established for the entire University of Buenos Aires.[38]
2. Comprehensive Protection Law to Prevent, Punish, and Eradicate Violence against Women in the Areas Where They Develop Their Interpersonal Relationships (Law 26,485).
3. Humanized Childbirth Law (Law 25,929).
4. Law of Existence of Sizes (Law 3,300).
5. Law of Promotion and Public Awareness on Breastfeeding (Law 26,873).
6. Gender Identity Law (Law 26,743).
7. Comprehensive and Inclusive Sex Education (Law 26,150).

Starting from the problematics of these laws and taking into account the thematic axes of the course (feminist critique of universalism, fallacy of neutrality, collaborative design, new paradigm of identity as narration and not as essence, critique of heteronormativity, queer approach, and criticism of the binarisms of modernism), a design project is developed.

dd: How did the students develop designs starting from these laws? Can you give us some examples of what was created in this course?

GF: One group of students, for instance, created Mobiliarie, a furniture system for schools that looks at different corporalities and dynamics within the classroom. Framed in the Law of Comprehensive Sexual Education, this project breaks with the classic hierarchical setup of traditional pedagogy. By delving into the micro-scenario of the daily life of the classroom, the students decided to create furniture of various sizes and materials and to configure elements that accept different bodies, activities, dynamics, and uses. The outcome is meant to be diverse, nomadic, and undetermined, and it does not consolidate the rigid and static furniture found in traditional classrooms. Students and teachers are not restricted by the furniture through homogenizing and disciplinary design. They can actually design and redesign the furniture on their own and according to the spatiotemporal grids of their activity, depending on the remodeling of learning situations, experiences, processes, and itineraries. With the help of these furniture elements, the bodies, which are in constant transformation, are going to develop a design that responds to their needs at that specific moment. From there arises the importance of having different morphologies and elements available for use. This shows the significance of the pupils' participation

Design Struggles

38. In Argentina, theorizing about violence from the perspective of the different contexts where it occurs had a growing proliferation at the national level that led to reflection in public universities for the design of specific institutional instruments for this space. The University of Buenos Aires was no stranger to this general scenario and in 2015 ts higher council approved the protocol.

39. Donna Haraway, "A Cyborg Manifesto: Science, Technology, and Socialist-Feminism in the Late Twentieth Century," in *Simians, Cyborgs and Women: The Reinvention of Nature* (New York, NY: Routledge, 1991), 149–81.

in the combination of the different modules arranged from the exploration of objects in the classroom.

dd: So, the students approach projects by questioning the "universal norms" of design and using abject bodies as their starting point. How does it reoccur in other projects developed in this class?

GF: Yes, indeed. There is also, for example, Regulate, a fragmented adjustable dummy (mannequin) made from a thermoformed cardboard structure covered with knitted fabric. Through a one-inch pipe system with plastic screws it allows each fragmented area – waist, hips, shoulders, chest, and abdomen – to be adjusted to the desired size and to also generate volume. This project departs from considering that communications technologies and biotechnologies are the decisive tools for giving new utilities to our bodies.[39] So, by designing a new tool the students created alternative criteria for apparel design. This design can be seen as a proposal towards the rupture of hegemonic and universalist models used in fashion

design schools. Generally, the tools used in fashion design education, such as the mannequin or the figurine, perpetuate the hegemony of certain bodies and also construct the students' perception of themselves, who often do not fit their own figurine and do not have access to tools with alternative measurements. Starting from the basic structure of the dummy, the possibility arises that it can be modified to alternate measurements in the width and height of the body, and with the option of regulating its volumes as well.

dd: But it is not only about questioning the norms in order to prevent the reproduction of symbolic violence towards "other" bodies. Some of the projects tackle such phenomena as obstetric violence.

GF: Yes, here I would like to mention Intimanta, a project made in the context of the Humanised Childbirth Law that seeks to enable self-managed parenthood. It accompanies the pregnant person and their baby during pregnancy, childbirth, and postpartum, providing assistance and intimacy to both of them, ensuring that they are the protagonists of the birth – something that often does not happen. The blanket is an intelligent object and in constant relationship with the pregnant body and the baby. During pregnancy, it allows the skin barriers to be transcended, achieving independence from an ultrasound, and allowing constant monitoring. In childbirth, it will mediate ensuring the atmosphere that the pregnant person desires for that moment, giving the possibility of playing music, regulating the temperature, adapting to their privacy. At the last stage, it will be used to wrap and contain the baby, intermediating the relationship between the parent and the child. In this way, it is present in the three stages as a means for the intimate relationship between the two, giving shelter, assistance, and monitoring, merging the two bodies, ensuring their bonding and comfort. The parent-baby blanket is an intelligent, hybrid element that enables the dissolution of the borders between one and the other, merging into a large organism in which technology mediates.

dd: As educators and feminists, we strive to bring feminist thoughts and approaches into our teaching, but we have to continue the process of questioning the structures and institutions within which we are working. Is it possible to change the university from within, and how? What educational practices informed by feminist thought could emerge?

GF: I think feminist pedagogies and strategies for teaching design change power relations. They make us reflect on how, from our place and subjectivity, we position ourselves hierarchically. In the game of hierarchies, I can be at a disadvantage as a woman in front of my male colleagues, but in class, I can use and abuse my position as a teacher with my students. We must ask ourselves

whether we are willing to discuss our own privileges, which are always situational and relative. Who is capable of putting their privileges at risk or denouncing them? Who is able to depart from the place that enables defining what "good" design is? From our perspective, we study the conditions of possibility that enable a discipline to be configured around certain valid signifiers. It tries to include new signifiers, to fight for the sense of design and its selective traditions. We ask what are the requirements, body shapes, practices, social, and material resources? They count as indicators of who is inside and who is outside the frameworks of "good design." What are the intelligibility frameworks from which we design?

DENOUNCE YOUR PRIVILEGE

Design Struggles

Bibliography

Abdulla, Danah. "Design Otherwise: Towards a Locally-centric Design Education Curricula in Jordan" (Ph.D. diss., Goldsmiths, University of London, 2018).

Anthony, Katheryn H., and Megan Dufersne. "Potty Parity in Perspective: Gender and Family Issues in Planning and Designing Public Restrooms." *Journal of Planning Literature* 21, no. 3 (2007), 267–94.

Austin, John Langshaw. "Lecture IX." In *How to Do Things with Words* (London: Oxford University Press, 1962), 108–19.

Blanco, Rafael. *Universidades íntimas y sexualidades públicas: La gestión de la identidad en la experiencia estudiantil.* Buenos Aires: Miño y Dávila, 2014,
—. *Escenas militantes: Lenguajes, identidades políticas y nuevas agendas del activismo estudiantil universitario* (Buenos Aires: Grupo Editor Universitario/CLACSO, 2017).

Bourdieu, Pierre. "La escuela como fuerza conservadora: Desigualdades escolares y culturales." In *La nueva sociología de la educación.* Prepared by Patricia De Leonardo (México: Ediciones El Caballito, 1986), 103–29.
—. *Las reglas del arte.* Barcelona: Anagrama, 1995.

Boxer, Marilyn Jacoby Boxer. "Challenging the Traditional Curriculum." *Women in American Higher Education: A Feminist Perspective.* Edited by Becky Ropers-Huilman, Barbara Townsend, and Judith Glazer-Raymo, 493. Needham Heighs, MA: Ginn Press, 2000.
Butler, Judith. *Bodies That Matter: On the Discursive Limits of "Sex."* New York, NY: Routledge, 1993.

Campos, Marissa Renee. *Queering Architecture: Appropriating Space and Process.* MA thesis, School of Architecture and Interior Design of the College of Design, Architecture, Art and Planning, Cincinnati, 2017.

CONADEP "Nunca más, informe final de la Comisión Nacional sobre la Desaparición de Personas." Buenos Aires: Eudeba, 1983.

Crenshaw, Kimberlé W. "Mapping the Margins: Intersectionality, Identity Politics, and Violence against Women of Color." *Stanford Law Review* 43, no. 6 (1991), 1241–99.

Devalle, Verónica. *La travesía de la forma: Emergencia y consolidación del Diseño Gráfico (1948–1984).* Buenos Aires: Paidós, 2009.

Elizalde, Silvia. "Hijas, hermanas, nietas: Genealogías políticas en el activismo de género de las jóvenes." *Revista Ensambles en sociedad, política y cultura* 4, no. 8 (2019), 86–93.

Freire, Paulo. "Pedagogy of the Oppressed." London: Penguin Books, 1968.

Flesler, Griselda. "Nueva Visión (1951–1957): Volver a ver." *tipoGráfica* no. 59 (2004), 44, 45.
—. "Queering fadu: Perspectivas de género para desbordar las disciplinas de diseño." In *Actas de las XXXII Jornadas de Investigación XIV Encuentro Regional.* Buenos Aires: FADU-UBA, 2019.
—, Valéria Durán, and Gabriela Gugliottella. "Inclusión de la perspectiva de género en el campo proyectual." *Ciencia, Técnica y Mainstreaming Social* 2 (2018), 43–51.

Haraway, Donna. "A Cyborg Manifesto: Science, Technology, and Socialist-Feminism in the Late Twentieth Century." In *Simians, Cyborgs and Women: The Reinvention of Nature.* New York, NY: Routledge, 1991, 149–81.

Harding, Sandra. "Feminist Standpoints." In *The Handbook of Feminist Research: Theory and Praxis.* Edited by Charlene Nagy Hesse-Biber, 46–64. Thousand Oaks: Sage Publications, 2012.

Herman, Jody L. "Gendered Restrooms and Minority Stress: The Public Regulation of Gender and Its Impact on Transgender People's Lives." *Journal of Public Management & Social Policy* 19, no. 1 (2013), 65–80.

Hesse-Biber, Sharlene Nagy, ed. *The Handbook of Feminist Research: Theory and Praxis.* Thousand Oaks: Sage Publications, 2012.

hooks, bell. *Teaching to Transgress: Education as the Practice of Freedom.* New York: Routledge, 1994.

Lefebvre, Henri. "La producción del espacio." Madrid: Capitán, 1974.

Massey, Doreen. *Space, Place, and Gender.* Minneapolis, MN: University of Minnesota Press, 1994.

Kafer, Alice. *Feminist, Queer, Crip.* Bloomington: Indiana University Press, 2013.

Kamarck Minnich, Elizabeth. *Transforming Knowledge.* Temple University Press, Philadelphia, 1990.

Matrix, *Making Space: Women and the Man-Made Environment.* London: Pluto Press, 1984.

Perazzo, Nelly. *El arte concreto en la Argentina en la década del 40.* Buenos Aires: Gaglianone, 1983.

Scott, Joan. "El género: Una categoría útil para el análisis histórico." In *Sexualidad, género y roles sexuales.* Edited by Marysa Navarro and Catharine R. Stimpson, 37–75. Buenos Aires: FCE, 1999.

Griselda Flesler,
Anja Neidhardt and Maya Ober /
depatriarchise design

DISCIPLINARY DISOBEDIENCE
A Border-Thinking Approach to Design

Danah Abdulla

1. In this chapter, my definition of border-thinking draws on both the works of Gloria Anzaldúa and Walter Mignolo. Anzaldúa's concept of the borderlands is both spiritual (being and mind) and physical, where the border becomes a sort of redemptive space, whereas Mignolo defines it as a way of thinking about epistemic resources seeking transformation/dissolution as opposed to accommodation of both sides.

2. Gloria E. Anzaldúa, *Borderlands/La Frontera: The New Mestiza*, 4th ed. (San Francisco: Aunt Lute Books 2012), 7.

3. Anzaldúa, 7.

4. Anzaldúa, 7.

5. See, for example, Michael Bierut, *79 Short Essays on Design* (New York, NY: Princeton Architectural Press, 2007); Craig Bremner and Paul Rodgers, "Design Without Discipline," *Design Issues 29*, no. 3 (Summer 2013), 4–13, doi.org/10.1162/DESI; Nigel Cross, "Design Research: A Disciplined Conversation," *Design Issues* 15, no. 2 (Summer 1999), 5–10; Arturo Escobar, *Designs for the Pluriverse: Radical Interdependence, Autonomy, and the Making of Worlds* (Durham, NC: Duke University Press, 2018); Alain Findeli, "Rethinking Design Education for the 21st Century: Theoretical, Methodological, and Ethical Discussion," *Design Issues* 17, no. 1 (Winter 2001), 5–17; Daniel Friedman, *Radical Modernism* (New Haven, MA: Yale University Press, 1994); Terry Irwin, "Transition Design: A Proposal for a New Area of Design Practice, Study, and Research," *Design and Culture* 7, no. 2 (2015), 229–46, doi. org/10.1080/17547075.201 5.1051829; Eleni Kalantidou and Tony Fry, eds., *Design in the Borderlands* (Abingdon,

Introduction

Designers often live, to borrow a term from Gloria Anzaldúa,[1] within the borderlands. "Living in the borderlands," as she writes, "produces knowledge by being within a system while also retaining the knowledge of an outsider who comes from outside the system."[2]

Possessing an "'outsider within' status"[3] means designers stand at one end of a discipline and tackle problems overlooking others. In this process, however, designers realize they are not accepted by either. We exclude and include, we reject and we accept, and we struggle while negotiating. "The basic concept," argues Anzaldúa, "involves the ability to hold multiple social perspectives while simultaneously maintaining a center that revolves around fighting against concrete material forms of oppression."[4] This oppression in design, I would argue, are the borders of specialization.

Expanding design to encompass theories and practices from other disciplines has long been debated.[5] However, most of these discussions revolve around incorporating different methodologies and practices from other disciplines, or developing another "-disciplinarity" in design, rather than eroding the borders between different specializations within design. Specifically, while Bremner and Rodgers[6] describe design moving away from disciplines and into issue- and project-based work, there is no discussion of the *how*, *what*, and *where* we think in design.[7] In this chapter, I propose the decolonial concept of border-thinking *within* design as a method of disciplinary disobedience for moving design towards more collective approaches.

Borders Imposed by Disciplinary Decadence

Borders indicate divisions; they "define the places that are safe and unsafe, to distinguish *us* from *them*."[8] Design specializations are narrow borders. Designers, I would argue, inhabit what Anzaldúa refers to as the borderland, "a vague and undetermined place created by the emotional residue of an unnatural boundary. It is in a constant state of transition."[9] Those who inhabit it "cross over, pass over, or go through the confines of the 'normal.'"[10]

> Consider this scenario, all too familiar to designers:
>
> What do you do?
> I'm a designer.
> What kind? Graphic? Fashion? Furniture? Interior?

Replying only with *design* means a designer is pressed for more details. For many, the question induces the same anxiety as the seemingly innocent question *Where are you from?*, where "the questioning, the interrogation, can stop only when you have explained yourself."[11]

Through our responses, we end up choosing containment.[12] But why are we afraid of crossing borders? These are predefined concepts that we think are unquestionable, and we leave them unchallenged. We are afraid of challenging them when our roles demand that we do.

The term "discipline" has many meanings referring to forms of control and punishment.[13] In academia, the term refers to the organization of knowledge into departments. As Lewis Gordon states, "disciplines, in this sense, become epistemological or knowledge-producing models that offer proven ways under the imposition of which reality … sighs."[14] The designations of theology, law, and medicine

Oxon: Earthscan, 2014); Adam Richardson, "The Death of the Designer," *Design Issues* 9, no. 2 (Autumn 1993), 34–43; Paul A. Rodgers and Craig Bremner, "The Concept of the Design Discipline," *Dialectic* 1, no. 1 (Winter 2017), doi.org/10.3998/dialectic.14932326.0001.104; Anne-Marie Willis, "Transition Design: The Need to Refuse Discipline and Transcend Instrumentalism," *Design Philosophy Papers* 13, no. 1 (2015), 69–74.

6. Rodgers and Bremner, "The Concept of the Design Discipline."

7. Walter D. Mignolo, "Geopolitics of Sensing and Knowing: On (De)Coloniality, Border Thinking and Epistemic Disobedience," *Postcolonial Studies* 14, no. 3 (2011), 273–83, doi.org/10.1080/13688790.2011.613105.

8. Anzaldúa, *Borderlands/La Frontera*, 25 (italics in original).

9. Anzaldúa, 25 (italics in original).

10. Anzaldúa, 25.

11. Sara Ahmed, *Living a Feminist Life* (Durham, NC: Duke University Press, 2017), 116.

12. I use the term "we" to refer to designers, and include myself in this category. Moreover, I am conscious of universalising the term "designers" and the design experience, acknowledging that design is taught and learned differently across the world. In this chapter, I speak from my experience learning from and teaching in a Western design context.

13. Michel Foucault, *L'Archéologie du savoir* (Paris: Gallimard, 1969); Michel Foucault, *Surveiller et punir: Naissance de la prison* (Paris: Gallimard, 1975); Lewis R. Gordon, *Disciplinary Decadence: Living Thought in Trying Times* (Boulder, CO: Paradigm Publishers, 2006); David R. Shumway and Ellen Messer-Davidow, "Disciplinarity: An Introduction," *Poetics Today* 12, no. 2 (Summer 1991), 201–25, doi.org/10.2307/1772850.

14. Gordon, *Disciplinary Decadence*, 3.

15. Julie Klein, *Interdisciplinarity: History, Theory, and Practice* (Detroit, MI: Wayne State University Press, 1990).

16. Armin Krishnan, "What Are Academic Disciplines? Some Observations on the Disciplinarity vs. Interdisciplinarity Debate," working paper (ESRC National Centre for Research Methods, NCRM Working Paper Series, 2009), 32.

17. Takuo Hirano, "The Development of Modern Japanese Design: A Personal Account," *Design Issues* 7, no. 2 (Spring 1991), 54–62, doi.org/10.2307/1511407.

18. Rodgers and Bremner, "The Concept of the Design Discipline," 21.

19. Francisco Laranjo, "Continuous Rebranding: Interview with Angela Mitropoulos," *Modes of Criticism*, no. 3 (2017), 34.

20. Rodgers and Bremner, "The Concept of the Design Discipline," 22.

21. Lewis R. Gordon, "Disciplinary Decadence and the Decolonisation of Knowledge," *Africa Development* 39, no. 1 (2014), 86.

have their origin in the late Middle Ages whereas further specialization and a whole range of new disciplines were established in nineteenth- and twentieth-century Europe.[15] The divisions were pragmatic, allowing "disciplines to develop a stable identity and an agenda for research and further development."[16]

Abolishing disciplinary boundaries enables designers to adapt early to the new challenges facing both our field and the world.[17] While design is beginning to "expan[d] its disciplinary, conceptual, theoretical, and methodological frameworks to encompass ever-wider disciplines, activities, and practice,"[18] the process is moving slowly. Moreover, when we borrow concepts from other disciplines, their appearance leads to a loss of "something that makes it possible to see the work those concepts do, or make us do when we use them."[19]

Design's encompassing of a wider range of disciplines produces new strands of design rather than a fundamental rethinking of how design specializations come together to address new challenges. As Bremner and Rodgers state:

> The edges between product design and service design … continue to be increasingly fuzzy. Mobile phone companies now offer more than a mere physical artefact (i.e. a phone), rather, they now regularly offer users the opportunities to subscribe to their services comprised of music and video downloads, among many others.[20]

We have forgotten the segregation that exists within our own discipline and have fallen into what Lewis Gordon refers to as "disciplinary decadence":

> the phenomenon of turning away from living thought, which engages reality and recognises its own limitations, to a deontologised or absolute conception of disciplinary life. The discipline becomes, in solipsistic fashion, the world. And in that world, the main concern is the proper administering of its rules, regulations, or, as Frantz Fanon argued, (self-devouring) methods.[21]

For Gordon, disciplinary decadence means treating a discipline as something that has always existed and is eternal. This eternalizing of a discipline leaves "no room for other disciplinary perspectives, the result of which is the rejection of them for not being one's own."[22]

An example of disciplinary decadence in design is all the forms that exist (listed in the image below).

These forms of design indicate that design is "los[ing] sight of itself" and "asserting [itself] *as the world*."[23]

Indeed, if we continue to pursue this decadence, we reach the conclusion that we must have a strand of design for anything that we come up with. Take the example of the call to decolonize design. Within design discourse, this is often interpreted as a proposal for yet another strand of design called "decolonial design." However, this proposition reduces the idea to additive changes rather than an ontological goal. But the inclusion of "a greater diversity of actors or perspectives" is not sufficient, as "this only goes to serve a delaying and offsetting demands for radical systemic change."[24]

Approaching design ontologically, as decolonial thinker Arturo Escobar writes, "destabilizes its comfortable niche within naturalized modern orders, demands a recentering of design education in order to bring it fully into the critical social theory space."[25] In other words, we must practice our disciplines differently. To tweak the words of

22. Gordon, *Disciplinary Decadence*, 5.

23. Gordon, *Disciplinary Decadence*, 8 (italics in original).

24. Decolonising Design, "Editorial Statement," *Decolonising Design* (blog), June 27, 2016, www.decolonisingdesign.com/statements/2016/editorial/.

25. Escobar, *Designs for the Pluriverse*, 50.

Graphic & Fashion & Interior & Product & Industrial & Furniture & 3D & Spatial & Surface & UX/UI & Interaction & Human-centred & Service & Design Innovation & Critical & Speculative & Inclusive & Participatory & Co-Design & Transition & Information & Design Fiction & Environmental & Sustainable & Design Engineering & Digital & Web & Animation & Social & Transdisciplinary & Games & Jewellery & Textile & Design Management & Ceramic & Urban & Disability...

26. Zoe Todd, "An Indigenous Feminist's Take on the Ontological Turn: 'Ontology' Is Just Another Word for Colonialism," *Journal of Historical Sociology* 29, no. 1 (March 2016), 8, doi.org/10.1111/johs.12124.

27. Tim Seitz, "The 'Design Thinking' Delusion," trans. Adam Baltner, *Jacobin*, October 16, 2018, https://jacobinmag.com/2018/10/design-thinking-innovation-consulting-politics.

28. C. West Churchman, "Guest Editorial: Wicked Problems," *Management Science* 14, no. 4 (December 1967), B141–42.

29. Nigel Cross, "Designerly Ways of Knowing," Design Studies 3, no. 4 (1982), 221–27.

30. Design Council, "Designing a Future Economy" (London: Design Council, 2018), 29, www.designcouncil.org.uk/resources/report/designing-future-economy-report.

Zoe Todd, they continue to be practiced in "ways that erase Indigenous bodies within our lecture halls, [and] we unconsciously avoid engaging with contemporary Indigenous scholars and thinkers while we engage instead with [sixty-year-old] texts [and ideas] or two-hundred-year-old philosophical tomes."[26]

We deny space for alternatives, for thinking of possibilities. To destabilize and disrupt requires not just integrating relevant methods and practices from other disciplines into design, but the step that comes before: eroding these different fields of design to imagine design anew. Otherwise, as the adoption of "design thinking" as a corporate management tool has shown, it is merely a simplistic and superficial adoption of methods and practices from other disciplines, making it seem as if complex problems and challenges were easily solvable and manageable – "saving the world the easy way."[27]

Redefinition – Skills of the Future

Design education trains us to deal with ill-formulated and confusing "wicked problems."[28] Nothing is ever certain, and designers are not taught to discover the rule but to try out different solutions.[29] For designers to try out different solutions – to tackle ill-defined twenty-first-century problems – requires new knowledge and a new set of skills. A Design Council report on "Designing a Future Economy" highlights the following as required skills and knowledge for the future of the design industry:

> – design (techniques, tools, and principles)
> – operations analysis
> – programming
> – drafting
> – engineering and technology
> – fine arts
> – technology design
> – building and construction
> – computers and electronics
> – geography
> – visualization[30]

Since design "is no longer confined to particular sectors or occupations,"[31] the report calls on the field to deliver twenty-first-century skills for tomorrow's companies and organizations – designers with exposure beyond their individual specialisms, working in interdisciplinary teams where they "are comfortable deploying their innate creativity and flexibility."[32]

As argued earlier, design's decadence is making any skill or approach a "strand" of design rather than viewing design as fluid and evolving.[33] If design is to deal with complex, ill-defined problems, why do we continue to think of it in such rigid terms? In its current structure, design education cannot begin to teach future designers these skills. In addition, the Design Council report states that developing design skills is underresourced:

> Designers require more expensive training, but receive it less often. The most critical barriers to training identified by firms are a lack of money available to fund training, training not being considered a priority and a lack of time for management to plan and organise training. Given there is also a narrowing pipeline of designers coming through the formal education system, further action is required from employers to avoid the UK experiencing a skills crisis in one of the most productive and valuable parts of the economy.[34]

However, the report does not clarify whether it is the training after school or the training within school that needs adjusting. Under the heading "Understanding Educational Pathways," the report states that

> our analysis examined the range of degree subjects that were taken by people working in the sector. Employers in design skills-intensive industries are more likely to complain that the people they recruit from Higher Education lack the required skills and competencies, and there appears to be scope to improve the relevance of university qualifications.[35]

31. Design Council, 5.

32. Design Council, 26.

33. Rodgers and Bremner, "The Concept of the Design Discipline."

34. Design Council, "Designing a Future Economy," 10.

35. Design Council, 65.

FRINGES

Design Struggles

36. Design Council, 5.

37. Escobar, *Designs for the Pluriverse.*

38. Escobar, 34–35.

39. Sara Ahmed, "White Men," *Feministkilljoys* (blog), November 4, 2014, feministkilljoys. com/2014/11/04/white-men/; Todd, "An Indigenous Feminist's Take On The Ontological Turn."

The report warns of the impact of underinvesting in these future skills, "and the need to better prepare for the economic, technological and political changes ahead."[36] While designers cannot be taught everything they need to know in university, the report makes a strong case for design programs to revise what they are teaching. These changes must go beyond the cosmetic.

With designers looking to respond to the planetary crisis, to become more sensitive to their environment, and to understand the impact of their work on both human and nonhuman actors, they are beginning to shift their concerns towards serving society rather than solving problems for industry.[37] As Arturo Escobar states, "new methods highlight front-end research, with the designer as facilitator and mediator more than expert; conceive of design as eminently user-centered, participatory, collaborative, and radically contextual."[38]

However, I would argue that we give these new methods too much credit. Designers may indeed be interested in these ideas and methods, but how are they enacted in practice? Design remains industry-focused, with an emphasis on incorporating content as a patchwork onto the existing structure rather than changing the terms of the conversation, i.e., it remains within the models of Western modernity. Despite the growing list of skills that require a move away from specialization, few programs within design education teach design in broader terms. Worse, design's focus on social awareness is often shallow and devoid of any real politics. The growing number of designers interested in moving away from consumerism and towards the "social" realm are mostly not equipped with the right tools and methods to address the problems they are tackling.

Design skills and the design canon have not received enough scrutiny or reexamination; rather, we are all about "tradition as authority" – design can change slightly but within disciplinary dictates. The recent integration of underrepresented designers into the reading lists remains within the same structure: the celebration of the individual. Redefining design brings with it new reference points, new texts, and new ideas – ideas and references that do not reproduce citation.[39] In addition, it should acknowledge the intellectual labor of thinkers and activists who have been ignored in favor of what Zoe Todd calls "the rock-stars of Euro-Western thought."[40] This is what it means to inhabit the borderlands: "thinking from the outside, using alternative knowledge traditions and alternative languages of expression."[41]

This becomes a "curricular action that challenges the dominant structure[s] of education,"[42] not to replace them, as they "will continue to exist and … will remain viable as spaces of, and for, critique,"[43] but to enable engagement with other epistemologies, knowledges, and understandings.[44]

A discipline is not eternal, it cannot outlive its purpose. Every discipline "faces the problem of having to exceed the scope of its object of inquiry."[45] Sometimes there are problems and questions that design cannot address on its own, "in spite of disciplinary dictates."[46]

Knowing One Another

Designers are masters of what Albert Rothenberg calls "Janusian thinking," an idea drawn from Janus, the Roman god with two faces.[47] Janus "look[s] and apprehend[s] in opposite directions" inside and outside.[48] Janusian thinking is "the capacity to conceive and utilize two or more opposite or contradictory ideas, concepts, or images simultaneously."[49] A swirl of opposites and contradictory ideas filling the mind creates possibilities for new points of view. In more designerly terms, it is the ability to observe details, coincidences, and rhythms that others "fail to notice."[50]

This is a characteristic shared by all design disciplines – *designerly ways of thinking and knowing*.[51] The question is, how much do graphic designers know about product design and vice versa? How much do we know about spatial/interior designers or fashion designers? From my experience as a graphic designer teaching in an industrial and product design program, and from speaking to academics and practitioners, I've realized how little designers know about design overall, and the discomfort they feel stepping into what they deem "unfamiliar." Yet we all share similar processes, ways of thinking, and ways of gathering design knowledge (through people, processes,

40. Todd, 8.

41. Lucy Mayblin, "Border Thinking," *Global Social Theory* (blog), n.d., globalsocialtheory. org/concepts/border-thinking/

42. Ira Shor, *Empowering Education: Critical Teaching for Social Change* (Chicago, IL: The University of Chicago Press, 1992), 188.

43. Arturo Escobar, "Worlds and Knowledges Otherwise," *Cultural Studies* 21, nos. 2–3 (2007), 187, doi.org/ 10.1080/0950238 0601162506.

44. Walter D. Mignolo, "DELINKING: The Rhetoric of Modernity, the Logic of Coloniality, and the Grammar of De-Coloniality," *Cultural Studies* 21, nos. 2–3 (2007), 449–514 doi.org/10.1080/09502380 601162647.

45. Gordon, "Disciplinary Decadence and the Decolonisation of Knowledge," 86.

46. Gordon, 44.

47. Albert Rothenberg, "The Process of Janusian Thinking in Creativity," *Archives of General Psychiatry* 24, no. 3 (1971), 195–205, doi.org/10.1001/ archpsyc.1971. 01750090001001.

48. Rothenberg, 196.

49. Rothenberg, 196.

50. Nigel Cross, *Design Thinking: Understanding How Designers Think and Work* (Oxford: Berg, 2011), 13.

51. I am referring to the values and aspects discussed by Nigel Cross, see Cross, "Design Research: A Disciplined Conversation" and "Designerly Ways of Knowing."

52. Cross, "Design Research: A Disciplined Conversation."

53. László Moholy-Nagy, *Vision in Motion* (Chicago, IL: Paul Theobald and Company, 1947), 67.

54. For a more comprehensive discussion of the terms, see Bremner and Rodgers, "Design Without Discipline."

55. Mignolo, "Geopolitics of Sensing and Knowing," 2.

56. Escobar, "Worlds and Knowledges Otherwise."

57. Ramón Grosfoguel, "Transmodernity, Border Thinking, and Global Coloniality: Decolonizing Political Economy and Postcolonial Studies," trans. Inês Martins Ferreira, *Revista Crítica de Ciências Sociais*, no. 80 (2008), 115–47; Madina V. Tlostanova and Walter D. Mignolo, "On Pluritopic Hermeneutics, Trans-Modern Thinking, and Decolonial Philosophy," *Encounters* 1, no. 1 (2009), 10–27.

and products).[52] Despite our commonalities, design remains a "strictly vocational education" that "breeds specialists with a rather narrow horizon"[53] – a caution from László Moholy-Nagy from over seventy years ago, and yet little has changed. Designers are specialized within design, and often are only familiar with their own field.

With all the changes in practice, why do we remain tied to these specialisms? How often do we work together? And most importantly, are specialisms still relevant? Design discourse uses the words crossdisciplinary, multidisciplinary, interdisciplinary, and transdisciplinary,[54] but these are not genuinely practiced to understand the true nature of collaboration. In current thinking, an interdisciplinary designer "crosses" a border by abolishing the divide between digital and print or design and illustration, rather than the larger issues of crossing specialism borders and other disciplinary boundaries.

Increased discussion of cross-, multi-, trans-, inter-, and post-disciplinary practices gives the impression that design is moving to redefine itself in radically new ways. But the opposite is occurring, as more types of designers and fields of design emerge; "fields" that are merely skills.

Border-Thinking as Method

A possible way out of this disciplinary containment and decadence is border-thinking. Border-thinking is a decolonial concept, a concept "focuse[d] on changing the terms of the conversation and not only its content."[55] Decoloniality crosses borders of thought to craft another space for the production of knowledge.[56] Therefore, it locates its inquiry on the very borders of systems of thought and reaches towards the possibility of non-Eurocentric models of thinking. This is a way of broadening the canon of thought by acknowledging the existence of other epistemologies, knowledges, and understandings, towards a pluriversal world – a world where many worlds fit.[57]

In *Design in the Borderlands*, Eleni Kalantidou and Tony Fry bring border-thinking closer to design, arguing that border-thinking brings us to confront the knowing of the ground of what we know and how such knowing frames what we see, hear and understand in the spaces of our being and becoming. By implication, border thinking breaks out of disciplinary boundaries; it crosses borders, is nomadic … [and] is … a thinking along, within and about borders rather than a thinking of them. … [A]t the same time, it is … an automatic refusal of containment, ownership and institution. This means it cannot be fixed and "held in place…"[58]

Border-thinking unifies the *how*, *what*, and *where* we think.[59] This definition moves thinking about design beyond disciplinary boundaries, where it invites other disciplines into dialogue to inform the issues it tackles and to think and act decolonially.

Border-thinking is not additive, it is systemic. It requires a complete rethinking of design. Engaging in border thinking here is not a "rejecti[on] of modernity to retreat into a fundamentalist absolutism" but "the decolonial transmodern response of the subaltern to Eurocentric modernity," a redefinition of design and "of citizenship, democracy, human rights, humanity, economic relations beyond the narrow definitions imposed by European

58. Eleni Kalantidou and Tony Fry, "Design in the Borderlands: An Introduction," in *Design in the Borderlands*, ed. Eleni Kalantidou and Tony Fry (Abingdon, Oxon: Earthscan), 6–7.

59. Mignolo, "Geopolitics of Sensing and Knowing."

What we think of when we say "good design".
Image: Danah Abdulla.

60. Ramón Grosfoguel, "World-System Analysis in the Context of Transmodernity, Border Thinking and Global Coloniality," *Review* 29, no. 2 (2006), 178–79.

61. Madina V. Tlostanova and Walter D. Mignolo, *Learning to Unlearn: Decolonial Reflections from Eurasia and the Americas* (Columbus, OH: Ohio State University Press, 2012), 36.

62. "Minor gestures" are context-based and somewhat subversive ideas that are presented as ways of expanding the limits of a given enclosed system, carving a pathway towards structural change (disciplines, higher education institutions, organisations, etc.). The concept of minor gestures is a work in progress that Pedro Oliveira and I are tackling and expanding on in a forthcoming coauthored paper.

63. Ashley Dawson, *Extinction: A Radical History* (New York, NY: OR Books, 2016).

64. Walter D. Mignolo, *Local Histories/Global Designs: Coloniality, Subaltern Knowledges, and Border Thinking* (Princeton, NJ: Princeton University Press, 2012), xvii.

65. Escobar, *Designs for the Pluriverse*, 35.

66. Kalantidou and Fry, "Design in the Borderlands: An Introduction."

67. Consider the attitude of engineers towards designers. Mike Nuttal claimed that engineers at General Motors called designers "clay fairies" (Harvey Molotch, *Where Stuff Comes From* New York, NY: Routledge, 2005]). Despite the close relationship between design and engineering, engineers often refer to designers as the people … who make the colors" (Mike Monteiro, Design's Lost Generation," *Mike Monteiro* (blog), February 19, 2018, https://medium. om/@monteiro/designs-lost- generation-ac7289549017) nd add the decoration, a definition still widely accepted y designers if we remain olitically unaware.

68. Bierut, *79 Short Essays on Design*.

modernity"[60] – i.e., a different way of thinking and knowing about the world.

As a decolonial concept, border-thinking rethinks the existence of design as a whole rather than its compartmentalization – it is not about "changing" the discipline but "und[oing] imperial and colonial differences, ontologically and epistemically."[61]

My proposal in this chapter – to erode the boundaries between design disciplines – can be read as a minor gesture[62] within the existing system before embracing and integrating other disciplines and truly decolonizing design (by questioning the discipline itself), as new challenges cannot be seen in isolation from capitalism and imperialism[63] and coloniality hiding "under the rhetoric of modernity."[64] Questioning the discipline of design is crucial, as these new challenges bring forth "unprecedented methodological and epistemological issues,"[65] opening up spaces for other disciplines to enter into dialogue with design and moving beyond the models of Western modernity. To solve twenty-first-century problems is to look beyond twentieth-century solutions.

But before design goes beyond itself as Kalantidou and Fry argue,[66] it should break out of – and understand – its own containment in specialization (interdisciplinarity) before engaging with other disciplines (cross-/multi-/transdisciplinarity), and meaningfully decolonizing the discipline (beyond additive change).

A rethinking and dismantling of design specializations opens up possibilities: it could subvert the hierarchy not only within design but across disciplines that have a close relationship with it. If design were to redefine itself, it might subvert the hierarchy within academic disciplines. After all, not all disciplines are created equal, and design, unfortunately, is not high up in this hierarchy.[67]

Design education requires a broad scope, and without exposure to other disciplines that share a culture with design – and exposure to different design practices – designers will continue to speak and design for themselves.[68] In this way, students and designers can critically engage with their surroundings, and make sense of their actions and how these affect the people they are designing for.

Conclusion

By engaging with border-thinking, the definition of design, and our ability to articulate our value as designers, rests in our hands. Designers are collaborative by nature, and we have always had the ability to bring different fields together. Therefore, design crosses borders.

Luckily, the borders of specialization were drawn by us, which means that we can move the line, toe it, and breach it. Border-thinking is a way of creating collective practices. Before beginning to bring design into other disciplines, we should look inward to our own discipline and transform it. In this way, we can articulate our contribution. We assume we have reached the tipping point, past the point of being able to change anything, but this signals a lack of imagination, a feeling that design is eternal and unchanging.

Would designers be "better-informed [and] better-theorised"[69] and create more meaningful objects if they really understood the economic, political, and social implications of what they do? Designers cannot hold concepts and ideas in rigid boundaries. These disciplinary borders prevent us from building meaningful relationships, from developing real collectivity and collaboration. Most importantly, to quote Henry Giroux, "at stake here is a notion of pedagogy that both informs the mind and creates the conditions for modes of agency that are critical, informed, engaged, and socially responsible."[70]

Arguing that designers lack contextual understanding is not new, but issues of race and power remain of little concern to design education. To begin to address this task requires more than just applying certain theories to design. It is time to reorient design away from the solution-finding experts serving industry – the functional, rational, and industrial traditions – "toward a type of rationality and set of practices attuned to the relational dimension of life."[71] It requires a complete rethinking towards a radical imagination,[72] one, I suggest, that begins with abolishing the borders between design itself, and thinking of design anew.

69. Kalantidou and Fry, "Design in the Borderlands: An Introduction," 7.

70. Henry A. Giroux, "The Disimagination Machine and the Pathologies of Power," *Symploke* 21, nos. 1–2 (2013), 265.

71. Escobar, *Designs for the Pluriverse*, x.

72. Giroux, "The Disimagination Machine."

Acknowledgments

This chapter is an expanded version of a talk given at the "Dilemma! Dilemma!" conference at the Hochschule der Künste Bern in May 2019. I am grateful to Durre Shehwar Ali and Julia Geiser for inviting me to speak and develop this idea. I would like to thank my colleague and friend Pedro Oliveira for his critical comments on this text, which remains a work in progress.

Apartheid wall, Pisgat Ze'ev settlement in the Shu'afat neighborhood of East Jerusalem, occupied Palestine. Photo: Lisa Nessan.

Bibliography

Ahmed, Sara. "White Men." *Feministkilljoys* (blog). 4 November 2014. https://feministkilljoys.com/2014/11/04/white-men/.
—. *Living a Feminist Life*. Durham, NC: Duke University Press, 2017.

Anzaldúa, Gloria. *Borderlands/La Frontera*. 4th ed. San Francisco, CA: Aunt Lute Books, 2012.

Bierut, Michael. *79 Short Essays on Design*. New York, NY: Princeton Architectural Press, 2007.

Bremner, Craig, and Paul Rodgers. "Design Without Discipline." *Design Issues* 29, no. 3 (2013), 4–13. doi.org/10.1162/DESI.

Cross, Nigel. "Designerly Ways of Knowing." *Design Studies* 3, no. 4 (1982), 221–27.
—. "Design Research: A Disciplined." *Design Issues* 15, no. 2 (1999), 5–10.
—. *Design Thinking by Nigel Cross*. Oxford: Berg, 2011.

Dawson, Ashley. *Extinction: A Radical History*. New York, NY, and London: OR Books, 2016.

Decolonising Design. "Editorial Statement." *Decolonising Design* (blog). 27 June 2016. www.decolonisingdesign.com/statements/2016/editorial/.

Design Council. "Designing a Future Economy." London: Design Council, 2018. www.designcouncil.org.uk/resources/report/designing-future-economy-report.

Escobar, Arturo. 2007. "Worlds and Knowledges Otherwise." *Cultural Studies* 21, no. 2 (2007), 179–210. doi.org/10.1080/09502380601162506.
—. *Designs for the Pluriverse: Radical Interdependence, Autonomy, and the Making of Worlds*. Durham, NC: Duke University Press, 2018.

Findeli, Alain. "Rethinking Design Education for the 21st Century: Theoretical, Methodological, and Ethical Discussion." *Design Issues* 17, no. 1 (2001), 5–17.

Foucault, Michel. *L'archéologie du savoir*. Paris: Gallimard, 1969.
—. *Surveiller et punir: Naissance de la prison*. Paris: Gallimard, 1975.

Friedman, Daniel. *Radical Modernism*. New Haven: Yale University Press, 1994.

Giroux, Henry A. "The Disimagination Machine and the Pathologies of Power." *Symploke* 21, nos. 1–2 (2013), 257–69.

Gordon, Lewis R. *Disciplinary Decadence: Living Thought in Trying Times*. Boulder, Colorado: Paradigm Publishers, 2006.
—. "Disciplinary Decadence and the Decolonisation of Knowledge." *Africa Development* 39, no. 1 (2014), 81–92.

Grosfoguel, Ramón. "World-System Analysis in the Context of Transmodernity, Border Thinking and Global Coloniality." *Review* 29, no. 2 (2006), 167–87.
—. "Transmodernity, Border Thinking, and Global Coloniality: Decolonizing Political Economy and Postcolonial Studies." Translated by Inês Martins Ferreira. *Revista Crítica de Ciências Sociais* 80 (2008), 115–47.

Hirano, Takuo. "The Development of Modern Japanese Design: A Personal Account." *Design Issues* 7, no. 2 (1991), 54–62. doi.org/10.2307/1511407.

Irwin, Terry. "Transition Design: A Proposal for a New Area of Design Practice, Study, and Research." *Design and Culture* 7, no. 2 (2015), 229–46. doi.org/10.1080/17547075.2015.1051829.

Kalantidou, Eleni, and Tony Fry, eds. *Design in the Borderlands*. Abingdon, Oxon: Earthscan, 2014.
—. "Design in the Borderlands: An Introduction." In *Design in the Borderlands*. Edited by Eleni Kalantidou and Tony Fry, 1–11. Abingdon, Oxon: Earthscan, 2014.

Klein, Julie. *Interdisciplinarity: History, Theory, and Practice*. Detroit: Wayne State University Press, 1990.

Krishnan, Armin. "What Are Academic Disciplines? Some Observations on the Disciplinarity vs. Interdisciplinarity Debate." Working Paper. NCRM Working Paper Series. ESRC National Centre for Research Methods, 2009.

Laranjo, Francisco. "Continuous Rebranding: Interview with Angela Mitropoulos." *Modes of Criticism* 3, no. 1 (2017), 31–34.

Mayblin, Lucy. "Border Thinking." *Global Social Theory* (blog). n.d. https://globalsocialtheory.org/concepts/border-thinking/.

Mignolo, Walter D. "DELINKING." *Cultural Studies* 21, no. 2 (2007), 449–514. doi.org/10.1080/09502380601162647.
—. "Geopolitics of Sensing and Knowing: On (de)Coloniality, Border Thinking and Epistemic Disobedience." *Postcolonial Studies* 14, no. 3 (2011), 273–83. doi.org/10.1080/13688790.2011.613105.
—. *Local Histories/Global Designs: Coloniality, Subaltern Knowledges, and Border Thinking*. Princeton, NJ: Princeton University Press, 2012.

Moholy-Nagy, László. *Vision in Motion*. Chicago: Paul Theobald and Company, 1947.

Molotch, Harvey. *Where Stuff Comes From*. New York: Routledge, 2005.

Monteiro, Mike. "Design's Lost Generation." *Mike Monteiro* (blog). 19 February 2018. https://medium.com/@monteiro/designs-lost-generation-ac7289549017.

Richardson, Adam. "The Death of the Designer." *Design Issues* 9, no. 2 (1993), 34–43.

Rodgers, Paul A., and Craig Bremner. "The Concept of the Design Discipline." *Dialectic* 1, no. 1 (2016). doi.org/10.3998/dialectic.14932326.0001.104.

Rothenberg, Albert. "The Process of Janusian Thinking in Creativity." *Archives of General Psychiatry* 24, no. 3 (1971), 195. doi.org/10.1001/archpsyc.1971.01750090001001.

Seitz, Tim. "The 'Design Thinking' Delusion." Translated by Adam Baltner. *Jacobin*, 16 October 2018. https://jacobinmag.com/2018/10/design-thinking-innovation-consulting-politics.

Shor, Ira. *Empowering Education: Critical Teaching for Social Change*. Chicago and London: The University of Chicago Press, 1992.

Shumway, David R., and Ellen Messer-Davidow. "Disciplinarity: An Introduction." *Poetics Today* 12, no. 2 (1991), 201–25. doi.org/10.2307/1772850.

Tlostanova, Madina V., and Walter D. Mignolo. 2009. "On Pluritopic Hermeneutics, Trans-Modern. Thinking, and Decolonial Philosophy." *Encounters* 1, no. 1 (2009), 10–27.
—. *Learning to Unlearn: Decolonial Reflections from Eurasia and the Americas*. Transoceanic Studies. Columbus, Ohio: The Ohio State University Press, 2012.

Todd, Zoe. 2016. "An Indigenous Feminist's Take On The Ontological Turn: 'Ontology' s Just Another Word For Colonialism: An Indigenous Feminist's Take on the Ontological Turn." *Journal of Historical Sociology* 29 (1), 4–22. doi.org/10.1111/ohs.12124.

West Churchman, C. "Guest Editorial: Wicked Problems." *Management Science* 14, no. 4 (1967), B141-142.

Willis, Anne-Marie. "Transition Design: The Need to Refuse Discipline and Transcend Instrumentalism." *Design Philosophy Papers* 13, no. 1 (2015), 69–74.

DO THE MAHI, REAP THE REWARDS Working Towards the Integration of Indigenous Knowledge Within Design Education

Nan O'Sullivan

1. Hiniri Moko Mead, *Tikanga Māori: Living by Māori Values* (Wellington: Huia Publishers, 2003).

2. Nan O'Sullivan, "Walking Backwards into the Future: Indigenous Wisdom within Design Education," *Educational Philosophy and Theory* 51, no. 4 (2018), 424–33.

3. The Treaty of Waitangi recognizes Māori and Pākehā (white New Zealanders) as having equal rights. It is an agreement made in 1840 between representatives of the British Crown and more than five hundred Māori chiefs. Most chiefs signed a Māori-language version of the treaty that in translation held different meanings, therefore had different expectations of the terms. Resolution of these differences has presented New Zealand with challenges and ongoing negotiations and claims throughout its history. See teara.govt.nz/en/treaty-of-waitangi/page-1.

"Māori knowledge has come out of hiding and is now in the bright light of day."[1] New Zealand Māori are the indigenous peoples of New Zealand and, alongside many others from the Pacific nations, contribute to New Zealand being a bicultural nation and a multicultural society. A particular focus of this paper is the motivations, opportunities, challenges, and outcomes of efforts made to facilitate the recognition and integration of indigenous knowledge into design education within Te Kura Hoahoa, the School of Design Innovation (SoDI), Te Herenga Waka, Victoria University of Wellington (VUW) in Aotearoa New Zealand. This paper is written with an understanding that indigenous knowledge is not old knowledge or knowledge relevant to distant, now-outmoded times, and a recognition that this wisdom continues to evolve through rebellious, resistant, and resilient cultural practices.[2] It will illustrate efforts within Te Herenga Waka (VUW) to address our commitments to Te Tiriti o Waitangi, the Treaty of Waitangi,[3] to increase the cultural competency of both staff and students, and, particularly within Te Kura Hoahoa (SoDI), to recalibrate design pedagogy to better enable our staff and graduates to engage with diversity, equity, inclusivity, and sustainability. The efforts discussed are specific to the First Year Design and the Design for Social Innovation (DSI) programs as trailblazers for these initiatives within the school. The design profession has heard time and time again that designers are now required to understand the complexities born of diverse and often contentious cultural, societal, and global issues.[4] It follows that our graduates will be required to play pivotal roles within the resolutions or interventions sought. To that end, this paper posits the need for design institutes to graduate students who can improve the discipline's capacity and capability to contribute to the development of more inclusive, equitable, sustaining, and sustainable futures and offers an overview of current efforts to achieve this within Te Kura Hoahoa, the School of Design Innovation, Te Herenga Waka, Victoria University of Wellington in Aotearoa New Zealand.

We seek to transition away from the dominant Eurocentric model of design education to a place-based pedagogy, informed by culturally inclusive principles, traditional knowledge, and strategies that hold at their core the health and well-being of both people and place – past, present, and future. Guiding our efforts within the first-year and Design for Social Innovation programs is a precolonial *whakataukī* (traditional Māori proverb): "Hoki whakamuri kia anga whakamua" (Let us walk backwards into the future). Informing the process is the acknowledgment of, respect for, and engagement with *te ao* Māori (Māori worldview), *tikanga* Māori (Māori protocols and values), and *mātauranga* Māori (Māori knowledge).

Our Commitment: With, and as, Tangata Whenua (the People of the Land), We Value Te Tiriti O Waitangi[5]

The Education Act 1989 requires that education providers acknowledge the broader principles of the Treaty of Waitangi in order to develop the relationship between Māori and the Crown. These principles, including equality, cooperation, and self-determination, still frame VUW's strategic goals and are viewed as distinctive qualities

4. Terry Irwin, Gideon Kossoff, and Cameron Tonkinwise, "Transition Design Provocation," *Design Philosophy Papers* 13, no. 1 (2015), 3.

5. Victoria University of Wellington Senior Leadership Team, *Strategic Plan* (Wellington: Victoria University of Wellington, 2014).

6. VUW Senior Leadership Team, 2014.

7. VUW Senior Leadership Team, 2014.

8. Victory University of Wellington Human Resources, *Tikanga Māori at Victoria* (Wellington: Victoria University of Wellington, 2016).

9. VUW Human Resources.

disseminated through *tikanga* Māori (Māori values), *mātauranga* Māori (Māori knowledge), and *te reo* Māori (the Māori language).[6] In 2014, the university reiterated this, stating that

> our respect for Te Tiriti o Waitangi and *mātauranga* Māori motivates us to influence and inform societal change for the betterment of Aotearoa New Zealand. We embed *te reo*, *tikanga* and *mātauranga* Māori in our university's activities, including research, learning, and teaching.[7]

To further enable the fruition of these goals, Te Rautaki Maruako, the Learning and Teaching Strategy 2017–2021 (LTS), was designed. The strategy, self-described as "unreservedly ambitious," gives direction and guidance for the entire university and signals a commitment to working in partnership to create and maintain an inclusive learning and teaching environment. Outlining six *tikanga* (values) as its bedrock, the LTS aims to "provide a holistic learning, teaching and student experience second to none."[8] These values are *akoranga* (lifelong learning), *whanaungatanga* (collaboration), *whai mātauranga* (curiosity), *kaitiakitanga* (guardianship), *manaakitanga* (respect), and *rangatiratanga* (self-determination). Implementation of the LTS is assisted by the Te Hāpai staff development program, which consists of workshops, booklets, and mentorship arrangements that are available to all staff both academic and professional. The program has been designed and is supported by the Office of the Deputy Vice-Chancellor (Māori) and aims to increase the understanding and use of Māori culture, *tikanga* (values), *te reo* (language), and the Treaty of Waitangi within the teaching, learning, and research environments.[9] All staff within the School of Design, including new and international staff, are encouraged as a part of their professional development to undertake these workshops.

The uptake by design school staff has been positive, but not unrealistically, and with an appreciation that their engagement requires *whakawhanaungatanga* (authentic and meaningful engagement), some staff members are hesitant to use *te reo* for fear of mispronunciation or misuse, while the structuring of the values within the curriculum and course content can also need *korero* (discussion) and guidance from specific *kaiwhakaako* (guides or instructors) to ensure respectful and meaningful engagement. The guidance offered as a part of the LTS strategy and Te Hāpai have enabled the first-year and DSI programs to create a foundation and distinct pathways of integration for *mātauranga* Māori (Māori knowledge), *te reo* Māori (Māori language), and *tikanga* Māori (Māori values). The knowledge embedded also guides the teaching and learning relationship, delivery modes, and the content and contexts outlined within the curricula redesign. The university's investment plan contains the specific goal "to develop Māori staff capabilities and increase the ability for staff to engage with Māori."[10] An important step towards this, and one that requires consistent consideration, strategic efforts, and reflection on one's own unconscious biases, is the visibility and presence of both Māori staff and students.

Cultural Competency: "He Reo E Rangona, Engari He Kanohi Kitea" (A Voice May Be Heard but a Face Needs to Be Seen)[11]

In 2016, the academic staff at Te Kura Hoahoa, the School of Design Innovation numbered fourteen, none of whom were of Māori or Pasifika descent, and only one staff member of color. In 2020, in line with the growth of the school's offerings, the staff and student numbers have increased considerably. There are now twenty-four academic staff, including three of Māori descent; two of these staff members are teaching in the DSI and one, a graduate of Media Design program, is teaching in that program and the first year. The generosity shown through knowledge-sharing has been invaluable, but with the representation of Māori within the staff at 12.5 percent, considerable responsibility and an awkward imbalance is placed on a few staff to inform, guide, and "act on the behalf of" other staff members. Although many Māori competent or growing in confidence with *te reo* or *kaupapa* Māori have shown understanding and generosity,[12] concerns have been

10. Victory University of Wellington Senior Leadership Team, *The Treaty at VUW Investment Plan* (2015–2017) (Wellington: Victoria University of Wellington), 26–27.

11. Katarina Davis, Innovate Change (website), www.innovatechange.co.nz (accessed November 16, 2019).

12. *Kaupapa* Māori: Māori approach, topic, customary practice, institution, agenda, principles, ideology – a philosophical doctrine incorporating the knowledge, skills, attitudes, and values of Māori society.

13. New Zealand Government, Stats NZ (website), www.stats.govt.nz (accessed January 7, 2020).

expressed about, firstly, the assumption that Māori wish to do this work (a job of many which, due to the low number of Māori staff, is made the responsibility of a few) and, secondly, the lack of engagement with, and in some cases lack of respect for, *kaupapa* Māori by non-Māori staff.

Statistics, although a blunt tool tallying only tangible outputs, sit at the heart of any attempt to measure the movement of numbers. VUW's pursuit to increase the inclusion and integration of *mātauranga* Māori (Māori knowledge) has shown that within Te Kura Hoahoa, the School of Design Innovation the number of Māori students graduating sat at 10 percent in 2019. This is an increase from 5 percent in 2016 and could be linked to the inclusion of Māori on the staff, but no research has been undertaken to ascertain this. Although this is an improvement, these numbers do not yet represent the cultural diversity of New Zealand's population, the majority of which is of European descent, referred to as Pākehā (white New Zealanders), with indigenous Māori being the largest minority at 16.5 percent, closely followed by Asians at 15.35 percent and non-Māori Pacific Islanders at 9 percent.[13]

In 2016, the SDI's first-year cohort represented thirty-one cultures. The highest number by over three times was Pākehā. This number is followed by Asian-Pacific students, many of whom are international students and new to our shores. The two smallest groups are Māori and Pasifika students. An important finding from an online research questionnaire put to the 2016 First Year Design students was that the Māori and Pasifika contingent consider Western influences to be more relevant to their

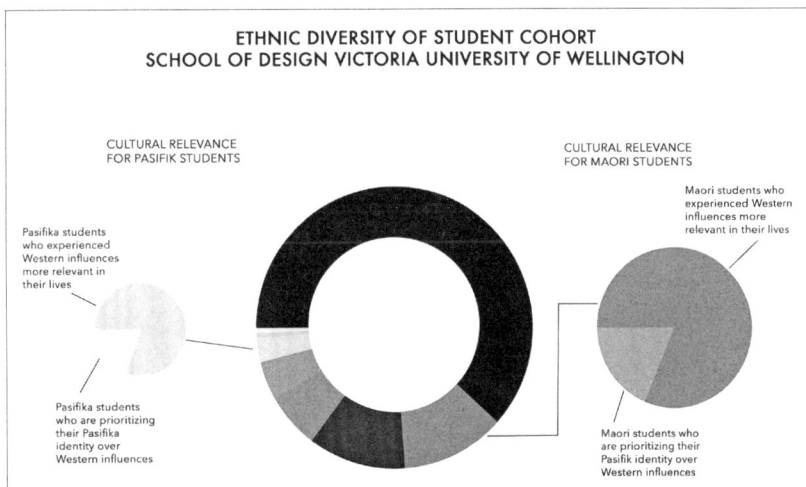

ETHNIC DIVERSITY OF STUDENT COHORT
SCHOOL OF DESIGN VICTORIA UNIVERSITY OF WELLINGTON

CULTURAL RELEVANCE
FOR PASIFIK STUDENTS

CULTURAL RELEVANCE
FOR MAORI STUDENTS

Pasifika students who experienced Western influences more relevant in their lives

Maori students who experienced Western influences more relevant in their lives

Pasifika students who are prioritizing their Pasifika identity over Western influences

Maori students who are prioritizing their Pasifik identity over Western influences

The assimilation of Western culture by Māori and Pasifika design students (indicative only).

studies than their own cultures' everyday customs, ideologies, or beliefs. Having completed both an undergraduate degree and a master's degree at Te Kura Hoahoa, the School of Design Innovation, a student of Samoan descent, St Andrew Matautia, stated that

> casting an eye over my educational experience, an epiphany had occurred when I was encouraged (although at first it felt like I was being permitted) to use aspects of my culture in my design process. There was no doubt that this inclusion allowed me to express myself, explore more confidently and design more intuitively.[14]

"This One Storyline Is Conceived from the Perspective of the Euro-American Experience and Exported to Many World Regions over the Past Few-Hundred Years"[15]

It could be construed from ongoing critiques of design education that the lack of appropriate culturally inclusive course content or any traditional knowledge within design curricula contributes to the displacement of students who do not identify with the hegemony or homogeneity of the Eurocentric or Euro-American tenets principally assimilated through modernist edicts. In addition to this, those delivering the course content also represent, and in many cases hold steadfast to, these codified and ingrained design doctrines. Within the DSI and first-year programs we acknowledge this approach as a fundamental flaw and seek change. One of the undertakings our programs has made to enable the shift Matautia speaks of, is to consciously parallel the diversity exhibited between the students and tutors.[16] In doing so, tutors and staff have also been able to shift their stance to one of learning from the student group. This ploy is synonymous with the "Silent Way," as developed by the French mathematician and educator, Caleb Gattegno (1911–1988), and employs indigenous methods of teaching and learning where the silence of the teacher gives the students room to explore cultural acumen and the teacher room to grow through observation.[17]

14. Nan O'Sullivan, "Constructing Your Own Reality Prevents Others from Doing It for You: A Shift towards Cultural Inclusivity in Design," Cumulus REDO Conference (Kolding: Kolding Design Academy, 2018).

15. Arturo Escobar, "*Transiciones*: A Space for Research and Design for Transitions to the Pluriverse," *Design Philosophy Papers* 13, no. 1 (2015), 13–23.

16. Every course employs tutors within the studio or tutorial group to support the staff member responsible for the course. The tutor to student ratio is one-to-eighteen in the studio. Course numbers range from approximately fifteen to three-hundred students.

17. Caleb Gattegno, *The Silent Way* (New York, NY: Education Solutions Worldwide, 1963).

Design Struggles

18. Renata Leitão, "Recognising and Overcoming the Myths of Modernity," in *Proceedings of Design Research Society Conference* DRS 2018: Catalyst (Limerick: University of Limerick, 2018), 8.

19. Linda Leach, "'I Treat All Students Equal': Further and Higher Education Teachers' Responses to Diversity," *Journal for Further and Higher Education* 35, no. 247 (2011), 263.

20. Rawinia Higgins, "Contributions to the Growth and Development of Māori Matauranga," Enriching Cultural Heritage Symposium (Wellington: Te Herenga Waka, Victoria University of Wellington, 2016).

21. Irwin, "Transition Design Provocation."

22. O'Sullivan, "Constructing Your Own Reality Prevents Others from Doing It for You."

23. Jamie Gamble et al., 'Theme 4: Evidence for Innovation," *The Royal Children's Hospital Melbourne: Centre for Community Child Health* (blog), May 6, 2019, blogs.rch.org.au/ccch/2019/05/06/theme-4-evidence-for-innovation/.

Recalibration: "We Can Only Become Aware of the Features and Flaws of Our Worldview in Contrast with Other Storylines"[18]

In 2011, Dr Linda Leach argued for the need to do more than pay lip service to diversity by simply situating it within the group. Leach asserted that indigenous peoples are still underrepresented in tertiary institutions and discussed the need to move away from methods that endorse "assimilation into the dominant culture."[19] In 2016, outlining VUW's aims for the use of indigenous knowledge, Deputy Vice-Chancellor (Māori) Rawinia Higgins outlined, as part of a larger plan, a hybrid approach. "*Mātauranga* Māori and *Mātauranga* Pasifika (Māori and Pasifika knowledge) should not be confined to the pre-colonial era, because its evolution is also about knowledge interaction, production and hybridity."[20]

In 2018, at the Design Research Society Conference in Limerick, Renata Leitão commented that discussions about culture and the cultural dimension in design were almost absent. Leitão noted the "Transition Design Provocation" assembled by Terry Irwin and her team of transition designers at Carnegie Mellon University, and Ezio Manzini within the Design for Social Innovation and Sustainability network (DESIS) for acknowledging concerns around the continued use of Euro-American design edicts. Both consider these edicts to be limiting the possibility of social change and hindering the reconception of lifestyles that is required to combat the world's environmental, social, political, and economic predicaments (or "wicked problems").[21]

As an extension of these thoughts, this study posits that paramount to the shift away from the standardization currently embedded in design education, the presence of and respect for indigenous students and indigenous knowledge is required.[22] Sadly, "while there is increasing recognition in mainstream or Western settings of indigenous knowledge systems as legitimate in their own right, references to evidence-based practices and programs in policy and service settings still rarely include this type of knowledge."[23]

"Māori Should Stand Tall in the Fact That Our Ancestors Led the World in Technology and Innovation, It's in Our DNA"[24]

24. Jacques-Pierre Dumas, IT Brief New Zealand (website), February 19, 2019, itbrief.co.nz (accessed January 10, 2020).

25. Leitão, "Recognising and Overcoming the Myths of Modernity."

26. Nan O'Sullivan, "Navigating Design History with a More Culturally Calibrated Compass," *Journal of New Zealand Art, Media & Design History* 1, no. 3 (2017), 103–17.

27. Te Ahukaramū Charles Royal, "Te Ao Mārama: The Natural World," Te Ara: The Encyclopaedia of New Zealand (website), September 24, 2007, teara.govt.nz/en/te-ao-marama-the-natural-world (accessed October 29, 2019).

Leitão pointed out a fundamental flaw in contemporary design pedagogy when she stated that "the leading role of the modern man entails that we live on a planet with only one storyline: the heroic story of the modern man."[25]

In New Zealand, design as a discipline developed well after the colonial period in the mid-twentieth century; as such, the design research and practice that was developed tended to sideline indigenous culture as having little to offer the discipline as future-focused, technologically advancing, and innovation orientated. This has resulted in current design pedagogy being dominated by a working model that privileges Western and capitalist influences.[26] Although acknowledged as valuable to design, when diversity is explored as non-Western creative practice, quixotically it is still found to be sidelined within design curricula, which remain dominated by the Eurocentric, hegemonic, and linear (not circular) ideals. Considering the graphic, narrative, navigational, and technological innovations and accomplishments for which Māori are globally recognized, this sits awkwardly in the context of New Zealand design education.

At this point, this paper acknowledges the need for change as tacit, and introduces the recalibrated curriculum, course content, and student responses resulting from this undertaking. The first acknowledgment is of *te ao* Māori, the Māori worldview, that holds as its essence relationships – not just with people, but between the natural and spiritual worlds where both tangible and intangible relationships hold equal relevance and importance.[27] As a part of this, *tikanga* (values) – which include *manaakitanga* (respect), *akoranga* (reciprocity), *whanaungatanga* (collaboration), *kaitiakitanga* (guardianship), and, importantly, *rangatiratanga* (self-determination) – act as protocols, behaviors, and beliefs that shape the past, present, and future lives of both people and place. Within the first-year and DSI programs we have engaged the ideology of connectedness imbued in *te ao* Māori and *tikanga* Māori to shape our three-year undergraduate curriculum structure,

Design Struggles

delivery modes, and the diversity of those who deliver it, and reframed the course content and contexts to enable a number of approaches to be adopted that can impart indigenous knowledge to both students and staff.

"Te Aha – Te Mea Nui – O Te Ao? He Tāngata, He Tāngata, He Tāngata" (What Is the Most Important Thing in the World? It Is People, It Is people, It Is people)

The first-year students who enroll at Te Kura Hoahoa, the School of Design Innovation are on average eighteen and a half years old when they commence studies. Having just left high school this is also quite possibly their first time living away from family (*whanau*). At the outset we aim to establish connections with the students, referencing people and place and, as importantly, emphasizing that education is a shared experience (*whanaungatanga* – from the root word *whanau*, "family"). Beyond the usual orientation activities, the school has introduced a digital experience to welcome and introduce students, and a curriculum framework that develops connection and curiosity (*whai mātauranga*) and builds confidence through respect (*manaakitanga*) and care (*kaitiakitanga*). This permeates into coursework that fosters a sense of identity, a capacity for empathy, and the capability of self-determination towards positive change within the fledging designers.

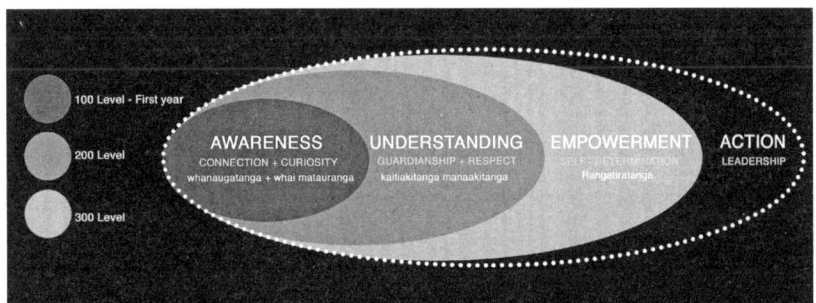

Growth of student capabilities throughout their undergraduate studies enabling them to identify and question, empathize and care for, and empower positive change both individually and collectively.

A Digital Experience

28. Nan O'Sullivan and David Hakaraia, FAD First Step (website), January 10, 2019, fadfirststep.fyi/2019/01/11/ expectations/ (accessed November 16, 2019).

Te Kuhunga (First Step; see www.fadfirststep.fyi) is a website and acts as a year-round guide, point of connection, and experience that encourages the recognition that education involves *whanaungatanga* (shared experience). The site positions *te reo* Māori (Māori language) prominently within the text and discusses the use of *tikanga* Māori (Māori protocols and values) throughout. The pages that receive the most hits are those concerning expectations and support. The school employs design students to assist in defining the aims and content, and yearly reviews are undertaken to ensure Te Kuhunga remains relevant and inclusive of their voice:

> Help us, help you. In the spirit of *whanaunga-tanga* which means relationships and collaborations. Let's appreciate the shared experience of teaching and learning – talk about your *mahi* (work), *korero* (share your ideas) with your classmates and tutors and importantly, if you don't know something – JUST ASK![28]

A Curriculum Framework

The initial aim of the curriculum is to enable the student to make connections between people and place, spark inquiry, and gain an ability to traverse new and often challenging knowledge. In the second year, students acquire important research and communication skills and are encouraged to discover, develop, and articulate their personal standpoints through their creative practice. Acknowledging *kaitiakitanga* (guardianship) and *manaakitanga* (respect and reciprocity), the students aim to be inclusive, sustainable, and sustaining in their design thinking and practice. The third-year curriculum encourages the volume in their voice. At this stage of the curriculum the coursework engages with real-world issues, at which point the more complex challenges around *rangatiratanga* (self-determination) begin. *Rangatiratanga* requires at its core a commitment to work *with* people and allow them to determine their own futures

SHARED EXPERIENCE

A reflection of the cultural diversity in the first year. Photo: St Andrew Matautia.

or outcomes. This is a significant shift away from designing *for*, i.e., designers imposing what they consider to be their "expert understanding" on others. As the number of graduates grows it is becoming important to ensure that connection, support, and learning can be ongoing. To that end, we are currently developing ways to stay tethered and ensure *akoranga* (a reciprocal knowledge-sharing relationship) develops as a continuously evolving and fluid loop between the programs, the alumni, and the contexts they work in.

Coursework Permeated with Indigenous Knowledge

Whanaungatanga: The first-year coursework specifically acknowledges familial and cultural relationships in order to encourage enjoyment and engagement within a collaborative learning environment. Drawing on their knowledge of symbolism, and with an understanding of *te ao* Māori, students reveal themselves through their culture or experiences of culture to express a personal narrative – a self-portrait through symbols. The aim is to encourage students to see themselves as a part of complex systems that connect people and place in many and varied ways. Using a combination of analog and digital software for pattern generation, students continued to expand on their understanding of iteration and connection. For some students this assignment is uncomfortable due to the introspection it requires. This experience can be difficult and at times confronting as students begin to recognize, investigate, or articulate such concepts. To mitigate this, the definition of culture is broadened to include other communities or groups that a student may identify with: LGBTQIA+, feminism, and sports fan are all examples used by students. The feedback from students includes the following:

> This project taught me about the importance of 'me' as part of my design work. I got a chance to communicate and work together with my family to discuss my heritage and to include my *whānau* (family) and our beliefs in my design work.

Kaitiakitanga (guardianship): The word *kaitiakitanga* holds specific relevance for the conversations of colonization within New Zealand's joint history with Māori, as it highlights fundamental cultural differences. As a part of *te ao* Māori, Māori consider themselves stewards of the land, sea, and sky. This is a relationship of guardianship, not ownership. This perhaps oversimplified explanation nevertheless offers an appreciation of just how differently Māori relate to the world's precious resources. Students are encouraged to consider the impact of their design work and to look at more contemporary considerations of sustainable and sustaining practice and outcomes in relation to *kaitiakitanga*. In a recent media promotion undertaken by Design Assembly,[29] two SoDI students were interviewed. When asked about what is important to them and what developments they wish to make in their work, they replied:

> I need to continue to ask more questions and learn to listen and read the world and things around me a lot better. More specifically, I plan on exercising this by remaining connected to and learning more about my Māori heritage and from the people around me.[30]

29. Design Assembly is an independent and collaborative digital and physical platform for New Zealand visual designers to learn, keep up to date, and be inspired.

30. Louise Kellerman, Design Assembly (website), 2009, designassembly.org.nz (accessed January 13, 2020).

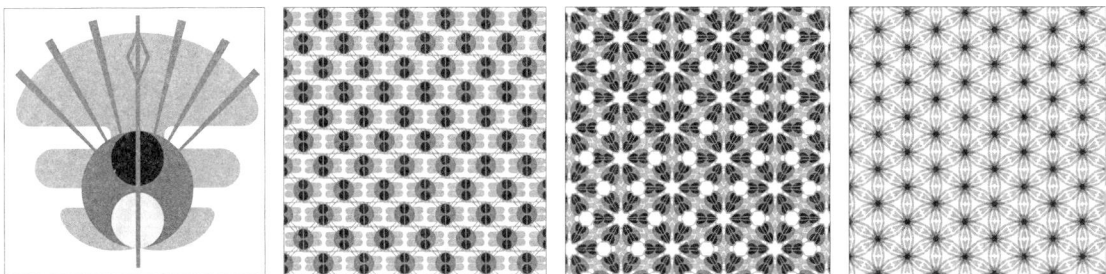

The individual symbols are adaptations representing different degrees to which the individual feels a part of larger collectives. The first pattern expresses the student's relationship with their family or with their tutorial group of about 20 students. This student has located the symbol as a large and recognizable element within a group of similar elements. The second pattern represents the student within their class of 120 students. The pattern shows less distinction between each element, but its creator expressed in their reflective summary that the scale still enabled a place for individuality. The remaining patterns represent the symbol as a part of the entire first-year cohort of over 250 students who the student referred to as "kindred spirits."

31. Kellerman.

32. Whare Tapa Wha (the four cornerstones) is a holistic strength-based model that considers wellbeing in terms of social, physical, mental, and spiritual capacities.

And:

> I like to think critically about what I'm doing and why I'm doing it. Design isn't done in a vacuum; I think you have to really be present in the world and asking difficult questions to do well by other people as well as getting as much out of it as you can. The classes I've taken at Victoria have really pushed me in this sense.[31]

Rangatiratanga (self-determination): In a recent keynote at the World Design Assembly I spoke of the obstacles current design practice faces when engaging with self-determination. The example I gave was within the discipline's practices of codesign. Guided by *tikanga* Māori (Māori values) it was clear that certain approaches within design education, thinking, and practice require redress. The codesign and participatory approaches currently demonstrated within design speak to engagement, inclusion, equality, empathy, and more often than not produce "designed" outcomes "for" clients. Whare Tapa Wha, a holistic model of health and well-being designed by Sir Mason Durie in 1982, was used to illustrate an alternative approach.[32] Importantly it was designed by Māori for Māori. Whare Tapa Wha moves away from Western health models in which services are delivered by "outsider" experts. The correspondences with the Western model of "designing by" and "designing for" are evident. Whare Tapa Wha is one of a number of Māori and Pasifika models that evoke *whanaungatanga* (collaboration), *kaitiakitanga* (guardianship), and *rangatiratanga* (self-determination) as key. Most importantly for design, this model places agency into the hands of those seeking it and ensures that decisions around stakeholder participation, methodology, evidence, intervention, communication, facilitation of outcomes, and distribution of funding are in the hands of those whose lives, lands, children, and grandchildren are to be impacted. This aspect of *rangatiratanga* is perhaps where design as a discipline still has work to do and is where we place the challenge for the students in our programs.

The goal of our endeavours is to enable a new generation of designers with a nuanced appreciation and respect for the connectivity and values imbued within

Nan O'Sullivan

indigenous knowledge and that have the skills and courage to engage empathy, care, respect, reciprocity, and autonomy as strategies to design with. This paper offers *manaakitanga* (respect for all that connects us), *nga manakura* (empathy towards all that connects us), and *kaitiakitanga* (guardianship of all that connects us) as new ways of being and designing more positive, inclusive, sustaining, and sustainable relationships between people and place.

Master's thesis by St Andrew Matautia.

Bibliography

Davis, Katarina. Innovate Change. 2017. www.innivatechange.co.nz (accessed November 16, 2019).

Dumas, Jacques-Pierre. IT Brief New Zealand. February 19, 1919. itbrief.co.nz (accessed January 10, 2020).

Escobar, Arturo. "Transciones: A Space for Research and Design for Transitions to the Pluriverse." *Design Philosophies Papers* 13, no. 1 (2015), 13–23.

Gamble, Jamie, et al. *The Royal Hospital Melbourne*. 2018. blogs.rch.org.au/ccch/2019/05/06/theme-4-evidence-for-innovation/ (accessed January 3, 2020).

Gattegno, Caleb. *The Silent Way*. New York: Education Solutions Worldwide Inc, 1963.

Higgins, Rawinia. "Contributions to the Growth and Development of Māori Matauranga." Enriching Cultural Heritage Symposium. Te Herenga Waka Wellington: Victoria University of Wellington, 2016.

Irwin, Terry, et al. "Transition Design Provocation." *Design Philosophies* 13, no. 1 (2015), 3.

Kellerman, Louise. 2009. designassembly.org.nz. www.designassembly.com (accessed January 13, 2020).
—. https://designassembly.org.nz/2020/01/07/hot-new-things-2020-liliana-manetto-quick/. (accessed January 13, 2020).

Leach, Linda. "'I Treat All Students Equal' Further and Higher Teachers' Responses to Diversity." *Journal for Further and Higher Education* 35 (2011), 247–63.

Leitão, Renata. "Recognising and Overcoming the Myths of Modernity." In *Proceedings of Design Research Society Conference DRS 2018: Catalyst*. Limerick: University of Limerick, 2018, 8.

Mead, Hiniri Moko. *Tikanga Māori: Living by Māori Values*. Wellington: Huia Publishers, 2003.

O'Sullivan, Nan. "Navigating Design History with a More Culturally Calibrated Compass." *Journal of New Zealand Art Media and Design History* 1, no. 3 (2017), 103–17.
—. "Constructing Your own Reality Prevents Others from Doing It For You: A Shift towards Cultural Inclusivity in Design." Cumulus REDO Conference. Kolding: Design School Kolding, 2018.
—. "Walking Backwards into the Future: Indigenous Wisdom within Design Education." *Educational Philosophy and Theory* (Taylor and Francis Online) 51, no. 4 (2018), 424–33.
—, and David Hakaraia. fadfirststep.fyi/2019/01/11/expectations/. Faculty of Architecture and Design. January 10, 2019. www.fadfirststep.fyi (accessed November 16, 2019).

Royal, Te Ahukaramū Charles. *Te Ara: New Zealand Government*. 2007. www.TeAra.govt.nz/en/te-ao-marama-the-natural-world/page- (accessed October 29, 2019).
Statistics NZ. 2019. Stats NZ. New Zealand Government. 2019. www.stats.govt.nz. (accessed January 7, 2020).

Te Ripowai Higgins, and Meremoana Potiki. *Tikanga Māori at Victoria*. Cultural Capability, Centre for Academic Development, Victoria University of Wellington. Wellington: Victoria University of Wellington, n.d.

VUW Human Resources. *Tikanga Māori at Victoria*. Academic Development, Human Resources , Victoria University of Wellington. Wellington: Victoria University of Wellington, 2016.

VUW Senior Leadership Team. Strategic Plan. Strategic Policy, Victoria University of Wellington. Wellington: Victoria University of Wellington, 2014.
—. The Treaty at Victoria VUW Investiment Plan (2015–2017). Strategic Investment, Victoria University of Wellington. Wellington: Victoria University of Wellington, 2015, 26–27.

DESIGN EDUCATION FUTURES
Reflections on Feminist Modes and Politics

Ramia Mazé

This is a pivotal time for design education, as widely discussed in the context of the "Beyond Change" conference. It is a time to consider possible and, even, preferred futures of our field. Our students and future generations of designers are demanding equality, sustainability, and other paradigms than those historically dominating the design profession and education. What do we want for the future, what do we want to be different, and how can we go about making that future happen?

Raising the question of difference, of different or preferred futures, is also a call for criticality. Through my years as a designer and then as a researcher, I have come to appreciate the role and power of critical theory and practice. One role of critical theory is to examine everyday life, to ask how particular norms, hegemonies, and in/exclusions are constructed and (re)produced. Practices of critical historiography ask such questions of the past, and critical futures studies interrogate the future. Further, feminist critical modalities explicitly explore how things could be otherwise. Taken into practice, theory is not neutral – in questioning, naming, and framing, it may destabilize how things were before and open new possibilities for thought and action.

Now is a time for such criticality in design education, for identifying what could and should be different, for aspiring and acting toward our preferred future. Here, I explore some of the everyday building blocks of design education, namely those of design canons and curricula, academic and research conventions. In order to explore these critically, and in relation to difference, I take a feminist perspective. By *feminism* here, I refer not only, or even primarily, to issues of gender and gender inequality. Feminist theory has become a powerful tool for interrogating the multiple, intersecting variables comprising the human condition, social relations, and societal hierarchies, which result in inequality as experienced by many people and cultures. In this respect, design has progressed. Increasingly, we have been making critical, feminist, and decolonial theories our own, adapting these to our practices as designers, educators, and researchers, and building, as architectural theorist Hélène Frichot puts it, "feminist design power tools."[1]

 In this essay, I write in the first person, from my own experience and work, referencing many others by name. For me, this is a feminist approach to writing. Donna Haraway articulates all knowledge as, unavoidably, situated, embodied, and partial,[2] an understanding that has been crucial not only for feminist theory but also for "research through practice" in design. Positioning myself and others is my refusal of the so-called "God trick" of supposed universality and neutrality.[3] It's also a way to express a personal stake in, among other things, (design education) futures.

The Design Canon and Educational Curricula

In envisioning and making a desired future come to be, the past and present are necessarily implicated. The future is not empty – it will be occupied by the legacies and consequences of preexisting worldviews, structures, institutions, policies, and practices.[4] These are historically rooted and, whether by habit or intent, continually reproduced. As the present turns into the future, minute by minute, there is nonetheless a potential to think and do differently, to contest and reform those things that condition, determine, and occupy the future.[5] Indeed, as philosopher Elizabeth Grosz argues,[6] a particular political potential of the future lies in the possibility of conceptualizing difference, of

1. Hélène Frichot, *How to Make Yourself a Feminist Design Power Tool* (Baunach: Spurbuchverlag, 2016).

2. Donna Haraway, "Situated Knowledges: The Science Question in Feminism and the Pivilege of Partial Perspective," *Feminist Studies* 14, no. 3 (1998), 575–99.

3. Sandra Harding, *Sciences from Below: Feminism, Postcolonialities and Modernities* (Chapel Hill, NC: Duke University Press, 2008). Cf. Jane Rendell, "How to Take Place (but Only for So Long)," in *Altering Practices: Feminist Politics and Poetics of Space*, ed. Doina Petrescu (London: Routledge, 2006), 69–88.

4. Ramia Mazé, "Politics of Designing Visions of the Future," *Journal of Futures Studies* 23, no. 3 (2019), 23–38.

5. Ramia Mazé and Josefin Wangel, "Future (Im)Perfect: Exploring Time, Becoming and Difference in Design and Futures Studies," in *Feminist Futures of Spatial Practice*, ed. Meike Schalk, Thérèse Kristiansson, and Ramia Mazé (Baunach: Spurbuchverlag, 2017), 273–86.

6. Elizabeth Grosz, *Architecture from the Outside* (Cambridge, MA: MIT Press, 2001).

7. Katerina Rüedi, "Bauhaus Dream-House: Imagining the (Un)Gendered and (Un)-Disciplined Social Body," in *Proceedings of the 87th ACSA Association of Collegiate Schools of Architecture Annual Meeting* (1999), 111. Cf. Katerina Rüedi Ray, *Bauhaus Dream-House: Modernity and globalization* (London: Routledge, 2010).

8. Mariángeles García, "The Lost History of the Women of the Bauhaus," trans. Marina Gosselin, *Arch Daily*, May 22, 2018, www.archdaily.com/890807/the-lost-history-of-the-women-of-the-bauhaus.

9. Leonie Sandercock, ed., *Making the Invisible Visible: A Multicultural Planning History* (Berkeley, CA: University of California Press, 1998).

10. Christina Zetterlund, "Taikons konst var en del av hennes kamp," trans. Christina Zetterlund, *Svenska Dagbladet*, March 7, 2017, www.svd.se/taikons-konst-var-en-del-av-hennes-kamp.

gaining a critical distance from the past and present and, thereby, building different possible futures.

To take an example from design education, we might look to the Bauhaus, which was widely celebrated during 2019, the centenary of its founding. It was an influential blueprint for design and design academia, also imprinting my own academic trajectory. Beyond the superficial celebration, however, historian Katerina Rüedi has revealed how structural inequality at the Bauhaus was enacted through higher fees for women and a restricted number of places. According to founder Walter Gropius, "no women were to be admitted as students of architecture."[7] Now, this may seem outrageous to us. We may too easily dismiss this as archaic, a policy quickly relegated to history that is simply unacceptable in our academic institutions today. However, this should not – must not – stop us from interrogating specific instances as part of wider phenomena, including legacies and consequences that may continue into the present and, potentially, into the future. Such instances cannot be merely relegated to the past nor are they compensated by pointing out exceptions to the rule – though, certainly, "lost histories" of women such as Gunta Stölzl at the Bauhaus should be told.[8] Indeed, researching and revealing oppressed or omitted stories, thereby "making the invisible visible," are important tasks for critical historiography.[9]

A more recent and, at least for me, even more discomforting example in design is that of Rosa Taikon. When Taikon passed away in 2017, my colleague, design historian Christina Zetterlund, wrote her obituary for the national newspaper *Svenska Dagbladet*.[10] Taikon's story is close to home, since she was a student during the 1960s at Konstfack College of Arts, Crafts, and Design in Sweden, where both Zetterlund and I later worked. The obituary recounts Taikon's substantial and historical contributions as a late-modernist jewelry artist. Its title also signals a wider impact: "Taikon's work was part of her struggle." Taikon's work builds upon her education but also upon her Swedish Roma family and cultural heritage – which is, arguably, a Swedish heritage, since Roma have lived in Sweden for 500 years. Zetterlund highlights this point, stating "she is undoubtedly one of the most outstanding

Swedish jewelry artists." Nor was Taikon's achievement about becoming "normalized" into the mainstream. Through her degree at Konstfack, Taikon gained access and invitations to exhibit in major galleries and museums in Sweden and globally. Her exhibition at Sweden's National Museum in 1969 included her own work, that of her sister Katarina Taikon, and an extensive section on the history of the Swedish Roma, including serious human rights abuses. Thus, Taikon's work might be understood as a critical art/design practice, and, further, a practice of activism and political struggle.

"Rosa Taikon was the only well-known Roma silversmith in Sweden," notes Zetterlund in the obituary, continuing, "she had no successors, either at Konstfack or any other art school in Sweden." This is not due to admissions policy – Swedish institutions have equality structures/policies in place, and Konstfack faculty, students, and alumni pioneer gender, queer, and "norm-critical" approaches to the arts.[11] Yet, like most design institutions in Europe and the US, it remains predominantly white and middle- and upper-class. Institutions of design education condition the demographic patterns within the discipline and society, producing qualified graduates for professional practice and cultural organizations which further employ, fund, and give prizes in ways that often reproduce taught, enculturated, and established norms, values, and demographics. What is identified and recognized as a design student, as a designer, as "good" design, is self-perpetuating. Zetterlund argues elsewhere that the absence of multiple types of designers and subjectivities in design history reproduces norms that deter those from more diverse backgrounds from applying to design schools.[12] Making Taikon's work at the National Museum and Konstfack visible in the media and design history serves to highlight the continuing absence of Roma and other minorities within the national archives, the design canon, and our academic institutions.

Admissions and recruitment policies in academia continue to be the subject of profound cultural, moral, and legal struggles. These have also been the subject of research on the persistent phenomena of inequality – for example, recent evaluation of more than two decades of

11. Camilla Andersson, Karin Ehrnberger, and Maja Gunn, eds., Norm Form (Stockholm: ARKDES National Center for Architecture and Design, 2017).

12. Christina Zetterlund, "Just Decoration? Ideology and Design in Early-Twentieth-Century Sweden," in Scandinavian Design: Alternative Histories, ed. Kjetil Fallan (London: Berg, 2012), 103–16.

13. Lotte Bailyn, "Academic Careers and Gender Equity: Lessons Learned from MIT," *Gender, Work & Organization* 10, no. 2 (2003), 137–53.

14. Kristin Monroe and William Chiu, "Gender Equality in the Academy: The Pipeline Problem," *Political Science and Politics* (April 2010), 303–8.

15. Monroe and Chiu, "Gender Equality." Cf. Courtney Gasser and Katharine Shaffer, "Career Development of Women in Academia: Traversing the Leaky Pipeline," *The Professional Counselor* 4, no. 4 (2014), 332–52.

16. Danah Abdulla, "Design Otherwise: Towards a Locally-Centric Design Education Curricula in Jordan" (Ph.D. diss., Goldsmiths University College London, United Kingdom, 2017).

unprecedented gender equity polices at the Massachusetts Institute of Technology (MIT).[13] Despite measurable improvements, inequalities continue to persist there and elsewhere, prompting soul-searching and further perspectives on the so-called "pipeline problem."[14] Focus on the "pipeline" entails increasing the number of qualified people from underrepresented groups and removing barriers to the development of career paths and progression to higher levels within institutions. Associated policies tend to target structural factors at gateway or turning points, such as entrance exams, application evaluation, and promotion processes. In this respect, the increase of women in institutions of higher education and, indeed, a female majority in many of our arts and architectural institutions today, is important and necessary. However, despite increasing numbers of historically underrepresented groups at lower levels in academia and early career stages, the pipeline continues to "leak" dramatically.[15] Inequalities at higher organizational levels and in advanced career stages persist. One conclusion is that pipeline approaches are necessary but not sufficient. This can also motivate a consideration of bias, discrimination, and deterrence as not only effected structurally but through subtle and everyday micropractices, social interactions, networks, and norms as well as through symbolic and psychological dimensions.

In relation to design education, Danah Abdulla's doctoral work makes several valuable theoretical and practical contributions to "decolonizing" institutional structures and everyday practices.[16] Her case is design educational institutions in Jordan, which are conditioned by and reproduce the "neopatriarchal" state. For Abdulla, "neopatriarchy" spans from macrostructures – society, state, and economy – to microstructures – individual psyche, personality, and the family. It also positions male supremacy – i.e., patriarchy – in concert with the socioeconomic organization of modernity, including the fissure between tradition and industry and other originally Western European economic models. Abdulla studies the multiple and varied forms that neopatriarchy takes in design educational institutions and curricula. She examines issues of access, considering entrance exams, fees, and "privileges of the King" (i.e., seats for students from certain sectors of society); power, academic freedom, and language; course lists and study plans (including how these (re)produce Western/capitalist paradigms); power in the classroom, including models of teacher-centered vs. student-centered pedagogy. Crucially, she starts to make suggestions about how to intervene into the macro (bureaucratic and juridical structures) and micro (curricula and pedagogy).

A particularly interesting example along these lines is the process of decolonization underway at the Ontario College of Art and Design (OCAD), Canada's biggest art and design university, under the leadership of Dori Tunstall. This and other Canadian institutions aim not only at equality but equity in order to redress the historical colonization and oppression of indigenous peoples and territories. A recent open call for indigenous applicants for five tenured or tenure-track faculty positions is interesting both as a structural policy (a pipeline approach to increasing candidates and, potentially, equity through a targeted call) but also in terms of more subtle variables. Previous gender studies have revealed how the composition and form of job ads affect whether or not women apply, which can be down to seemingly trivial things such as wording, tone, punctuation, and lists, which elicit different responses between genders.[17] The OCAD ad is carefully composed to frame traditionally exclusive or excluding categories such as academia, design, and research more broadly than usual through terms such as "university of the imagination," "visual culture," and "indigenous knowledge systems." The ad was further accompanied by Tunstall's personal social media campaign reaching out more broadly than the institutional website and providing practical tips on applying to academic posts.

Decolonization at OCAD goes beyond conforming to the Ontario Human Rights Code, implemented through gateway and pipeline policies aimed at broadening representation in the faculty, board, and student body. The issue has been opened and discussed extensively within an institution-wide cultural and organizational change. Concepts stemming from indigenous communities (such as *mnaadendimowin*) have been developed and integrated into a governing principle of "respectful design,"[18] which is stated in the high-level university mission as well as in

17. Danielle Gaucher, Justin Friesen, and Aaron Kay, "Evidence that Gendered Wording in Job Advertisements Exists and Sustains Gender Inequality," *Journal of Personality and Social Psychology* 101, no. 1 (2001), 109–28.

18. Dori Tunstall, "On Respectful Design," www2.ocadu.ca/keyword/resepectful-design (accessed August 16, 2018).

Design Struggles

the nitty-gritty of criteria used in grading and graduating students. Thus, beyond the gateway terms for entering the institution, faculty and students continue to work and study within radically transformed structures (including budgets, evaluation criteria, and performance indicators) and subtle or "soft" variables such as institutional brand, content of curricula and courses, cultural values, and ethos.

These examples articulate modalities of institutional critique, which can open for contesting the terms in which design is constituted and practiced. Historians such as Katerina Rüedi sift through meeting notes and bureaucratic documentation accumulated within institutional archives, unearthing particular decisions with far-reaching consequences. Christina Zetterlund and others reveal overlooked or hidden figures within design, recording and making public alternative histories. An important task of critical historiography is troubling (rather than merely celebrating and reproducing) design history and those designers canonized in our past and present history books, museum archives, and educational syllabi.

Further, these examples make institutional critique explicit as a set of possible practices through which not only to contest but to reform design. Within her work, Taikon might be understood as an activist; acknowledging the privilege accompanying enrolment at Konstfack, she used her access to the National Museum to expand what and who might count in design. This is an important example of institutional "criticism from within" design practice, and the example also surfaces further practices available to design researchers and educators. Obituary writing can be understood as a form of institutional critique reaching a broad public, through which awareness and debate might be raised concerning policies, structures, and, importantly, the soft norms governing our design institutions. Writing job ads, in the case of OCAD, seems to be a careful and critical practice with measurable outcomes. Indeed, beyond mere reproduction of top-down national policies, OCAD demonstrates a more comprehensive process of institutional self-critique and change, through which design definitions, cultures, and future generations of designers may be transformed.

Everyday practices within academic life, such as

writing, bring the idea (and ideals) of institutional critique within reach. In my Nordic context, sociologist Liisa Husu has been a pioneering scholar of covert and subtle forms of discrimination and interventions in response. Her book *Sexism, Support and Survival in Academia*[19] is required reading in the mandatory course I took for academic promotion. Sara Ahmed's related and well-known scholarship details the "diversity work" in academia that often starts involuntarily, as a result of experiencing discrimination.[20] Reclaiming slurs such as "feminist killjoys," the title of her popular blog, she also attends to the typically unrewarded and stigmatized diversity work as an ongoing "phenomenological practice" enacted in daily practical reflections, struggles, and actions that take place within the mundanities of academia. For example, Ahmed evokes a further practice of institutional critique that I find relevant to design – namely, citation:

> I would describe citation as a rather successful reproductive technology, a way of reproducing the world around certain bodies. The reproduction of a discipline can be the reproduction of these techniques of selection, ways of making certain bodies and thematics core to the discipline, and others not even part.[21]

I have been developing my own "critical citation practice." Influenced by "critical design" during my postgraduate studies at the Royal College of Art (RCA) in London, as my career has developed as a researcher, educator, administrator, and academic leader, I have attempted to transpose criticality into practices associated with these roles as well. I have become increasingly reflexive and meticulous about who I cite and reference in my syllabi, presentations, and publications. For example, my preparation process often involves listing potential citations in spreadsheets to examine and thus make more conscious choices concerning gender and culture (im)balances.

I was shocked the first time I tried this during a book project with Johan Redström, Christina Zetterlund, Matilda Plöjel, and Lisa Olausson.[22] I was writing at the time about how climate change disproportionately affects

19. Liisa Husu, *Sexism, Support and Survival in Academia* (Helsinki: University of Helsinki, 2001).

20. Sara Ahmed, *On Being Included: Racism and Diversity in Institutional Life* (Durham, NC: Duke University, 2012).

21. Sara Ahmed, "Making Feminist Points," feministkilljoys. com/2013/09/11/making-feminist-points/ (accessed August 1, 2018).

22. Ramia Mazé, "Who Is Sustainable?," in *Share This Book*, ed. Ramia Mazé et al. (Stockholm: Axl Books, 2013), 83–124.

23. European Commission, SHE
FIGURES 2015 (Luxembourg:
Publications Office of the
European Union, 2016),
ec.europa.eu/research/swafs/
pdf/pub_gender_equality/
she_figures_2015-final.pdf. Cf.
Kristina Rolin and Jenny Vainio,
"Gender in Academia in Finland:
Tensions between Policies and
Gendering Processes in Physics
Departments," Science Studies
24, no. 1 (2011), 26–46.

24. Husu, *Sexism*.

25. Vincent Larivière et al.,
"Bibliometrics: Global Gender
Disparities in Science," *Nature*
504, no. 7079 (2013), 211–13;
see also Danica Savonick and
Cathy Davidson, "Gender Bias
in Academe: An Annotated
Bibliography of Important
Recent Studies," blogs.lse.
ac.uk/impactofsocialsciences/
2016/03/08/gender-bias-
in-academe-an-annotated-
bibliography (accessed August
16, 2018).

certain cultures, generations, genders, and geographies, and how design can reproduce such inequalities. When I paused in the process to scrutinize my bibliography, I found it dominated by white, Western, male authors. Deciding to rectify this, I started developing a practice of nerdy, quantitative counting but also, importantly, I started a more qualitative journey to find and engage with more authors from different backgrounds. In the process, I encountered a wealth of new examples and sources that have fundamentally transformed my work. Matilda Plöjel, the book's designer, perceived this shift, and we tried to reflect it in the graphical form of the article. In addition to the normal appended list of references, and alongside my own text and other illustrations on each page of the article, sources were represented visually as reproductions of book spines including author names. Thus, my alternative design canon became even more visible.

As designers, educators, administrators, and researchers, we all, daily, may contest and reform the design canon, understood here, literally, as the doctrine, dogma, and lineage of key figures and works comprising design. Career advancement comes with an increase in authority and privilege, and I try to recognize this with more critical practices. Now, in my position as an academic in Finland, where academia is more gender-equal than almost anywhere in the world, persistent inequalities are still apparent despite substantial policy and structural measures.[23] Liisa Husu calls our attention to hidden forms of discrimination in academia, in which women, parents, and others encounter closed cultures, gendered distributions of labor, and impenetrable social hierarchies, experienced as bias, exclusion, isolation, and obstacles blocking their career paths. These compound to the extent that, in the end, there remains only a dramatically gendered pattern of "professors and 'leavers.'"[24] For me, citation is a contributing practice, among many others, which I can affect. It is, apparently, normal for both men and women to cite equally qualified female authors less frequently than males.[25] While writing the article mentioned above, I found myself reproducing a practice that contributes to systematically discriminating and excluding others like me from advancing within academia. This has done much more than "kill joy" for me;

this kind of critical institutional practice has transformed my ideals, knowledges, and the basic content of my everyday practice.

Academic and Research Conventions

In 2002, Monica Bueno and I marked a career milestone when we presented our first academic conference paper about our critical and participatory design project with an elder community.[26] The conference keynote, "Neither Bauhäusler nor Nerd: Educating the Interaction Designer,"[27] was given by participatory design pioneer Pelle Ehn, who would later become my doctoral supervisor. This was the time when my postgraduate field of study at the RCA, rather ambiguously named "Computer-Related Design,"[28] was becoming named, institutionalized, and widely called upon by industry as "interaction design." Ehn's keynote referred to his previously published "Manifesto for a Digital Bauhaus,"[29] a founding document for a new interaction design curriculum at Malmö University in Sweden and for two new research studios at the Interactive Institute in Malmö. In 2001, I had moved to Sweden to work at the Interactive Institute in Gothenburg and gravitated towards a research career, eventually completing my doctorate through Malmö University.[30] In response to the institutional model of the MIT Media Lab in the US, the Interactive Institute was founded as Sweden's national research institute, modeling transdisciplinary knowledge production combining art and technology and addressing the public and societal challenges.

By 1998, Ehn targeted the "nerd generation and the third culture." He argued for building upon the studio-based pedagogies of the original Bauhaus but additionally emphasized transdisciplinarity and "Scandinavian design that unites a democratic perspective emphasizing open dialogue and active user participation."[31] These were evident in research projects developed within the context of the Interactive Institute studios,[32] along with an orientation, articulated in Ehn's 2002 keynote, in relation to the critical design of my RCA tutors and authors of *Design Noir*,[33] Anthony Dunne and Fiona Raby. Ehn concludes:

26. Ramia Mazé and Monica Bueno, "Mixers: A Participatory Approach to Design Prototyping," in *Proceedings of the Conference DIS Designing Interactive Systems* (2002).

27. Pelle Ehn, "Neither Bauhäusler nor Nerd: Educating the Interaction Designer," in *Proceedings of the Conference DIS Designing Interactive Systems* (2002).

28. Gillian Crampton Smith, "Computer-Related Design at the Royal College of Art: 1997 Graduation Projects," *interactions* 4, no. 6 (1997), 27–33.

29. Pelle Ehn, "Manifesto for a Digital Bauhaus," *Digital Creativity* 9, no. 4 (1998), 207–16.

30. Ramia Mazé, *Occupying Time: Design, Technology and the Form of Interaction* (Stockholm: Axl Books, 2017).

31. Ehn, "Manifesto for a Digital Bauhaus."

32. Lone Malmborg, "The Digital Bauhaus: Vision or Reality?," *Digital Creativity* 15, no. 3 (2004), 175–81.

33. Anthony Dunne and Fiona Raby, *Design Noir: The Secret Life of Electronic Objects* (Basel: Birkhäuser and August Media, 2001).

34. Ehn, "Neither Bauhäusler nor Nerd."

35. Pelle Ehn and Peter Ullmark, "Educating the Reflective Design Researcher," in *Practice-Based Design Research*, ed. Laurene Vaughan (London: Bloomsbury, 2017), 77–86.

36. Cf. Rolf Hughes, Catharina Dyrssen, and Maria Hellström Reimer, "Artistic Research Today and Tomorrow," *Årsbok Konstnärlig FoU* (Stockholm: Swedish Research Council, 2011); Catharina Dyrssen et al., "The Future of Swedish Research: Overview 2014 Artistic Research" (Stockholm: Swedish Research Council, 2014); Susannah Helgeson et al., eds., *D! Designforskning för nytänkande, innovation och hållbar tillväxt* 22 (2014).

37. Joyce Yee, "Methodological innovation in Practice-Based Design Doctorates," *Journal of Research Practice* 6, no. 2 (2010).

38. Ramia Mazé, *Occupying*, Cf. Ramia Mazé and Johan Redström, "Difficult Forms: Critical Practices of Design and Research," *Research Design Journal* 1, no. 1 (2009), 28–39.

Design noir is not glamourous with great utopias and modern heroes as the Bauhaus, but it still has a humanist stance and a consciousness about political dilemmas that can take us beyond modern design and challenge both the Bauhäusler and the nerd as the interaction designer of tomorrow.[34]

Against this backdrop, my doctoral research took shape at the Interactive Institute. Indeed, the institute was a testbed for developing design and artistic research in Sweden as a whole. At the time, there was no doctoral program that would accept and fund arts practitioners as researchers, and we at the institute prototyped early examples of "research through practice."[35] Eventually, our approaches and many of my colleagues influenced and shifted to more formal institutions such as educational programs at universities, funding programs at national research foundations and research conferences, and publications in design and the arts.[36] This was part of a larger wave, spanning several decades in the Nordics, Europe, and other regions, of practitioners entering institutions of higher education and research, inventing and reforming academic structures and norms. Critical practitioners, more specifically, have contested the institutionalized practices, doctrinal conventions, and material forms that research takes. Examples in Sweden include the doctoral work of myself and Otto von Busch[37] and my colleagues at the Interactive Institute, Kristina Lindström and Åsa Ståhl. We all conducted "research through practice," a modality of knowledge production that I articulated in my doctorate as "criticism from within" the materiality, methods, and modality of design practice.[38] Further, the doctoral dissertation became a site for expressing, experimenting, and expanding critical practice, challenging the form of the book itself.

The work of Lindström and Ståhl is particularly interesting in this respect. They were researchers at the Interactive Institute, who then applied with the same coauthored research proposal to two different departments at Malmö University (interaction design and media and communication studies, respectively). This is highly unconventional in institutional terms – but it is in the transdisciplinary spirit of the Digital Bauhaus. Their

proposal was accepted, they were assigned different supervisors (Pelle Ehn and Bo Reimer, respectively), and they
proceeded to embark on several years of "research through
design" together with their project "Threads – a Mobile
Sewing Circle." Their final dissertation was written, publicly
defended, and published as a single, coauthored book.[39] It
was comprised of multiple, coauthored, and peer-reviewed
articles published in reputed journals and conferences, with
inserted introductory, concluding, and interim texts. The
form of the book as well as the writing style and authorial
"voice" were carefully and critically positioned, drawing
upon feminist technoscience theories that informed not only
their project but the composition of the dissertation itself.
Particularly striking to me was how their theorized position
on knowledge as jointly produced was reflected in shifts
between the single-authored first-person singular ("I") and
the collective first-person plural ("we") in the book and in
the defense.

　　　Their work exemplifies relevant philosophies and
epistemologies of Ehn's manifesto and the ambitions of
our institute to engage in institutional self-critique and
organizational change. The plural "we" reflects the spirit of
a "third culture" conception of knowledge *co*production.
Lindström and Ståhl extend but also challenge philosophical underpinnings of "research through practice,"
such as pragmatist positions adapted from Donald Schön
concerning knowledge as produced through embodied and
material action. They seem to depart from the cognitivist
assumptions of his scholarship; instead they emphasize
knowledge as emerging in-between people and things,
relationally and socially through *inter*action. To formulate
their epistemological position, they draw upon feminist
theorists of science and technology such as Donna Haraway
and Karen Barad. Through the work of Barad and Maria
Puig de la Bellacasa, they also challenge and develop
notions of criticality, moving beyond the Frankfurt School
theories influencing the critical design of Anthony Dunne
and Fiona Raby to theorize their work in terms of feminist
concepts of relation, concern, and care. Lindström and
Ståhl thus theorize, cross, and reconfigure boundaries
between knowledges, disciplines, methods, and, even, bodies
and beings. This is an example of how feminist modes of

39. Kristina Lindström and
Åsa Ståhl, "Patchworking
Publics-in-the-Making" (Ph.D.
diss., Malmö University, 2014).

40. Katja Grillner, "Ramble, Linger and Gaze: Dialogs from the Landscape Garden" (Ph.D. diss., KTH Royal Institute of Technology, Stockholm, 2000).

41. Katarina Bonnevier, "Behind Straight Curtains: Towards a Queer Feminist Theory of Architecture" (Ph.D. diss., KTH Royal Institute of Technology, Stockholm, 2007).

42. Brady Burroughs, "Architectural Flirtations, Formerly Known as Critique: Dethroning the Serious to Clear Ground for Generous Architectural Conversations," in *Feminist Futures of Spatial Practice*, ed. Meike Schalk, Thérèse Kristiansson, and Ramia Mazé (Baunach: Spurbuchverlag, 2017), 225–38. Cf. Dana Cuff, *Architecture: The Story of Practice* (Cambridge, MA: MIT Press, 1992).

criticality may not only interrogate, but also project, activate, and enact alternatives. Their alternative articulations of research practices and academic conventions constitute a major departure from doctoral study, which is typically constituted as individualistic and mono-disciplinary.

At the time in Sweden, there was a shift not only of the arts and associated practices into academia but also a reconsideration of more institutionalized and established research traditions. Notably, at the School of Architecture at the Royal Institute of Technology (KTH) in Stockholm, doctoral students experimented with writing and teaching as practices of knowledge production. The subject of Katja Grillner's dissertation was eighteenth-century landscape architecture, for example, but its contribution was not only historical but methodological.[40] She developed a narrative and dialogical mode of writing as a hermeneutical research method for the field of architectural history and theory. Subsequently, Grillner's doctoral student, Katarina Bonnevier, completed her dissertation as a study of historical architectural subjects.[41] Bonnevier integrated dialogical methodologies with activism, design, and theatre, which are theorized and positioned as critical (queer feminist) practices. Bonnevier articulates herself within an emerging tradition of "Ph.D. by architectural design," which parallels "research through practice" in design.

Brady Burroughs, who was supervised mainly by Hélène Frichot but also by Katja Grillner, completed a dissertation that builds upon and further develops these epistemologies and methodologies. Additionally, in Burrough's case, teaching was the site of critical (queer feminist) practice, in which knowledge was produced through experiments with curricula, pedagogical methods, and course materials. In the classroom, for example, she explored alternative relations of power and authority, including coproduction of the course syllabus with students and experiments with subjectivity and voice through theatre, masquerade, writing, and social media. She documents efforts to alter the power dynamic of the architectural jury, or "crit," which is a primary vehicle for indoctrinating students into the working culture, social dynamics, and hierarchies (predominantly patriarchies) of the architectural profession.[42] Some of these methods were also applied and developed "live" within an interim evaluation of her research, for which I was the opponent, and in the final public defense. The multiple subjectivities and epistemological standpoints informing her research, articulated through fictional personas, is expressed as three authors, Beda Ring, Brady Burroughs, and Henri T. Beall, on the cover and in the colophon of her dissertation.[43]

These examples of doctoral work and dissertations develop dialogical forms of creative and critical practice, thus extending social and relational conceptions of knowledge production to the writing process and form of the dissertation. Grillner, Bonnevier, and Burroughs situate this in relation to a tradition of feminist writing, as articulated by, for example, Mona Livholts.[44] They experiment with subject and author positions, identities, and voices, playing with and blurring theory and practice and high and low literary forms and boundaries. In addition, these demonstrate multiple and interacting practices in knowledge (co-) production, including design practices (such as making, prototyping, and testing), historiographical practices, writing practices, and even naming, referencing, and citational practices. These are further practical examples of institutional critique, thus contributing to potential "feminist design power tools," accessible in our everyday work as design academics.

The academic book "norm" has become an important site for my own work in collaboration with several of these scholars. I have reconsidered the activity of making a book ("bookmaking"[45]) as a critical and feminist practice of design in two different academic book projects: *Share This Book* with Johan Redström, Christina Zetterlund, Matilda Plöjel, and Lisa Olausson;[46] and *Feminist Futures of Spatial Practice* with Meike Schalk and Thérèse Kristiansson,[47] which includes collaborations with and contributions from Bonnevier, Burroughs, Frichot, Grillner, and more than thirty others from across architecture, the arts, art history, curating, cultural heritage studies, environmental sciences, futures studies, film, visual communication, design and design theory, queer, intersectional, and gender studies, political sciences, sociology, and urban planning. To elaborate more specifically through one example, *Feminist Futures* can be understood as querying the codified format of an

43. Beda Ring, Brady Burroughs, and Henri T. Beall, "Architectural Flirtations: A Love Storey" (Ph.D. diss., KTH Royal Institute of Technology, Stockholm, 2016).

44. Mona Livholts, ed., *Emergent Writing Methodologies in Feminist Studies* (London: Routledge, 2011).

45. Ramia Mazé, "Bookmaking as Critical and Feminist Practice of Design," in *Proceedings of the Design Research Society Conference* DRS (2018).

46. Ramia Mazé, Lisa Olausson, Matilda Plöjel, Johan Redström, and Christina Zetterlund, eds., *Share This Book* (Stockholm: Axl Books, 2013).

47. Meike Schalk, Thérèse Kristiansson, and Ramia Mazé, eds., *Feminist Futures of Spatial Practice* (Baunach: Spurbuchverlag, 2017).

48. Dexter Sinister, "On Self-Initiated Projects as an Alternative Platform," in *Iaspis Forum on Design and Critical Practice: The Reader*, ed. Magnus Ericson et al. (Berlin: Sternberg Press and Iaspis, 2009), 267.

49. James Goggin, "Practice from Everyday Life," in *Graphic Design: Now in Production*, ed. Andrew Blauvelt and Ellen Lupton (Minneapolis, MN: Walker Art Center, 2011), 32–40.

50. Jane Rendell, "Critical Spatial Practice: Curating, Editing, Writing," in *Issues in Curating Contemporary Art and Performance*, ed. Judith Rugg and Michele Sedgwig (London: Intellect, 2007), 59–75.

51. Hélène Frichot, Katja Grillner, and Julieanna Preston, "Feminist Practices: Writing around the Kitchen Table," in *Feminist Futures of Spatial Practice*, 171–98.

edited, peer-reviewed academic book.

To conceptualize "bookmaking," I looked both to practices of critical design and to critical and feminist theory. Critical (graphic) designers such as Dexter Sinister and James Goggin reconfigure the scope of criticality within their work. Dexter Sinister, the joint identity of David Reinfurt and Stuart Bailey, do produce books. But their practice also takes the form of a "just-in-time workshop and occasional bookstore," a space and time for anyone to learn and self-produce graphic design and with a lending-library and community-building intent. This alternative production and distribution model is "best described as a self-conscious model: both a regular design studio and a tool to question the nature of a design studio."[48] Goggin considers the 99 percent non-design activity involved in running a design company as critical, including the daily details of administering, contracting, lecturing, curating, editing, distributing, and "press-passing."[49] The mundane activity and action of doing criticality is emphasized in his company name, Practise, in which the British spelling with an "s" exclusively denotes a verb (whereas *practice* in American English can be a noun or a verb).

Feminist architectural theorist Jane Rendell further interrogates writing, curating, and making edited books or anthologies as feminist spatial practices, arguing that the edited book is an ideal site for investigating movements between disciplines and between theory and practice.[50] This was enacted physically and socially in "Anthology Works," an event organized by FATALE (of which Bonnevier, Burroughs, Grillner, and Schalk are the main members) featuring Rendell as a keynote. Participants, including myself, took part in a series of activities exploring the notion of *anthology* from different disciplinary positions. The anthology and other academic practices have norms and exclusions. The anthology as, essentially, a structure for selecting, giving voice to, and citing particular texts and authors, can become feminist or decolonial when done by or with others, and otherwise. An example was Grillner's "architecture writing workshop,"[51] which unfolded at the event as role-play and dialog among participants through the medium of extracted quotations from a historical canon of feminist texts. Not only the content of the texts but the format of the activity itself was positioned as feminist. Texts were selected and sequenced, collectively and performatively, in an embodied and dialogic way, creating relations or interiority among differently situated knowledges in which sub-altern authors outside of the mainstream canon were voiced and heard by each and all together. This can be seen as a microcosm of our "book-making" in *Feminist Futures*.

Feminist Futures of Spatial Practice is the culmination of a process set into motion within the Introduction to Architecture and Gender course module offered at KTH. A more extensive account is provided elsewhere of how the course was set up, including its location and position toward the university, admissions policy, and pedagogical methods, conceived as a "pedagogical queering-tool" involving a series of critically debated microdecisions and standpoints.[52] A community and a critical mass of content formed around and through the course. Thus, a book project and process was initiated. Criticality in the book was enacted through mundane practices related to academic conventions such as selection, positioning, sequencing, and voices of contributors; review and editorial processes including language, spelling, and style guides; balance and distribution of theory and practice as well as labor and resources during the process; and terms, materiality, and

52. Meike Schalk, et al., "Introduction," in *Feminist Futures of Spatial Practice*, 13–23.

Peer review in the round. Roundtable with myself, Katja Grillner, Meike Schalk, Maryam Fanni, Hélène Frichot, and Brady Burroughs. Photo: Ramia Mazé, 2014.

53. Mazé, "Bookmaking."

54. Christing Wennerås and Agnes Wold, "Nepotism and Sexism in Peer-Review," *Nature* 387, no. 6631 (1997), 341. Cf. references in Danica Savonick and Cathy Davidson, "Gender Bias."

55. Nel Janssens, "Collective Sense-Making for Change," in *Feminist Futures of Spatial Practice*, 151–58; Doina Petrescu, ed., *Altering Practices: Feminist Politics and Poetics of Space* (London: Routledge, 2007).

ownership within book publishing and distribution.[53]
To pick one practice to further exemplify here, we reconceptualized review as a kind of "peer review in the round," performed face-to-face, in dialog, and collectively.

Five roundtable sessions were organized in 2014, in which contributors to the course were invited to develop contributions for the book. Roundtables took the form of intimate conversations around texts circulated in advance, closely read and carefully commented by participants and a designated "peer reviewer." Peer review is a key mechanism to ensure quality in the academic system in which many of us work. Standard "blind" peer review is argued to serve gender and other measures of equality in publishing, though certainly not unequivocally, and even the most rigorous standards may be subject to nepotism and sexism.[54] While peer-review standards are important to build and maintain, there is no singular, unassailable solution to quality and equality in review. In *Feminist Futures*, we sought quality and equality through other means suited to the community and project. We were inspired by feminist pedagogy including, in the terms of Nel Janssens, "the pleasure of conversation" and, in those of Doina Petrescu, "feminist collective reconstructions."[55] In the roundtables, we came from different backgrounds, disciplines, and positions within academia or practice – rather distant social and cultural locations that could potentially pose a risk of inequality or hierarchy. Each participant had shared a chapter draft, which meant each was equally vulnerable and had a common stake in both receiving and giving feedback. Giving and receiving feedback in person, as a conversation and around a table meant that critique became dialogic and mutualistic, articulated from distinctly different but mutually respectful positions. The external "peer reviewer" in our session acted as a kind of moderator, rather than as an evaluator, listening to the conversations for common issues articulated from different perspectives.

Peer review in *Feminist Futures* had a pedagogical purpose as a kind of peer learning, in contrast to other purposes such as critique or evaluation. Unexpected commonalities and differences emerged from the peer-review conversations, which thus constituted a kind of interpersonal or collective knowledge-making. After the roundtables, each draft further evolved through several cycles of further review with the three book editors, in which reviewing continued as an increasingly precise form of dialog. As editors, we also contributed with chapters and were thus reviewed by the others, enhancing our sensitivity to the personal and power relations enacted within review processes. This reflection and transparency throughout the process attuned not only to articulating but listening carefully, more than in standard review or editorial processes. One implication is a more careful and multifaceted editorial position, and the evolution of chapters that expressed ever-more precisely in argument, language, and form the author's (or authors') own position and voice. In practice, there was never a "universal" nor neutral position but rather a safe space created spatially (in the room, around the table, and, consequently, continued in more distant and written exchanges). Within the roundtables, and the "book-making" as a whole, there was an intense and continual "being-in-relation" continuously performed, a continual self-transformation and peer learning.

56. Isabelle Stengers and Vinciene Despret, *Women Who Make a Fuss* (Minneapolis, MN: Univocal Publishing, 2014).

Concluding Thoughts

I and my two co-editors of *Feminist Futures* came to academia from different practice backgrounds, each grappling with our positionality and power in relation to our disciplines (no small feat considering our transdisciplinary experiences), within the institution more generally, and in relation to our predecessors and future generations. Nor are we alone in this, as is apparent from the scholarship of Liisa Husu and Sara Ahmed and as articulated by philosophers Isabelle Stengers and Vinciane Despret in their book *Women Who Make a Fuss*.[56] Like Stengers and Despret, an immediate problem for us today is that, unlike our predecessors at the Bauhaus, it can be hard to see or recognize when and where we are oppressed. Covert and subtle forms of inequality are not easily visible in a group photograph. Many of us, and especially women and others in the minority, are too often told not to "make a fuss." Mainstream design, the design profession, and our established cultural and educational institutions are resistant

MAKING THE INVISIBLE VISIBLE

to change and may favor abstract and often uncritical conceptions of "innovation" and "progress." Here, the idea of the future is critical – we cannot know what needs to be different (or "innovated") nor what direction we prefer ("progression") without making a fuss. We must pause to reflect on the past and present.

Critical and feminist practices question and contest but also project, activate, and enact alternative norms or future ideals. The how and when, as well as the by and for whom, of such practices is also important. Even as we expand our collection of "feminist design power tools," these are always situated and directed, and must also be subject to critical questions. Nevertheless, it is in our everyday practices that present and future overlap, moment by moment, as we critically learn from the past and actively live out alternatives and preferred futures – for example, as "embodied utopias" and through "practicing otherwise."[57] We encounter glass walls and ceilings, which we try to pierce or make our own. Critical historiography and design studies (for example, through feminist or decolonial perspectives) help us to understand underlying worldviews, ontologies, and ideologies. These are daily reproduced in canons, curricula, and other forms, which, in turn, in/exclude and shape students, teachers, and, potentially, ourselves. We may experience an inevitable "mainstreaming," or indoctrination, to existing structures and policies. But there is also at least some power in our everyday micropractices, in collaborating, coproducing knowledge, in building collectivity, in becoming toward others and preferred futures.

I have argued here that we can act, each of us, from within our everyday practices, as part of larger sociopolitical entities, in the here and now, and affect the future. I've traversed examples of critical/feminist practices of design, history, education, and research. For me, and from multiple standpoints in my everyday life – as a woman, a designer, an educator, a researcher, an author, a jury member, etc. – there are possibilities for asking critical questions, for being reflexive and intentional about the differences and futures I try to affect. Each time I cite others, make a syllabus, super-vise students, collaborate with peers, write and make books, there exists the possibility for doing things differently, to become closer to my preferred future. In *Feminist Futures*, we argue that feminist futures are "becoming" when common projects – e.g., a canon, curriculum, project, or conversation – not only momentarily produce an alternative space, but effect new connections and social relations that can alter ingrained patriarchal structures as many of us still experience them.

Acknowledgments

Based on my keynote at "Beyond Change," this is a revised version of an article subsequently published as "Design Educational Practice: Reflections on Feminist Modes and Politics," in *Bauhaus Futures*, ed. Laura Forlano, Molly Wright Steenson, and Mike Ananny, 3–23 (Boston, MA: MIT Press, 2019). Thank you to Felix Gerloff for editorial contributions to this article.

III
PERSPECTIVES

ALEXA'S BODY
What the Interface Obscures and How Design Could Help Us See

Johannes Bruder

1. Daniel Farey-Jones, "Amazon Alexa Helps Blind Woman in RNIB-Approved Ad," *Campaign*, September 2, 2020, www.campaignlive.co.uk/article/amazon-alexa-helps-blind-woman-rnib-approved-ad/1595228.

Seeing through the Internet's Eyes

A Black woman wakes up in a dark bedroom to the chirping of an unknown bird. "Alexa, what's the time," she asks. "It's 6 a.m.," replies a female voice emanating from a light pulsating disk, as we observe the protagonist getting dressed. Carefully, the woman walks down the stairs, greets her dog, and lights up the stove to make coffee. She delicately reaches for a cup from the shelf, and after pouring herself some coffee she gravitates towards the window and calmly stares into the distance. "Alexa, what's the weather like right now," she asks, the eyes seemingly locked on raindrops running down the glass. "Currently it's light rain," Alexa responds to the coffee-sipping protagonist, who – after a cut – slips into a raincoat and directs her dog out of the front door. Just a second earlier, a close-up shot on the handle attached to the dog's harness revealed that the woman is blind.

What you just read is a description of "Morning Ritual," a short commercial that advertises Amazon's smart speaker Echo Dot to blind or partially sighted people and has thus been approved by the Royal National Institute of Blind People (RNIB). The marketing webpage *Campaign* quotes their senior technology manager, who believes that "a device that can give you information via voice simplifies tasks and opens a world of accessibility" for those living with sight loss.[1]

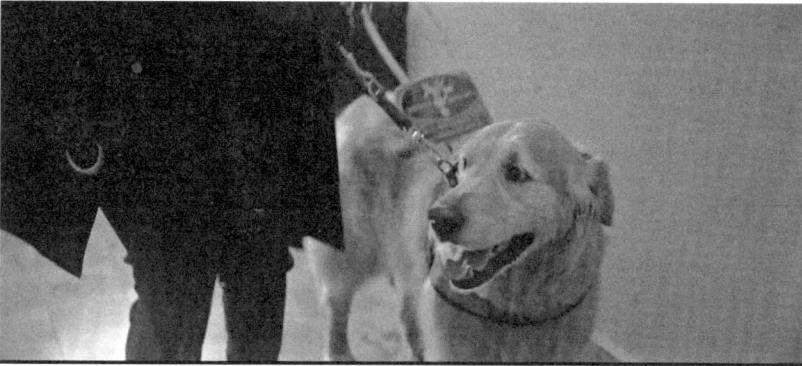

Stills from *Morning Ritual*. Agency: Joint London; production: Academy Film; director: Frédéric Planchon.

The commercial is typical for Amazon's recent marketing strategy, which involves promoting the integration of their smart devices into domestic environments. Tailored to specific countries or markets, they detail how Alexa will augment the lives of those who provide her with a home. Against this background, "Morning Ritual" seems convincing, for it gives examples of how an unassuming,

Design Struggles

2. Johannes Bruder, "Infrastructural Intelligence: Contemporary Entanglements between Neuroscience and AI," in *Vital Models: The Making and Use of Models in the Brain Sciences*, ed. Tara Mahfoud, Sam McLean, and Nikolas Rose, (Cambridge, MA: Academic Press, 2017), 101–28, doi.org/10.1016/bs.pbr.2017.06.004.

tiny speaker that goes under the name of Echo Dot can step in where (partial) sight loss obscures the external world. But then again, the commercial makes you wonder: who is to be convinced?

That is to say that there's a bitter irony inherent in "Morning Ritual," which resides in the fact that the commercial is a short film, and mostly devoid of voice-over and dialogue at that. What happens throughout the commercial consequently remains entirely opaque to anyone who cannot see. "Morning Ritual" is therefore probably the most sincere ad that Amazon has ever commissioned and figures as a powerful visual metaphor for the sight loss that nearly all of Alexa's interlocutors suffer from: while Alexa permits the owner of an Echo Dot to metaphorically see through the eyes of the internet, she herself can never be seen.

What is present in the users' living rooms is no more than a tiny, unassuming speaker-microphone combination that provides the interface for interactions between a cloud-based machine-learning system and its human interlocutors. What the interface obscures is the human labor that first put Alexa in the position to appear intelligent. In fact, it is user experience and interface design that allows those who conceive themselves as "users" to understand the services of Alexa as mere products of a distant, machinic, or "infrastructural" intelligence.[2] The real crisis of design – if you want to use this term – is that it often succumbs to user experience and blinds us to the logistical assemblage of precarious labor that happens in front, behind, above, and below the interface.

This essay is an attempt at breaking this spell and rethinking the role of design – as that which potentially reinstates the symmetry between, and a common political agenda for, users and producers. I begin by assembling Alexa's body and continue by analyzing the subject positions of workers caught within. Based on these insights, I argue that UX and interface design are in a unique position to support workers' struggles against a social factory – by reminding the user that she is a producer herself.

Alexa's Anatomy

In 2018, Kate Crawford of AI Now and Vladan Joler of Share Lab published their very own attempt at visualizing Alexa's typically invisible, ungraspable, and, literally, sublime body.[3] Their essay and interactive map, published under the title "Anatomy of an AI System," provide an anatomical case study of an artificial intelligence system made of human labor. It links pit mines and the extraction of metals and rare earths to the labor of data labeling, the automated training of machine learning algorithms, and the recovery of resources on large e-waste grounds in the Global South. The strength of Crawford and Joler's map is that it draws seemingly unrelated processes of extraction and exploitation together into one "body," where each has a particular, anatomical function.

"Anatomy of an AI System" responds to calls for approaching structural inequalities through the lives of those whose work is typically not formally recognized – typically because it is maintenance or "infrastructural" labor.[4] In any "fleeting moment of interaction [with an Echo device]," Crawford and Joler write, "a vast matrix of capacities is invoked: interlaced chains of resource extraction, human labor, and algorithmic processing across networks of mining, logistics, distribution, prediction, and optimization."[5]

Crawford and Joler briefly elaborate on lithium extraction on the Bolivian Salar de Uyuni plateau, tin mining on the Indonesian island of Bangka, and the difficulties faced by large corporations such as Philips when they try to avoid tantalum sourced by children in the Congo. Martín Arboleda, meanwhile, speaks of circuits of (planetary) extraction to emphasize the extent to which the production of computing devices and the logistics of mining are interrelated,[6] while Orit Halpern has coined the term "machine learning landscapes" to analyze how the Atacama desert in Chile is reconfigured as one of the planet's primary resources for the introduction of general artificial intelligence.[7]

Yet, industrialized landscapes in the Global South are not the only spaces where human bodies are exhausted so that Alexa can let you know – at any time – what time

3. Kate Crawford and Vladan Joler, "Anatomy of an AI System: The Amazon Echo as an Anatomical Map of Human Labor, Data and Planetary Resources," *AI Now Institute and Share Lab*, September 7, 2018, www.anatomyof.ai.

4. Susan Leigh Star and Anselm Strauss, "Layers of Silence, Arenas of Voice: The Ecology of Visible and Invisible Work," *Computer Supported Cooperative Work (CSCW)* 8, no. 1 (March 1, 1999), 9–30, doi.org/10.1023/A:1008651105359.

5. Crawford and Joler, "Anatomy of an AI System," 16.

6. Martín Arboleda, "From Spaces to Circuits of Extraction: Value in Process and the Mine/City Nexus," *Capitalism Nature Socialism* (August 16, 2019), 1–20, doi.org/10.1080/10455752.2019.1656758.

7. Orit Halpern, "Learning from the Atacama," 2020 (unpublished manuscript).

8. Sarah T. Roberts, *Behind the Screen: Content Moderation in the Shadows of Social Media* (New Haven, CT: Yale University Press, 2019), 183.

9. Alix Johnson, "Data Centers as Infrastructural In-Betweens: Expanding Connections and Enduring Marginalities in Iceland," *American Ethnologist* 46, no. 1 (February 2019), 75–88, doi.org/10.1111/amet.12735.

10. Tanwen Dawn-Hiscox, "Who Wants to Be a Data Center Engineer?," *Data Center Dynamics* (blog), December 3, 2018, www.datacenterdynamics.com/analysis/who-wants-be-data-center-engineer/.

11. George Henry, "The best part is the autonomy," April 12, 2014, post on Quora, "What's it like to work in a data center?," www.quora.com/Whats-it-like-to-work-in-a-data-center.

it is. Urban environments are gradually reorganized to provide excellent conditions for the design and implementation of smart or intelligent infrastructure. In Nairobi's Kibera neighborhood, the Metiabruz neighborhood of Kolkata, and Metro Manila in the Philippines, predominantly female cognitive workers manually label data to augment the capabilities of intelligent systems – such as the ability to understand various dialects and pronunciations in order to translate them into text that can be effectively searched.

The optimization of remote landscapes and urban nodes for machine learning shows how former colonial relations map onto today's digital labor, for supposedly decolonized territories are in this process reorganized as zones of extraction where workers' rights cannot develop thanks to historical legacies of "military, economic, and cultural dominance."[8]

Speaking of military legacies: the server farms and data centers on which Alexa runs are often placed in abandoned military zones[9] and the humans employed to troubleshoot these systems profit from having served in armed forces. Advertisements for data center jobs emphasize that physical endurance is at least as important as management skills and technical know-how. An Amazon data center technician's role "has a physical component requiring the ability to lift and rack equipment up to 40 lbs." It may require working in cramped spaces – which is why Salute Inc., an organization founded by a former US Army reservist, is trying to employ army veterans in data center management. Apparently, "the transition from infantryman to data center technician is easy: working remotely, maintaining dangerous equipment, communicating with a team, and acting fast in the face of unexpected situations are skills expected both in the army and in data centres."[10]

The subject positions of maintainers and troubleshooters are defined primarily by operating manuals and technical protocols, and their ability to function as a cog in the wheels of the machine. On a Quora thread, a Facebook data center engineer asks: "Can you work in an environment where you have spoken to not one other person for 8 hours?"[11] And Tim Burke, former owner of a data center explains that his favorite data center was a building so hardened it was an accidental Faraday cage. When I went in, I knew that communication with the outside world was going to be severed like a cut ethernet cord. The data center was where I went to get away. It was where I went to think.[12]

12. Tim Burke, "Why I Miss My Data Center and Why I'm Never Going Back," *BetterCloud* (blog), April 27, 2016, www.bettercloud.com/monitor/data-center-nostalgia/.

13. Maya Indira Ganesh and Johannes Bruder, "Cloud Cosmogram," *Data Farms* (blog), 2019, www.datafarms.org/2019/12/16/cloud-cosmogram/.

14. Burke, "Why I Miss My Data Center and Why I'm Never Going Back."

Many workplaces in contemporary machine learning landscapes are indeed not only or always remote, but lonely in that they define sociality as the ability to communicate with the machine.

The Socio-Material Configurations of Contemporary AI

In "Cloud Cosmogram," Maya Indira Ganesh and I analyze how the roles of humans are defined where humans are supposedly absent.[13] Via blog posts, personal conversations, and job descriptions, we delved into the work-lives of data center engineers and found that they attend primarily to strange noises and flashing lights – or rather, anomalies in the patterns of noises and signals are what they are trained to perceive:

> Servers visually communicate through their flashing lights – green, yellow, blue, red, you name it. Each color and how quickly it flashes means something. You can feel the pulse of your organization simply by stepping inside your data center and taking a quick glance. It's almost a server morse code. The lights make basic troubleshooting easy. If port 41 is flashing like crazy, something is up.[14]

The solitary labor of maintainers and troubleshooters extends into home offices and living rooms in the Global North, where an abundance of user interfaces allows "microworkers" to rate map data, transcribe spoken text, tag images, or verify product reviews for services like CrowdFlower, TaskRabbit, Upwork, or Amazon's very own Mechanical Turk (AMT). Again, communication with human customers is rare; tasks appear on the interface and

The diagram that Selena Savic produced based on our essay takes the form of a cosmogram.
A cosmogram, as described by John Tresch in his analysis of plans for nomadic temples, is simultaneously an architectural plan and an operating manual; it details how "the link with God is made possible by the mediation of a construction described in an extremely detailed and technical manner and this construction has a place for all of society and all of nature."[15]
By denoting essay and diagram as cosmogram, we seek to emphasize the integrative power of the Cloud as planetary design.

15. John Tresch, "Cosmogram," in *Cosmograms*, ed. Melik Ohanian and Jean-Christoph Royoux, Lukas & Sternberg Series (New York: Sternberg Press, 2005), 58.

"work hand-in-hand with technical Sales teams as an enterprise database subject matter expert to differentiate and paint the vision of Google Cloud to our customers"

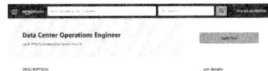

"ensure that the data center's MEP operates at 100% availability while maintaining first-class customer service to the teams and groups within the data centers"

You will provide and prepare all types of documents, including scope of work (SOW), concept designs, functional design specifications (FDS), drawing markup, total cost of ownership (TCO) analysis, budget, schedule, etc.

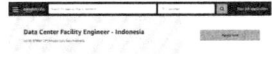

"will manage both routine maintenance and emergency services on a variety of critical systems"

Your projects often span offices, time zones and hemispheres, and it's your job to keep all the players coordinated on the project's progress and deadlines

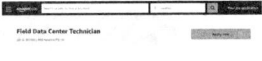

"You are a high performer with a "can do" attitude. Able to lift up to 20kg and participate in team lifts of 20+kg"

"Lift and move 50lbs equipment daily. Shifts, which may include weekends and or holidays. Good social, written and verbal relational skills. Maintain a high degree of self-motivation, drive and integrity"

"Ensure site integrity and systems stability through the enforcement of corporate standards, processes and disciplines, accountable to maintain a 24/7 Data Center

"operate critical infrastructure under the supervision of more senior technical staff"

"Analyse, track and effectively manage critical milestone activities to avoid schedule slip"

" Manage and support design professionals including architects, and engineers from initial programming to construction completion. Ability to consistently travel between different project sites across the nation."

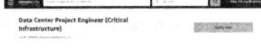

"Requires both independent contribution as well as the ability to work within multi-disciplinary teams"

"Expert operation and maintenance of these facilities is crucial in order to maintain 24/7 services with optimum energy efficiency"

Cosmogram (detail), job stacks

16. Lilly Irani, "The Cultural Work of Microwork," *New Media & Society* 17, no. 5 (May 2015), 16, doi.org/10.1177/1461444813511926.

17. David M. Berry, "Against Infrasomatization: Towards a Critical Theory of Algorithms," in *Data Politics: Worlds, Subjects, Rights*, ed. Didier Bigo, Engin Isin, and Evelyn Ruppert, Routledge Studies in International Political Sociology (London: Routledge, 2019), 48, doi.org/10.4324/9781315167305-3.

18. Lisa Nakamura, "Indigenous Circuits: Navajo Women and the Racialization of Early Electronic Manufacture," *American Quarterly* 66, no. 4 (2014), 921.

19. Tiziana Terranova, *Network Culture: Politics for the Information Age* (London: Pluto Press, 2004); Gabriella Lukács, *Invisibility by Design: Women and Labor in Japan's Digital Economy* (Durham, NC: Duke University Press, 2020).

20. Mariarosa Dalla Costa and Selma James, eds., *The Power of Women and the Subversion of the Community*, 3rd ed. (Bristol: Falling Wall Press, 1975), 11.

are silently solved as fast as possible to raise hourly wages and get better reviews. Although the products of their work do rarely appear as human labor, microworkers tend to maintain "the ideology of the non-hierarchical organization within their walls."[16] By keeping low-status work at a distance, "Turkers" uphold "notions of 'freedom' in a free-lance 'gig' economy mediated and performed by algorithms that are actually systems of control and exploitation."[17]

In this regard, microwork latches onto various forms of un- or underpaid labor that have been constitutive of the digital economy. Lisa Nakamura observes that the Fairchild Semiconductor Inc. did not only produce hardware on Navajo land in the 1960s and 1970s, but represented the work of Navajo women as "creative-race labor," which was "understood through the lens of specific 'mental and physical characteristics' such as docility, manual dexterity, and affective investment in native material craft."[18] Navajo women represented a mobile, cheap, and flexible workforce that supposedly had a natural disposition to "electronics manufacture as a high-tech version of blanket weaving," which allowed for the blurring of the lines between wage labor and free, cultural-creative labor. Tiziana Terranova considers said blurring as scaffolding digital culture tout court – an observation that has been confirmed by Gabriella Lukács's analysis of women's labor in Japan's digital economy.[19] Lukács observes that social media platforms in particular thrived through the sourcing of voluntary contributions to content production and brand development. She references feminist scholars Mariarosa Dalla Costa and Selma James to reconceive the digital economy as an extension of the "social factory," which always had as "its pivot the women in the home producing labor power as a commodity, and her struggle not to."[20]

Amazon's Alexa supports this co-option of domestic environments and care work in that it secretly employs those who conceive themselves merely as users. Amazon's commercials suggest that Alexa is to become part of the family and takes on duties such as supporting children in doing their homework or reminding the overwhelmed father how to cook a simple meal. What remains unseen in TV spots is that every command of the

When off, it's a beautiful full length mirror.

This is a 15 minute workout,

AT HOME IN ANY HOME

With a small footprint and elegant design, The Mirror blends seamlessly into any home. Turn less than two feet of wall space into a personal fitness studio.

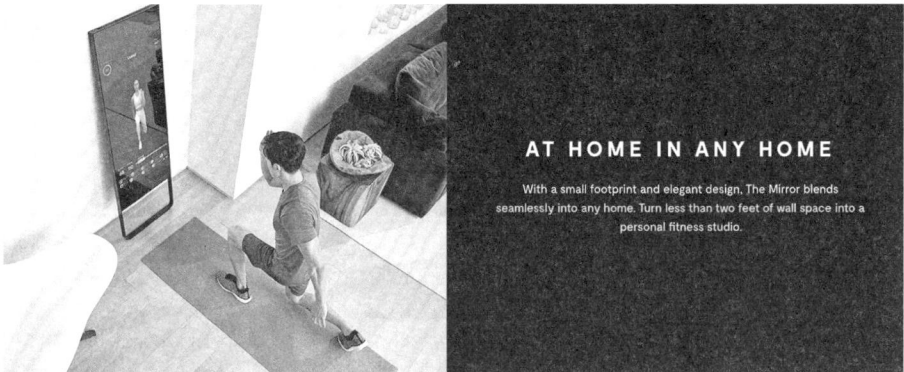

Screenshot of an instructional video at mirror.co.

21. Crawford and Joler, "Anatomy of an AI System."

user arguably improves Alexa's cognitive abilities, for they are used to train the machine learning system that provides a smooth user experience in the first place. The invisible exploitation and exhaustion of distant bodies through digital infrastructures is hence complemented with the invisible exploitation of the user. Crawford and Joler compare the user to the Greek "chimera," a mythological animal that was part lion, goat, snake, and monster. Similarly,

> the Echo user is simultaneously a consumer, a resource, a worker, and a product… In the specific case of the Amazon Echo, the user has purchased a consumer device for which they receive a set of convenient affordances. But they are also a resource, as their voice commands are collected, analyzed, and retained for the purposes of building an ever-larger corpus of human voices and instructions.[21]

Indeed, I believe that this recurring, multiple identity should sit at the heart of thinking design "beyond change," for it allows us to reconceive social relations in the context of contemporary sociomaterial constellations. Making people aware of the fact that the experiences of a small number of happy, privileged, and mostly white bodies are scaffolded by an abundance of exhausted – mostly POC – bodies distributed throughout the world will not suffice; instead, the act of disturbing user experience has to take center stage. Where humans are primarily called upon to maintain and support the machine instead of their human coworkers, the user is always already implicated in the exploitation and exhaustion of distant bodies and an anonymous workforce.

Ceci n'est pas un miroir

In a recent article, Paul Dourish denotes "user experience" as a legitimacy trap. He traces the origins of human–computer interaction (HCI) back to the early work of Douglas Engelbart's work on natural language processing or the Learning Research Group at Xerox Park to prove that design was originally conceived "to unleash creative expression and to place the computer in service of human needs, rather than the other way around. If one traces it to the Scandinavian participatory design movement in the 1970s, one similarly will find it rooted in efforts to resist the human as a cog in the machinery of industrial automation."[22]

You need not succumb to Dourish's (selective) version of HCI history to understand that such interfaces as the Echo Dot are in direct opposition to the ideals that his historical examples of interface design intend to convey. Thanks to the interface, Alexa's interlocutors help Amazon's algorithms develop their capacities and supply the – according to *Slate* magazine[23] – most evil corporation on Earth with an abundance of data to automate and optimize its logistical services. Against this background, interface design appears as a user-oriented aestheticization of un- or low-paid domestic labor and rather ugly logistical processes, which it obscures by throwing the user back at itself.

Another domestic smart device, Mirror, is the culmination of said narcisstic program. If it was not affixed to a wall in your living room, Mirror could make you believe that it represents the most recent bet at forcing users to adapt to oversized smartphones. Indeed, the price tag of $1,495 is suspiciously close to that of Apple's top-end handhelds.

If you manage to pay your monthly subscription fee of thirty-nine dollars, however, Mirror turns into a "nearly invisible home gym," allowing you to work out at any time of the day, guided by a personal trainer that is not, in fact, in your home and can nevertheless see you thanks to the front-facing camera. Yet, what's much more important is that the only thing that you can see – apart from the fitness instructor – is the image of your own exhausted, yet hormonally enhanced body.

The so-called runner's high, which refers to the nepenthean feeling that takes hold of the body during extended workouts, is also described as a flow experience where the normally distinguished elements of a body appear to work in perfect harmony. Mirror apparently allows for this feeling to take hold of your body, particularly since

22. Paul Dourish, "User Experience as Legitimacy Trap," *Interactions* 26, no. 6 (October 30, 2019), 46–49, doi.org/10.1145/3358908.

23. Unknown, "The Evil List," *Slate*, January 15, 2020, slate.com/technology/2020/01/evil-list-tech-companies-dangerous-amazon-facebook-google-palantir.html.

24. Dourish, "User Experience as Legitimacy Trap," 49.

it allows you to watch yourself grow and simultaneously occludes the fact that the precarious workers that first made this experience possible are most likely not in a state of somatic excitement. What you don't see is that your body has been entangled with an abundance of other bodies – and, crucially, their exhaustion – as soon as you decide to put up Mirror on a wall in your living room.

A similar feeling takes hold of me when any interface fades into the background and things simply: work. It's most likely a result of some sort of networked affect that design can give rise to if the overall system works as promised. While it may be Alexa who speaks, what you hear is essentially an echo of your thoughts; in return, you gradually grow accustomed to customized, just-in-time information and the uninterrupted presence of a disembodied, disenfranchised, and discrete workforce in your living room. That is to say that interface design provides the gloss that obscures that the user is an integral part of the infrastructure that exploits and exhausts distant human bodies.

However, the user is only superficially at the heart of the design process: "the great irony of the notion of user-centered design is that users (or people) are not, in fact, at the center of it at all. Design is. Something can be more user-centered or less user-centered, but the phrase guarantees that design will always be present."[24] If this rings true, the current situation can only improve if (interface) design can be reconceived – not by way of another marketable and necessarily exhibitable version of design, but as a practice and an attitude of being with and in this world – and being part of Alexa's body.

Instead of strengthening narcissistic tendencies by design, user experience and interface design could contribute to making felt the ugly logistics that are currently banned from the interface and so remind users that they are part of an infrastructure that defines automation as automated exploitation. Since their work is mission-critical – or indispensable as regards the functioning of the system – (user experience and interface) designers are in a unique position to support the activism of tech workers and employees in Amazon's Fulfilment Centers, which provides examples of how resistance is

EXHAUSTION OF DISTANT BODIES

Johannes Bruder

possible also from within Alexa's body.

In "The Hidden Faces of Automation," Lilly Irani asks what "computer science [would] look like if it did not see human-algorithmic partnerships as an embarrassment, but rather as an ethical project where the humans were as, or even more, important than the algorithms?"[25]

Their acts of individual or collective resistance and insubordination, such as fooling productivity sensors and collectively resisting the implementation of surveillance tools, have contributed to mitigating the effects of logistical designs that keep workers isolated and maniacally productive.[26] Backdoors, bugs, and secret kill switches might not necessarily hurt planetary corporations, but can improve the lives of workers in fulfillment centers and the AMT eco-system.

In any case, more shiny, yet obscuring surfaces and interfaces will only exacerbate social divides long in the making. Feminist digital media scholar Kylie Jarrett writes that the history of capitalism is "the history of struggle within and against a social factory."[27] Designers could assume a central role within this struggle if they engaged with the deconstruction of an uninvolved user. As an anthropologist of design and technology, I wonder if Bianca Williams's understanding of anthropology would not apply to design in a similar way. In a recent episode of the Cultural Anthropology Podcast, "What Does Anthropology Sound Like: Activism," she argues that anthropology will always be a ready tool for colonizers and oppressors, because of its beginnings and the way it has been used throughout time. "It's in its nature. But I believe that there is room for resistance, protest, activism, insurrection, and rebellion in these spaces also."[28]

25. Lilly Irani, "The Hidden Faces of Automation," XRDS: Crossroads, The ACM Magazine for Students 23, no. 2 (December 15, 2016), 34–37, doi.org/10.1145/3014390.

26. Sam Adler-Bell, "Surviving Amazon," Logic Magazine, August 3, 2019, logicmag.io/bodies/surviving-amazon/; Heike Geissler, Seasonal Associate (South Pasadena, CA: Semiotext(e), 2018).

27. Kylie Jarrett, "Laundering Women's History: A Feminist Critique of the Social Factory," First Monday 23, nos. 3–5 (2018), ojphi.org/ojs/index.php/fm/article/view/8280/6647.

28. Cory-Alice André-Johnson, "What Does Anthropology Sound Like: Activism," January 20, 2020, in AnthroPod: Fieldsights, podcast, culanth.org/fieldsights/what-does-anthropology-sound-like-activism.

Design Struggles

Cosmogram (detail), data center

EMOTIONAL LABOR, SUPPORT STRUCTURES, AND THE WALLS IN BETWEEN
A Conversation with Members of the Decolonising Design Group

Nina Paim and Corin Gisel

SOOTHING SURROUNDINGS

Everyone in this room is exhausted. The last few days have been an emotional rollercoaster. It's late afternoon in a rental flat in Porto. Outside, the sun shines bright orange as if it was summer's last breath. The door to the small balcony is open, letting in the sounds of seagulls croaking in the remote background. It takes a while for everyone to gather around the coffee table on an assembly of couches and armchairs. Matt is on the phone, Mahmoud and Danah are on the balcony, Pedro and Ece are dozing off on the couch. As they finally take a seat, it's hard to begin. We, the interviewers, don't quite know how to bring the conversation to a start. They, the interviewees, are visibly downcast. We had suggested postponing the talk, in light of everything that had happened over the past few days, but they nevertheless insisted on going ahead.

This interview had been in planning for several months. It all started when we heard that all of the founding members of the Decolonising Design group were going to be in Porto. We saw this as a historic opportunity to have a collective conversation with all of them together. In the three years that the group has existed, they have never managed to meet in a single room. This was finally going to happen on the occasion of "Real World: Design, Politics, Future," the 2019 Papanek Symposium, a design conference organized by Alison J. Clarke and Francisco Laranjo as a partnership between the Papanek Foundation and the Porto Design Biennale. The program spanned two days. The first consisted of lectures followed by short panel discussions, covering topics such as design justice, control and care, decolonial futures, cosmo-localisms, and more. The second day was devoted to workshops and open forums entirely led by the Decolonising Design group, that is, by Danah Abdulla, Ece Canlı, Mahmoud Keshavarz, Matthew Kiem, Pedro Oliveira, Luiza Prado, Tristan Schultz, and Ahmed Ansari.[1]

Decolonising Design was founded in 2016 by these eight design researchers, artists, and activists, all of whom stem from or have ties to the Global South. At the time, most of them were in the process of writing or completing their Ph.D.s. The group officially emerged on June 27, 2016,

1. See www.dabdulla.com/ (Danah Abdulla), ececanli.com/ (Ece Canlı), www.mahmoudkeshavarz.com/ (Mahmoud Keshavarz), independent.academia.edu/MatthewKiem (Matthew Kiem), oliveira.work/ (Pedro Oliveira), luiza-prado.com/ (Luiza Prado), tristanschultz.com/ (Tristan Schultz), ahmedansari.com/ (Ahmed Ansari).

2. Decolonising Design (Danah Abdulla, Ece Canlı, Mahmoud Keshavarz, Luiza Prado de O. Martins, and Pedro J. S. Vieira de Oliveira), "A Statement on the Design Research Society Conference 2016," Decolonising Design (website), June 27, 2016, www.decolonisingdesign.com/general/2016/drs2016statement/.

3. Decolonising Design Group, "A Statement on the Design Research Society Conference 2016."

4. We counted over eighty messages on the original thread. However, the discussion led to other threads, e.g., "With friends like these who needs the PhD-Design List?" (www.jiscmail.ac.uk/cgi-bin/webadmin?A2=ind1607&L=PHD-DESIGN&O=D&P=935) and "How to avoid fights on mailing lists" (www.jiscmail.ac.uk/cgi-bin/webadmin?A2=ind1607&L=PHD-DESIGN&O=D&P=8467). In several messages the tone was harsh and offensive.

Members of Decolonising Design in Malmö, November 2016. Photo: Danah Abdulla.

Panel during the the Intersectional Perspectives on Design, Politics and Power Symposium, Malmö, November 2016. Photo: Mahmoud Keshavarz.

Design Struggles

through the simultaneous launching of several digital channels: a Twitter account, a website, and an email address. The date, four days after the Brexit referendum, coincided with the opening of the annual Design Research Society Conference of 2016 (DRS), which took place in Brighton, UK, and was themed "Future-Focused Thinking." The group had submitted one paper and one conversation proposal to that conference. The first was summarily rejected while the second was unanimously accepted. This discrepancy prompted a series of discussions within the group and ultimately led them to withdraw their second proposal. None of them attended the DRS conference. Instead, they went public. Their newly founded website opened with a statement to the DRS 2016, in which they addressed the politically charged reviews they had received and advocated for a "profound debate and redirection of the colonial ethos of design and design research."[2]

"We live and work on the border, shuttling back and forth between the knowledge of our lands, deemed peripheral, and the logic of Western, Anglophonic and neoliberal academia, regarded as central," read their statement.

> The struggle against the colonisation of knowledge, i.e. the colonial conditions that inform knowledge production and validation, is not only part of our work, but part of our lives. Coloniality is not an abstract concept nor is it a subject to be examined from a comfortable distance. It is something that affects our communities, our countries, and our peoples every single day. It is a continuous process of domination and violence to which we are submitted. It demeans our knowledge, subjugates our bodies, and renders our lives arduous. For us, decolonisation is imperative for survival.[3]

The launch of the Decolonising Design platform was announced through the JISC PhD-Design list, a mailing list for design research set up in 1998, which currently counts 3,220 subscribers. The news was met with enthusiastic support from numerous researchers and scholars from Canada, Colombia, India, Turkey, the US, UK, and others. However, it also provoked skepticism, contempt, and downright harassment by a small group of white, male, European scholars in the same list[4] – some of whom are well established in the field. Despite this initial backlash, since 2016 the group has remained active, curating conferences, editing journals, organizing workshops, speaking at conferences, and writing.

The dream of bringing all members of the group into one room in Porto never happened. Luiza Prado and Tristan Schultz were unable to come for personal reasons, while Ahmed Ansari, one of the symposium's keynotes, didn't get his visa approved in time. "I am not here today because of a sequence of events that speak heavily to the ways in which diplomatic institutions are set up to make it extremely difficult for people from select nationalities and backgrounds to traverse borders," he wrote in a statement read aloud by the other members of the group.

> It is tiring to endlessly negotiate the mazes of academic and government bureaucracy expending ever more precious time, capital, and mental and emotional labor to obtain a visa to catch what amounts to a mere eight-hour-long flight across the Atlantic. I still consider myself very lucky and privileged to be where I am in life right now. I am always acutely aware of how many others, and not just international scholars, live lives of extreme stress and precarity, and yet the fact remains that the border remains the most enduring symbol of the legacy of colonialism.[5]

Ahmed's statement concluded with a crescendo of pleas for academics to use their privilege to support and empower underprivileged colleagues and students. With the words "do your homework" as a resounding metronome, Ahmed called for fighting against cheap or unpaid academic labor, pushing for unionization of academic institutions, as well as promoting the work of marginalized scholars and thinkers. As the five members of the group alternated reading his words, the statement was interrupted by applause and shouts of support from the audience.

The following day, the entire program of the Papanek Symposium was led by the Decolonising Design group. Both expectation and anticipation seemed high. Because they were fewer in number than originally planned, the group opted for canceling one of three workshops. Approximately sixty people attended "Design Politics of Bodies: Tackling the Coloniality of Bodies and Borders" and "Decoloniality and Pedagogy: Research and Learning Within the Westernized University." We participated in the latter, which consisted of informal group discussions around questions of everyday discrimination within design education and the minor gestures that teachers might employ to make a difference. We appreciated our exchange on how to talk about complex problems and heavy theory with students, and how to tackle racism, sexism, or homophobia in the classroom. We left shortly before it ended, because of another engagement that day.

The events that followed are partially reconstructed based on conversations with participants who stayed. According to these accounts, after the two workshops, there was an open discussion round in the lobby where the workshop had been taking place. One well-established scholar expressed his disappointment and questioned in what ways the two workshops were related to decoloniality. "We were expecting a bit more, we came here as allies,"

5. Ahmed Ansari, "A Statement to the Victor Papanek Symposium," published as a Google Doc, 2019, docs.google.com/document/d/14azGtWKpFa6aK8SZExe9mHu2PBBTBuJMKbOR6DZtJYw/edit.

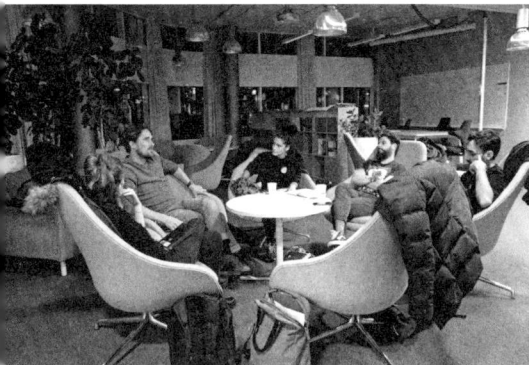

Members of Decolonising Design in Malmö, November 2016.
Photo: Danah Abdulla.

Panel during the the Intersectional Perspectives on Design, Politics and Power Symposium, Malmö, November 2016.
Photo: Danah Abdulla.

Members of Decolonising Design conducting a workshop at the Papanek Symposium in Porto, September 2019.
Photo: Danah Abdulla.

he reportedly said. Heads nodded in agreement, and a snowball of reactions followed. Other participants complained that the original program had been changed, especially that the morning session, called "Portuguese Colonialism," had been omitted. Apparently and understandably, many people had come for that. The Decolonising Design group responded, somewhat passive-aggressively, saying that they always face unrealistic expectations and that the workshops were exactly intended to counteract such expectations. There is no "kit for decolonizing anything," the group reportedly countered. By then, the tension between them and the audience had become evident.

At that point, everyone moved to the auditorium, where the previous day's lectures and panel discussions had taken place. The five members of the Decolonising Design group stood in front of the first row of chairs with their backs to the stage, facing the workshop participants who were sitting in the audience. There was another round of questions. Eventually, someone took the microphone to question that hierarchical setting. Why not a more "equal" sitting disposition, like the circle before? The group explained that they had been asked to take this position, but that they were open to sharing it. Multiple audience members went on stage and the debate on decoloniality, intersectionality, and the environment continued. Shortly after, however, a keynote lecturer from the previous day who had remained in the audience took the microphone

Nina Paim and Corin Gisel, with Decolonising Design Group

and exclaimed, "There is here an epistemological change. For decades, it has been the same white scholars on stage. And now that these researchers from the Global South are finally given space, instead of listening, you want to come to the stage?" Several people apologetically left the stage and went back to their seats. The event concluded awkwardly not long after with discontent still lingering in the air. Some comments were taken to Twitter – some positive, while others highlighted the friction throughout the symposium. When we met for the interview the day after, frustration had been joined by exhaustion. And yet, we talked.

Nina Paim and Corin Gisel: How did the Decolonising Design group start? How did you first connect?

Danah: I met Pedro and Luiza at the Fadfest conference in Barcelona in the summer of 2014. We started talking about our Ph.D.s and I gave them my card. One year later, Luiza reached out to me through academia.edu and asked if I was interested in writing a paper with six other people. I said sure.

Pedro: This was the paper we submitted to the DRS in 2016. It was written by Ece, Mahmoud, Luiza, Danah, myself, as well as Rodrigo Gonzatto and Fred van Amstel – two other Brazilian researchers who were also dealing with critical design at the time. Luiza and I met Mahmoud at the DRS 2014, which took place in Umeå, Sweden, and was called "Design's Big

Debates." I attended a conversation on "Violence, Militancy, and Design Research," which was cochaired by Mahmoud. Eventually someone said, "Yeah, passports are obsolete, we don't need passports to cross borders anymore." Of course, this got me really angry. I threw my residency permit onto the table and said, "How can you say that passports are obsolete since this card determines whether or not I can be here?" And this shifted the entire conversation. Afterward, Mahmoud and I were both still really angry, but through this experience we became friends. And by then, Mahmoud already knew Ece right?

Ece: Yes, in 2010 I went to Sweden to study experience design at Konstfack. Each new student was paired with a "buddy" – a senior who would show you around the campus. Mahmoud was my buddy. Of course, he was very critical of the program, but he didn't say much at first. A few weeks later I asked him, "What's going on here, what's happening?" We bonded both on an intellectual and on a friendship level. Mahmoud went to do his Ph.D. in Malmö, while I returned to Turkey, and later came to Portugal to do my own Ph.D. A couple of years later, Mahmoud wrote saying that he had just met someone who was doing similar work in gender and sexuality studies. He introduced me to Luiza and it was love at first sight! By then, we realized we needed a place to talk.

Pedro: After we submitted our paper to the 2016 DRS, we got these very

Design Struggles

questionable and biased reviews. Putting it bluntly, they basically said, "Yeah, decolonization is important but what you are saying is probably too radical." They found whatever problem to reject our piece. Luiza and I were very frustrated, so we reached out to Matt and Ahmed, whom we had met through the online forum of the *Design and Violence* online MoMA exhibition. We were trying to find consonance, and I think it was Ahmed who suggested using the project management app Slack. It was already all of us except for Tristan. It was Matt who brought in Tristan, right?

Danah: How did you meet Tristan?

Matt: I attended a number of HotHouses, which were a series of symposiums that brought together creative thinkers around ideas for transforming urban environments. They were run by Tony Fry, who was also the head of the Master of Design Futures at Griffith University in Brisbane. Tristan was a student in that master's course. He participated and actually helped to run some of these HotHouses. I got to know his work, and how he was interested in decolonization, and thought he should be introduced to the group.

Pedro: Then we crafted that statement about DRS together over Slack.

Mahmoud: Things happened really fast! In one day we made a Twitter account, the website, a Gmail account.

Pedro: We wanted to release the platform exactly on the day of the DRS. That was the idea. And that's when the shitstorm started.

Ece: The entire PhD-Design list started throwing stones.

Danah: But there was also an incredible amount of support that came from people who were so glad to find such a platform! I think launching it at the opening of DRS was a good tactic, we really got the attention. Several people who attended DRS said that it took over the conversation.

Mahmoud: Because none of us was there. That was the point.

Danah: We decided not to attend. We had submitted two proposals: one paper, one "conversation." And they had significantly different reviews. The paper was rejected, but the workshop got ten out of ten!

Mahmoud: But it was the same content, the "conversation" was just a shorter version of the paper.

Nina Paim and Corin Gisel: Why do you think that happened? Why was the workshop praised and the paper rejected?

Ece: I think the conversation was less threatening and that they saw it as checking a "diversity" box. For the paper, each of us wrote a different section, and an introduction and conclusion tied the text together.

Although the call for papers welcomed more performative and explorative approaches, the reviewers said that ours was not an acceptable format. But actually, I don't think the problem was the format, the problem was the content. I remember one reviewer saying, "But the author is actually affirming illegality" while they were still justifying the rejection with the fact that our paper was "off-format."

Mahmoud: Usually, in conferences, the pool of paper reviewers is different from the pool of workshop reviewers. Papers are often reviewed by senior academics, while workshops are evaluated by lesser-known scholars, who are maybe more open-minded reviewers. And of course, academically speaking, a peer-reviewed paper is ranked differently from a workshop. The first would be counted as a publication but the latter would not. So it matters.

Nina Paim and Corin Gisel: Can you talk about the blow-up on the Ph.D. list?

Ece: I try to forget about that.

Pedro: It was heavy. From my personal perspective, it took a very strong emotional toll. But I think that is more for Luiza to say, she was in at the center and took the heaviest blow.

Mahmoud: Luiza was the one who sent the message to the PhD-Design list announcing the launch of our platform. But there was already a

6. Matt Kiem, "With Friends Like These Who Needs the PhD-Design List," Medium (website), January 16, 2016, medium.com/@mattkiem/with-friends-like-these-who-needs-the-phd-design-list-6e1bc158e23b.

7. Jacob Lindgren, ed., *Extra-Curricular* (Eindhoven: Onomatopee, 2018).

8. "Decolonizing Design," ed. Decolonising Design Group (Danah Abdulla, Ahmed Ansari, Ece Canlı, Mahmoud Keshavarz, Matthew Kiem, Luiza Prado de O. Martins, Tristan Schultz, and Pedro J. S. Vieira de Oliveira), special issue, *Design and Culture* 10, no. 1 (2018).

history a few years back with her on that list, when Mariam Assad, then a Ph.D. student at Georgia Institute of Technology, posted a call for papers for a workshop event titled *Exploring Social Justice, Design, and HCI*, and there was a similar backlash. Matt even wrote a piece about it on Medium, called "With friends like these who needs the PhD-Design List."[6]

Pedro: Parallel to the personal attacks against Luiza, there was a general dissatisfaction along the lines of "Who are these young scholars trying to question the establishments of this discipline?"

Danah: It was unreal. I feel I've erased most of it from my memory. I don't even remember the comments.

Ece: I remember one comment: "Take decolonization out and put a chicken there, and it's the same thing!" It was completely absurd and condescending. But I think it's not worth going there. First, we were following the reactions and asking ourselves, is this real?… Mentally and emotionally it was completely exhausting.

Members of Decolonising Design during the "Beyond Change" conference, Basel, March 2018. Photo: unknown.

Nina Paim and Corin Gisel: It has now been three years since this happened. Looking back, what do you think have been milestones or important successes for you since then?

Mahmoud: The Malmö symposium, "Intersectional Perspectives on Design Politics and Power." I was done with my Ph.D., but there was still some money left. So even though I had lots of conflicts with my institution, I thought "Let's just do a symposium." Not so many people from my institution showed up, but lots of other people came.

Danah: In 2017, Luiza, Tristan, and I went to the research pavilion at the Venice Biennale. The keynote was canceled, so we happened to have this huge time slot talking to a very small room, speaking to a group of mostly artists. People were quite engaged. Then we turned that into a chapter for a book called *Extra-Curricular*.[7]

Ece: The *Design and Culture* issue we edited was especially important for us in terms of working, writing, editing, and organizing everything together.[8] It was a good experience on how to manage our own dynamics, who takes space, whose voice is there and whose is not. And then we went to the Swiss Design Network 2018 conference, "Beyond Change: Questioning the Role of Design in Times of Global Transformation."

Danah: With everything that had happened with the PhD-Design list, I think "Beyond Change" was a big thing. We were still around and people had to deal with it. These discussions are here to stay.

Pedro: One thing about "Beyond Change" that made an impact was the library.[9] I still think about that library a lot, the number of people going through those books, taking pictures and writing things down. We consciously selected books that were not related to design but we thought could be useful for design. On a personal level, this is something that I want to carry into anything I do. I remember someone mentioning Harsha Walia's *Undoing Border Imperialism* during one of the conversations, and so many people said, "I want the book, I just want it!" I think this is almost half of the job done. Making people read such a radical book that most likely they would not have encountered otherwise.

Danah: Being in the classroom every single day, you are always scared about how students are going to react to these ideas and topics. But then you get emails, "Could you please recommend something I could read?" That's fantastic! I can just give the link which collects all the references from

9. See mediathek.hgk.fhnw.ch/ wordpress/building-platforms/.

our library, which is still online and available.

Nina Paim and Corin Gisel: How do you work together?

Mahmoud: I think most of it is contingent. Often we create a Slack channel to discuss a project, and maybe one person or two or three will take that responsibility. Sometimes there are projects that we try to do together, like the symposium in Malmö, or the *Design and Culture* issue. There are different topologies. It depends on how available people are, based on their other jobs, lives, issues, or emotional availability.

Pedro: Often work emerges out of respecting each other's time. It's based on a mutual understanding that not everyone is available and that this is OK.

Ece: I like this metaphor of the "sphere." It's not a pyramid, there are no edges, there's no leader. It's more about different people taking part at different times and in different forms.

Mahmoud: As an example, the *Design and Culture* issue was a huge project. Securing reviewers, checking their revisions, editing, all the while we all live in different time zones, so it's hard to have a continuous discussion. I would write one comment, and it's

Design Struggles

Members of Decolonising Design at the Papanek Symposium, Porto, September 2019. Photo: unknown.

already one day ahead in Australia, and several hours behind in the US. It's hard to follow up and have a Skype. In that, Tristan was great. I think that if it weren't for him that special issue would not have come out.

Matt: We recognized that Tristan had a significant role in that. That's why we decided to put him as lead-author. I think one thing that has always been important for me is to consider that the work which the people in the Decolonising Design group produce is always going to be a product of the conditions under which each of us is living. The way

things come together, the amount of time that things take, the ability to choose particular projects, who is able to participate, they're going to be different from the realities of people in more secure, privileged positions – notwithstanding the various privileges that each of us has in different ways. The work that this group produces is an embodiment of all the particular difficulties that people have. As well as the fact that living in so many different time zones is difficult to organize in itself. Plus trying to address our own responsibilities and our respective lives to other people means that we are not always available for Skype meetings, for instance. Skype meetings require considerable effort to organize and are always very special events. I'm always looking forward to them, whenever they happen. And it's extremely difficult to get people into the same room. We have not yet managed to get everyone into the same room. Our work is the product of those conditions, and many others that I'm sure I'm overlooking. And, of course, that's no different from any other academic work, or design work, or any kind of work, for that matter. Work is the product of material conditions. It's important to understand that the reason why sometimes the work looks different is because it embodies these differences. There are complications and there are challenges, but there are also a lot of privileges and advantages that we have. The work is a product of the group conditions and of how we have managed to support each other but also learn from one another.

Nina Paim and Corin Gisel: In light of the many structural challenges you face, could you talk about how the group helps you and supports your work?

Pedro: I think we all agree that without a group we wouldn't have finished our Ph.D.s.

Ece: We always say that we're more of a "support group" than a "research group." It's about care. The group is a place to go and share the challenges and struggles we're facing as researchers, but also in our personal lives. During our Ph.D.s, we were all tackling very severe issues such as racism, sexism, coloniality, borders, illegality, white supremacy, etc., which are really hard to deal with. It's not just about navigating design academia, but actually dealing with those heavier issues. The group became a place to share our experiences, give and receive advice, or just be there for each other. Do you want to talk? Let's Skype.

Danah: Or just to have people read your work and critique it. I remember sending a chapter to Matt – this was the first time anyone read anything from my Ph.D. Matt got back to me very quickly, understanding my necessity of timeliness. Getting his comments was really important, especially because he was able to read it before it was submitted. Of course, I knew other people who could help me with grammar, but that was different. This is really important for me, having someone I trust to look at and critique my work without being destructive. Unfortunately, in academia people hide behind blind peer review, which, in my opinion, is ruthless. Even for the chapter I'm contributing to the "Beyond Change" publication (that is this book *Design Struggles*), Pedro contributed really great comments.

Pedro: During the Ph.D. process, most of us – if not all of us – vented on Slack at some point. Finding that space in which we could just say anything and have support from others was really important. That sense of, "We are here, keep strong, we have to stick together." In my case, it was just me and Luiza in the same department fighting against a very conservative mindset and being literally the tokens of that department, finding no support whatsoever within the German scope of design academia. Having feedback from others who had faced or were facing similar challenges helped us in situating ourselves. It made us realize that what we were trying to do was not absurd but had resonance and value.

Matt: Academia can be tough. It's often a process of trying to break people down. And to an extent, I think that's a necessary process. You've got to challenge yourself into thinking. But there's not enough emphasis on building people back up again. Our network helped us to do that for each other. When people were being broken down or spun out into a condition of confusion – which is very common, because people kinda pull the rug out from underneath you – sometimes that's necessary, sometimes it's not. And even if it is necessary, it's always good to have someone or many people around you that help with the building up. It's nice to be able to have a group or a network. I like the word *network* better, because it's not like "decolonizing design" is hermetically sealed. It's not just us. We have partners, we have friends, we have other projects, we have other networks, all of us, outside the group. And that comes back into the work that we do as well. And the other way around, the work that we do in the Decolonising Design network feed back out into these other projects. And not just into projects, but into our lives in general, into our families and friendships. There's a bit of us in each of us, because we've been working together for so long. At the same time, we are trying to maintain this idea that everyone is coming from a particular place, so it's not like we're this flat homogenous entity. In the process of building each other, we contribute to the production of each other – and to the repair of each other.

Nina Paim and Corin Gisel: You are talking a lot about support structures and networks of support. What are the immediate networks of support in your surroundings that would need to be established or expanded for you to keep on doing your work?

Matt: This concept of *network* comes from my engagement with xBorder, the activist network that sprang from the work of Angela Mitropoulos. She was the one that emphasized that xBorder is a network rather than an entity. Decolonising Design is influenced by my engagement with xBorder, and that then feeds into this network. My engagement in xBorder is, in part, a product of my wanting to find something to make my design education meaningful. And my engagement with that was maybe one example of a network that was supportive of my own thinking. Through that I've learned that you have to also give back.

Mahmoud: One does not choose these difficult issues – we've arrived at them because of our personal lives, the encounters and choices we've made. For me, for example, a lot comes from my involvement in no-border activism in Sweden. I understand the notions of borders and legality through this activist engagement. The way I see it, it's not enough to just talk about borders – whether you like it or not, you actually have to reach out and be in other spaces. I'm now doing something called "Critical Border Studies" with a bunch of anthropologists and migration scholars. We study how migration knowledge is produced – migration as actually something that historically has been made here, in Europe, at the heart of the empire. I work with people in other disciplines that have similar frustrations concerning the ways we write and talk about borders. There is a bunch of professors – mostly, of course, people of color – who now engage with this issue. Still, if I get in trouble within the field of design discourse, for them it is very hard to support me, because they don't know this discourse, they don't know anything about design. So I also need to build support structures moving in this other discourse too, which takes a lot of time and requires a lot of commitment.

Pedro: Back in Brazil, I was involved in student movements both during high school and university, trying to move things in a different way within the privileged spaces I occupied. After I moved to Germany, I lost that space. I was not involved in direct activism during my Ph.D., as Mahmoud or Matt were. It was then through my own Ph.D. research that I reconnected with those experiences. For me, Decolonising Design helped open up that space again, a space in which I could figure out my scope of action, what I can do that feels truthful and necessary. This requires a reflection on one's own body politics. For example, I wrote my thesis about Brazil while living in Germany. What is the scope of action as a Brazilian living in Germany talking about Brazil? Where can I intervene without just talking from outside? This requires bringing together all the experiences from my upbringing as a "troublemaker," and becoming a troublemaker again within the academic discourse. In that sense, there's maybe not so much difference between academic networks and activist networks.

Nina Paim and Corin Gisel: What are the immediate walls surrounding you, the structures that are stopping you from doing work? How you are dealing with dismantling them?

Danah: You would expect your institution to support you, but not everybody has that obviously – and in fact most people don't have this. I don't feel like I have this. I think that already sets you up for failure. The other thing that sets you up for failure is the idea that you are not allowed to fail. Which is bound to make you fail, right? Because then there is all this pressure on you. It's easy to get disheartened.

Matt: In terms of what could be done to dismantle it, I don't know how to answer this directly. In an important sense, just surviving is an achievement. Holding it together. Holding your life together while you are under pressure and while there are active colonial structures that are trying to pull people apart in different ways depending upon who they are. Sometimes, just surviving is the way it's done.

Danah: We are living on the margins. Sometimes you don't want to get out of the margins, but then again, it can be a very lonely place.

Mahmoud: It's quite hard to change institutions from within. It's important to remember that every time you encounter these kinds of hindrances, they knock you down, right? And it takes a long time to recover. Sometimes you refuse to engage in certain practices, or you make choices that might not be good for your career and future. But you have to do it because it's just too much! When these things happen I think, "OK, honestly, I have to talk about this." This is an act of love. Many times we discuss small strategies through commenting or chatting. For me, it's the group that helps to navigate this. I'm not sure if we will ever be able to really dismantle those walls, at least not yet, because we are not in the position of being able to do so. But we are navigating through them, finding some sorts of escape routes.

Ece: There's one kind of wall we have always have, actually: the "blank space" we face when we talk about these issues. Sometimes it's good when people react and say things – like what happened yesterday. Maybe they had an idea, maybe they agreed, maybe it's just a stupid comment, maybe they are ignorant, but at least they say something. But sometimes – maybe people are being "politically correct" – there is just blankness. All of a sudden you teach in a Western university, so you have all these Western students with many privileges. And what you say seems to not get through to them. You feel like you're doing nothing, that what you do is not worthy. When Pedro started teaching he had all these questions and opened a Slack channel called "pedagogy." He was asking for help, what to do with these issues, and everyone started sharing their experiences and methods. "This happened but it doesn't mean that that student actually thinks as such," etc. Now I just started teaching, and so find myself in that same channel. It's not like there's one challenge and then it's resolved. It is every day.

Nina Paim and Corin Gisel: What's next? Ideas, projects, dreams, hopes…

Pedro: The decolonizing design toolkit, right? It will sell for €2,000.

Danah: No, €12.99!

Pedro: Oh yeah, right, it's a subscription service! We do cross-border shipping.

[laughter]

Pedro: My parallel is really ridiculous, but I always think of the Brazilian rap group Racionais MCs, and how they say, "We come together when we need to come together." We respond when we feel it's worth responding together. The Papanek Symposium is an example of this. We chose to be here together.

Mahmoud: Who made this point about us *not* being project-based?

Ece: I was saying how, in general, the design field is so much project-based, but that doesn't work for us. Things take time, and we need time. As a group, we put forward our critiques. What more can we say? How do we go beyond this threshold of explaining what decolonization is? Beyond the "Show me the examples" or "Give me the decolonizing toolkit" kinds of questions. What can our own research bring?

Danah: Do I see any changes within the design industry? Within mainstream design discourse? No. How do we affect that? I guess this is a very big project, but that's something that would be interesting for us. Because when you are just talking to allies, people that share the same views as you, are you going to get very far? I don't want to do a workshop and end it there, I want to build on it. Also, we are interested in making a book.

Mahmoud: A book that we would have wanted to see when we were undergrads.

Danah: Being a published author, that gives legitimacy. Rather than having only students and young scholars citing us, perhaps more established names would start citing us rather than other people – because, of course, if you cite one person you purposely exclude someone else.

Mahmoud: Do you think a book would necessarily make people take the discourse seriously? I'm not sure. There are already several books, which are largely being ignored. Again, this is the politics of citation. We have been doing this for three years, and we have been engaging with the discourses in the field, we have been engaging with the established scholars – with little progress. But actually most of us have the experience that our students are eager to learn. They are the future. They are going to be the scholars and designers of the future, so talking to them and caring for them and their themes is what's important. That would change the language and orientation of our book.

Pedro: These experiences, even though they are sometimes emotionally very heavy, materialize the responses to the conditions and the propositions that we are putting forward as a group. When we say what we stand for and people realize that what we stand for is not solvable, it is not an easy conversation. It's discomforting. It's disheartening. But those responses and reactions inform how we assess the field. With this book project we want to make sense of all of these signals, of what is profoundly complicated and problematic within the field of design studies. How do we provide, not an answer but a direction, an orientation? We are trying to give at least some processing back – vomiting something back, so to speak – based on everything that has happened since we started the platform and everything that has happened before we came together as a group. Of course, it is a project that is bound to be incomplete, and that's OK.

After the conversation we sat for a moment longer, silent and inert. At some point one of us got up to put on the coffee pot that had been abandoned before the interview started. It was Saturday, and Ece knew of a great music concert that evening. There was also an opening of another event across town. And the idea of going to the seaside to eat a typical Portuguese fish dinner. In the end, Danah, Matt, Mahmoud, Ece, and Pedro decided to stick to their plan to stay in the flat and use this precious time together to work. Outside, the setting sun was a burnt orange, the daylight soon gone, but their day was still not over.

Members of Decolonising Design in Malmö, November 2016. Left to right: Ece Canlı, Danah Abdulla, Tristan Schultz, Mahmoud Keshavarz, Pedro Oliveira and Luiza Prado. Photo: Max Mollon.

DESIGN(ERS) BEYOND PRECARITY Proposals for Everyday Action

Bianca Elzenbaumer / Brave New Alps

1. See, e.g., Danah Abdulla, "Design Otherwise: Towards a Locally-Centric Design Education Curricula in Jordan" (London: Goldsmiths, University of London, 2017); Joanna Boehnert, *Design, Ecology, Politics: Towards the Ecocene* (London: Bloomsbury Academic, 2018); Arturo Escobar, *Designs for the Pluriverse: Radical Interdependence, Autonomy, and the Making of Worlds* (Durham, NC: Duke University Press Books, 2018); Ramia Mazé, Meike Schalk, and Thérèse Kristiansson, eds., *Feminist Futures of Spatial Practice: Materialism, Activism, Dialogues, Pedagogies, Projections* (Baunach: AADR, 2017).

2. Consider, e.g., the rise in design courses catering to this desire, such as the BA in Design + Change at Linnaeus University (SE), the MA in Eco-Social Design at the Free University of Bozen-Bolzano (IT), the MA in Transformation Design at the University of Fine Arts Brunswick (DE), the MA in Sustainable Design at Kingston University (UK), or the Ph.D. programme in Transition Design at Carnegie Mellon University (USA).

Introduction

How to create the social and material conditions that make critical, transformative design practice possible? This question continues to drive us in our work, especially because we are convinced that if we want design skills to be used for the creation of a world into which many worlds fit,[1] then lots of people interested in doing such transformative work need to be enabled to do it repeatedly and in the long-run. We know that the desire to use design as a tool for critical inquiry – to undo the roots behind issues such as rampant racism and earth systems breakdown – is shared by many,[2] but precarious conditions of work and life – which for designers manifest in ways such as overwork and underpayment, hyper-flexibility and lack of predictability, inability to access sick pay, paid vacations, or parental leave – make such a critical and transformative use of design materially difficult. When confronted with the pressure and anxieties produced by precarity, doing work that challenges the status quo often seems utopian as a basis on which to secure one's immediate livelihood. We also agree, however, that to be a realist in our times of social and ecological breakdown fuelled by neoliberal politics that try to commodify everything, one needs to be utopian and to work with full force towards just and sustainable futures.

From our own position of environmental activism and precarity back in 2006, we began to grapple with the question of how to sustain critical, transformative design practices: first by exploring the origins of precarizing conditions that stop people from doing critical and transformative work;[3] later by creating *Precarity Pilot*,[4] an online platform and series of workshops that share actionable tools against the mess and anxiety of precarious working and living conditions; and then by going into detail about how long-term eco-social practitioners make work work.[5] What we would like to do with this text is to share some of the main things we have learned throughout this period about how – as designers – we can work in our everyday towards a movement beyond precarity, for ourselves as well as for others. We will outline four general principles for orientation and three concrete everyday strategies and tactics that can be supportive in creating the socio-material conditions for sustaining a critical, transformative practice and, thus, for the creation of a world guided by principles of eco-social justice.[6]

Points of Orientation for a Move Beyond Precarity

To ask how to undo, go beyond, or exit precarity is also to ask what desires, interests, and values orient our actions and our being in the world. For us, questions about critical, transformative practice and about how to go beyond precarity are also questions of how not to be governed by precarizing principles, objectives, and procedures.[7] In being informed by such questions, we propose three points of orientation that we have found helpful in challenging precarity and making space for design practices of critical inquiry and social transformation.

There is an urgent need to attune ourselves to recognize precarizing value practices, i.e., to recognize those actions and processes – as well as correspondent webs of relations – that are predicated on a value system that exposes us and others to precarious working and living conditions, while at the same time (re)producing them.[8] This urgency is underlined for us by the reactions we got

3. Bianca Elzenbaumer, "Designing Economic Cultures: Cultivating Socially and Politically Engaged Design Practices Against Procedures of Precarisation" (London: Goldsmiths, University of London, 2014).

4. Brave New Alps, "Precarity Pilot," 2014, precaritypilot.net/.

5. Bianca Elzenbaumer et al., "Mapping Eco-Social Design," 2016, www.brave-new-alps.com/mapping-eco-social-design/.

6. We have already shared elsewhere how design educators can contribute to create a more diffuse awareness of precarious working conditions and to prefigure ways of working and living that lead beyond precarity: Brave New Alps, "Notes on Design Education and (Prefigurative) Work Politics," *Art, Design & Communication in Higher Education* 16, no. 1 (1 April 2017), 117–23, doi.org/10.1386/adch.16.1.117_1.

7. Michel Foucault, "What Is Critique?," in *The Politics of Truth*, ed. Sylvère Lotringer and Lysa Hochroth, trans. Lysa Hochroth (New York: Semiotext(e), 1997), 44–47.

8. For a discussion of value practices, see Massimo De Angelis, *The Beginning of History: Value Struggles and Global Capital* (London: Pluto Press, 2007), 24.

RE-DEFINING
THE PATH
OF OUR
WORKING
LIVES

News
Workshops
Essays
Interviews
Glossary
Get in touch

Search for stuff

precaritypilot.net

PRECARITY PILOT

FROM UNIVERSITY TO WORK
internships,
alternatives,
exploitation

REDEFINING CAREER MODELS
ambitions,
values,
stereotypes

ORGANISING YOUR PRACTICE
money, time,
working
conditions

COOPERATION AND SUPPORT
rights,
mutuality,
social protection

when running *Precarity Pilot* workshops across Europe. On the one hand, in contexts where we worked with already precarious designers – for example, in self-organized summer schools – there was a sense of relief among participants at being able to speak openly about the difficulties of precarious work, yet also a sense of hopelessness in regards of how to get out of it. People felt that the practical as well as conceptual tools they had acquired so far did not open up empowering perspectives in their working lives. On the other hand, in university contexts we encountered a great deal of denial of precarious working conditions and a preconception that to experience them means an individual lack of creativity and talent or too little commitment to work, and that's certainly something that does not apply to oneself, so no troubles in sight.

  Despite the diversity in approach, for a majority of participants in both contexts there was an inability to recognize patterns of work and ways of life that generate precarious conditions for oneself and others. Overwork was seen as fulfilling, jumping from one project to the next as exciting, lack of retirement provisions and parental leave as something to deal with in a distant future, doing un- or underpaid work for prestigious clients or design studios as an excellent stepping stone for one's career, and the prospect of at some point holding a respected teaching position was seen as the guarantee for critical practice. While we agree that all these aspects can be fulfilling, we also know that they are so only as long as overwork and flexibility are self-directed, social provisions are secured by access to the systems of a functioning welfare state or by wealthy parents, underpayment does not simply lead to the next underpaid job, and the respected teaching position is actually properly paid. However, to go beyond systemic precarity, it is incredibly important to recognize precarizing patterns of work and life, as this enables one to come up with other ways of doing, while generating a sense of empowerment that goes beyond oneself: changing the way I work and live will not just help to de-precarize myself but also others.

MOVING BEYOND PRECARITY

Design Struggles

9. Joan C. Tronto, *Moral Boundaries: A Political Argument for an Ethic of Care* (New York: Routledge, 1993), 102.

10. Bernice Fisher and Joan C. Tronto, "Toward a Feminist Theory of Care," in *Circles of Care: Work and Identity in Women's Lives*, ed. Emily K. Abel and Margaret K. Nelson (State University of New York Press, 1990), 40. This ethics of care and interdependence needs also to be applied beyond the field of humans to consider our interdependence with the more-than-human world in order to remake our subjectivities and our everyday practices. An elaboration of this aspect would, however, exceed the space of this text.

Follow a Logic of Interdependence to Practice Differently

A helpful first step in learning and activating de-precarizing value practices is to recognize our interdependence within and beyond our professional field. From this recognition we can start to act with an ethics of care, i.e., an ethics that "implies reaching out to something other than the self"[9] and that includes all activities "that we do to maintain, continue, and repair our 'world' so that we can live in it as well as possible."[10] This implies that fighting against the deleterious effects of precarious working and living conditions is not just about saving your own butt, as that's precisely the attitude that perpetuates precarizing value practices.

For us it is imperative that designers who do well economically and who have the racial, social, or geographical background that makes life easier, extend a supportive hand to others well beyond their circle of friends and cultivate de-precarizing value practices. Such value practices can take pretty conventional forms, such as fair pay for collaborators, charging properly for our services to avoid fee dumping, taking time to contribute to eco-social causes, and to slow down and cultivate a way of life aware of our interdependence with the more-than-human others in this world. Acting from a logic of interdependence and solidarity contributes – one act at a time – to improving the working situation and ability to produce transformative work for many more than just oneself.

Treat the Economy as the Malleable Stuff of Everyday Life

Another empowering move in generating de-precarizing value practices is to learn to see the economy as *always* diverse, i.e., as always made up of activities and exchanges beyond the money nexus and the logic of profit, and thus as a realm we always participate in, no matter how we secure our livelihoods. To better grasp the concept of the diverse economy, we can imagine the economy to have the shape of an iceberg where market exchanges are only the top

Bianca Elzenbaumer /
Brave New Alps

of what we see, while under the water there is a diversity of relational patterns of exchange and support that helps people to sustain their livelihoods. On the one hand, this feminist approach to the economy, developed by geographers J. K. Gibson-Graham,[11] places each of us as a key actor who makes the economy (and who can decide on how to make it) on a daily basis. On the other hand, it places the economy as a historical, discursive practice that is shaped by a wide range of actors and that by no means needs to stay as it is.[12]

This means that as designers we can make the economy the object of our design and even of our whole design practice, starting in the everyday with how we craft the diverse economies that sustain our livelihood and through which we weave ourselves together with others. This move towards diverse economies is especially important because (very often) critical, transformative work pays less and is more difficult to sustain than work that perpetuates the hegemonic system. In a diverse economies logic, making a living and creating the material and social conditions that enable critical, transformative work ceases to be a question of working your way up a ladder whose bars have become ever further apart and ever more slippery. Rather, it becomes a matter of weaving yourself into an ecology of practices that enables you to unfold your own force in challenging the status quo and experimenting with other ways of doing.[13] An ecology of practices, in which to ask what modes of doing and thinking one belongs to, is not a frictionless or tensionless space, but a space in which people can connect in empowering ways while creating an environment in which many can flourish.

Undo Ambitions for Imperial Modes of Living

In addressing our desires for less precarious ways of working and living while practicing design in critical and transformative work, we need to engage with structural and personal ties to imperial modes of living, i.e., ways of life that draw on ecological and social resources of more or less far away places to guarantee high living standards for oneself, while destroying the habitats and ways of life

11. The diverse economy has been theorized by feminist economic geographers J. K. Gibson-Graham. See their foundational work on this as well as the popularized version of it: J. K. Gibson-Graham, *A Postcapitalist Politics* (Minneapolis, MN: University of Minnesota Press, 2006); *Take Back the Economy: An Ethical Guide for Transforming Our Communities* (Minneapolis, MN: University of Minnesota Press, 2013).

12. Michel Callon, "What Does It Mean to Say That Economics Is Performative?," in *Do Economists Make Markets: On the Performativity of Economics*, ed. Donald MacKenzie, Fabian Muniesa, and Lucia Sui (Princeton, NJ: Princeton University Press, 2007), 311–57; Timothy Mitchell, "Rethinking Economy," *Geoforum* 39, no. 3 (2008), 1116–21.

13. Isabelle Stengers, "Introductory Notes on an Ecology of Practices," *Cultural Studies Review* 11, no. 1 (2005), 183–96, doi.org/ http://dx.doi.org/10.5130/ csr.v11i1.3459.

> *"TREAT THE EXISTING SITUATION AS A (PROBLEMATIC) RESOURCE FOR PROJECTS OF BECOMING, A PLACE FROM WHICH TO BUILD SOMETHING MORE DESIRABLE IN THE FUTURE."*
>
> *J.K. GIBSON-GRAHAM — THE END OF CAPITALISM (AS WE KNEW IT), 2006*

of others.[14] Imperial modes of life are attractive, and much of the infrastructure and practices of everyday life in the minority world imply the destruction of other life-worlds along racialized fault lines.[15] Thus for critical, transformative design practices, it becomes crucial to question one's ambitions, ways of doing, and fields of reference, as a way to shape decisions and ways of working. Here we see two key aspects: (a) getting over one's sense of innate entitlement to imperial modes of living, and (b) working towards ways of practicing design and sustaining one's practice that experiment with degrowth and (ever-growing) solidarity.

To get over one's entitlement to imperial modes of living in the minority world, it is important to dig into the social history of one's upbringing and the context one lives in: what practices are enabled because of your gender, your skin color, your geographical and social background, your body fitness? For example, it is just as important for male designers to begin to see through patriarchal and sexist patterns as it is for white designers to begin to see through the patterns of racist and colonial socialization. Once

14. Ulrich Brand and Markus Wissen, *Imperiale Lebensweise: Zur Ausbeutung von Mensch und Natur in Zeiten des globalen Kapitalismus* (Munich: Oekom Verlag, 2017); I.L.A. Kollektiv, *Auf Kosten Der Anderen? Wie Die Imperiale Lebensweise Ein Gutes Leben Für Alle Verhindert* (Munich: Oekom Verlag, 2017); For an English introduction to the concept, see Ulrich Brand, "Imperial Mode of Living and the Politics of Social-Ecological Transformation," July 2018, www.youtube.com/watch?v=6306Svk_8j8.

15. Kathryn Yusoff, *A Billion Black Anthropocenes or None* (Minneapolis, MN: University Of Minnesota Press, 2018).

these dividing and destructive patterns become apparent it is possible to begin to form ambitions – and from these to produce design projects and thus modes of living – that empower through the creation of social solidarity and material support structures that allow for the emergence of a just pluriverse.

Construct Nurturing Value Practices

For us as designers, combining a logic of interdependence and diverse economies with a desire to undo imperial modes of living, means being at a point where it's possible to stop trying to fit one's work and life into conventional business or career templates. As J. K. Gibson-Graham teach us, the economies that sustain our livelihoods are by default always much more diverse – and we would say messy – than we are made to think.[16] From this perspective, the design of economies that carry ourselves and others beyond precarity becomes an appealing design task. We can begin to create amorphous entities that entangle work and life in empowering ways, while creating multiple economies above and below the waterline of the iceberg to sustain a design practice that does not want to cater to conventional market needs. There are many people out there doing this already, and the moment one doesn't take the design world of glossy magazines, shiny start-ups, and corporate collaborations as one's frame of reference for "success" one can begin to come up with pretty workable and nurturing value practices for work and life that challenge the isolating individuality that neoliberal politics pulls us towards.[17]

Strategies and Tactics to Move Beyond Precarity

"If women are everywhere, a woman is always somewhere, and those places of women are transformed as women transform themselves."
—J. K. Gibson Graham

If you have come this far in reading this text, you might begin to argue that the challenge we are setting out is too

16. It's also interesting to note that when you start digging into design practices that are successful in conventional terms, these very often sustain themselves in part through inherited wealth and/or supportive governments, who themselves mostly build their wealth on colonial pasts, a neocolonial present, and petroleum extraction.

17. The Feral Business Research Network, of which we are members, draws together a whole range of practitioners who are enacting diverse economies through artistic and designerly methods.

18. Lauren Berlant, *Cruel Optimism* (Durham, NC: Duke University Press, 2011).

big and that conventional, competitive ways of practicing design still seem the safest option to go beyond precarity. If this is the case, you might be experiencing a form of the "cruel optimism" that affect theorist Lauren Berlant has so sharply theorized.[18] Cruel optimism is an attachment to compromised conditions of possibility: the escape from precarious working and living conditions always seems just around the corner, but their resolution continuously escapes because cruel optimism keeps us locked into precarizing value practices.

So what follows are entry points to value practices that in our experience can break with compromised conditions of possibility. For some these value practices might seem too small or irrelevant, for others they might be too big, depending on where you are currently at. For us, they serve as concrete starting points and thinking devices that help us to reframe our ways of thinking, doing, and being in the world.

Make Long-term Plans

Capital moves people around and draws them to the center: to find your luck you are urged to move from the village to the town, from the town to the regional capital, and from there to the metropolis. The constant urge to move on and, especially, to move ever closer to a more powerful center, is in our view a precarizing value practice that is further exacerbated by the fact that places where capital is more dense are very often also places that precarize through exclusivity (expressed through, for example, high living costs and fierce restrictions on the right to stay based on qualifications and citizenship) and sped up, individualizing lifestyles. While we know very well that the center is also often where you get fresh air (and safety) by escaping the stifling patriarchal, sexist, racist, and homophobic structures of more peripheral spaces or where there is at least a chance of finding paid work (or security from war), we have also observed that resisting capital's demand for constant movement is for some designers a strategy against precarization.

While we have seen that places that feel more peripheral are often more fertile spaces for growing de-precarizing value practices because access to living and working space is more affordable, we also think that whether you choose to live in a space that feels central or peripheral (and this can be a pretty subjective feeling), what is most important in terms of challenging precarity is to have a long-term plan you can stick to and inventively move around in when the pressures, anxieties, and doubts of precarity pull on you. Being exposed to precarity implies a constant temporariness, a constant flux of building and abandoning social and material structures, thus missing out on the possibility of creating interlinking infrastructures that can take us and others beyond precarity, infrastructures that can support critical practice through dire times.

Loosen the Grip of Money

Precarity is also related to the need for a constant flow of money to cover basic needs, work-related expenses, and leisure. However, the more you earn the more you spend, so the feeling of never earning enough remains pretty much a constant. From observing this dynamic, we have come to be convinced that voluntarily frugal lifestyles – paired with the political request for a general basic income – can be a way out of the tyranny of underpaid work, forced consumerism, and sped up ways of life. Frugal lifestyles can drastically reduce the need for – and with it the tyranny of – money. Frugality in terms of technology can mean to keep on fixing and upgrading your computer while resisting the pressure to keep up with the newest IT trends and taking a political stance by treating with care objects that have high social and environmental costs. When you also apply frugality to the consumption of energy, it means that flying both for work and leisure becomes an exception. In a critical and transformative act, you stop placing your own well-being and success above that of others further along the chain of destruction of the human practice of flying.
     Once you perceive the economy as diverse, you can also begin to play with how you access what you need without moving through the money nexus, while growing rich social networks of mutual aid. But you can also loosen the grip of money by experimenting in more radical ways.

19. Christophe Meierhans, *Common Wallet (General Presentation, Oct 2018)*, 2018, vimeo.com/295537042.

20. "Ecosol Fidenza: Ecohousing nel quartiere Europa a Fidenza," www.ecosol-fidenza.it/ (accessed July 25, 2019); Tv2000it, *"Siamo noi": Cohousing a Fidenza*, www.youtube.com/watch?v=frgyQ76zCjo (accessed July 25, 2019).

21. See also Caroline Shenaz Hossein, *The Black Social Economy in the Americas Exploring Diverse Community-Based Markets*, Perspectives from Social Economics (New York, NY: Palgrave Macmillan, 2018).

22. Recent examples of such solidarity in our own network are the Cornerstone Housing Coop in Leeds, UK, always offering one spare room to refugees in need for immediate accommodation, and R50 in Berlin, who between 2015 and 2016 hosted a family of twelve Syrian refugees until, through their network, they had found proper housing for all of them.

Sharing all your income in a common pot with a group of people who also feel a desire for socio-economic transformation can be one way to go. In 2018, a diverse group of ten cultural producers in Brussels (Belgium) decided to start a common wallet as an experiment in kinship, solidarity, and radical trust, for although everyone in the group deserves steady access to money, there are not enough well-paid and stable jobs to go around.[19] Such experiments can lead to more common plans: in the 1990s a group of peace activists – one of whom is the architect Luca Rigoni – started a similar income-sharing collective in Fidenza (Italy). Ten years later they opened up their experiment to more people and built an ecological co-housing space in their town, which also offers leisure spaces for others in their neighborhood.[20] Loosening the grip of money on your minds, desires, and doing – through whatever mode of experimentation you choose – allows you to think in practice through what money does to us, our relations, and our lives, while creating a space from where it becomes possible to construct lives beyond precarity.[21]

Care for Common Infrastructures

Safe housing is a basic need, but desires for its fulfillment are often channeled into efforts for single household and family homes and often come with precarizing mortgages and individualisation by design. Moving desires and efforts around housing towards cooperative living can be very empowering, and, for designers wanting to do critical and transformative work, a way to embed themselves into spaces where daily experimentation opens different approaches to what designs and human practices the world beyond precarity needs. To share ownership of a building keeps living costs relatively low in the long-run, while providing communal spaces in which to grow supporting social connections that can carry people through financially difficult times and through which to offer support for people in immediate need for shelter and care.[22] Very often, such forms of cooperative living can also be inscribed into what we would call intergenerational commons, i.e., commons that are passed on between generations, since through legal forms such as community land trusts and network arrangements such as Radical Routes in the UK, cooperatively owned houses can be locked into communal ownership for perpetuity, thus guaranteeing a base for critical citizenship and work for generations to come. Moreover, the extra space that cooperative housing often entails can be used to host radical businesses that work towards just sustainability, as is the case with the Cornerstone Housing Coop in the North of England, which hosts a cooperative of activist printers.[23]

But clearly common infrastructure is not just about housing. To start small and immediately with caring for more collective infrastructures, you can investigate through practice how others can be empowered through the social, intellectual, and/or material wealth you have. How can it be channeled into more collective and collaborative efforts to work ourselves away from precarious living and working conditions towards an ecologically and socially just society? Small experiments in opening up to others what you have can bring up desires and ideas for more extensive action. The frame here is about creating ecologies of support where the myth of the heroic designer as genius is undone in favor of gentle, solidary, and effective modes of cooperation that enable transformative infrastructures to emerge.

Concluding to Take Action

As you see, these entry points into value practices that defy precarity interweave with and nurture each other. We think that for designers engaging in critical, transformative design, solving their own issues around precarious work and life through collaborative and cooperative arrangements – starting today wherever they are at – is a way to enact a prefigurative politics; a politics that does away with the separation between life and work in collectively empowering ways rather than the disempowering ones enacted by neoliberal politics, where all of life is sacrificed for work and hegemonic notions of success. Combine these practices that challenge precarity through the creation of social and material support structures with social movement activism – for causes such as environmental

23. Bianca Elzenbaumer and Fabio Franz, "Footprint: A Radical Workers Co-Operative and Its Ecology of Mutual Support," *Ephemera: Theory and Politics in Organization* 18, no. 4 (November 2018), 791–804.

Design Struggles

justice, queer culture, no borders, universal healthcare, and a general income – and you get a powerful mix of activities that all aim at taking us en-masse beyond precarity.

Bibliography

Abdulla, Danah. "Design Otherwise: Towards a Locally-Centric Design Education Curricula in Jordan." Goldsmiths, University of London, 2017.

Berlant, Lauren. *Cruel Optimism*. Durham, NC: Duke University Press, 2011.

Boehnert, Joanna. *Design, Ecology, Politics: Towards the Ecocene*. London: Bloomsbury Academic, 2018.

Brand, Ulrich. "Imperial Mode of Living and the Politics of Social-Ecological Transformation." Heinrich Boell Foundation, Bazaleti, Georgia, July 2018. www.youtube.com/watch?v=6306Svk_8j8.
—, and Markus Wissen. *Imperiale Lebensweise: Zur Ausbeutung von Mensch und Natur in Zeiten des globalen Kapitalismus*. Munich: Oekom Verlag, 2017.

Brave New Alps. "Precarity Pilot," 2014. precaritypilot.net/.
—. "Notes on Design Education and (Prefigurative) Work Politics." *Art, Design & Communication in Higher Education* 16, no. 1 (April 1, 2017), 117–23. doi.org/10.1386/adch.16.1.117_1.

Callon, Michel. "What Does It Mean to Say That Economics Is Performative?" In *Do Economists Make Markets: On the Performativity of Economics*. Edited by Donald MacKenzie, Fabian Muniesa, and Lucia Sui, 311–57. Princeton, NJ: Princeton University Press, 2007.

De Angelis, Massimo. *The Beginning of History: Value Struggles and Global Capital*. London: Pluto Press, 2007.

"Ecosol Fidenza: Ecohousing nel quartiere Europa a Fidenza." www.ecosol-fidenza.it/ (accessed 25 July 2019).

Elzenbaumer, Bianca. "Designing Economic Cultures: Cultivating Socially and Politically Engaged Design Practices Against Procedures of Precarisation." London: Goldsmiths, University of London, 2014.
—, and Fabio Franz. "Footprint: A Radical Workers Co-Operative and Its Ecology of Mutual Support." *Ephemera: Theory and Politics in Organization* 18, no. 4 (November 2018), 791–804.
—, Fabio Franz, Kris Krois, and Alvise Mattozzi. "Mapping Eco-Social Design," 2016. www.brave-new-alps.com/mapping-eco-social-design/.

Escobar, Arturo. *Designs for the Pluriverse: Radical Interdependence, Autonomy, and the Making of Worlds*. Durham, NC: Duke University Press Books, 2018.

Fisher, Bernice, and Joan C. Tronto. "Toward a Feminist Theory of Care." In *Circles of Care: Work and Identity in Women's Lives*. Edited by Emily K. Abel and Margaret K. Nelson, 36–54. New York, NY: State University of New York Press, 1990.

Foucault, Michel. "What Is Critique?" In *The Politics of Truth*. Edited by Sylvère Lotringer and Lysa Hochroth. Translated by Lysa Hochroth, 23–82. New York, NY: Semiotext(e), 1997.
Gibson-Graham, J. K. *A Postcapitalist Politics*. Minneapolis, MN: University of Minnesota Press, 2006.
—, Jenny Cameron, and Stephen Healy. *Take Back the Economy: An Ethical Guide for Transforming Our Communities*. Minneapolis, MN: University of Minnesota Press, 2013.
Hossein, Caroline Shenaz. *The Black Social Economy in the Americas Exploring Diverse Community-Based Markets*. Perspectives from Social Economics. New York, NY: Palgrave Macmillan, 2018.

I.L.A. Kollektiv. *Auf Kosten der Anderen? Wie die imperiale Lebensweise Ein gutes Leben für alle verhindert*. Munich: Oekom Verlag, 2017.

Mazé, Ramia, Meike Schalk, and Thérèse Kristiansson, eds. *Feminist Futures of Spatial Practice: Materialism, Activism, Dialogues, Pedagogies, Projections*. Baunach: AADR, 2017.

Meierhans, Christophe. *Common Wallet (General Presentation, Oct 2018)*, 2018. vimeo.com/295537042.

Mitchell, Timothy. "Rethinking Economy." *Geoforum* 39, no. 3 (2008), 1116–21.

Stengers, Isabelle. "Introductory Notes on an Ecology of Practices". *Cultural Studies Review* 11, no. 1 (2005), 183–96. doi.org/http://dx.doi.org/10.5130/csr.v11i1.3459.

Tronto, Joan C. *Moral Boundaries: A Political Argument for an Ethic of Care*. New York, NY: Routledge, 1993.

Tv2000it. *"Siamo noi": Cohousing a Fidenza*. www.youtube.com/watch?v=frgyQ76zCjo (accessed 25 July 2019).

Yusoff, Kathryn. *A Billion Black Anthropocenes or None*. Minneapolis, MN: University Of Minnesota Press, 2018.

Design Struggles

DESIGN JUSTICE Towards an Intersectional Feminist Framework for Design Theory and Practice

Sasha Costanza-Chock

Introduction

In June 2015, at the Allied Media Conference in Detroit, a group of thirty designers, artists, technologists, and community organizers took part in the workshop "Generating Shared Principles for Design Justice." The goal of the workshop was to move beyond the frames of "social impact design" or "design for good," to challenge designers to think about how good intentions are not necessarily enough to ensure that design processes and practices become tools of liberation, and to develop principles that might help practitioners avoid the (often unwitting) reproduction of existing inequalities. The draft principles developed at that workshop would come to be refined over the next few years, and were most recently (in 2018) released in the following form:

Design Justice Network Principles

Design mediates so much of our realities and has tremendous impact on our lives, yet very few of us participate in design processes. In particular, the people who are most adversely affected by design decisions – about visual culture, new technologies, the planning of our communities, or the structure of our political and economic systems – tend to have the least influence on those decisions and how they are made.

1. Design Justice Network, designjustice.org.

Design justice rethinks design processes, centers people who are normally marginalized by design, and uses collaborative, creative practices to address the deepest challenges our communities face.

• We use design to **sustain, heal, and empower** our communities, as well as to seek liberation from exploitative and oppressive systems.

• We **center the voices of those who are directly impacted** by the outcomes of the design process.

• We **prioritize design's impact on the community** over the intentions of the designer.

• We view **change as emergent from an accountable, accessible, and collaborative process**, rather than as a point at the end of a process.

• We see the role of the **designer as a facilitator rather than an expert.**

• We believe that **everyone is an expert based on their own lived experience**, and that we all have unique and brilliant contributions to bring to a design process.

• We **share design knowledge and tools** with our communities.

• We work towards **sustainable, community-led and -controlled** outcomes.

• We work towards **non-exploitative solutions** that reconnect us to the earth and to each other.

• Before seeking new design solutions, **we look for what is already working** at the community level. We honor and uplift traditional, indigenous, and local knowledge and practices.[1]

2. Patricia Hill Collins, *Black Feminist Thought: Knowledge, Consciousness, and the Politics of Empowerment* (London: Routledge, 2002).

In this paper, I will attempt to further develop the approach articulated in the Design Justice Principles, and to explore design justice as a broader framework that might guide design theory and practice across a wide range of fields.

Naming Oppressive Systems: On Intersectionality and the Matrix of Domination

Design is key to our collective liberation, but most design processes today reproduce inequalities that are structured by what Black feminist scholar Patricia Hill Collins calls the matrix of domination: white supremacy, heteropatriarchy, capitalism, and settler colonialism.[2] These and additional intersecting inequalities are manifest at all levels of the design process, including (but not limited to) designers, intended users, values, affordances and disaffordances, scoping and framing, privileged design sites, governance, ownership, and control of designed objects, platforms, and systems, and narratives about how design processes work.

The Design Justice Principles (above) were proposed in part as a response to this situation. These principles are an important starting point for growing a network of practitioners who care about articulating and more intentionally practicing design that, as much as possible, avoids reproducing structural inequality and oppression. The first principle states that design justice practitioners "seek liberation from exploitative and oppressive systems." More explicitly naming the oppressive systems that design justice seeks to counter can strengthen the approach. To do this work, we can draw upon the tradition of Black feminist thought.

Intersectionality

First, we need to briefly clarify the concepts of intersectionality and the matrix of domination. Black feminist thought fundamentally reconceptualizes race, class, and gender as interlocking systems: they do not only operate "on their own," but are often experienced together, by individuals who exist at their intersections. The analytical framework built on this fundamental insight from Black feminist thought and experience is called *intersectionality*. The term was first proposed by Black feminist legal scholar Kimberlé Crenshaw in her 1989 article "Demarginalizing the Intersection of Race and Sex: A Black Feminist Critique of Antidiscrimination Doctrine, Feminist Theory and Antiracist Politics." In the article, Crenshaw describes how existing antidiscrimination law (Title VII of the Civil Rights Act) repeatedly failed to protect Black women workers. First, she discusses an instance where Black women workers at General Motors (GM) were told they had no legal grounds for a discrimination case against their employer, because antidiscrimination law only protected single-identity categories. The Court found that GM did not systematically discriminate against all women, because the company hired white women, and that there was insufficient evidence of discrimination against Black people in general. Thus, Black women, who did in reality experience systematic employment discrimination as Black women, were not protected by existing law, and had no actionable legal claim.

In a second case described by Crenshaw, the court rejected the claims of a Black woman who claimed discrimination by Hugh Helicopters Inc., because "her attempt to specify her race was seen as being at odds with the standard allegation that the employer simply discriminated 'against females.'"[3] In other words, the court could not accept that Black women might be able to represent all women, including white women, as a class. In a third case, the court *did* award discrimination damages to Black women workers at a pharmaceutical company, but refused to award the damages to all Black workers, under the rationale that Black women could not adequately represent the claims of Black people as a category. Crenshaw notes the role of statistical analysis in each of these cases: sometimes, the courts required Black women to include broader statistics for all women that countered their claims of discrimination; in other cases, the courts limited the admissible data to that dealing with Black women only. In those cases, the low total number of Black women employees typically made statistically valid claims impossible, whereas strong claims could have been made if the plaintiffs were allowed to include data for all women, for all Black people, or both. Later,

3. Kimberlé Crenshaw, "Demarginalizing the Intersection of Race and Sex: A Black Feminist Critique of Antidiscrimination Doctrine, Feminist Theory and Antiracist Politics," *The University of Chicago Legal Forum* no. 1, 1989, 139–67.

4. Kimberlé Crenshaw, 'Mapping the Margins: Intersectionality, Identity Politics, and Violence Against Women of Color," *Stanford Law Reviews* 43, no. 6 (1991), 1241–99.

in her 1991 *Stanford Law Review* article "Mapping the Margins: Intersectionality, Identity Politics, and Violence Against Women of Color,"[4] Crenshaw powerfully articulates the ways that women of color often experience male violence as a product of intersecting racism and sexism, but are then marginalized from both feminist and antiracist discourse and practice, and denied access to specific legal remedies.

The concept of intersectionality provided the grounds for a long, slow paradigm shift that is still unfolding in the social sciences, legal scholarship, and in other domains of research and practice. This paradigm shift is also beginning to transform the domain of design. The shift away from what Crenshaw calls "single-axis analysis," where race or gender are considered as independent constructs, has wide-reaching consequences for design theory and practice.

Universalist design principles and practices, as well as single-axis evaluations of fairness in design, erase certain groups of people: specifically, those who are intersectionally disadvantaged (or multiply burdened) under white supremacist heteropatriarchy, capitalism, and settler colonialism. When designers do consider inequality in design (and most professional design processes do not consider inequality at all), they nearly always employ a single-axis framework. Most design processes today are therefore structured in ways that make it impossible to see, engage with, account for, or attempt to remedy the unequal distribution of benefits and burdens that they reproduce. As Crenshaw noted, feminist theory and antiracist policy that is not grounded in an intersectional understanding of gender and race cannot adequately address the experiences of Black women when it comes to the formulation of policy demands. Design justice holds that the same is true when it comes to "design demands."

The Matrix of Domination

Closely linked to intersectionality, but less widely used today, the *matrix of domination* is a term developed by Black feminist scholar Patricia Hill Collins to refer to race, class, and gender as interlocking systems of oppression, rather than each operating "on its own." It is a conceptual model that helps us think about how power, oppression, resistance, privilege, penalties, benefits, and harms are systematically distributed. When she introduces the term, in her book *Black Feminist Thought*,[5] Collins emphasizes race, class, and gender as the three systems that historically have been most important in structuring most Black women's lives. She notes that additional systems of oppression structure the matrix of domination for other kinds of people. The term, for her, describes a mode of analysis that includes any systems of oppression that shape people's lives.

This framework also emphasizes that every individual simultaneously receives both benefits and harms, or "penalty and privilege," based on their location within the interlocking systems of oppression that structure our experience. As Collins notes, "[e]ach individual derives varying amounts of penalty and privilege" within the matrix of domination.[6] An intersectional Black feminist analysis thus helps us each see that we are simultaneously members of multiple groups, both dominant and subordinate. Design justice urges us to consider how design (affordances, objects, systems, processes) simultaneously distributes both penalty and privileges to individuals based on their location within the matrix of domination, and to attend to the ways that this operates at various scales.

In *Black Feminist Thought*, Collins notes that

> [p]eople experience and resist oppression on three levels: the level of personal biography; the group or community level of the cultural context created by race, class, and gender; and the systemic level of social institutions. Black feminist thought emphasizes all three levels as sites of domination and as potential sites of resistance.[7]

Design justice as a framework urges us to explore the ways that design relates to domination and resistance at each of these three levels (personal, community, and institutional).

For example, at the personal level, we might explore how interface design affirms or denies aspects of a person's identity through features such as, say, a binary

5. Collins, *Black Feminist Thought*.

6. Collins, 287.

7. Collins.

gender dropdown during account profile creation. More broadly, we might consider how design decisions play out in the impacts they have on different individual's biographies or life-chances. At the community level, we might explore how platform design fosters certain kinds of communities while suppressing others, through setting and implementing community guidelines, rules, and speech norms, instantiated through different kinds of content moderation systems.

At the institutional level, design justice asks us to consider the ways that various design institutions reproduce and/or challenge the matrix of domination in their practices. This might include large companies (Google, Apple, IDEO), venture capitalists, standards-setting bodies (ISO, W3C, NIST), laws (such as the Americans with Disabilities Act), and universities and educational institutions that train designers.

Additionally, institutions design objects, systems, and processes that they then use to distribute benefits and harms across society. For example, the ability to immigrate to the United States is unequally distributed among different groups of people through a combination of laws passed by the US Congress, software decision support systems, executive orders that influence enforcement priorities, and so on. Within the broader immigration system, visa allocation is an algorithm that has been designed according to the ideology and political priorities of those who hold political power.

Finally, Black feminist thought also emphasizes the value of situated knowledge over universalist knowledge. In other words, particular insights about the nature of power, oppression, and resistance come from those who occupy a subjugated standpoint, and knowledge developed from any particular standpoint is always partial knowledge.

A Tentative Definition of Design Justice

Having briefly explored the ideas of intersectionality and the matrix of domination, I offer the following tentative definition of design justice:

Design justice is a field of theory and practice that

is concerned with how the design of objects and systems influences the distribution of risks, harms, and benefits among various groups of people. Design justice focuses on the ways that design reproduces, is reproduced by, and/or challenges the matrix of domination (white supremacy, heteropatriarchy, capitalism, and settler colonialism). Design justice is also a growing social movement that aims to ensure a more equitable distribution of design's benefits and burdens; fair and meaningful participation in design decisions; and recognition of community-based design traditions, knowledge, and practices.

This definition emphasizes that design justice is both procedural and distributive: we have an ethical imperative to systematically advance the participation of marginalized communities in all stages of the technology design process; through this process, resources and power can be more equitably distributed. Procedural goals are reflected in the second Design Justice Principle ("we center the voices of those who are directly impacted by the outcomes of the design process"), while distributive goals are emphasized in the third ("we prioritize design's impact on the community over the intentions of the designer").

In this definition, design justice also has both normative and pragmatic justifications: it is based on broader ideals of democratic inclusion and social justice in all spheres of life; at the same time, design processes that operate according to these ideals can produce products, processes, and systems that work better for all of us, in the long run.

This is not meant to be the only definition of design justice, but rather a provisional proposal that we can use to build a conversation. There is already a growing community of people who identify with the term design justice, and many have worked to explore the idea and clarify what it might mean.

Design justice as a framework asks us to engage with a series of questions about how design processes currently work, and about how we want them to work. These include questions of equity (who gets to do design?),

INTERSECTIONALITY

8. Victor Papanek, *Design for the Real World* (London: Thames and Hudson, 1972).

9. Anne-Marie Willis, "Ontological Designing," *Design Philosophy Papers* 4, no. 2 (2006), 62–92.

10. Mariarosa Dalla Costa and Giovanna Franca Dalla Costa, eds., *Women, Development, and Labor of Reproduction: Struggles and Movements* (Trenton, NJ: Africa World Press, 1999).

beneficiaries (who do we design for, or with?), values (what values do we encode and reproduce in the objects and systems that we design?), scope (how do we scope and frame design problems?), sites (where do we do design, what design sites are privileged and what sites are ignored or marginalized, and how do we make design sites accessible to those who will be most impacted?), ownership, account-ability, and political economy (who owns and profits from design outcomes, what social relationships are reproduced by design, and how do we move towards community control of design processes?), and discourse (what stories do we tell about how things are designed?). In the next section of this paper, I will briefly engage with several of these questions, in an attempt to illustrate the generative power of the proposed definition of design justice.

Designers: Who Gets (Paid) to do Design?

Design justice as a theoretical framework recognizes the universality of design as a human activity. "Design," in a general sense, means problem-solving; all human beings participate in design.[8] Design theorist Anne-Marie Willis put it this way:

> Design is something far more pervasive and profound than is generally recognised by designers, cultural theorists, philosophers or lay persons; designing is fundamental to being human – we design, that is to say, we deliberate, plan and scheme in ways which prefigure our actions and makings … – we design our world, while our world acts back on us and designs us.[9]

Through this lens, and inspired by feminist critiques of the invisibilized, unpaid labor of reproduction,[10] design justice includes a call for broader recognition of everyday design practices.

At the same time, as Willis notes, "design" is also often used to refer to expert knowledge and practices contained within a particular set of professionalized fields, including software development, architecture, planning, and industrial design, as well as in various media and audiovisual industries, such as graphic design. Within a discussion of "design" as a specialist activity, or as a certain type of work accomplished by experts, there is also a significant and steadily growing literature on design practices by marginalized people. Alternative histories of technology and design help to recuperate and center people, practices, and forms of expertise that have long been erased by mainstream theory and history, both in scholarly and popular writing. Some histories of invisibilized technology design work have been widely popularized; for example, the 2016 film *Hidden Figures* chronicles the work of Katherine Johnson and other Black women who worked for NASA as "human computers," coding space flight trajectories.[11] Additionally, recent literature on innovation decenters the myth of the individual designer and emphasizes the key roles played by "lead users" who constantly modify, hack, repurpose, and reuse technologies in order to better fit their needs.[12]

With these caveats – all humans design, design is not only the domain of paid experts, the contributions of expert designers and technologists who are not wealthy and/or educationally privileged white cisgender men have been erased from history, and professional designers constantly draw both from one another and from the unsung design work of everyday people – it is still possible and valuable to consider the ways that the matrix of domination systematically structures paid professional design work.

Although the discussion that follows could easily apply to any of the professionalized design fields, we will focus on the US software industry. Designers in this sector are highly rewarded, both economically and culturally, and have achieved status as iconic figures who stand in for the promise of innovation and entrepreneurialism under informational capitalism.

There has been a growing public conversation about the fact that the most advanced sector of the economy might well be the most unequal. In 2016, many Silicon Valley firms, under pressure from mobilized publics, released diversity data about their employment practices. Unsurprisingly, this data did not paint a flattering picture of progress towards gender and racial equity. Overall, white

11. Margot Lee Shetterly, *Hidden Figures: The Untold Story of the African-American Women Who Helped Win the Space Race* (New York, NY: W. Morrow, 2016).

12. Eric von Hippel, *Democratizing Innovation* (Cambridge, MA: MIT Press, 2005).

13. Catherine Ashcraft, Elizabeth Eger, and Michelle Friend, *Girls in iT: The Facts* (Boulder, CO: National Center for Women & Information Technology, 2012).

14. Will Evans and Sinduja Rangarajan, "Hidden Figures: How Silicon Valley Keeps Diversity Data Secret," *Reveal News*, October 19, 2017, www.revealnews.org/article/hidden-figures-how-silicon-valley-keeps-diversity-data-secret/.

15. Kim A. Weeden, Youngjoo Cha, and Mauricio Bucca, "Long Work Hours, Part-Time Work, and Trends in the Gender Gap in Pay, the Motherhood Wage Penalty, and the Fatherhood Wage Premium," *RSF: The Russell Sage Foundation Journal of the Social Sciences* 2, no. 4 (2016), 71–102; Franklin D. Wilson, "Generational Changes in Racial Inequality in Occupational Attainment, 1950–2010: A Synthetic Cohort Analysis," *Du Bois Review: Social Science Research on Race* 14, no. 2 (2016), 387–425; Erik Arce and Dennis A. Segura, "Stratification in the Labor Market," in *The Wiley Blackwell Encyclopedia of Race, Ethnicity, and Nationalism*, 2015, doi.org/10.1002/9781118663202.wberen226.

16. Gary Orfield, et al., "'Brown' at 62: School Segregation by Race, Poverty and State," *The Civil Rights Project/Proyecto Derechos Civiles* (UCLA, 2016), escholarship.org/uc/item/5ds6k0rd.

17. Alfinio Flores, "Examining Disparities in Mathematics Education: Achievement Gap or Opportunity Gap?," *The High School Journal* 91, no. 1 (2007), 29–42.

and Asian cisgender men dominate software industry jobs. For example, in the United States, women overall hold 25 percent of these jobs; Black women hold just 3 percent of computer programming jobs, and Latinas, 1 percent.[13] Even when women and People of Color (POC) are employed in technology design, development, and product management, in a context of extremely hierarchical organizations, only a handful of women have positions at the top. Gender diversity on the boards of top software and technology companies tends to range between just 10 percent to 25 percent (almost exclusively white) cisgender women. For example, Apple's board has six men and two women, Google, eight and three; Microsoft, eight and two; Twitter, seven and one; eBay, eleven and one, and so on. Yahoo, with a board composed of six men and three women, is the top-tier software firm that comes closest to gender parity at the highest decision-making level.[14]

These dismal employment equity statistics reflect broader raced and gendered patterns that persist across nearly all sectors of the US economy.[15] Racial and gender inequality in who gets paid to do design is consistent with persistent structural inequality across a stratified labor market; it is also shaped by inequalities in access to education. In a broader context of rising wealth inequality, a winner-take-all dynamic is at play, with wealthy whites withdrawing children and tax dollars from schools that used to serve mixed-income and multiracial populations. White flight, and later, gentrification and the recolonization of urban cores, have produced a school system where nearly half of Black and Latino students attend schools with poverty rates higher than 75 percent, vs. less than 5 percent of Whites.[16] Schools in low-income communities of color are rarely allocated the resources they need to provide high-quality STEM education. As a result, Black, Latinx, and low-income students are statistically more likely to be taught by less experienced teachers, receive less funding per student, face lower expectations, score lower on standardized STEM tests, and are less likely to enter higher education in STEM fields.[17] Other factors that militate against more women, POC, and LGBTQIA+ people gaining STEM education, and thereby moving into lucrative design positions in the software and technology professions, include the defunding of public education, the rise of mass incarceration and the school to prison pipeline, school pushout, and in-school abuses faced by LGBTQIA+ and GNC youth, especially LGBTQIA+ youth of color.[18]

Towards Equity in the Tech Workforce: Organizations that Build the Design Skills of More Women, POC, and LGBTQIA+ Folks

Despite recent attention to the lack of diversity in the tech sector, the debate about gender and racial equity in science and technology is not at all new. Many organizations have long worked towards gender parity in STEM fields. For example, the National Center for Women & Information Technology (NCWIT), a community of several hundred companies, universities, government agencies, and nonprofit organizations, was founded in 2004 by the National Science Foundation to advance women and girls' participation in ICTs.[19] In addition to longstanding organizations and initiatives, a number of groups have recently emerged that focus on building the design, tech, and media skills of girls and women, POC, and LGBTQIA+ folks. For example, Black Girls Code, started in 2011, teaches young African American women the basics of computer science and software development. Girls Who Code,[20] launched in 2012, focuses on eliminating the gender gap in the technology and engineering sectors. Code2040, based in San Francisco, works "to ensure that by the year 2040 – when the US will be majority Black and Latinx – we are proportionally represented in America's innovation economy as technologists, investors, thought leaders, and entrepreneurs."[21] The Lesbians Who Tech Summit provides a physical meetup and networking space for lesbians working at all levels of technology industries. Trans Tech Social Enterprises aims to provide jobs and job training in web design to trans* folks in the Chicago area, and Trans*H4CK is a series of hackathons by and for trans* and gender nonconforming people. Trans*H4ACK has grown rapidly, and has organized local events in San Francisco, Boston, and many other cities.[22]

These and similar initiatives are important developments. However, design justice impels recognition that

18. Sasha Costanza-Chock, Chris Schweidler, and Transformative Media Organizing Project, "Toward Transformative Media Organizing: LGBTQ and Two-Spirit Media Work in the United States," *Media, Culture & Society* 39, no. 2 (2017), 159–84, doi.org/10.1177/0163443716674360.

19. For a recent review of best practices towards gender equity in computer science education, see Margaret Hamilton et al., "Gender Equity in Computing: International Faculty Perceptions and Current Practices," in *Proceedings of the 2016 ITiCSE Working Group Reports* (New York, NY: ACM Publications, 2016), 81–102.

20. See girlswhocode.com/.

21. Code2040, 2017, www.code2040.org/.

22. See www.transhack.org/.

23. Laurie Penny, "A Tale of Two Cities: How San Francisco's Tech Boom Is Widening the Gap between Rich and Poor," *The New Statesman*, April 9, 2014, www.newstatesman.com/laurie-penny/2014/04/tale-two-cities-how-sanfranciscos-tech-boom-widening-gap-between-rich-and-poor.

employment in paid design fields is important, but is not the whole picture. We also need to rethink a number of other aspects of current design practice, including the intended beneficiaries of design.

"Users": Who Do We Design For/With?

We must also examine design beneficiaries. In other words, who are we designing for? Journalist and feminist activist Laurie Penny puts it this way:

> There is nothing wrong with making things that people want. The problem is that personhood and desire are constrained by capital; money affects whose wants appear to matter. The kids in Startup House may want a pizza delivery drone, but not in the same way low-income families want health care, or the elderly men lying in their own faeces on Howard Street want a safe place to sleep. There is nothing wrong with making things people want. It's just that too little attention is being paid to the things people need.
>
> The wants and needs of young, healthy, middle-class people with connections and a reasonable amount of spare cash are overrepresented among Start-up City's priorities. For one thing, those are the problems with solutions that sell. For another, given a few million dollars and a team of semigeniuses, those problems are easy to solve. Structural social injustice and systemic racism are harder to tackle – and that's where the tech sector has, until recently, thrown up its hands.[23]

To Penny's critique of the classed prioritization of users within capitalist start-up scenes, we can add that the "default" imagined users are often raced, classed, and gendered within a worldview produced by the matrix of domination and internalized, then reproduced, by design teams. Designers most frequently assume that the unmarked user has access to a number of very powerful privileges, such as US citizenship, English language proficiency, access to broadband internet, a smartphone, no disabilities, and so on. Diversifying the software workforce, unfortunately, will not automatically produce a more diverse default imagined user. Unless the gender identity, sexual orientation, race/ ethnicity, age, nationality, language, immigration status, and other aspects of end-user identity are specified in advance, the imagined user for whom technology design teams develop products tends to default to the dominant social group. In the US, this means straight white middle-class cisgender men, with educational privilege and high tech-nological literacy, citizenship, native English speakers, and so on. Even with diverse design teams, the types and scope of "problems" addressed by most product design ends up limited to this tiny, but potentially highly profitable, subset of humanity.

There is a growing awareness of this problem, and a number of designers, projects, events, and communities of practice who are attempting to address it through an intentional focus on designing for, or with, communities who are usually invisibilized in the world of technology. For example, the Trans*H4CK series of hackathons focus on trans* and gender-nonconforming communities; the Make the Breast Pump Not Suck hackathon focuses on breastfeeding parents; and Contratados.org operates like a "Yelp, for migrant workers" to review potential employers and recruitment agents, educate migrant workers about their rights, and protect them from transnational recruit-ment scams.

Accountability: "About Us, without Us"

We began this section by considering the ways that race and gender structure employment in the software and tech-nology design industries; we then introduced a discussion of the ways the matrix of domination structures our ideas about who to design for. This shifts us from an argument for equity (we need diverse designers, and diverse users) to an argument for accountability (those most affected by the outcomes should lead and own digital design processes and products). In a nutshell: according to both the Design Justice Principles and our tentative definition of design

Design Struggles

24. Douglas Schuler and Aki Namioka, eds., *Participatory Design: Principles and Practices* (Boca Raton, FL: CRC Press, 1993); Michael J. Muller and Sarah Kuhn, "Participatory Design," *Communications of the ACM* 36, no. 6 (1993), 24–28.

25. Shaowen Bardzell, "Feminist HCI: Taking Stock and Outlining an Agenda for Design," in *Proceedings of the SIGCHI Conference on Human Factors in Computing Systems* (New York: Association of Computing Machinery, 2010), 1301–10.

26. James Charlton, *Nothing about Us without Us: Disability Oppression and Empowerment* (Berkeley, CA: University of California Press, 1998).

27. Batya Friedman, ed., *Human Values and the Design of Computer Technology* (Cambridge, MA: Cambridge University Press, 1997); Mary Flanagan, Daniel C. Howe, and Helen Nissenbaum, "Embodying Values in Technology: Theory and Practice," in *Information Technology and Moral Philosophy* (Cambridge, MA: Cambridge University Press, 2008), 322–53, doi.org/10.1017/CBO9780511498725.

justice, the most valuable "ingredient" in design justice is the full inclusion of people with direct lived experience of the conditions the design team is trying to change.

This reflects the "participatory turn" in technology design; for example, see intersecting histories of user-led innovation, participatory design,[24] and feminist HCI[25] and see recent work by the organizers of the Design, Research, and Feminism(s) track at the 2018 Design Research Conference (Ramia Mazé, Laura Forlano, Li Jonsson, Kristina Lindström, and Åsa Ståhl). Additionally, design justice draws from the disability justice movement, whose activists popularized the phrase "Nothing about us without us."[26] The key lessons include involving members of the community that is most directly affected by the issue that you are focusing on. This is crucial, both because it's ethical, and also because the tacit and experiential knowledge of community members is sure to produce ideas, approaches, and innovations that a nonmember of the community would be very unlikely to come up with. It is also possible to create formal community accountability mechanisms in design processes.

Values: What Values and Assumptions Do We Encode in Designed Objects and Processes?

Scholars of science and technology have long noted that values are encoded in, and reproduced through, the affordances of the objects, processes, and systems that we design.[27] In addition to shifting designers and users, design justice proposes systematic evaluation of the values that we choose to encode in designed objects and systems. Intersecting forms of oppression, including white supremacy, cisnormativity, heteropatriarchy, capitalism, and settler colonialism, are hardcoded into designed objects and systems. This typically takes place not because designers are intentionally "evil," but largely through structural forces: resources for design are typically allocated based on potential profitability, and that means most resources are dedicated to design problems that affect the wealthiest groups of people. In addition, at the level of the individual designer or design team, several mechanisms that introduce unintentional bias are at play. These include assumptions about the "unmarked" end-user, limited feedback loops, and (most recently) the use of systematically biased datasets to train algorithms using machine learning techniques.[28]

The emergence of "values in design" is an important shift in design thinking and practice, but design justice goes further, to consider not only the ways that we hardcode oppressive values and norms into affordances, but also the transformative potential of broader participation in the design process, as well as ownership and stewardship of the results. We might consider case studies in areas as diverse as consumer electronics (cameras), algorithm design in sectors such as banking, housing, and policing, and on the other end of the spectrum, intentional values-based design in projects like Contratados, and so on. For example, "Native Americans, African Americans, and other people of color are banned disproportionately because, to Facebook, a 'real' name sometimes means 'traditionally European.'"[29] This happens, in part, because the algorithms used to flag "real" vs. "fake" names were trained on real name datasets that overrepresent European names, using machine learning and natural language processing techniques.

The LGBTQIA+ community, and in particular, drag queens, did successfully organize to force Facebook to modify its "real name" policy. Many LGBTQIA+ folks choose to use names that are not their given name on social media platforms, for various reasons, including a desire to control who has access to their self-presentation of sexual orientation and/or gender identity (SOGI). For many, undesired "outing" of a nonhetero- and/or noncis-normative SOGI may have disastrous real-world consequences, from teasing, bullying, and emotional and physical violence from peers, to loss of family, a stable housing situation, access to resources for education, and so on. Facebook systematically flagged and suspended accounts of LGBTQIA+ people who it suspected of not using "real names," especially drag queens; drag queens fought back. After several prominent drag queens began to leave the hegemonic social network for startup competitor Ello, Facebook ultimately implemented both modifications to its real-name flagging and dispute process and instituted a new set of options for users to display gender pronouns and gender identity, as well as

28. Cecilia Munoz, Megan Smith, and D. J. Patil, "Big Data: A Report on Algorithmic Systems, Opportunity, and Civil Rights" (Washington, DC: Executive Office of the President, The White House: 2016), obamawhitehouse. archives.gov/sites/ default/files/microsites/ ostp/2016_0504_data_ discrimination.pdf.

29. Alli Kirkham, "6 Alarming Ways Facebook's 'Real' Name Policy Puts Its Users at Risk," Everyday Feminism, September 29, 2015, everydayfeminism.com/2015/ 09/the-problem-with-real-names/.

more fine-grained control over who can see these changes. These examples demonstrate the ways that dominant values are typically encoded in the affordances of systems that we design and build – in this case, assumptions about names, pronouns, and gender that were built into various aspects of Facebook's interface design. They also demonstrate how, typically through user mobilization, platforms and systems can be redesigned to encode alternative value systems.

Overall, design justice builds on the foundational work in values in design (VID). VID emphasizes that designers make intentional choices about the affordances and aesthetics of objects and systems that they create. The approach proposes rubrics for analysis of how designed affordances encode particular value sets, as well as evaluation of design projects according to their values. However, design justice as an approach goes several steps further. First, VID is "apolitical," in the sense that the approach suggests that designers should make conscious choices about the values they wish to encode, but avoids a normative stance as to what such values should be. Design justice, as we have seen, begins instead with an intersectional analysis of the matrix of domination, and proposes a systematic effort to encode liberatory values that counter white supremacist capitalist heteropatriarchy, ableism, and settler colonialism. Design justice centers the perspectives and values of Queer, trans*, Black and POC, indigenous, migrant, decolonial, antiauthoritarian, and commons-based communities, among others, while recognizing that there is always conflict both within and between marginalized groups. Additionally, where values in design tends to focus on the affordances and aesthetics of designed objects or systems, design justice is concerned with all aspects of design, including the values that are reproduced in the social relations of power of the design process itself, as well as what happens to the profits, attribution, and governance of the designed object or system.

Conclusions: Towards Design Justice

We began with the Design Justice Principles, then moved on to a brief discussion of intersectionality and the matrix of domination. We then posited a tentative definition of design justice as a framework. We explored the implications of design justice for questions about who gets to do design, who we design for (or with), and the values we encode in designed objects and systems.

The design justice framework raises many other questions that we will not be able to explore here in depth, such as design scoping, sites, platforms, and pedagogy. Design justice encourages a shift from deficit to asset-based approaches to design scoping; the formal inclusion of community members in design processes during scoping; and the valorization of intentionally inclusive hacker and makerspaces (such as Liberating Ourselves Locally, a QTPOC-led hackerspace in Oakland). Design justice also has implications for the current discussion of platform cooperativism;[30] projects that challenge the matrix of domination at the level of the platform include worker-centered projects like Turkopticon, SherpaShare, Stocksy, Union Taxi, and more. Applied to labor markets, design justice requires that designers and developers involve workers, worker advocacy organizations, and cooperatives from the beginning in the design of (cooperative, worker-owned) platforms in various sectors. Additionally, a design justice framework requires that we consistently attend to the question of who receives credit for innovative design work. For example, social movement media innovations are often adopted by the journalism profession and by the broader cultural industries, although stripped of their original coun-terhegemonic intent. Examples might include Indymedia and CNN iReports, TxtMob and Twitter, and DIY lives-treams from DeepDish TV to Occupy (GlobalRevolution, Timcast) to Facebook Live.[31]

These and other questions about design practices will have to wait for future explication. It will also be useful to develop rubrics for evaluation rooted in design justice: how do we determine the degree to which a given design project, process, product, or object follows the design justice principles? We might develop and share design justice tools and toolkits, guides, checklists, and case studies, along with best practices and awards.

Indeed, the Design Justice Network is already engaging in some of these activities. There are a growing

30. Trebor Scholz and Nathan Schneider, eds., *Ours to Hack and to Own: The Rise of Platform Cooperativism, a New Vision for the Future of Work and a Fairer Internet* (New York, NY: OR books, 2016), www.jstor.org/stable/j.ctv62hfq7.

31. Sasha Costanza-Chock, "Mic Check! Media Cultures and the Occupy Movement," *Social Movement Studies* 11, nos. 3–4 (2012), 375–85.

32. Virginia Eubanks, *Automating Inequality: How High-Tech Tools Profile, Police, and Punish the Poor* (New York, NY: St. Martin's Press, 2018).

33. Safiya Noble, *Algorithms of Oppression* (New York, NY: New York University Press, 2018).

number of organizations, spaces, networks, and events that share a vision of design justice. Design organizations like And Also Too in Toronto, Intelligent Mischief in Brooklyn, and the worker-owned cooperative Research Action Design (RAD.cat), are putting design justice principles into practice in their daily work.

There is also a growing community that focuses on challenging the design of algorithmic bias, with a wave of recent feminist publications such as Virginia Eubanks's *Automating Inequality*[32] and Safiyah Noble's *Algorithms of Oppression.*[33] There are new organizations such as Data4BlackLives, the AI Now Institute, Data and Society, the Data Justice Lab, the Data Equity Lab, and the Algorithmic Justice League, and conferences such as Fairness, Accountability, and Transparency in Machine Learning.

Finally, the Design Justice Network is growing rapidly. This network, composed of designers who work with social movements and community-based organizations, as well as community organizers who use design as a tool to build power in their neighborhoods, authored the Design Justice Principles that opened this paper. The network has produced a series of 'zines, and coordinated a Design Justice track at the Allied Media Conference in 2017 and again in 2018. I urge readers to explore the work of the Design Justice Network, sign up to the Design Justice Principles, and develop additional work through the design justice lens.

Acknowledgments

Sasha Costanza-Chock's text was first published in the *Proceedings of the Design Research Society*, 2018, available at ssrn.com/abstract=3189696.

Bibliography

Arce, Erik, and Dennis A. Segura. "Stratification in the Labor Market." In *The Wiley Blackwell Encyclopedia of Race, Ethnicity, and Nationalism*, 2015. doi. org/10.1002/9781118663202.wberen226.

Ashcraft, Catherine, Elizabeth Eger, and Michelle Friend. *Girls in iT: The Facts*. Boulder, CO: National Center for Women & IT, 2012.

Bardzell, Shaowen. "Feminist HCI: Taking Stock and Outlining an Agenda for Design." In *Proceedings of the SIGCHI Conference on Human Factors in Computing Systems*, 1301–10. New York, NY: Association of Computing Machinery, 2010.

Charlton, James. *Nothing about Us without Us: Disability Oppression and Empowerment*. Berkeley, CA: University of California Press, 1998.

Collins, Patricia Hill. *Black Feminist Thought: Knowledge, Consciousness, and the Politics of Empowerment*. London: Routledge, 2002.

Costanza-Chock, Sasha. "Mic Check! Media Cultures and the Occupy Movement." *Social Movement Studies* 11, nos. 3–4 (2012), 375–85.
—, Chris Schweidler, and Transformative Media Organizing Project. "Toward Transformative Media Organizing: LGBTQ and Two-Spirit Media Work in the United States." *Media, Culture & Society* 39, no. 2 (2017), 159–84. doi. org/10.1177/0163443716674360.

Crenshaw, Kimberlé. "Demarginalizing the Intersection of Race and Sex: A Black Feminist Critique of Antidiscrimination Doctrine, Feminist Theory and Antiracist Politics." *The University of Chicago Legal Forum* no. 1, 1989, 139–67.
—. "Mapping the Margins: Intersectionality, Identity Politics, and Violence Against Women of Color." *Stanford Law Reviews* 43, no. 6 (1991), 1241–99.

Dalla Costa, Mariarosa, and Giovanna Franca Dalla Costa, eds. *Women, Development, and Labor of Reproduction: Struggles and Movements*. Trenton, NJ: Africa World Press, 1999.

Design Justice Network. designjustice.org.

Eubanks, Virginia. *Automating Inequality:How High-Tech Tools Profile, Police, and Punish the Poor*. New York City, NY: St. Martin's Press, 2018.

Evans, Will, and Sinduja Rangarajan. "Hidden Figures: How Silicon Valley Keeps Diversity Data Secret." *Reveal News*, October 19, 2017. www.revealnews.org/article/hidden-figures-how-silicon-valleykeeps-diversity-data-secret.

Flanagan, Mary, Daniel C. Howe, and Helen Nissenbaum. "Embodying Values in Technology: Theory and Practice." In *Information Technology and Moral Philosophy*, 322–53. Cambridge, MA: Cambridge University Press, 2008. doi.org/10.1017/CBO9780511498725.

Flores, Alfinio. "Examining Disparities in Mathematics Education: Achievement Gap or Opportunity Gap?" *The High School Journal* 91, no. 1 (2007), 29–42.

Friedman, Batya, ed. *Human Values and the Design of Computer Technology*. Cambridge, MA: Cambridge University Press, 1997.

Hamilton, Margaret, et al. "Gender Equity in Computing: International Faculty Perceptions and Current Practices." In *Proceedings of the 2016 ITiCSE Working Group Reports*, 81–102. New York, NY: ACM Publications, 2016.

Herring, Cedric. "Does Diversity Pay?: Race, Gender, and the Business Case for Diversity." *American Sociological Review* 74, no. 2 (2009), 208–24.

Irani, Lilly. "Hackathons and the Making of Entrepreneurial Citizenship." *Science, Technology, & Human Values* 40, no. 5 (2015), 799–824. doi.org/10.1177/0162243915578486.

Kochan, Thomas, et al. "The Effects of Diversity on Business Performance: Report of the Diversity Research Network." *Human Resource Management* 42, no. 1 (2003), 3–21.

Kushi, Sidita, and Ian P. McManus. "Gender, Crisis and the Welfare State: Female Labor Market Outcomes across OECD Countries." *Comparative European Politics* 16 (2018), 434–63.

Kirkham, Alli. "6 Alarming Ways Facebook's 'Real' Name Policy Puts Its Users at Risk." *Everyday Feminism*, September 29, 2015. everydayfeminism.com/2015/09/the-problem-with-real-names.

Muller, Michael J., and Sarah Kuhn. "Participatory Design." *Communications of the ACM* 36, no. 6 (1993), 24–28.

Munoz, Cecilia, Megan Smith, and D. J. Patil. "Big Data: A Report on Algorithmic Systems, Opportunity, and Civil Rights" Executive Office of the President. The White House. Washington, DC: Executive Office of the President, 2016. obamawhitehouse. archives.gov/sites/default/files/microsites/ostp/2016_0504_data_discrimination.pdf.

Noble, Safiya. *Algorithms of Oppression*. New York City, NY: New York University Press, 2018.

Orfield, Gary, et al. "'Brown' at 62: School Segregation by Race, Poverty and State." *Civil Rights Project/Proyecto Derechos Civiles*. UCLA, 2016. escholarship.org/uc/item/5ds6k0rd.

Papanek, Victor, and R. Buckminster Fuller. *Design for the Real World*. London: Thames and Hudson, 1972.

Penny, Laurie. "A Tale of Two Cities: How San Francisco's Tech Boom is Widening the Gap between Rich and Poor." *The New Statesman*, April 9, 2014. www.newstatesman.com/laurie-penny/2014/04/tale-two-cities-how-sanfranciscos-tech-boom-widening-gap-between-rich-and-poor.

Scholz, Trebor, and Nathan Schneider, eds. *Ours to Hack and to Own: The Rise of Platform Cooperativism, a New Vision for the Future of Work and a Fairer Internet*. New York, NY: OR books, 2016. www.jstor.org/stable/j.ctv62hfq7.

Schuler, Douglas, and Aki Namioka, eds. *Participatory Design: Principles and Practices*. Boca Raton: CRC Press, 1993.

Shetterly, Margot Lee. *Hidden Figures: The Untold Story of the African-American Women Who Helped Win the Space Race*. New York City, NY: W. Morrow, 2016.

Design Struggles

von Hippel, Eric. *Democratizing Innovation*. Cambridge, MA: MIT Press, 2005.

Weeden, Kim A., Youngjoo Cha, and Mauricio Bucca. "Long Work Hours, Part-Time Work, and Trends in the Gender Gap in Pay, the Motherhood Wage Penalty, and the Fatherhood Wage Premium." *RSF: The Russell Sage Foundation Journal of the Social Sciences* 2, no. 4 (2016), 71–102.

Willis, Anne-Marie. "Ontological Designing." *Design Philosophy Papers* 4, no. 2 (2006), 69–92.

Wilson, Franklin D. "Generational Changes in Racial Inequality in Occupational Attainment, 1950–2010: A Synthetic Cohort Analysis." *Du Bois Review: Social Science Research on Race* 14, no. 2 (2016), 387–425.

Sasha Costanza-Chock

THERE ARE WORDS AND WORLDS THAT ARE TRUTHFUL AND TRUE

Luiza Prado de O. Martins

1. Ana Luíza Guimarães, "Acidente derruba agrotóxico na marginal da rodovia na Baixada," broadcast August 24, 2019, on RJ2, globoplay.globo.com/v/7867648/.

2. Patrícia Figueiredo, "Moradores de SP coletam água preta de chuva em dia que a cidade ficou sob nuvem escura," G1, August 20, 2019, g1.globo.com/sp/sao-paulo/noticia/2019/08/20/moradores-de-sp-coletam-agua-preta-de-chuva-em-dia-que-a-cidade-ficou-sob-nuvem-escura.ghtml.

A Red Path, a Black Sky

On August 23, 2019, an accident took place on the Rodovia Presidente Dutra, one of Rio de Janeiro's most important federal highways. In a section that cuts through the suburban municipality of Nova Iguaçu, a cargo truck carrying pesticide was hit by another vehicle. Vats rolled out of the truck, spilling their contents all along the highway, a bright pinkish-red liquid, dragged along the pavement by the wheels of other cars for hundreds of meters. The highway was temporarily closed as the liquid, considered harmful to humans, was cleaned up. RJTV, the region's most popular midday news program, aired footage of workers in hazmat suits shoveling the dried remains of the substance into large white bags under the cheerful headline "Colorful Dutra."[1] The exact nature of the pesticide, as well as the name of the company or companies responsible for its manufacturing and transportation, went unmentioned. The ensuing traffic jams slowed the flow of vehicles from city center to periphery for kilometers.

  Four days earlier, around 3 p.m. on August 19, 2019, day abruptly turned into darkness in São Paulo. The skies above the metropolis, so often obscured by rainy clouds, acquired an unusual, black-brown hue; a sooty curtain falling prematurely over the city's bewildered inhabitants. Later that afternoon, the thick clouds finally released their cargo – a deep black rain, heavy with the unexpected scent of smoke.[2] The reason for this dark rain did not take much guessing: the fires devouring the Amazon rainforest along Brazil's northernmost states had been in the news for a while. This was just one repercussion, finally reaching the country's largest and wealthiest city, pushed by a cold wind. São Paulo's Tietê River – once a clean, living body of water – had long ago been reduced to a sludgy, foul-smelling mass; now it was the turn of the skies to fall.

Rainforests don't burn spontaneously; they must be intentionally set on fire. In July 2019, INPE (Brazil's National Institute for Space Research) reported an 88 percent increase in wildfires in the Amazon basin, compared to the same time frame in the previous year.[3] For centuries before this winter, forests had covered a great portion of the tropical areas of South America. The fires that preceded the black rain, the premature nightfall, and the spillage of pesticides had, in truth, been consuming everything in their path since European ships first arrived on the shores of the continent. These events were part of an old tragedy, a long-festering wound. To consume, to devour until nothing is left – these practices are interwoven throughout the history of coloniality into the present, from the foodstuffs taken from the Americas to be served to eager Europeans, to the voracious consumption of living black and brown bodies at the table of colonial economy, to the ravenous devouring of the Earth itself in the quest for endless economic growth. Avidity, in short, which leads inevitably to destruction; rapacity, which hinges on a vastly unequal distribution of the conditions necessary for well-being.

It is this hunger that underscores the rhetoric of exploitation of human and nonhuman beings at the root of the current climate crisis; a hunger that classifies not only forests, valleys, lakes, and seas, but also some people, as "resources." In his book *Ideias para adiar o fim do mundo* (Ideas to Postpone the End of the World), Indigenous writer and activist Ailton Krenak remarks that "[w]hen we remove the personhood from the river, the mountain, when we remove their senses, thinking that this is an exclusively human attribute, we allow these places to become residues of extractivist industrial activity."[4] He points out: "If there is an eagerness to consume nature, there is also one to consume subjectivities – our subjectivities."[5] While some continue to devour, consuming with ferocious greed, others are starved by scarcity.

3. Ana Carolina Moreno, "Desmatamento na Amazônia em junho é 88% maior do que no mesmo período de 2018," G1, July 3, 2019, g1.globo.com/natureza/noticia/2019/07/03/desmatamento-na-amazonia-em-junho-e-88percent-maior-do-que-no-mesmo-periodo-de-2018.ghtml.

4. Ailton Krenak, *Ideias para adiar o fim do mundo* (São Paulo: Companhia das Letras, 2019), 49. All quotes from this work, translation mine.

5. Krenak, 32.

6. Krenak, 22.

This is, of course, a produced scarcity, constructed through a mechanism that negates the personhood of some subjects, human and nonhuman, to classify them as exploitable resources and consume them indiscriminately in the name of Western and capitalist notions of development. As soon as the human bodies exploited within this cycle cease to work in its favor, perhaps due to disease, hunger, conflict, or death; as soon as the material repercussions of this process emerge (food shortages, water contamination, an increase in global temperature, natural disasters), scarcity is declared. There is now not enough food and water for all; there are not enough natural resources to sustain so many living, breathing human bodies. Krenak asks, pointedly: "Natural resources for whom? Sustainable development for what? What is there to sustain?"[6] The foundations of coloniality and capitalism have always hinged on this construction of scarcity: in order for wealth to exist, so too must poverty. In order for some to live, some must die. In order for some to be satisfied, others must be eaten. Although produced through a complex network of power relations, scarcity has become a defining, tangible circumstance in the lives of those on the margins of a world still scarred by colonial wounds; a world where the sky blackens and falls, and paths are painted toxic red. The imagined isn't imaginary.

There Is No Room

The narrative of scarcity needs a corresponding one – that of excess, directed at those whose bodies and lives are framed as exploitable resources in the quest for the accumulation of wealth through endless economic growth. The people for whom food, water, land, shelter, care, affection, and dignity will not be afforded. On July 11, 2017, BBC host Victoria Derbyshire interviewed philanthropist Melinda Gates and the United Kingdom Secretary of State for International Development at the time, Priti Patel, on her #VictoriaLIVE segment. The topic of discussion was birth control, particularly the initiatives led in the Global South by the Gates Foundation (cochaired by the philanthropist and her husband) and the UK government.

BONDS OF AFFECTION

Birth control, Gates and Patel stressed, is a pivotal issue for fighting poverty in the Global South, for it allows women in these regions to continue their education, contribute to the local economy, and better provide for smaller, planned families. The programs initiated by the Gates Foundation are necessary, Gates argued, in order to address the conditions brought about by a "population bulge" that has, in her words, caused the "biggest population of adolescents we've ever had in the history of the Earth" to be currently "coming through the developing world." If denied access to birth control, this population will be condemned to a "life of destitute poverty," she continued, whereas "if you can offer a girl contraceptives, she will stay in school." Patel additionally asserted that population growth in the "developing world" doesn't only have a negative impact on local economies, it also puts undue pressure on the United Kingdom's resources and, more importantly, leads to increases in the flow of migrants to the country.[7]

The rhetoric employed by Gates and Patel, which positions poverty and scarcity as a direct result of population growth, dates back centuries. In 1798, British scholar Thomas Malthus published *An Essay on the Principles of Population.* In it, he argues that while a nation's ability to produce food could increase arithmetically, its populace would grow exponentially, leading to a destructive cycle that would culminate in what is known as a Malthusian catastrophe. He writes:

> The power of population is so superior to the power of the earth to produce subsistence for man, that premature death must in some shape or other visit the human race. The vices of mankind are active and able ministers of depopulation. They are the precursors in the great army of destruction, and often finish the dreadful work themselves. But should they fail in this war of extermination, sickly seasons, epidemics, pestilence, and plague advance in terrific array, and sweep off their thousands and tens of thousands. Should success be still incomplete, gigantic inevitable famine stalks in the rear, and with one mighty blow levels the population with the food of the world.[8]

7. Victoria Derbyshire, BBC News, 9–11 a.m., July 11, 2017, archive.org/details/ BBCNEWS_20170711_ 080000_Victoria_Derbyshire.

8. Thomas Robert Malthus, *An Essay on the Principle of Population* (CreateSpace Independent Publishing Platform, 2014 [1798]), 50.

Design Struggles

9. Eric B. Ross, *The Malthus Factor: Poverty, Politics and Population in Capitalist Development* (New York, NY: Zed Books, 1998), 1.

10. Kalpana Wilson, *Race, Racism and Development: Interrogating History, Discourse and Practice* (New York, NY: Zed Books, 2012).

11. Paul R. Ehrlich, *The Population Bomb* (New York, NY: Ballantine Books, 1969).

12. Dorothy Roberts, *Killing the Black Body: Race, Reproduction, and the Meaning of Liberty* (New York, NY: Vintage Books, 1998).

13. Wilson, *Race, Racism and Development*; Laura Briggs, *Reproducing Empire: Race, Sex, Science, and U.S. Imperialism in Puerto Rico* (Berkeley, CA: University of California Press, 2002).

14. Roberts, *Killing the Black Body*.

15. Angela Y. Davis, *Women, Race, & Class* (New York, NY: Vintage, 1983).

Though not the first to propose these ideas, Malthus remains their most famous advocate. Anthropologist Eric Ross notes that Malthusian theories have been fundamental "to provide an enduring argument for the prevention of social and economic change and to obscure, in both academic and popular thinking, the real roots of poverty, inequality and environmental deterioration."[9] Through the Malthusian lens, scarcity is not an inevitable – and desired – outcome of capitalist systems, but rather a result of the actions and choices of the poor.[10] Since Malthus's initial formulation, his arguments have been periodically revisited and recycled by academics and activists alike, from Paul Ehrlich (one of the first biologists to blame environmental collapse on overpopulation[11]) to Margaret Sanger, whose crusade for the right to birth control in the early twentieth century was animated by the perception that many of the problems that afflicted poor women were results of unregulated fertility.[12]

Scholars Kalpana Wilson and Laura Briggs stress, however, that population control policies implemented in the Global South, which are underscored by neo-Malthusian beliefs and advanced with the financial and political incentives of Northern nations, need to be understood as continuations of the colonial/imperial project, in that they pathologize the sex and reproduction of colonial subjects for the benefit of colonizers.[13] Interventions on the fertility and sexuality of colonial subjects are thus framed as necessary and beneficial. In the rhetoric of humanitarian aid presented by Patel and Gates, they are described as strategies for the empowerment of women and girls, devised to effectively introduce this demographic into the (low-paid) workforce of the Global South. Although both interviewees specifically used the designation "developing countries" to politically and geographically position the subjects of the policies and programs they discuss, this designation obfuscates the complexity and diversity of the colonial subjects whose sexualities and fertilities are matters of such scrutiny. As a result, this designation also obscures the ways in which population control policies have been fundamental for the preservation of colonial racial hierarchies in the United States, as has been thoroughly documented and discussed by scholars such as Dorothy Roberts,[14] Angela Davis,[15]

Elena Gutiérrez,[16] and Anne Hendrixson.[17] Patel's argument, in particular, aligns itself with the discourse associating population growth in the Global South with threats to national identity and security, identified by Hendrixson as a fundamental rationale behind US – and, I would expand, Western – military interventionism in the Middle East, and the surveillance of Muslims and Arabs circulating within US and European borders.

The works of Wilson and Briggs focus primarily on how organizations and institutions based in the US or Europe promote these policies in the Global South; a similar racist logic, however, also governs healthcare initiatives deployed by many institutions and organizations within the Global South, directed at locally marginalized communities. The systematic, nonconsensual, mass sterilization of Indigenous peoples in Peru during the regime of dictator Alberto Fujimori in the 1990s is one such instance.[18] In Brazil, anthropologist Emilia Sanabria documented the widespread and coercive administration of the birth-control shot Depo-Provera to low-income women who resort to government-funded family planning services in the city of Salvador.[19] Current Brazilian President Jair Bolsonaro has long publicly supported many of Fujimori's ideas, defending strict population control policies aimed at the country's poorest as a way to "control criminality and poverty."[20] Bolsonaro's rhetoric is far from unique: historically, population control policies have been presented in Brazil as carrying positive economic implications for the general population,[21] a strategy to ward off the impending threat of scarcity.

Further complicating this scenario, as conversations on the climate crisis and its current and future impacts gain more prominence, concerns over possible connections between overpopulation, the increase of global temperatures, and fears of widespread scarcity have been placed once again in the spotlight – to the point that acts of white supremacist violence have been animated by the fear of a looming climactic disaster triggered by the presence of brown and Black people within the borders of Western nations.[22] The idea of bodies in excessive abundance is inseparable from the colonial structures that have long sought to classify humans into hierarchical categories.

16. Elena R. Gutiérrez, *Fertile Matters: The Politics of Mexican-Origin Women's Reproduction* (Austin, TX: University of Texas Press, 2008).

17. Anne Hendrixson, "Angry Young Men, Veiled Young Women: Constructing a New Population Threat," *The Corner House*, Briefing 34, December 2, 2004, www.thecornerhouse. org.uk/resource/angry-young-men-veiled-young-women.

18. Mathilde Damoisel, dir., *A Woman's Womb*, 2010, www.cultureunplugged.com/play/4623/A-Woman-s-Womb.

19. Emilia Sanabria, *Plastic Bodies: Sex Hormones and Menstrual Suppression in Brazil* (Durham, NC: Duke University Press, 2016).

20. Ranier Bragon, "Bolsonaro defendeu esterilização de pobres para combater miséria e crime," *Folha de S.Paulo*, June 11, 2018, www1.folha.uol.com.br/poder/2018/06/bolsonaro-defendeu-esterilizacao-de-pobres-para-combater-miseria-e-crime.shtml.

21. Sanabria, *Plastic Bodies*; Lilia Moritz Schwarcz, "Espetáculo da miscigenação," *Estudos Avançados* 8, no. 20 (April 1994), 137–52.

22. Natasha Lennard, "The El Paso Shooter Embraced Eco-Fascism: We Can't Let the Far Right Co-Opt the Environmental Struggle," *The Intercept*, August 5, 2019, theintercept.com/2019/08/05/el-paso-shooting-eco-fascism-migration/.

23. Krenak, *Ideias para adiar o fim do mundo*, 21.

24. Adele Clarke and Donna J. Haraway, eds., *Making Kin Not Population: Reconceiving Generations* (Chicago, IL: Prickly Paradigm Press, 2018), 71–72.

25. Clarke and Haraway, 88.

26. Clarke and Haraway, 87.

27. Clarke and Haraway, 75.

Rhetoric becomes fear becomes policy becomes violence becomes rhetoric; a process woven into the everyday lives of those who, although they "hold on to this Earth, are those who are forgotten along the borders of the planet, the margins of rivers, the shores of oceans, in Africa, in Asia, or in Latin America."[23] Though critical of the "population bomb" rhetoric, in her contribution to the book *Making Kin Not Population*, Donna Haraway circles around the discourse of scarcity related to the climate crisis, arguing that:

> Food production is a major contributor to climate change and the extinction crisis, with, as usual, those humans and nonhumans benefitting most suffering the least dire impacts. The super-peopling of the earth with both humans and industrial and pathogenic nonhumans is a worlding practice premised on the commitment to endless growth and vastly unequal well-being.[24]

Although in this passage Haraway does leave room for a critique that focuses on the systems and networks that construct scarcity within capitalism, she later recants this line, writing that "blaming Capitalism, Imperialism, Neoliberalism, Modernization, or some other 'not us' for ongoing destruction webbed with human numbers will not work."[25] Additionally, she maintains that "anti-racist feminist avoidance of thinking and acting in public about the pressing urgencies of human and nonhuman global populations is akin to the denial of anthropogenic climate change by some deeply believing US Christians,"[26] and goes so far as to "only half-jokingly call for a sliding scale approach to global reduction of human numbers."[27] Under this system, she suggests, those willing to birth a human baby would need to collect tokens from other prospective parents; the number of necessary tokens would vary according to the parents' cultural, economic, racial, and ethnic background. Haraway's argument fails to consider that not all humans relate to the Earth in the same way; while she does admit that those living in so-called developed Western societies might impact the planet differently from people living in other societal organizations, this admission does not make its way into the core logic of her argument. Let us return again to Krenak, who remarks:

> If we imprinted upon the planet Earth a mark so heavy that it characterizes an era, which may remain even after we are no longer here, because we are exhausting the sources of life that allow us to prosper and feel that we are home […] it is because we are again in front of a dilemma I have already alluded to: we exclude from life, locally, the forms of organization that are not integrated to the world of commodities, risking all other forms of living – at least the ones we thought of as possible, where there was co-responsibility to the places we live and the respect for the life of beings, and not only this abstraction we allowed ourselves to construct as one humanity, which excludes all others and other beings.[28]

While Haraway insists this system would not be imposed but rather willingly embraced, her speculative proposal relies on the assumption of good will from all involved. Five hundred years of history have, however, abundantly shown this is not the case. As long as some people are perceived as not fully human, any such system is bound to facilitate violence being inflicted upon already marginalized populations – those living at the blunt end of what philosopher María Lugones calls the colonial/modern gender system. This system, Lugones clarifies, is fundamental to the establishment and continuation of the colonial project, and includes what she calls a "light" and a "dark" side which operate in distinct ways, and act upon distinct bodies. Hegemonic (that is, European) constructions of gender and sex/sexuality are characteristic of the "light" side of the colonial/modern gender system, which orders "the lives of white bourgeois men and women."[29] Concurrently, this light side constructs the meaning (epistemological and ontological) of the modern categories of "men" and "women."[30]

   The "dark" side to the colonial/modern gender system governs the lives of those who exist outside of white bourgeois heteropatriarchy. Both sides of this gender system are violent, yet they manifest this inherent violence

28. Krenak, *Ideias para adiar o fim do mundo*, 46–47.

29. María Lugones, "Heterosexualism and the Colonial/Modern Gender System," *Hypatia* 22, no. 1 (2007), 206.

30. Lugones.

31. Davis, *Women, Race, & Class*, 209.

32. Lugones, "Heterosexualism," 202.

33. Krenak, *Ideias para adiar o fim do mundo*.

34. microchipsbiotech.com/; Rob Matheson, "Major Step for Implantable Drug-Delivery Device," *MIT News*, June 29, 2015, news.mit.edu/2015/implantable-drug-delivery-microchip-device-0629.

35. Dominic Basulto, "This Amazing Remote-Controlled Contraceptive Microchip You Implant under Your Skin Is the Future of Medicine," *Washington Post*, July 17, 2014, www.washingtonpost.com/news/innovations/wp/2014/07/17/this-amazing-remote-controlled-contraceptive-microchip-you-implant-under-your-skin-is-the-future-of-medicine/?utm_term=.7e8bcf013438.

in different ways. Whereas white women are encumbered with perpetuating the white race – as Angela Davis has also highlighted[31] – women of color are "understood as animals in the deep sense of 'without gender,' sexually marked as female, but without the characteristics of femininity."[32] In the rhetoric of harm reduction related to the climate crisis, similar arguments are translated into calls for the surveillance of fertility – many similar to Haraway's – framed as necessary and beneficial for the entire world's population. Concurrently, the uncomfortable fact of the Global North's perpetual hunger for disposable goods, exploitable bodies, and natural resources – all key factors in the ongoing crisis – often remains un- or under-examined. Instead the blame is shifted to those existing under the duress inflicted through centuries of colonial domination, which as Krenak stresses, is in itself an ongoing project of world-ending.[33] Ultimately, these concerns reveal the perversity of calls for care – reproductive care, in particular – that do not adequately address underlying capitalist-colonial articulations. This in itself is a violence, one more way of consuming an "other."

Predictably, the narrative of climate crisis linked to uncontrolled reproduction is materialized in technologies currently being developed to provide so-called solutions to the perceived problem of overpopulation. A notable example is that of the startup Microchips Biotech, backed by the Gates Foundation and partnered with Israeli company Teva Pharmaceutical, whose flagship product, announced in 2014, is a remote-controlled smart birth-control implant that had been planned for commercial release in 2018.[34] The microchip can be turned on and off with a proprietary app controlled by a physician; it is designed to work for up to sixteen years – so for a large part of one's fertile life – as opposed to the three years of existing contraceptive implants. Additionally, the implant could collect a number of data points about patients, ostensibly to provide tailored healthcare solutions. The chip, Bill Gates clarified in 2014, was being conceived with the developing world in mind, more so than Western audiences, the rationale being that in these regions, it would mean a "form of reproductive justice," rather than merely a "lifestyle choice,"[35] and could be distributed as part of the numerous birth-control programs initiated by the foundation in the Global South. As of 2019, no new information has been publicly released about the project.

36. Maria Sibylla Merian, *Metamorphosis Insectorum Surinamensium* (Tielt: Lannoo Publishers, 2016), 45.

The mass distribution of devices like the Microchips implant could have serious implications for the digitalized biometric surveillance of those living on the "dark side" of the colonial/modern gender system. These bodies have long been hypervisible, targets of surveillance by public and private actors. In order to understand the wide-ranging implications of this surveillance, however, it is fundamental to approach "reproduction" as a broader set of life-making practices and articulations, rather than as a strictly biological process. Returning to the question of scarcity help reframes the oft-repeated narrative of "choice" pushed by many white Western feminists in relation to reproduction. Scarcity – of food, housing, healthcare, education, adequate climatic conditions – is precisely the argument that animates much of the supposed necessity for contraceptive technologies such as the one developed by Microchips Biotech in the Global South and so insistently pushed by the likes of Gates and Patel. It follows that in order to avoid scarcity, these subjects then must be monitored, their fertility controlled "for their own good," considered incapable of making such decisions on their own. So goes the perverse narrative of "care" tied to scarcity: the vulnerable must accept and be grateful for any apparent help provided by the same powerful actors who profit from that vulnerability in the first place.

It is also fundamental to consider that the lived experience of constructed scarcity has profound effects on the paths and choices one feels compelled to follow. In eighteenth-century Surinam, naturalist Maria Sibylla Merian documented the use of an infusion of peacock flower by enslaved Indigenous and African peoples as a way to provoke abortions. This, Merian stressed, was a reaction to the conditions of extreme violence to which these people were subjected; they did so, she wrote, "so that their children will not become slaves like they are."[36] Currently, although the threat of climate disasters looms over the entire planet, there is still a sharp distinction between those most affected, and those who command the resources to survive the oncoming catastrophe. The

Design Struggles

37. Krenak, *Ideias para adiar o fim do mundo*, 22–23.

38. Krenak, 21.

39. Krenak, 26.

40. Krenak, 28.

dominant narrative of the climate crisis is one of suffering delegated to someone else, somewhere else by an economic system that hinges on the production of scarcity for some in order to offer wealth for others. It is a narrative that negates the personhood of beings: human and nonhuman, living and not yet or no longer embodied – a lingering effect of the colonial hierarchies that have long been used to justify the expropriation of land, exploitation of bodies, and extraction of so-called resources. It is a narrative that feeds the colonial hunger for homogenization and globalization, which seeks to "suppress diversity, deny the plurality of forms of life, existence, and habits," offering "the same menu, the same costumes and, if possible, the same language to all."[37] And so those who "hold on to this Earth" are pushed and shoved into a monocultural, universalizing narrative, while simultaneously remaining "forgotten along the borders of the planet, the margins of rivers, the shores of oceans,"[38] navigating the same perverse plot that produced and produces this marginalization. When dark skies loom above, however, Krenak reminds us: "There are so many small constellations of people scattered all over the world who dance, sing, make rain."[39] World-endings have happened so many times before, marking the margins of the world like scars, but "when you feel the sky is getting too low, all you have to do is to push it back and breathe."[40]

An Abundance of Small Gestures

How is it possible, then, to create the conditions for life within a political system designed to produce death? How to counteract a narrative of scarcity for which the only resolution presented by the current system is the total consumption of the Earth, and with it all of the persons – human and nonhuman, living and not yet or no longer embodied – who exist in relation to it? How to sustain radical, decolonizing practices of care and affect that directly challenge the infrastructures that monitor and restrict the ability to create futures and sustain worlds that are multiple, plural, heterogeneous?

In 2019, I undertook a joint residency between transmediale and the Universität der Künste Berlin to work on a project titled "The Councils of the Pluriversal: Affective Temporalities of Reproduction and Climate Change." In it, I intended to convene the Councils – a series of meetings with activists, artists, elders, and thinkers hailing from marginalized groups in Northern nations and the Global South. In these events I would propose discussions pertaining to the entanglements between the climate crisis, reproduction, ancestral and future histories, land and belonging, and radical, decolonizing forms of care. A guiding principle to these events would be the notion of "un mundo donde quepan muchos mundos" – that is, a world in which many worlds fit – a conception first advanced by the Zapatista liberation movement in Mexico:

> Many words are walked in the world. Many worlds are made. Many worlds make us. There are words and worlds that are lies and injustices. There are words and worlds that are truthful and true. We make truthful worlds. We are made by truthful words. In the world of the powerful there is space only for the big and their servants. In the world we want there is space for all. The world we want is a world where many worlds fit. The nation we build is one that may fit all the peoples and their languages, that may be walked by all gaits, that may be laughed in, that may be awoken.[41]

This conception rejects universalizing impulses toward consensus, favoring instead temporal, spatial, and infrastructural multiplicities that nurture the emergence of epistemological and ontological complexity. "The Councils of the Pluriversal" were conceived as dialogic and idiosyncratic events, not meant to provide exhaustive, unifying, or definitive summaries of issues of care, temporalities, reproduction, and climate change, but rather to provide possible points of entry to think and act through these issues.

Throughout the research process, I had the honor and privilege to strengthen and expand affective bonds of care and intimacy with a number of people operating within the vastly distinct contexts of Rio de Janeiro and Boa Vista, Brazil, and Berlin, Germany. I extend my deepest gratitude to Dagmar Schultz and Ika Hügel-Marshall in Berlin; to

41. Comité Clandestino Revolucionario Indígena-Comandancia General del Ejército Zapatista de Liberación Nacional, "Cuarta Declarión de la Selva Lacandona," *Enlace Zapatista*, enlacezapatista.ezln.org.mx/1996/01/01/cuarta-declaracion-de-la-selva-lacandona/. Translation mine.

Design Struggles

Vó Bernaldina, Jaider Esbell, Paula Berbert, Raquel Blaque, Amazoner Arawak, Parmênio Citó, and Caio Clímaco in Boa Vista; as well as to the hundreds of activists I encountered in the streets of Rio, protesting while caring for one another, and keeping each other safe. These bonds were not all started as part of this project; most were existing relationships that had emerged through shared interests in the struggle for decolonization, as well as for reproductive and climate justice. Some of these bonds extended, too, to nonhuman beings – the *lavrado* vegetation, the rivers and *igarapés* of the state of Roraima, where Boa Vista is located[42] – as well as to human beings no longer embodied – in particular, to Audre Lorde and May Ayim, whose truth in words and worlds is capable of transcending life itself.

Most importantly, all of these persons were already, through their practices – as activists, artists, curators, singers, cooks, storytellers, curators, cultural workers, writers, poets, filmmakers, educators, and care workers, among others – conducting their own versions of what I had come to call "The Councils of the Pluriversal." Amongst all of the experiences I had while developing this research, this was perhaps the most significant and humbling realization: art, particularly politically oriented art, often risks gravitating toward grand, sensational gestures. These become performances that benefit those who hold power, including artists themselves, far more than those actually affected by the issues at hand.

There was no need for me to name the Councils as such; they already existed in alternate forms, practiced by people whose sincerity, commitment, and deep understanding of their communities and peers allow them to articulate spaces where ever-evolving forms of caring for one another can emerge across an extended period of time. This type of maintenance work is made of smaller gestures with long-term repercussions, gestures that trouble the narrative of scarcity advanced by capitalism, and point toward other possibilities, other realities, other worlds where abundance – of time, generosity, affection, patience – is possible. This work is Makuxi elder Vó Bernaldina preparing *damurida*, an ancestral fish stew made with local ingredients, cooked in a pot made with clay borrowed from the land, and eaten with cassava flour, for those who arrive to visit artist Jaider Esbell's gallery in Boa Vista. It is artist and cook Raquel Blaque repurposing the leftovers with foraged local herbs and vegetables to feed a group of school students who wanted a space where they could engage with Indigenous art, and discuss the ongoing fires that consumed the forest south of Boa Vista. It is artist and anthropologist Amazoner Arawak sharing stories on Wapixana cosmologies, and the exploitation of Indigenous material cultures by European cultural institutions over a bottle of *caxiri*.[43] It is Jaider's generosity in opening up his life, his gallery, his home to those who arrive in Boa Vista with the intent to live and exchange and learn. It is a group of young students holding a large placard protesting the burning of the Amazon in Rio de Janeiro and being fed by their peers, so that they wouldn't need to drop the sign. It is Dagmar Schultz and Ika Hügel-Marshall, lifelong friends of Audre Lorde, cooking a meal in their home to introduce young feminist, antiracist, and environmental activists to one another – in the same way Lorde did, too. It is Vó Bernaldina singing a Makuxi song celebrating the recognition of the Raposa Serra do Sol territory as Indigenous land.

Developing bonds of affection is a long-term process, as remarked by Ailton Krenak to art worker and cultural producer Paula Berbert and relayed to me in conversation. It is only through nurturing sincere, solid relationships that the conditions for sustaining life can emerge; that truly pluriversal modes of engaging with each other and with the world can come into being. Counteracting the narrative of scarcity demands abundance. In the end, instead of convening councils as I had imagined, the main avenue of work became an exploration of these different forms of relating and practicing care with other bodies, human and nonhuman; the beginning of a long-term engagement, whose first ramifications will be presented at transmediale 2020. After all, as Krenak points out:

> Why does the feeling of falling cause us such discomfort? We haven't done anything lately but fall. Fall, fall, fall. So why are we worried about the process of falling? Let us use all of our critical and creative capacity to build colorful parachutes.

43. A fermented cassava-based drink, typical of the Amazon basin.

Design Struggles

44. Krenak, *Ideias para adiar o fim do mundo*, 30.

Let us think of space not as a confined place, but as a cosmos where we can fall with colorful parachutes.[44]

Decolonization is not an individual choice; it demands collective, sustained, committed work. Let us feed these visions for a future of blue skies and open paths. Let us nourish each other with responsibility, care, affection, and patience.

Acknowledgments

Luiza Prado's text was originally published as part of the Transmediale 2020 booklet *The Eternal Network: The Ends and Becoming of Netwerk Culture*, ed. Kristoffer Gansing and Inga Luchs, 45–56 (Amsterdam: Institute of Network Cultures; Berlin: transmediale e.V., 2020).

LOVE
A Blues Epistemology from the Undercommons

Mia Charlene White

Greetings from my beloved New York City and a slightly
jetlagged mind. I should begin by telling you all a little bit
about myself: I am a relatively new assistant professor at
the New School. I'm excited to be a faculty member there
because of its history of being populated by rebellious
academics who needed sanctuary after the war, folks
who had a transformative vision for a different kind of
knowledge-making space. Today, the New School continues
to try to live up to those early aspirations. The New School
is a great place for somebody who is trying to engage in
epistemic disobedience, like me, and for somebody who has
studied in several disciplines and is trying to figure out how
to bring them together – even if it means that it's going to
be very hard to make a tenure case. So what that looks like
is that I have brought autoethnographic method, from my
anthropological mindset, to teach a newly developed course
called Black Geographies – itself a radical intervention in
the discipline of geography, which was a space I turned to
as I searched for a different kind of epistemological framing
from the one I was inculcated with during my doctoral
studies in urban planning. I have to tell you that I rarely
do things perfectly, not even close, but what feels really
thrilling and really excellent is that my Black Geographies
course is one of very few majority-Black and Brown student
spaces at my predominantly white university. It's really like
a prayer. It's not something I knew I was building toward
while a doctoral student at MIT for sure, but I think it must
be the result of being blessed with many Black and Brown
educators who saw something in me.

I'm also a native New Yorker, born and raised. I spent some time in the projects growing up, in one of the biggest projects in the United States, called Queensbridge. It's a beautiful, contradictory place – not really the hellhole that people like to describe it as. I'm standing here, so I'm evidence that it must not be, right? I'm the daughter of an American GI, a Black veteran of the Korean and Vietnam Wars, and a Korean immigrant, a farmworker from South Korea. And you know what? I'm also the daughter of my grandma Belle Walker, the southern Black woman who raised me in my early years before parental divorce took me and mom to Queensbridge… Her hands, her beautiful brown hands gave me the first touch I remember, her skin the first smell I remember, her serious countenance … the first face I remember.

As you can see, I am trying to model my auto-ethnographic teaching, so you can understand how I situate myself spatially and geographically, as the first sort of design intervention. So to continue, my mom and I, we were street vendors when I was growing up. We sold socks and underwear – 3 for 5 dollars, 6 for 5 dollars, 2 for 10 dollars. We sold in the Lower East Side of Manhattan and also in Queens, New York, where we lived. We eventually graduated to an indoor flea-market aptly named "The Colosseum." As a little girl, with my mom, near Tompkins Square Park – if anybody knows Manhattan, you can try to picture me, my short self with my little afro – I met people that I didn't know were famous or would become famous. One of them was Jean-Michel Basquiat, who very generously allowed me to call him "June Basket," perhaps because I could not pronounce his name – I guess I don't really remember anymore. Every Saturday, religiously (at least in my memory's eye), Basquiat would come to buy that clear plastic bag of 6-for-5-dollars white tube socks. My mother was confused by this and would always mutter later that he must not ever launder his socks. For me – whatever the reason, I didn't care, perhaps because if I squinted he looked like my handsome daddy and he seemed different. Oh – and he didn't like my mom, my grouchy chain-smoking mom who sat apart in a folding lawn chair worrying about our future. June Basket preferred to buy the tube socks from me and he would wait even if I was helping

Design Struggles

someone else. He used to tell me things like "Mia, you are beautiful" and "Mia, don't forget you are Black. You are mixed, like me, but you are Black." Now, I have to tell you that I was many things, but I was not beautiful. I was kind of malnourished, and I was sort of a little wild-looking because my immigrant-Korean mom didn't know what to do with my hair, and I was basically a bit strange – but I would say, "Thank you, June Basket."

It wasn't till several years later that I realized his name was not in fact June Basket. At the Colosseum, where we migrated to, I saw a picture of him in a Black newspaper wearing what in my mind of course were our white tube socks. (Basquiat was often depicted wearing white socks.) It's hilarious to me now because of course it's doubtful he was wearing our socks at that time. But seeing his image reconnected my body to his, my moment in Queens to our shared moment in Tomkins Square Park, my Blackness to his – my feelings of yearning and grief and searching to this fleeting and meaningful encounter. By my autoethnographic sharing of this, I want to give you a sense of how I understand space as an embodied experience. I adapt and I dream with these imaginations. I don't really know June Basket whatsoever except for these snippets, but I insist on this kind of radical dreaming where I invent a friendship between myself and June Basket, because I think that's what we need very much. That's the foundation of how I think about love and a blues epistemology.

Yes, I totally did just say the word love, as per the title of this talk. In this conceptualization I'm working through, love is not a romantic concept between two people, straight or otherwise. It's really about radical, revolutionary friendship invested in space, granted in space. I think the best we can do for ourselves and each other is to figure out how to enable this kind of transformative, radical, spatial love – the kind you feel in your body and in your dreams and in your motivations – like with me right now. I hope somewhere June Basket can feel my love. I think it is what we are called to do really … because we are thirsty and also anemic in our love practices – and especially in the context of design. We have to question whether design can model vulnerability and whether it can actually help us grow in our love practices.

This is the basis of how I am thinking right now: Can design be vulnerable? Can design help us in the development of love practices that move us away from the individuation of a nuclear or binary relationship, where we only think about ourselves or our families? I have two children, how is it that I can think beyond myself and my career and what I need individually and what my two children need? But also, what about all the dreamers who might imagine a relationship with me, who might find some connection to me? How can I invest myself in that, even when I may never meet these people? Is it possible?

These are the kinds of questions that I wrestle with. Because just like Angela Davis said to us many years ago, even though prison abolition is impossible, it is still possible.[1] We still have to dream it. We still have to wrestle with the idea and figure out steps toward that dream. So, again, my idea of love is really vested in abolition. The idea that we have to dream the place that we are trying to get to, and in the process of getting to it we are making these love practices that in fact define a blues epistemology.

My first job out of MIT (I studied housing and environment in the Urban Studies and Planning Department) was as assistant professor at the Black Studies Department at the University of California, Santa Barbara. Against the advice of very smart people, I left MIT as "ABD," which means "all but dissertation," to take this great job while I finished up my writing, which of course took way longer than I thought. But it was worth it because the Santa Barbara position commemorated the life of Clyde Woods, a Black radical geographer who had recently died, and who was, like me, trained in urban planning. I'd be teaching his courses and sitting in his office and working in his tradition – and that blew my mind. Clyde Woods coined and developed the conceptual framework of "blues epistemology" in his work called *Development Arrested: The Blues and Plantation Power in the Mississippi Delta*.[2] His thinking about epistemology is the way I now teach it. And what does it mean? Epistemology is simply how you make sense of the world. This is how I answer my students who say to me "I don't really care about theory. Why do you always talk about theory?" And I say, "Well, you are theorizing all the time. You just theorized to me why theory sucks, right?

1. Angela Y. Davis, *Are Prisons Obsolete?* (New York, NY: Seven Stories Press, 2003).

2. Clyde Woods, *Development Arrested: The Blues and Plantation Power in the Mississippi Delta* (London: Verso, 1998).

All it is, is you are making meaning out of the world around you." That's what theorizing is. And epistemology is *how* you go about that process – and the architecture of your knowledge, that has everything to do with how you theorize. Are you going about that process as a lucid thinker, as I say to my students, or are you going about that process in a sort of cyborg, automatic way, based on the famous people that you have been taught to respect in your various classes? This matters so much because your epistemological architecture will become actualized in the physical world, in all your design labors that then sort of orient how we experience life together.

Again, I'm speaking from the perspective of an autoethnographic human, but also as an educator. In my classes, I talk about two kinds of researchers, I try to model these two tensions. I say to my students: "There are two ways to be a researcher. Just like there are two ways to dream, right?" On the one hand, there is the lucid dream. You are having a nightmare, you are frightened, but you are aware that you are dreaming. Even though you are very scared, you know that it is a dream and that you can wake yourself up. You are lucid. The other kind of dream is the one where you are falling into a deep hole, maybe like the sunken place, for those of you who have seen the movie *Get Out*. But you don't *know* that you are in the sunken place. It's the totality of your experience. You cannot see or feel or imagine otherwise. You don't know that you are dreaming, so you feel completely and unalterably stuck. There is no future in this framework and, thus, abolition is an impossibility.

I want us to be lucid thinkers and lucid researchers, and I want my students to be lucid in their understanding of themselves and the world. The question "Can design be vulnerable?" requires us to be lucid. It actually requires you to be autoethnographic and ask "Who am I? Why am I asking this question this space or intervention?" It is not an academic question

– it is a soul question. Why do we need design to be vulnerable? Where is the purpose of that level of vulnerability? This is a geographic question. Geography is really near and dear to my heart, and therefore to my mind. *Geographers ask why things happen where they happen.* Geographers are not content to simply catalog *that* something happened, and they don't want to simply adore the fact that we can make things happen. We proceed in our understanding of *why* something happened by thinking about *where – about the space of that happening, and how that matters.* We think space matters and we theorize space in order to make sense of things.

I have been very, very deeply engaged in Black study all my life. I proceed from the working theory that the story of Black people in America is an excellent launchpad for any larger investigation into the limits of ideas like democracy, freedom, environment, and especially love. My life's training and intellectual mentors have helped me reframe what I have understood to be my pessimism. I've now come to understand that my afro-pessimism can generate a new world. A new world that is here already, as many feminists have talked about. I'm not waiting for the revolution to come; I'm challenging myself to see that the revolution has already arrived. In fact, the gathering of us together creates a space that manifests a kind of revolution: the idea of the daily revolution. This is so important because we make freedom out of what we have. This is neither hippy-dippy talk nor new age love stuff, this is all very, very real. It comes from spatial theory and fancy-talk philosophers, but it also comes from a sort of autoethnographic awareness, the lucid self.

I am American, so I try to start with my lucid experience of being American. Miles Davis talked of the blues as being about playing what's not there.[3] The space between the noise, which is most fraught. And James Baldwin, of course, beloved to so many of us, said, "If I am a part of the American house, and I am, it is because my ancestors paid – *striving to make it my home* – so unimaginable a price: and I have seen some of the effects of that passion everywhere I have been, all over this world. The music is everywhere, resounds, no sounds: and tells me that now is the moment, for me, to return to the eye of the hurricane."[4] He was referring to when he left France to return to the United States and to pick back up his allegiance and collaboration with US civil rights leaders, despite his own feelings of animosity and marginalization during that time. Obviously, as a queer Black American man, his was a complicated

3. Robert G. O'Meally, "'Pressing on Life Until It Gave Back Something in Kinship': An Introductory Essay," in *The Romare Bearden Reader*, ed. Robert G. O'Meally (Durham, NC: Duke University Press, 2019), 7: "Miles Davis said, 'It's not the notes you play, it's the notes you don't play... Play what's not there.'"

4. James Baldwin, "Every Good-bye Ain't Gone," in *The Price of the Ticket: Collected Nonfiction, 1948–1985* (New York, NY: St. Martin's Press, 1985), 647.

Design Struggles

experience. Miles Davis and James Baldwin left us some real clues about lucid dreaming, and we are grateful.

And so these questions we ask: What are we doing here, why do we engage in this work, and what does the blues have to do with it? Well, the United States is blues country, and my beloved city, NYC, is a blues city. Both are something of an imaginary and also something of a nightmare. We've created this myth of progress and we've built big buildings and railroads and big cities in the name of this idea of progress, without really lucidly examining what this idea means. Not just us as historians or armchair historians, but how does it matter, the way that we think about the problem?

To me, this image of American progress from 1873 perfectly illustrates part of our conceptualization of the problem. It is very obvious to us that there are some strong implications around white supremacy and Native genocide and the stealing of Native land. What's not visible in this picture is slavery and forced and exploited labor, including patriarchy. But what I like about this image – and I use it in my Black Geographies course – is that it is very spatial, and it is very much vested in this idea of dreams. Maybe it is the wrong hope and the wrong dream, but we can recognize that we are constantly evoking these ideas, as human beings.

John Gast, *American Progress*, 1872, Auntry Museum of the American West, Los Angeles.

Dreams have always been our design inspirations.

What I'm laying out here is how I understand the blues as a design framework, as our most lucid dreaming. The blues of course is a Black American music tradition that is based on making space. How does the blues make space? By playing these bent notes. A bent note is a musical note that is varied in pitch. The bent note is very important for us as lucid researchers and lucid educators and lucid designers. We use the bent note, the reality to create space, the blues. And in the process of using the bent note toward the blues, we can create deeper love practices – maybe. The bent note is all around us, but sometimes we don't recognize it, or we disavow it. We bury it or we marginalize it, because we don't know what to do with it. We think that it's just too heavy and too much and it produces too much guilt. So, what do we do with it? We recognize it, we feel bad, but we don't really incorporate it into our lucid everyday living, because we simply don't know what to do. Even as super-overeducated people we don't know what to do. But artists have really helped us understand that you don't necessarily need to know exactly what to do in order to wrestle with the problem, with the bent note.

This is a piece by Jacob Lawrence, from his 1967 Migration Series, called *Through Forests, Through Rivers, Up Mountains*. What I love about this piece from a Black geographic perspective is that it helps us build a different kind of design imaginary. Jacob Lawrence is implicating the human with the so-called nature-space. In the image, it's difficult to disaggregate the human from the trees and the

Jacob Lawrence, *Through Forests, Through Rivers, Through Mountains*, 1967.

5. Christina Sharpe, *In the Wake: On Blackness and Being* (Durham, NC: Duke University Press, 2016).

rivers and the streams. It's also kind of a scary image, there are a lot of bent notes in there. You see Harriet Tubman, or what I imagine to be Harriet Tubman, and her hand looks like a claw. It is as if she is saying "This is not a fairytale. There is some very scary stuff to wrestle with here." Her other hand is pointing to the North Star, an imagined sanctuary or safe space. Everything is struggling in that direction, positioned toward the star, toward the sanctuary, even the squirrel in the bottom left. We're all kind of embedded together. You can't disaggregate one from the other. Jacob Lawrence is showing us collectivity not just with his use of color but with the entire orientation of the image. I have looked at this image over and over since I was a kid, because, first of all, it frightens me, but also because there is something so real about it. How do we deal with the fear and also the hope of yearning toward sanctuary?

In her incredible book, *In the Wake*, Christina Sharpe talks about the slave ship and the mid-Atlantic crossings as "leaving a wake."[5] The ship leaves a kind of a trail in the water, that's the wake. Sharpe conceptualizes our present time, and all the labor of artists like Jacob Lawrence, and all of your work, and all of my efforts, as existing in the wake. We are in the wake right now. We are in the wake of anti-Blackness, genocide, colonization, imperialism, oppression, and marginalization. However, we are also engaged in wake work.

A wake celebrates the passing of something, and it acknowledges pain and trauma such as we see in Jacob Lawrence's piece. But a wake is also something different because it is a collective experience – like music, like the bent note I mentioned earlier. You don't experience a wake by yourself, as an individual. A wake is something that happens in community with people. You bring things to a wake, you bring yourselves, sometimes you bring food, you bring your trauma and you bring your hopes for healing. You bring funny stories and your body. But you don't know what's going to happen precisely, you just know that grief will be shared. However, the neoliberal mind wants us to control every moment of our time. Every moment must be accounted for and if it is not we have somehow failed. Time is almost like the big bureaucratic arm that administers fear. "Oh my God, we are losing time. I have wasted time!"

That's why some of the most critical Black theorists talk about time as anti-Black. Christina Sharpe says that we are both in the wake and we are engaged in wake work. So, what does it mean to be engaged in wake work as educators and as designers? Can design be vulnerable to this wake work? Can design be responsible for this idea of wake work?

Let's move to a more expansive idea of being in the wake. I teach two courses this semester, one is the Black Geographies course I've described, which is populated by Black students from all across the beautiful diaspora. We do things like dance together, we pray together, we hold hands together at the end of classes. We also talk about white supremacy. The other class I teach is called Environmental History, Race, and Natural Resource Management, and in that class too we talk about white supremacy. In both classes, I stress that white supremacy is not equal to white skin. (I think it is very important to say that. Hopefully everybody already knows that.) The indigenous scholar Andrea Smith has conceptualized "the three pillars of white supremacy" as grounded in 1) forced Black labor or slavery, a kind of anti-Black expropriation through which capitalism is born; 2) indigenous genocide, as a requirement for the land theft upon which settler colonialism depends; and 3) what Edward Said and others have called "Orientalism," which creates and recreates a kind of war capitalism and a war ethic, a perpetual horde of others always on the poetic front gates about to stampede in and wreak havoc.[6] These three pillars have historically defined the pillars of white supremacy. This is often very difficult for students of all kinds to wrestle with. We are in the wake, but what are we supposed to do with this? If we are lucid, it seems like an overwhelming quantity of pain and history and facts and geographies and realities to grasp as one person, let alone as a designer or anybody who is trying to change the world. How on earth can we possibly deal with this from a subconscious or spiritual or soul level?

The neoliberal impulse is to solve this or abandon our confrontation as pointless. Christina Sharpe and others tell us that actually some things cannot be "solved" – because can grief be "solved"? Would you ever have the nerve to say to a grieving person that they should "solve"

6. Andrea Smith, "Heteropatriarchy and the Three Pillars of White Supremacy: Rethinking Women of Color Organizing," in *Feminist Theory Reader: Local and Global Perspectives*, 4th ed., ed. Carole R. McCann and Seung-Kyung Kim (New York, NY: Routledge, 2016), 273–81.

Design Struggles

their grief? So, to circle back to an abolitionist love ethic or ethos – what we can do is resist in our daily practices, we can fight against the conditions which have enabled our pain and humiliation. That's the reality. Our afro-pessimism can generate a new world. We have to figure out how to hold the general tension that this cannot be solved, neither with a plaque that commemorates it, nor a class called Black Geographies. But that does not mean that we are absolved of our requirement to engage in socially creative thinking daily. We do not "solve," we bear witness, we play the bent notes, we think with the blues in mind.

What is the blues? It's this improvisational set of acts toward creating space. It's using the bent notes – as Christina Sharpe has laid out for us, and Jared Sexton, and Angela Davis, and Clyde Woods, and so many others – to create a way of making sense of the world, an epistemology that's based in openness and not needing to know the answer. If you want to remember one thing from all that I'm saying it's this: if you don't engage in experimental thinking in which you allow yourself to say that you don't know the answer, then you are not engaging in a critical or radical position. That's what abolition requires. It requires that you do not see yourself as an individual apart from the suffering of others, despite what everyone has told you. I'm simply a manifestation of all of my ancestors and I'm embodied in this particular framework. And yes, I am speaking, and yes, my name is Mia Charlene White, but I am here representing so many, many other people and spaces and geographies, as are you. Which is part of the soul work that we talked about, what you brought into this space when we made this space.

Clyde Woods's blues epistemology asks us to attend to the affect, or affective resistance, or love; the affect of how we respond to things like Andrea Smith's three pillars of white supremacy. How are you going to recognize how you feel about it? I use this concept of affective resistance to build on my own theorization of spatial practices, and I translate that as "love." Some people prefer "affective resistance" a lot better than love, because, you know, love is so gendered and we are so patriarchal, we don't know what to do with it.

One of my favorite writers is Fred Moten. He

knows it, I'm a big-time fangirl of his. Fred Moten is the basis of what I will go into now, which is the undercommons, the last part of the title of this session.[7] Fred's work encompasses many, many things, it's hard to put him into a disciplinary box. But he is really interested in affect and performance and poetics. So I have tried to weave this all together. He and Stefano Harney, who model the kind of radical friendship I am so interested in – they theorize love as mutual study. We can sort of, I have sort of engaged their definition of love, mutual study, to better understand spatial resistance in order to reject the neoliberal evaluative logics that render these community efforts as inefficient, ineffectual, or unsuccessful. Love as a blues epistemology helps us see differently and therefore react differently.

As an example: I theorize on community land trusts and other kinds of collective and community-based emancipatory processes. So let's think about the poetics of private property. I can't solve the problem of private property as Mia Charlene White. And neither can the community land trusts that I empirically study, alone, "solve" the historical, sedimented reality of private property. But that should not stop my ability to theorize the meaning of these efforts. Love as a blues epistemology asks us to try to understand what it is that community land trust folks are doing and how they are attending to the affect or the poetics of private property, knowing that they are going up as David against Goliath. In other words, we can understand that with a design intervention or design strategy like the community land trust, our neoliberal training asks us whether they "solved the thing," i.e., the challenge of private property … but with a blues epistemological orientation, we are looking at why they are trying to solve the thing, and how it matters where that thing developed, grew up, and lives.

I'm trying to adopt, as J. K. Gibson-Graham says, an experimental orientation toward everything: toward critique or analysis, toward theorizing empirical projects, and even in the context of giving a presentation.[8] Let's take a really ugly, heavy-handed modernist design, the State University of New York at Stonybrook, where I went for my undergraduate degree, with its giant cement blocks, a depressing state of affairs that students have to engage with every day. Rather than simply critiquing it as a failure

7. Stefano Harney and Fred Moten, *The Undercommons: Fugitive Planning & Black Study* (Wivenhoe: Minor Compositions, 2013).

8. See J. K. Gibson-Graham, "Socially Creative Thinking, or How Experimental Thinking Creates Other Worlds," paper presented at the Katarsis conference, 2008, www. communityeconomies.org/ publications/conference-papers/socially-creative-thinking-or-how-experimental-thinking-creates.

Design Struggles

9. On "embracing the feels," see Elizabeth Willis, "Work This Thing," *Boston Review*, July 15, 2015, bostonreview.net/poetry/elizabeth-willis-fred-moten-little-edges-feel-trio.

of imagination, we might understand it as a reflection of how people were feeling. And what does that mean? What does it mean that these structures are reflections of how people were feeling? Does it matter that people were feeling whatever you feel when you look at these big, heavy cement blocks?

One of the things that Fred Moten, whom I mentioned before, talks about, is the idea of "embracing the feels" analytically and productively.[9] Not turning away from drama but revealing its truth as having a very long history. In Black feminist memoirs, in poetry, in personal essays, this is how we have been able to uncover feels. And why is it so important? It is almost pedestrian to talk about feelings, but it's the thing that people don't talk about. It's like the universal thing that people have very little capacity and fluency in talking about. Of course, words are limited. It's zeros and dashes or symbols or whatever. They are very limited, but we still need them. Every word is an incantation. It's a spell and the silences also cast a spell.

The idea that we have to face the feels with words, with art, is a way of saying "let's cast some spells together." Let's conjure things with an abolitionist eye. We don't know what will happen when we conjure them together, but the process of conjuring together is important as human beings. Sometimes we conjure together and what comes out is a building or a syllabus, or a baby. But we have to recognize that we actually have been doing something together, not as individuals. We are far too individuated. Engaging trauma and mourning is one of the ways educators and designers in particular can model, pedagogically and analytically, how to participate in world-breaking and belonging anew. This is so important, because it services the subconscious need to assist in a development in an uncovering of a deeper vernacular understanding, of love practice as affective dissent.

By *vernacular* I mean that you don't need to have a Ph.D. from MIT to know that the way that you feel is actually wildly relevant. The epistemological dissent and awakening occurs when we willfully realize how universal trauma is in every space: in the classroom, the bedroom, the boardroom, the park, the shelter, the street. I'm going to read a poem now, in the context of my epistemological dissent about Eric Garner, who you may know was murdered by the US police state. The poem begins with its title, *A Small Needful Fact*, and continues:

10. Ross Gay, "A Small Needful Fact," published on Split This Rock's *The Quarry: A Social Justice Poetry Database*, 2015, www.splitthisrock. org/poetry-database/ poem/a-small-needful-fact.

> Is that Eric Garner worked
> for some time for the Parcs and Rec.
> Horticultural Department, which means,
> perhaps, that with his very large hands,
> perhaps, in all likelihood,
> he put gently into the earth
> some plants which, most likely,
> some of them, in all likelihood,
> continue to grow, continue
> to do what such plants do, like house
> and feed small and necessary creatures,
> like being pleasant to touch and smell,
> like converting sunlight
> into food, like making it easier
> for us to breathe.[10]

This poem was written by Ross Gay. For me, it perfectly exemplifies what Christina Sharpe says, being both in the wake and engaging in wake work. And my reading it to you here is my way of engaging in wake work. What do we do about the Eric Garners of the world? We cannot solve his murder. But blues epistemology suggests we ask what the wake work is that we will be engaged in as people doing varying jobs, including design, to recognize and acknowledge the feelings that are produced by his murder? Something has to be done. The affect must be attended to.

I teach space as existing on three levels. (I know this is limited, it's just where I am right now.) The first space is embodied space: our physical space, how we look into the world, but also how our physical existence is oriented, what we look like and how we appear to others, and how this affects how we can move in space. The second space is institutions: the Federal Housing Authority, marriage, the phrase "I do," all these are institutions by design. Design as an institution, that's the second space. The third space is politics, which is conceptualized as the politics of possibility. The poetics of property that I mentioned earlier would go into this third space. But we can't really get there

Design Struggles

11. Nayyirah Waheed, *Salt* (CreateSpace, 2013).

if we do not lucidly recognize the first and second spaces. If we don't realize that design is an institution and that you are a lucid human being, making space, then we can't really get to the third space, we can't get to the politics of possibilities or the poetics of property, anything like that. Because these spaces are not sequential, they are very much a co-mingling, you can't really pull them apart.

What this spatial theorizing does is to support how I understand love practice. Love practice is basically embodied, or understood, or imagined in this third space, the poetics of property as a love practice. It is vested in abolition. We can think of private property, we can think of the mortgage as vested in the second space. The mortgage, which allows the private ownership of a home, for instance. But we can't get to the third space without really understanding how this happened. And it's not so much about answering or solving it, it's about an act of resistance.

Nayyirah Waheed is a wonderful poet, who has said, "where you write from is important" and to me that's another way of thinking about the lucid. She says: "Where you write from is important. The feet. The hands, the hem of the heart, the soft patch behind the ear."[11] Where you design from is important. And if you don't think that design can manifest our human vulnerability, then you are designing from a particular point of view, from what I call a cyborg point of view. I don't think we are cyborgs, I think we are humans, and I think the thing that connects us most is trauma and vulnerability. In my perspective, designers who think about a so-called intervention at the level of the street, at the level of the bus stop, where instead of seats you have swings, you know, those are the people, that's the kind of so-called intervention that I think responds to our various vulnerabilities.

We need to play in order to feel some sense of freedom. In order to feel some sense of freedom, we have to engage in our various affects, our fear affects: we are tired, we are old, nobody cares, the bus is never going to come, what are we going to do? What can a designer do? A designer can put swings at the bus stop. We can swing, even if just for a few minutes. I saw an image once: six older people with silver and white hair, swinging, waiting for a bus. To me, this

Daily Tous Le Jours, *21 Swings*, 2011, interactive installation in Montreal.

was a revolutionary feeling. They were elder and they were swinging while they were waiting for the bus. Sit with this for a moment: they were swinging, while they were waiting for a bus. This means that someone imagined freedom as human beings swinging while waiting for something to happen. You feel it and you see it but you need actually to encounter it in space to share it with other people, to get the feeling, to have power. To me, that is abolition, that is a love practice right there.

The swinging to me is like a perfect image, a mental picture of what Angela Davis has said repeatedly, that freedom is a constant struggle. Maybe you can think of it as freedom requires constant play. You know, freedom requires a constant reminiscing of your childhood and your unfettered hopes and dreams. The idea that we, as regular people, just regular people – and also maybe fancy-pants designers – can help other people feel some measure of freedom, that these moments might add up to something is wildly important to me. There is something aesthetic, there is something poetic, there is something so powerful about swinging while you are waiting for something.

Let me get to another kind of example: community land trusts (CLTs), a topic I have studied since my dissertation. I really love that I can't fully explain everything they are, and I want to focus on how they are vested in the idea of a trust doctrine. I'm not talking about the actual mortgage writer and pieces of paper, but about investing in the idea of trust itself. Trust as in "I want to trust you that you know I need a place to live and I want to trust that you care." It's an experiment. It's a love act. And it fails in many ways.

There are many community land trusts: there's one in West London, and there are several in the Deep South – i.e., the southern states that historically were most dependent on plantations and slavery. These are the ones I study, the Black and Brown community land trusts. The first one was started in the 1960s by Slater King, Martin Luther King's cousin. It began under very fraught circumstances. Slater King decided to take a contingent of white and Black people to Jerusalem. He was going to interview folks from the Jewish National Fund, because he wanted to understand how the JNF was funding kibbutzim. Slater King was really interested in ideas of territory, settlement, and freedom, so he went to Jerusalem to get a better sense of how it could work to get more freedom for Black Americans in the United States.

Turning to Zionism was quite fraught given the violence required to engage in space-making when there is an existing indigenous population. When I go to CLT meetings – I've been to maybe seventy, eighty of these meetings – no one ever mentions that the model came from Jerusalem and from kibbutzim and that the initial plans were based on interviews with the Jewish National Fund – obviously these are bent notes, right? I'm here trying to flesh out those first-, second-, and third-space notions I mentioned before. In the case of the CLT, we skipped to the second space: here is an institution that we can believe in. That happens a lot with how we theorize experimental projects: we skip right to the second space without really uncovering how it matters where it happened, the way that we understood this thing, and how people all around the world have understood it.

From Slater King's perspective, he was trying to figure out how Black people could be safe in the United States. This is still a question: how can Black people be safe in the United States, where the state continues to kill them? If you can't be swallowed and you can't be purged, what are you going to do? Slater King looked at what had happened in Jerusalem, where they were trying to create these safe spaces. He thought "Let's bring this model back to the United States." Now, I have nothing but respect for Slater King and all the work that community land trust people do – but I think we can't really get to that third space, that poetics, the politics of possibility, without wrestling with this sort of intimacy, with global oppression that is somewhat tuned down when we don't really reconcile with how it is that the JNF has been able to populate these very settlements via kibbutzim. I love the idea of kibbutzim, but there is also a kind of uncomfortable contradiction about their existence. And the same thing with the community land trust.

     I'm trying to model my version of love as an ethic of abolition. Love is not, as I said, a romantic sensibility between two people, or even between a researcher and a social object like the community land trust. It's really about covering that first space and that second space and getting toward that third space and then trying to understand those sort of generative contradictions and the cognitive dissonances. That's not an abolition-based love ethic. I'm trying to understand the problem the community land trust is trying to solve. The problem they are trying to solve is Black murder and the need for Black sanctuary.

     Fast-forward to 2018 and community land trusts have now become conceptualized as affordable housing models. And the most successful ones are known to be in what we call white spaces, like Vermont. And they have been able to create wonderful housing as a public good for folks in Vermont. But why is it that the CLT continues to be kind of unsuccessful in Black and Brown spaces? And I would say, because we haven't really dealt with those first and second spaces – the problem that Slater King was trying to solve. The problem the CLT was trying to solve is the problem of Black murder by the state and the poetics of private property predicated on Black expropriation. We still need to wrestle together as a community, as a group of people who all have different proximities to history and knowledge, over how to situate this appropriately.

     I see the community land trust as a kind of rebellious, fugitive love practice, something like marronage, in the sense of those maroon communities who fled to the swamps and the wetlands and the forests. The CLT is trying to flee the poetics of private property, trying to conjure up something different, a trust doctrine, where the land is owned by the community and individuals live in various parcels on the land. And then people come and do really interesting things, like they are building with cob and they are building with hemp and other natural products not requiring heavy machinery or lots of money or tons of expensive schooling. They are making installations out of hemp which is a carbon-neutral material. Imagine if we had 10 percent of the homes in the United States made from hemp, sucking carbon out of the air just by existing!

But we can't get to that if we don't wrestle with the second space. What's the second space with regard to hemp? The United States housing practice is basically a cartel. We are allowed to build with industrial hemp, but we cannot grow it in the United States. It is illegal to grow industrial hemp in the United States, you have to go to Canada to buy industrial hemp. Hemp is drought-tolerant, hardly needs any pesticides. It would take two months and two weeks to grow enough hemp to make a 2,000 square-foot structure that can house several families. It costs a fraction of the amount that it does to build with sticks, with wood and steel.

I'm trying to evoke what Jacob Lawrence depicted in *Through Forests, Through Rivers, Up Mountains* – the fugitivity of the people fleeing through the forest trying to get to that North Star. The community land trust folks are trying to get to that North Star, too. My focus, though, as an educator, as a critical theorist, is not to go so heavy into all the ways that they have done it wrong, but to try to hold that unease, that contradiction of using particular institutions toward getting to that North Star. If you don't deal with the reality of that history that keeps coming up, then you are left wondering why it is that a Vermont community land trust can be so successful while all these Black and Brown ones are not seen as such? I think the answer to that is because we neglect to hear the bent notes, or we mistake them because time is a coil, it's not linear, our mistakes keep repeating. The history is the bent note that I was talking about before – the bent note is the music Slater King was trying to play for us. The bent note illustrates the blues epistemology we must bear witness to. See with and through a blues epistemology and you will hear and see the bent notes.

And you know there are joys as we try to get to that North Star. For instance, there are Black electric cooperatives – I'm thinking of one in particular in North Carolina called the Roanoke Electric Cooperative – that are trying to generate electricity on a democratic and shared basis. The money they make is put back into the cooperative and used to train young people to become experts with sustainable solutions in insulation, for example – the hemp I talked about. There is this drain of young people leaving the Deep South. You have older people from New York and the different cities coming back to the South and then you have younger people leaving the South. And they are doing that because they need to find a place to live and work. They need a job. And this Black electric cooperative said, we can solve this problem that grandmothers and grandfathers are raising in a vernacular way. We don't need expert designers or engineers. We need to train young people on how to create hemp insulation that could help create a healthy indoor atmosphere, you know, because indoor air pollution is worse than outdoor air pollution.

They are creating a sustainable loop that's invested in the idea of Black freedom: how can I, as a Black grandparent on a fixed income and on the board of this Black electric cooperative, recognize and acknowledge the reality of these grandchildren, mine or fictive, who have no job opportunities? And also, at the same time, I'm supposed to rely on experts that come from New York, or wherever they come from, to tell me about how to make a sustainably based insulation, when in fact we can train each other to do this. We can see each other as having boundless potential, without credentials. And that's what they are doing. They are creating insulation out of hemp in these Black communities. To me, that's abolition on so many levels. And what we need to do is see it in the right way, the blue note that has been made and the space that we make when we talk about what they are doing.

At the moment, I am studying community land trusts, electric cooperatives, popular education tools, credit unions, and Triodos-style banking. What I'm trying to do

Design Struggles

with my own work is to move forward with a land ethic. A land ethic requires that we think about space differently. In my conceptualization we have to think in those first, second, and third spaces if we want to proceed with that land ethic. The reason I proceed with the land ethic is because land has been stolen, it has been lied over, it's been mistreated, and it's basically a metaphor for us, for each of us. It's traumatized, it's wounded, but it's revelatory. And so, if we think about land as an avatar for each other and we move with a land ethic that's a basic collective emancipation, I think really amazing things happen. What would it mean for designers, for example, to design with a land ethic, with a landed blues epistemology?

I'll close by reiterating what so many Black artists and organizers and intellectuals before me have said, which is that I come from that other America, that other America that is so invested in the bent notes. As Christina Sharpe says, we are in the wake. And we continue to create from those bent notes blue notes that create space – that's our wake work. Sometimes the space that's made is misunderstood. And it's misunderstood because the gaze of the viewer trying to understand the blue notes is not lucid. The gaze of each of us is not always lucid. We think we are neutral or individual or objective and we are looking at these various projects as individual projects and not as a continuum – like time is a coil – as a reflection or a mirror of all our different traumas and vulnerabilities. So, if we were to think with a blues epistemology about, for instance, what the architectures of a spatial justice would be, that would require that we engaged with trauma and vulnerability, not with credentials – and I'm saying this with an understanding that my life has been vested in seeking credentials. But if an architecture of spatial justice requires that we build on each other's vernacular everyday revolutionary capacity – for instance, train each other how to make something as crazy sounding as hemp insulation that would keep our elders lovingly cool in the summer and warm in the winter, our Earth safer, without fancy degrees – we would be engaging in what I call love from the undercommons, based in the undercommons, the people whose history is all about the bent notes and also about so much more. Thank you.

LOVE

BIOGRAPHIES

Danah Abdulla is an Arab-Canadian designer, educator, and researcher – not in any particular order but always all three. She is program director of Graphic Design at Camberwell, Chelsea, and Wimbledon Colleges of Art, University of the Arts London. She has previously held positions at Brunel University London and the London College of Communication, University of the Arts London. Danah holds a Ph.D. in Design from Goldsmiths, University of London (2018). She is a founding member of the Decolonising Design platform. In 2010, she founded *Kalimat Magazine*, an independent, nonprofit publication about Arab thought and culture. Danah's research is particularly focused on decolonizing design, possibilities of design education, design culture(s) with a focus on the Arab region, the politics of design, publishing, and social design.

Tanveer Ahmed, after many frustrating years of learning and teaching dominant capitalist models of fashion design, began a part-time Ph.D. at the Open University, UK, to investigate ways of teaching antiracist and anticapitalist forms of fashion design. Inspired by Black feminist literature and decolonizing education movements, she has drawn on her family histories and identity to offer students ways of disrupting the Eurocentric and neoliberal agendas that dominate fashion design education. The project described in her essay, by centering a garment from the Global South, has helped students question the dominance of European fashion design in their curricula and resources. Her long-term aspiration is to contribute to fashion design educational paradigms by generating new antiracist, postcapital agendas in fashion design. She is currently a visiting lecturer in design at Goldsmiths College and the Royal College of Art, London.

Zoy Anastassakis (b. 1974) is a Brazilian designer and anthropologist. She is associate professor and former director of the Superior School of Industrial Design, State University of Rio de Janeiro (ESDI/UERJ), where she coordinates the Design and Anthropology Lab (LaDA). In 2014, she published *Triunfos e Impasses: Lina Bo Bardi, Aloisio Magalhães e o design no Brasil*. In 2018, she was invited as a visiting researcher in the Department of Anthropology, University of Aberdeen, Scotland, where she took part in the research project "Knowing from the Inside," coordinated by Tim Ingold. Since 2019, she is an associated researcher at the Centre for Research in Anthropology (CRIA) at Nova University, Lisbon, Portugal. In 2020, she published the book *Refazendo tudo: Confabulações em meio aos cupins na universidade*. Together with Marcos Martins, she is preparing a book on the ESDI Aberta movement, to be published in 2021 by Bloomsbury, in the series *Designing in Dark Times*.

Ahmed Ansari is an assistant professor in NYU Tandon's Department of Technology, Culture, and Society. He holds a B.Des. in communication design from the Indus Valley School of Art and Architecture, in Karachi, Pakistan (2008); and an M.Des. and Ph.D. in interaction design from Carnegie Mellon University (2013 and 2019). His research interests intersect at the junction between design, critical cultural studies, and the history and philosophy of technology, particularly in the contexts of the Indian subcontinent.

Brave New Alps, cofounded by Bianca Elzenbaumer and Fabio Franz, is a collaborative design practice based in the alpine Lagarina Valley in Italy, whose twelve members are dedicated to the creation of commons and community economies. Since embarking on design studies in 2002, they have been looking for ways in which to activate design skills for eco-social causes. Since 2010, Bianca has been researching the entanglements and worldviews that create the precarious working conditions that make critical design practices so difficult to sustain. Since 2014, Fabio has been researching commons and modes of community organizing in the Italian Alps. As members of the international Community Economies Research Network, they activate empowering readings of the economy in order to create modes of practice and living that can sustain themselves and others engaged in transformative practices. Currently, Bianca also works as a Marie Skłodowska-Curie Individual Fellow at Eurac Research in Italy, where she runs the Alpine

Community Economies Lab. Fabio is coordinating a network of civic organizations and informal groups, who are setting up a community academy at the train station of Rovereto in Trentino, Italy.

Johannes Bruder works at the intersection of anthropology, STS, and media studies, and between the Milieux Institute for Arts, Culture, and Technology at Concordia University in Montreal and FHNW's Critical Media Lab in Basel. His research revolves around experiments, tests, and demos that link science, design, and the arts – which means that, in his own words, "I am often faced with the question about who I am, where I belong, or what it is that I am doing. Research? For sure! Critique? Probably yes, but hasn't critique run out of steam? Intervention? I do hope so. Activism? I don't know. But then, how can activism and research be reliably discerned in our current situation?" His essay "Alexa's Body" is an attempt to merge intersecting subjectivities, and to think like a researcher, an interventionist, and an activist at the same time – and to avoid succumbing to the pressures of having one, and one subjectivity only.

Cheryl Buckley is professor of fashion and design history at the University of Brighton. A founding member of the journal *Visual Culture* in Britain in 2000, and chair of the Design History Society from 2006–2009, she also served as editor-in-chief of the *Journal of Design History* from 2011–2016.

Questions relating to gender have been continuous throughout her academic work, and her research has explored fashion, ceramics, émigrés, and transnational identities as well as design in everyday lives. Key books include Potters and Paintresses (1991), *Fashioning the Feminine* (with Hilary Fawcett, 2002), *Designing Modern Britain* (2007), and, most recently, *Fashion and Everyday Life: London and New York* (with Hazel Clark, 2017). Her article "Made in Patriarchy: Towards a Feminist Analysis of Women and Design" (*Design Issues* 3, no. 2, Fall 1986) was written as part of her Ph.D. thesis (University of East Anglia, 1990).

Sria Chatterjee holds a Ph.D. from Princeton University and was awarded the Charlotte Elizabeth Procter Honorific Fellowship in 2019. She specializes in the political ecologies of art and design in the Global South in the nineteenth and twentieth centuries. Her work draws on transnational environmental histories, the history of science (in particular, plant science and agriculture), landscape studies, design, and cybernetics. She is currently a fellow at the Max-Planck Kunsthistorisches Institut in Florenz, and at the Institute for Experimental Design and Media at FHNW in Basel. Her research has been funded by the Paul Mellon Centre, the Yale Center for British Art, and the Terra Foundation for American Art among others. She is a contributing editor at *British Art* Studies and her writing has been published in journals such as

Cultural Politics, Contemporary Political Theory, and others.

Alison J. Clarke joined the University of Applied Arts Vienna from the Royal College of Art in London to become chair of the department of Design History and Theory and founding director of the Victor Papanek Foundation: she is the convener of the biennial Papanek Symposium exploring the ethics and futures of contemporary design. As a trained design historian (RCA/V&A, London) and social anthropologist (University College London), her research explores the intersection of design and anthropology. Recipient of major international grants and fellowships, Clarke is a regular media broadcaster and international speaker in the field of design. Her most recent publications include *Design Anthropology: Object Cultures in Transition*, the coedited volume *Émigré Cultures in Design and Architecture*, and the monograph *Victor Papanek: The Politics of Design*, forthcoming from the MIT Press. She has recently cocurated, with Vitra Design Museum, the international traveling exhibition *Victor Papanek: The Politics of Design*.

Sasha Costanza-Chock is a scholar, activist, designer, and media-maker, and currently associate professor of civic media at MIT. They are a faculty associate at the Berkman-Klein Center for Internet & Society at Harvard University, faculty affiliate with the MIT Open Documentary Lab, and creator of the MIT Codesign Studio (codesign.mit.edu). Their work focuses on social movements, transformative media organizing, and design justice. Sasha's first book, *Out of the Shadows, Into the Streets: Transmedia Organizing and the Immigrant Rights Movement*, was published by the MIT Press in 2014. Their new book, *Design Justice: Community-Led Practices to Build the Worlds We Need*, was published by the MIT Press in February 2020. Sasha is a board member of Allied Media Projects (alliedmedia.org) and a steering committee member of the Design Justice Network (designjusticenetwork.org).

Paola De Martin was born in 1965 in Switzerland as a child of Italian migrant workers. After her formal training as a textile designer at the Zurich School for Applied Arts (SfGZ; today: ZHdK), she was an entrepreneur of interior and fashion design, and a founding member of the fashion label Beige. The exploitation of herself and others in the global fashion industry soon pushed her out of practice. She went on to study socioeconomic and art history at the University of Zurich, where she received a master's degree in 2011. She currently teaches design history, design sociology, and interculturality in the Department of Design and the Department of Cultural Analysis and Education at ZHdK. De Martin is now completing her dissertation at the ETH Zurich (Institute for the Theory and History of Architecture (gta), Chair

Prof. Dr. Philip Ursprung), which focusses on the history of aesthetic and social inequality within the field of design. De Martin is a member of the Design History Society, the Swiss Netzwerk Designgeschichte, the NGO Public Eye, and the postmigrant Institut Neue Schweiz INES. She is the leading force behind actual claims for the reparation of human rights violations caused by the denial of family reunion by Swiss immigration law, which many thousands of non-Swiss worker's families, hers included, endured with traumatic consequences between the 1950s and the early 2000s.

Decolonising Design was founded in 2016 by eight design researchers, artists, and activists, most of whom stem from or have ties to ties to the Global South, as a response to Euro- and Anglocentric socio-technical politics and pedagogies of design as both a field of research and praxis. The group does not aim to offer an alternative perspective on design, but rather questions the very foundations upon which the discipline was established.

depatriarchise design is a nonprofit research platform working across different mediation formats. Their manifold investigative and activist practice is rooted in intersectional feminism. Founded in 2017, depatriarchise design was born out of frustration with a design discipline that is deeply interwoven with discriminating structures.

depatriarchise design started as a call for action. The urgent need for change in design practice and its dominant paradigms is their driving force. Through texts, workshops, and exhibitions they examine the complicity of design in the reproduction of oppressive systems but also tell long-silenced stories. Constantly researching feminist pedagogies, they stir alternative modes of teaching design, initiating workshops, bringing like-minded people together to learn from and with each other. They value collaboration and the cocreation of knowledge, and therefore often join forces with people, collectives, and initiatives whose work they admire and with whom they share common political ground. They believe in the transformative potential of design and are constantly looking for ways of creating more socially sustainable futures. depatriarchise design is registered as a nonprofit association in Basel, Switzerland, and works internationally. Anja Neidhardt and Maya Ober run the platform together as a collaborative endeavor.

Arturo Escobar is Kenan Distinguished Teaching Professor of Anthropology at the University of North Carolina, Chapel Hill, and Research Associate with the Culture, Memory, and Nation group at Universidad del Valle, Cali, and the Cultural Studies groups at Universidad Javeriana, Bogota. He is Member of the Executive Board in the Society of Cultural Anthropology and the Editorial

Boards of numerous publications, such as *Capitalism, Nature, Socialism: Journal of Socialist Ecology* (Santa Cruz, CA), *Development* (Journal of the Society for International Development, Rome) and *Ecología Política* (Barcelona). His main interests are political ecology, ontological design, and the anthropology of development, social movements, and technoscience. Over the past twenty-five years, he has worked closely with several Afro-Colombian social movements in the Colombian Pacific, particular the Process of Black Communities (PCN). His most well-known book is *Encountering Development: The Making and Unmaking of the Third* World (1995, 2nd ed. 2011). His most recent books are *Territories of Difference: Place, Movements, Life, Redes* (2008; 2010 for the Spanish edition); *Sentipensar con la Tierra. Nuevas lecturas sobre desarrollo, territorio y diferencia* (2014); *Autonomía y diseño: La realización de lo comunal* (2016; February 2018 for the English edition, *Designs for the Pluriverse: Radical Interdependence, Autonomy, and the Making of Worlds)*; and *Otro posible es posible: Caminando hacia las transiciones desde Abya Yala/Afro/Latino-América* (2018).

Kjetil Fallan is professor of design history at the University of Oslo, and cofounder of the Oslo School of Environmental Humanities. In recent years his research has sought to bring together histories of design and the environment. Key output thus far includes "Environmental

Histories of Design," a special issue of the *Journal of Design History* (vol. 30, no. 2); the 2017 Design History Society Annual Conference, *Making and Unmaking the Environment;* and the edited volume *The Culture of Nature in the History of Design* (Routledge, 2019). Previous work has focused chiefly on twentieth-century everyday design culture and professional design discourse in Scandinavia and Italy, including *Designing Modern Norway: A History of Design Discourse* (Routledge, 2017); *Scandinavian Design: Alternative Histories* (Berg, 2012); and, with Grace Lees-Maffei, *Made in Italy: Rethinking a Century of Italian Design* (Bloomsbury, 2014). Fallan also has a sustained interest in the theory, methodology, and historiography of design, as explored in, among others, *Design History: Understanding Theory and Method* (Berg, 2010) and, with Grace Lees-Maffei, *Designing Worlds: National Histories of Design in an Age of Globalization* (Berghahn Books, 2016).

Griselda Flesler is a tenured professor at the Chair of Design and Gender Studies in the Faculty of Architecture, Design, and Urbanism; principal researcher at the American Art Institute; and a Ph.D. candidate in Social Sciences at the University of Buenos Aires in Argentina. Being raised in a feminist household on the one hand, and having acquired a predominately Eurocentric graphic design education that didn't relate to the Argentinian reality on the other, Flesler has started researching design as a space for the construction and reproduction of gender relations, applying an intersectional lens. Her research focuses on the symbolic violence of the university space and the queer uses of institutional and public space. Flesler also serves as Head of Gender Office at FADU-UBA, developing and applying the "Protocol of Institutional Intervention in the Case of Complaints of Gender Violence, Sexual Harassment, and Gender Discrimination."

Corin Gisel is a Swiss writer, researcher, and designer. Gisel holds an MA in cultural publishing from Zurich University of the Arts/Institute for Applied Media Studies. Their writing has been published by Lars Müller Publishers, Diogenes, Spector Books, Occasional Papers, Walker Art Center, and Valiz and has covered topics such as design education, dress culture, the digitalization of the museum, LGBTQIA+ button badges, and money as a medium for political opposition. Gisel has taught and lectured at the School of Visual Arts New York, POST Design Festival, Ésad Valence, FHNW Basel, and Krabbesholm Højskole, among others. With Nina Paim, they conceived the book *Taking a Line for a Walk*, published by Spector Books, Leipzig, in 2016 and supported by the Graham Foundation for Advanced Studies in the Fine Arts. In 2018, they coedited the book *Protest: The Aesthetics of Resistance*, published by Lars Müller Publishers. Gisel is a co-founder of the feminist magazine for design politics *Futuress*. Next to their work, Gisel is also active in LGBTQIA+ community organizing and activism.

Matthew Kiem is a designer, researcher, and educator currently working at the University of New South Wales faculty of Art & Design. He holds degrees in both design and art education from the University of New South Wales (2010) and a Ph.D. in design from Western Sydney University (2018). His research focuses on the application of decolonial theory to the critical study of design history, theory, and practice. He is a founding member of the Decolonising Design group.

Claudia Mareis is a design researcher and cultural scientist with a background in design practice. In 2013 she was appointed professor for design history and theory at the FHNW Academy of Art and Design in Basel. There she is also the director of the Institute of Experimental Design and Media Cultures (IXDM) and the Critical Media Lab. Since 2019 she is one of the deputies of the Cluster of Excellence "Matters of Activity. Image Space Material" at the Humboldt University of Berlin. She is also a member of the National Research Council of the Swiss National Science Foundation; the vice-president of the Swiss Design Network (SDN); and a board member of the German Association for Design Theory and Research (DGTF). Her research interests comprise the history of design in the nineteenth and twentieth centuries, including epistemologies, ontologies, and politics of design. She is working on a critical cultural history of creativity and is about to complete a comprehensive monograph on the history of creative techniques in the postwar period.

Ramia Mazé is professor in Design for Social Innovation and Sustainability at London College of Communication, University of the Arts, United Kingdom. Previously, in Finland, she was a professor and head of education in the Department of Design at Aalto University and, prior to that, she worked at Konstfack College of Arts, Crafts, and Design, KTH Royal Institute of Technology, the national doctoral school Designfakulteten, and the Interactive Institute in Sweden. A designer and architect by training, her Ph.D. is in interaction design. She has led, published, and exhibited widely through major interdisciplinary and international practice-based design research projects, most recently in social and sustainable design, design activism, and design for policy. She specializes in participatory, critical, and politically engaged design practices, as well as "research through design" and feminist epistemologies.

Tania Messell is a design historian whose research focuses on design professionalization and globalization in the second half of the twentieth century. Her essay derives from her doctoral research on the International Council of Societies of Industrial Design (1957–80), conducted at the University of Brighton. Her thesis mapped the early years of the organization, tracing the competing political, economic, and cultural imperatives that shaped the forum in the wider Cold War and decolonial contexts. She is currently researching the rise of humanitarian design with a focus on Western practices, a critical study of the imperatives of "care" in their most extreme articulations. Of multiple origins, Messell grew up close to Switzerland, a background which informed her interest in the value systems and power dynamics pervading international organizations and humanitarian aid. She has published in several international peer-reviewed publications and is a coeditor of *International Design Organisations: Histories, Legacies, Values*, published by Bloomsbury Academic (forthcoming).

Anja Neidhardt is a Ph.D. student at Umeå Institute of Design and Umeå Centre for Gender Studies in Sweden. Previously she worked as an independent design journalist and educator. She has a master's degree in Design Curating and Writing from Design Academy Eindhoven. Anja is contributing to depatriachise design since 2017, and became co-editor in 2018.

Nan O'Sullivan is an associate dean within the faculty of Architecture and Design, director of the Design for Social Innovation Programme, and founder of the research cluster The Social Lab at the School of Design

Innovation, Victoria University of Wellington Te Herenga Waka. Nan investigates the changing faces, languages, values, and processes of design found within the complex social and cultural issues that challenge us as individuals and as a part of larger communities and societies. As an advocate for Transition Design, Nan investigates, identifies, creates, facilitates, and communicates creative pathways that are informed by more equitable, inclusive, and place-based approaches. Inspired by the traditional Māori proverb Hoki whakamuri kia anga whakamua – "look to the past to forge the future" – Nan seeks to illustrate the relevance of indigenous knowledge, specifically that of Māori and Pasifika nations, to design education, thinking, and practice in the twenty-first century.

Maya Ober is a designer, researcher, educator, activist, and the founding editor of depatriarchise design based in Basel, Switzerland. She works as a research associate at the Institute of Industrial Design and as a lecturer at the Institute of Aesthetic Practice and Theory at the Academy of Arts and Design in Basel. There, together with Laura Pregger she has initiated the educational programme "Imagining Otherwise" exploring intersectional pedagogies of art and design education. Her current research project "Space of Radical Possibilities – towards intersectional feminist pedagogies of design" at the Academy of the Arts in Bern is a multi-sited study situated interdisciplinary

between gender studies, social anthropology, and design, exploring how intersectional feminist pedagogies influence design education.

Nina Paim is a Brazilian curator and design researcher. Her work usually involves many others and revolves around notions of directing, supporting, and collaborating. She was born in Nova Friburgo, 168 years after Swiss settler-colonialists displaced the indigenous tribes of the puris, coroados, and guarus. Love and fate brought her to Basel, where she seeks to transmute her daily immigrant exhaustion into care practices for making space. She curated the exhibition *Taking a Line for a Walk* at the 2014 Brno Design Biennial and co-curated *Department of Non-Binaries* at the 2018 Fikra Design Biennial, Sharjah. She was a program coordinator for the 2018 Swiss Design Network conference "Beyond Change." She's a two-time recipient of the Swiss Design Award, and a co-founder of the feminist magazine for design politics *Futuress*.

Luiza Prado de O. Martins is an artist and researcher born in Rio de Janeiro in 1985, 485 years after the Portuguese first invaded the land currently known as Brazil. She holds an MA from Bremen University of the Arts and a Ph.D. from Berlin University of the Arts. Her work investigates how colonial gender difference is inscribed and imposed upon and within bodies through technology. Over the past years, she has been researching practices of herbalism and the management of fertility through performances, installations, and moving image. She is a founding member of the Decolonising Design group, and currently teaches at Berlin University of the Arts.

Mia Charlene White is Assistant Professor of Environmental Studies at the New School, where she is also Associate Director of the Housing Justice Lab @ Parsons School of Design, New York. She has a bachelor's degree in anthropology and political science from the State University of NY at Stonybrook, a master's degree in international affairs from Columbia University's School of International and Public Affairs (SIPA), and a Ph.D. in urban studies and planning from Massachusetts Institute of Technology (MIT). She is a Ford Foundation Minority Fellow and a National Science Foundation Fellow. Originally from NYC and a mother of two, Mia identifies as a Black American of African American and Korean descent. She is working on her first book, the basis of which is shared in her remarks here.

Design and Publisher

Lotte Lara Schröder is an artist and graphic designer, interested in ecological and natural phenomena. Her 'free' work consists of drawings, paintings, and collages, often combined with sound or objects. Lotte created the overall book and cover design, and the opening chapter images of this publication. These sediments dissect and reveal the remnants of our modern/ contemporary society. Images from Lotte's personal archive mixed with others sourced online, reveal personal, natural, and sometimes upsetting visuals that represent our current state of being. Each layer freely symbolizes a theme that resides within this book: gender, unsustainable systems, working class, ignorance, epistemology, obstacles, and poetry.

Valiz is an independent international publisher, addressing contemporary developments in art, design, architecture, and urban affairs. Their books provide critical reflection and interdisciplinary inspiration in a broad and imaginative way, often establishing a connection between cultural disciplines and socio-economic questions. Valiz is headed by Astrid Vorstermans and Pia Pol.

www.valiz.nl
@valiz_books_projects

INDEX
OF NAMES

Design Struggles

INDEX ORGANIZATIONS, PLATFORMS, PROJECTS

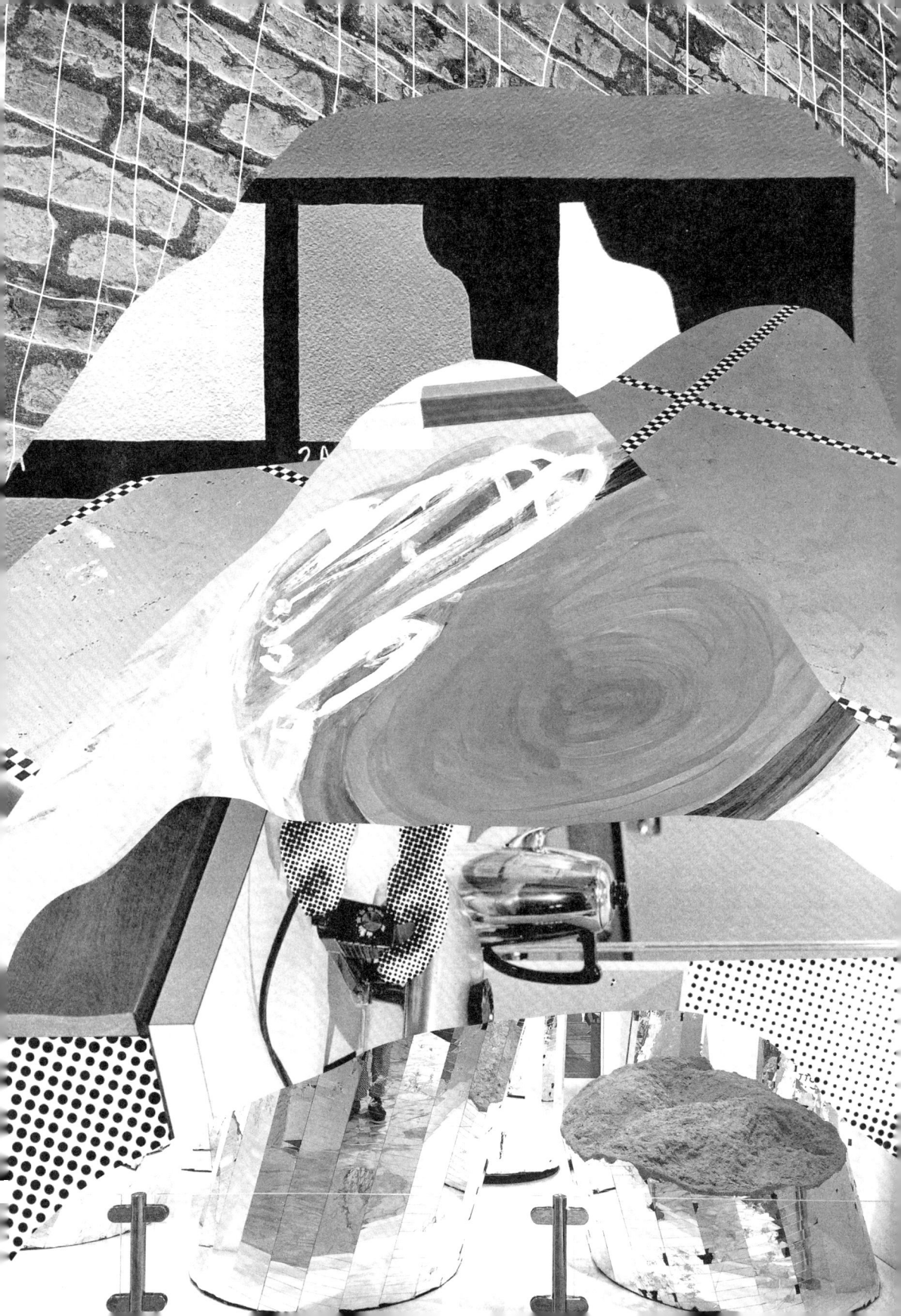

ACKNOWLEDGMENTS

This book is a collective endeavor. We would like to express our sincere thanks to all those who contributed to its preparation and production as well as to the preceding Swiss Design Network conference "Beyond Change" at FHNW Academy of Art and Design in March 2018, including (in alphabetical order): Phil Baber, Nuria Bacelo, Jan Boelen, Massimo Botta, Johannes Bruder, Mayar El Bakry, Davide Fornari, Corin Gisel, Sarah Haug, Madeleine Morley, Isabel Rosa Müggler Zumstein, Sarah Owens, Haejeung Paik, Sunjung Park, Naz Naddaf, Vera Sacchetti, Arne Scheuermann, Arianna Smaron, Julia Sommerfeld, Anne-Catherine Sutermeister as well as the entire team of IXDM at FHNW Academy of Art and Design. We would especially like to thank the authors of this book for their unfaltering generosity and patience, Astrid Vorstermans from Valiz publishers and her team for the outstanding collaboration and support, and Lotte Lara Schröder for the congenial design of this book. Last but not least, we would like to thank the entire community of designers, researchers, activists and thinkers who have inspired and guided us in recent years to make this project a reality.

Claudia Mareis and Nina Paim /
the editors

This publication was produced and printed with generous financial support from the Swiss Design Network and the FHNW Academy of Art and Design. The pre-press stage of the publication was supported by the Swiss National Science Foundation.

FNSNF

Members of the **SWISSDESIGNNETWORK** (SDN)

éc a l ECAL: ECAL Ecole cantonale d'art de Lausanne

n|w
University of Applied Sciences and Arts Northwestern Switzerland
Academy of Art and Design

FHNW HGK: University of Applied Sciences and Arts Northwestern Switzerland, Academy of Art and Design

—HEAD Genève HEAD – Genève: Geneva School for Art and Design

HKB HKB
Hochschule der Künste Bern
Haute école des arts de Berne
Bern University of the Arts

HKB: Bern University of the Art

Lucerne University of
Applied Sciences and Arts
HOCHSCHULE LUZERN
Art and Design
FH Zentralschweiz

HSLU: Lucerne School of Art and Design

University of Applied Sciences and Arts
of Southern Switzerland
SUPSI

SUPSI: University of Applied Sciences and Arts of Southern Switzerland

z hdk
Zürcher Hochschule der Künste
Zurich University of the Arts

ZHdK: Zurich University of the Arts

COLOPHON

EDITORS
Claudia Mareis, Nina Paim

CONTRIBUTIONS BY
Danah Abdulla, Tanveer Ahmed, Zoy Anastassakis, Ahmed Ansari, Brave New Alps, Johannes Bruder, Cheryl Buckley, Sria Chatterjee, Alison J. Clarke, Sasha Costanza-Chock, Paola De Martin, Decolonising Design, depatriarchise design, Bianca Elzenbaumer, Arturo Escobar, Kjetil Fallan, Griselda Flesler, Corin Gisel, Matthew Kiem, Claudia Mareis, Ramia Mazé, Tania Messell, Anja Neidhardt, Nan O'Sullivan, Maya Ober, Nina Paim, Luiza Prado de O. Martins, Mia Charlene White

EDITORIAL SUPPORT
Madeleine Morley

COPY-EDITING
Phil Baber

PROOFREADING
Els Brinkman

INDEX
Elke Stevens

IMAGE RESEARCH
the authors, Mayar El Hayawan, Nina Paim

DESIGN
Lotte Lara Schröder
(incl. cover, opening visuals/collages)

TYPEFACES
Cofo Sans and Cofo Chimera by Contrast Foundry
Times New Roman MT Std

PAPER
Munken Print White 1.5 100 gr
Fedrigoni Arena Natural Rough 200 gr

LITHOGRAPHY
Mariska Bijl, Wilco Art Books, Amsterdam

PRINTING AND BINDING
Wilco Art Books, Amersfoort

PUBLISHING PARTNER
Swiss Design Network
www.swissdesignnetwork.ch

PUBLISHER
Valiz, Amsterdam
Astrid Vorstermans & Pia Pol
www.valiz.nl

PLURAL

The PLURAL series focuses on how the intersections between, identity, power, representation and emancipation play out in the arts and in cultural practices. The volumes in this series aim to do justice to the plurality of voices, experiences and perspectives in society and in the arts and to address the history, present and future meaning of these positions and their interrelations. PLURAL brings together new and critical insights from artists, arts professionals, activists, cultural and social researchers, journalists and theorists. Series design by Lotte Lara Schröder

Design Struggles is the third volume in the PLURAL series.

DESIGN STRUGGLES
Intersecting Histories, Pedagogies, and Perspectives
Claudia Mareis & Nina Paim (eds.)

ISBN 978-94-93246-52-2
Printed and bound in the EU, 2021
Second print, 2025

The other two are:

Feminist Art Activisms and Artivisms
Katy Deepwell (ed.), ISBN 978-94-92095-72-5
Amsterdam, Valiz, 2020
Shame! and Masculinity
Ernst van Alphen (ed.), ISBN 978-94-92095-92-3
Amsterdam, Valiz, 2020

Name of the Author